MW00463083

PORTLAND
BEST PLACES

PORTLAND BEST PLACES

A discriminating guide to Portland's restaurants, lodgings, shopping, nightlife, arts, sights, outings, and annual events

Edited by Stephanie Irving
Introduction by David Sarasohn

Written by a team of
Portland writers

Sasquatch Books

Copyright © 1990 by Sasquatch Books
All rights reserved
Printed in the United States of America
Distributed in Canada by Raincoast Books Ltd.

Library of Congress Cataloging-in-Publication Data

Portland best places : a discriminating guide to Portland's
   restaurants, lodgings, shopping, nightlife, arts, sights, outings,
   and annual events / edited by Stephanie Irving ; introduction by
   David Sarasohn ; written by a team of Portland writers.
     p. cm.
   ISBN 0-912365-28-5 : $10.95
     1. Portland (Or.)—Description—Guide-books. I. Irving,
   Stephanie, 1962-
   F884.P83P67 1990   90-31965
   917.95′490443—dc20   CIP

Design by Jane Jeszeck
Cover illustration by Nick Gaetano
Interior illustrations by Jerry Nelson
Maps by Karen Schober
Typeset by Typeworks, Vancouver, BC, Canada

The Best Places guidebooks have been published continuously since 1975. Books in the Best
Places series read like personal guidebooks, but the evaluations given are based on numerous
reports from local and traveling inspectors. Final judgments are made by the editor. Our
inspectors never identify themselves (except over the phone) and never accept free meals or
other favors. The editor welcomes information from readers, as long as they have no financial
connections with the establishments concerned; a report form is provided at the end of the
book. *Northwest Best Places*, *Seattle Best Places*, *Portland Best Places*, and other Sasquatch
publications are available at bulk discounts for corporate giving, conventions, and fund-
raising; see the order form in the back of this book, or write Sasquatch Books for a catalog.

Sasquatch Books
1931 Second Avenue
Seattle, Washington 98101
Phone: (206) 441-5555

ACKNOWLEDGMENTS

First off, heartfelt thanks to the entire team of Portland reviewers: Doug and Jill Berry, Karen Brooks, Deborah Fairley, Bonnie Martin Fazio, Fran Gardner, D.K. Holm, Serena Lesley, Carol Morton, Tom Novick, Judy Peterson-Nedry, Pam Phillips, J. Kingston Pierce, Roger Porter, Terry Ross, Melissa Rossi, David Sarasohn, Tim Sills, Wendy Smith, Linda Tross, Laurie Underwood, and Martha Wagner. Their expertise and fearlessness help ensure a thorough and honest guidebook. Countless others have contributed leads and invaluable advice that add to the book's reliability. Essential to the project were the keen eyes of copyeditor Barry Foy and proofreaders Sally Anderson and Danielle McClellan, as well as the tirelessness and persistence of editorial assistants Kim Carlson, Kim Hill, and Jeff Sanders.

So, here it is: *Portland Best Places*, our snapshot of a city and a region, captured in the midst of dynamic change. Our coverage extends as far north as Vancouver, Washington, and south to West Linn, west to Beaverton, and east to Gresham. Our method is to poll a wide range of passionate fans of the city, reinspecting old favorite places and comparing notes on new ones. We have tried to organize the book around things that the people who live here like to do, rather than applying the universal categories usually found in guidebooks. Reviewers make anonymous visits, accepting no free meals, accommodations, or services. We are always on the lookout for the out-of-the-way, the little-advertised, the owner-operated, the bargain places, hoping that by publicizing these spots we can help ensure their survival. You can help, too: when you find a great spot, drop us a note (there's a report form in the back of this book) so we can investigate it and wonder how we could have missed it. Likewise, if you find we've misjudged a place, send us your corrections. We value your comments. Even if you're a tourist!

Stephanie Irving

TABLE OF CONTENTS

INTRODUCTION

The best place in Portland is a stretch of four or five blocks running under a bridge along First Avenue, in a neighborhood that at some hours you might want to avoid entirely. Big business here means the sale of macrame candle holders, and the most prominent restaurant space has had more identities than Meryl Streep. The buildings date from a time when Portland was called Stumptown and the suburbs produced cow chips instead of silicon ones.

Over the past decade or so, these buildings have been carefully restored, and riding down this street you might feel you're back in the time before world wars started getting numbered. That is, you might feel like that if the only way to ride down the street were not on one of the most modern mass transit systems in the country.

This is the best thing about Portland: it takes what it wants and leaves the rest, and if the resulting combinations don't look like those of other cities, Portland figures that's their problem. The city doesn't exactly live in a time warp, but in an era when most others seem to be trying out for "Lifestyles of the Rich and Uninhabitable" and every other West Coast city has been bursting its seams, Portland has managed to avoid megalopoly by lying low and pretending to be Wyoming.

Portland remained a secret its residents wanted to keep. Of course, like everything else, this is changing. Even with small cars and smaller houses, there are only so many people you can jam into California and, more recently, the Puget Sound area—and it's getting tough to hide a rose-colored city in between them.

Portland decided a while ago that it was neither going to abandon its downtown nor cover it with glass canyons. The wars over development that Seattle went through in 1989 had been fought in Portland 15 years before, and the resulting limits have not been taken lightly. In 1968, Portland poet William Stafford wrote, "Other people's neglect is our precious and abiding shell."

Today, the shell is cracking. Portland is being dragged into major metropolitan status. Even so, the city has managed to develop on its own terms, and it now has a small jewel of a center for the performing arts, nationally noted light rail service, and, as of 1990, a new convention center—despite the risk that those things will attract out-of-towners. At about the same time as the convention center, the three-block Pioneer Place will be completed, featuring Saks Fifth Avenue (the last Eastern haberdasher to make so dramatic an entrance was the Hudson's Bay Company). The RiverPlace project, with a promenade along the Willamette that has redefined the summer evening, is so popular that it's about to produce a sequel. So far, the cracking of the shell has made the city stronger.

The new openings will add to Portland's already unusual set of downtown landmarks. These were recently displayed to a visiting New York writer.

"Over there," he was told, "is the US BanCorp'building, popularly known as Big Pink," 40 stories the color of strawberry mousse, providing the mandatory fancy restaurant on top of a bank building. He murmured appreciatively.

"There," he was informed as he pivoted to the right, "is *Portlandia*," the 20-foot bronze woman that Portland thinks is what the Statue of Liberty could become if she'd just kick back a little. He again murmured appreciatively.

"And there," he was instructed, with his eyes directed toward a bloomingly bearded figure in a three-piece suit tearing toward City Hall on a bicycle, "is the mayor." This time, the visitor did not murmur appreciatively; in fact, it was some time before he could say anything at all.

Other than New York and its hey-look-at-me Ed Koch, there haven't been many cities whose choice of mayor said as much about them as Bud Clark says about Portland. It's not so much that no other metropolis would have elected a bicycle-riding tavern owner with no political experience to be mayor; it's that no other metropolis would even have *considered* it.

The secret may be getting out, but Portlanders still insist that a city is not for networking or catching planes to other places, but for living in. What they prize about the place is not its per capita income but its rivers, its neighborhoods, its live jazz, its microbreweries, and its pro basketball Trail Blazers. The last may be an acquired taste, but all the rest comes *naturally*—one of Portland's favorite words.

Speaking of taste, the food is also getting better. These days you can get a decent New York pizza, reasonable barbecue, flown-in lox, and tagliatelle al limone here. At the moment, the richest and most striking offerings come from Portland's Vietnamese community, but that may be temporary—the second generation of every Vietnamese restaurant family seems to be studying computers at Portland State. Another group of newcomers has also bolstered Portland's cuisine— namely, people who originally came here to teach or study at Reed College. Former Reedies show up in the kitchens, dining rooms, and management of a vast number of Portland restaurants.

But let's return to what I think is Portland's best place. At the center of what is now a National Historic District sits Skidmore Fountain. Portland's fondness for fountains is like Tulsa's for oil wells: the city seems to feel that despite all the water falling from the sky, you can never tell when you might run short. Some of the fountains that dot the downtown like mailboxes are themselves metal sculptures or are made of imported granite; the style of the Skidmore Fountain is 19th-Century Monumental, with drinking space for horses and an inscription reading, "Good Citizens Are the Riches of a City."

At any given time, some of Portland's riches will be juggling or jogging around— or wading in—Skidmore Fountain. Weekends, nine months a year, it's the center of an outdoor market. In decent weather—a term that Portlanders interpret broadly—the Saturday Market is jammed, although one suspects that most people pretending to ponder the purchase of hand-carved running-shoe trees are actually deciding between the Thai noodles and the skewered shrimp. Just a philosopher's stone's throw down the street is McCormick & Schmick's Seafood Restaurant, appreciated by thousands who have never even eaten there: through a vent above the kitchen, the smells of alder smoke and grilling salmon spill out onto Oak Street and First Avenue. There may be restaurants where Portland's fascination with its seafood is more elaborately cultivated, but there aren't many where the alder and salmon drift out and follow you down the street.

Down the middle of First Avenue runs MAX, the city's new light rail system, which presently makes tracks from Nordstom to the eastern suburbs—or, as a West Hills resident might put it, from the sublime to the ridiculous. MAX is fast and clean, and efficiently connects the two halves of the city divided by the Willamette River. Portland cherishes its river, though it has cultivated only one bank. The river's east side is a concrete tangle of freeway fettuccine, while on the west a riverside park ambles along for miles, drawing Portlanders like Goretex-covered lemmings.

On those rare days when clouds are not arranged to conceal the city from Soviet satellites—not to mention the sun—the city has two volcanoes on its horizon. One is perfect (for the moment, at least); the other is famous. That difference serves to remind Portlanders of what the rest of the world's values are like.

The perfect one is Mount Hood. It's about 40 miles away, but Portland's imagination long ago annexed it. It's the tallest point in the state (11,245 feet), but more importantly, it's an ever-present escape valve and reality check. When you can look over the city's rooftops and see Mount Hood every day—OK, maybe every fourth day—you're a little less interested in becoming Donald Trump.

The famous mountain, of course, is Mount St. Helens, which one day in 1980 decided to show the other Cascades what happens when matter is converted into energy. For a while, Portland daily weather bulletins included an ash report, the way Los Angeles meteorologists explain just which people should not risk breathing the local air on a particular day. These days, the volcano occasionally burps up a little cloud, but that's all; it has made its point. Since locals admire both nature and self-restraint, they are growing quite fond of Mount St. Helens.

City folk are equally fond of their neighborhoods. They aren't big—a fairly short drive will take you through four or five of them—but each has its own style, and its own shopping area, and even its own flag (although they're not flown much and are never burned). Neighborhoods range from areas where the telephone poles are covered with flyers for gay environmental protest meetings to areas where neighbors conduct local business at the laundromat to places where they give each other muscular nods while jogging. The residents of most of them have a strong sense of place, and know why they live there instead of in some other section where housing prices are comparable. In Portland, for the same amount of money you can live around the corner from a country-western bar or a vegetarian co-op; in either case, you'll probably know the owner by name.

On Saturdays, those Portlanders who don't leave the city get exotic by going to other neighborhoods. One that draws a considerable amount of attention is Hawthorne, which has not only its own cuisine but its own foreign policy. The surrounding houses could be in two dozen different neighborhoods, and the signs and flyers on Hawthorne Boulevard inform you in no uncertain terms that the Hawthorne neighborhood is pro baked goods and anti Contra. On Hawthorne, even someone who hand-cures sausages for sale to San Francisco still knows the people who buy from him in town. Even as the boutiques and cafes spread down the street, the area maintains its laid-back entrepreneurialism, a kind of prosciutto perestroika.

Hawthorne is a model of the balance that Portland tries to keep, bringing in the attractions of the rest of the world without becoming like the rest of the world. It's a balance that can—and around here, sometimes does—tilt fatally in either direction.

The city tries hard to maintain balance, or at least to keep it in sight. While other cities declare their intention to become world class, Portland tries to stay people-sized. And even in a time when both the people and the size are changing, Portland is hanging on.

David Sarasohn

HOW TO USE THIS BOOK

Star Rating System. Every place listed in this book is recommended. We rate restaurants and lodgings on a scale of zero to four stars (with half-stars in between), based on uniqueness, enjoyability, value, loyalty of local clientele, excellence of cooking, performance measured against goals, cleanliness, and professionalism of service.

(no stars) Worth knowing about, if nearby

★ A good place

★★ Excellent, some wonderful qualities

★★★ Distinguished, many outstanding features

★★★★ The very best in the region
(four establishments rate four stars in this edition)

Price Range. When prices range between two categories (for instance, moderate to expensive), the lower one is given. Call ahead to verify.

Expensive indicates a tab of more than $75 for dinner for two, including wine (but not tip), and more than $90 for one night's lodging for two.

Moderate falls between expensive and inexpensive.

Inexpensive indicates a tab of less than $25 for dinner, and less than $50 for lodgings for two.

Map References. The letter-and-number code listed after each phone number refers to coordinates on the fold-out maps included in this book. Single letters (as in F7) refer to the downtown Portland map; double letters (FF7) refer to the Greater Portland map on the flip side.

Checks and Credit Cards. Most establishments that accept checks also require a major credit card for identification. American Express is abbreviated as AE, Diners Club as DC, MasterCard as MC, Visa as V.

Addresses. Addresses are in Portland unless otherwise specified. If an establishment has two Portland-area locations, we list both addresses; if there are more than two, we list the original, downtown, or biggest branch, followed by the words "and branches."

Phone Numbers. All area codes are 503 except where indicated. Telephone numbers beginning with "1" are long-distance from Portland but still within the 503 area.

Indexes. There is a full index by page number at the back of the book. You'll also find handy indexes by category at the front of the "Bars" and "Nightclubs" sections of the Nightlife chapter and the Restaurants chapter. Bars are indexed by neighborhood and noteworthy features; nightclubs by neighborhood and type of music; restaurants by neighborhood, cuisine, and star rating.

"Kids" and "Free" Symbols. We have provided **KIDS** and **FREE** symbols throughout the book to indicate attractions and events that are especially suited to children or free of charge.

RESTAURANTS CONTENTS

RESTAURANTS

INDEX: STAR RATING

RESTAURANTS

Anne Hughes Coffee Room
Besaw's
Broadway Bakery and
  Bistro
Carnival
Coffee People Immediate
  Care Center
Dave's Delicatessen
Goose Hollow Inn
Hamburger Mary's

Helvetia Tavern
Humphrey Yogart
Johnny's Greek Villa
La Casa de Rios
La Patisserie
Marco Polo Garden
McCalls
Nick's Famous Coney
Island Food
O'Connor's

Produce Row Cafe
Rich's Restaurant
Sweet Basil
Uncle Chen
Who-Song and Larry's
  Cantina

UNRATED
Trios

INDEX: FOOD AND OTHER FEATURES

24 HOURS
Besaw's

AMERICAN
Benjamin's
Besaw's
Couch Street Fish House
Grand Cafe American
  Restaurant
Main Street Restaurant
McCalls
O'Connor's
Perry's on Fremont
Pharmacy Fountain
Vat & Tonsure

ATMOSPHERE
Alexis
B.Moloch's/Heathman
  Bakery & Pub
Casa U-Betcha
Delphina's
Greek Deli & Grocery
Jake's Famous Crawfish
L'Auberge
Rimsky-Korsakoffee
  House

BARBECUE
Doris' Cafe

BRAZILIAN
BJ's Brazilian Restaurant

BREAKFAST
Besaw's
Bijou Cafe
Boulevard Cafe
Bread and Ink Cafe
Broadway Bakery and Cafe

Caffe Fresco
Fat City Cafe
Foothill Broiler
Hamburger Mary's
Hawthorne Street Cafe
The Heathman Restaurant
  and Bar
La Patisserie
Marco's Cafe and Espresso
  Bar
Metropolis Cafe
The Original Pancake
  House
Ron Paul Catering and
  Charcuterie
Sweet Basil
Tabor Hill Cafe
Zell's: An American Cafe

BRUNCH: SUNDAY/WEEKEND
Atwater's
Bread and Ink Cafe
Esplanade at RiverPlace
  (Alexis Hotel)
Hands On Cafe
Harborside Restaurant

BURGERS
Besaw's
Bijou Cafe
Carnival
Fat City Cafe
Foothill Broiler
Giant Drive-In
Hamburger Mary's
Helvetia Tavern
L'Auberge (Sundays)
Nick's Famous Coney
  Island Food
O'Connor's

Perry's on Fremont
Stanich Ten-Till-One
  Tavern

CAJUN/CREOLE
Cajun Cafe and Bistro
Jake's Famous Crawfish

CAMBODIAN
Phnom Penh Express

CATERING
B. Moloch/The Heathman
  Bakery and Pub
Briggs and Crampton
Ron Paul Catering and
  Charcuterie
Jake's Famous Crawfish

CHEAP EATS
American Dream Pizza
Anne Hughes Coffee Room
Benji's
Bridgeport Brew Pub
Dan's West Coast Bento
Doris' Cafe
Dragoon's Deli
Escape from New York
  Pizza
Fat City Cafe
Formosa Harbor
Goose Hollow Inn
Helvetia Tavern
Hot Lips Pizza
Humphrey Yogart
Macheesmo Mouse
Nick's Famous Coney
  Island Food
Pharmacy Fountain
Phnom Penh Express

RESTAURANTS

Produce Row Cafe
Stanich Ten-Till-One
  Tavern
Taj Mahal
Yen Ha

CHILDREN: GOOD FOR
American Dream Pizza
Bridgeport Brew Pub
Carnival
Foothill Broiler
Formosa Harbor
Giant Drive-In
Hawthorne Street Cafe
Humphrey Yogart
Old Wives' Tale
Vista Springs Cafe

CHINESE
Chang's Mongolian Grill
Chang's Yangtze
Chen's China Clipper
Chen's Dynasty
Fong Chong
Formosa Harbor
Hunan
Marco Polo Garden
Uncle Chen

CONTINENTAL
Hidden House
Huber's
The Old Country Inn
Western Culinary Institute
Westmoreland Wine and
  Bistro

DESSERT AND COFFEE
Anne Hughes Coffee Room
Ashley's
Brasserie Montmartre
Bread and Ink Cafe
Coffee People Immediate
  Care Center
Gazebo Gallery-Restaurant
Grand Cafe American
  Restaurant
Humphrey Yogart
La Patisserie
Marco's Cafe and Espresso
  Bar
Paisley's
Panini
Papa Haydn

Rimsky-Korsakoffee
  House
Ron Paul Catering and
  Charcuterie
Tabor Hill Cafe

DIM SUM
Fong Chong

ETHIOPIAN
Jarra's Ethiopian
  Restaurant
Yacob's Rainbow

FRENCH
Cafe des Amis
Crepe Faire
L'Auberge
L'Ecurie

GOOD BAR FOOD
Chen's Dynasty
Delphina's
Esplanade at RiverPlace
  (Alexis Hotel)
Hall Street Bar and Grill
The Heathman Restaurant
  and Bar
L'Auberge
McCormick & Schmick's
  Seafood Restaurant
Remo's Ristorante Italiano
Thirty-One Northwest
Trios
Vat & Tonsure

GOURMET TAKEOUT/
DELICATESSEN
Dave's Delicatessen
Greek Deli & Grocery
Marco Polo Garden
Maya's Tacqueria
Panini
Ron Paul Catering and
  Charcuterie
Vista Springs Cafe

GREEK
Alexis
Berbati
Greek Deli & Grocery
Johnny's Greek Villa

INDIAN
Indigine

Kashmir
Plainfield's Mayur
Taj Mahal

INVENTIVE ETHNIC
Bread and Ink Cafe
Briggs and Crampton
Eddie Lee's
Hands On Cafe
Indigine
Metropolis Cafe
Pinot Ganache
Ron Paul Catering and
  Charcuterie
Thirty-One Northwest
Westmoreland Wine and
  Bistro

ITALIAN
see also Pizza
Delphina's
Lotsa Pasta
Genoa Restaurant
Panini
Piccolo Mondo
Remo's Ristorante Italiano
Riccardo's Restaurant &
  Espresso Bar
Ristorante Medici

JAPANESE
Bush Garden
Dan's West Coast Bento
Fuji
Ginza
Ichidai
Koji Osakaya Japanese
  Fish House
Kyoto
Obi
Sumida's
Uogashi
Zen

JEWISH/KOSHER
Dave's Delicatessen
Dragoon's Deli

LATE NIGHT
*serves food past 11pm
  weekends, at least; see
  also 24-Hour*
Besaw's
Brasserie Montmartre
Hamburger Mary's

La Casa de Rios
La Patisserie
Papa Haydn
Remo's Ristorante Italiano
The Ringside

LEBANESE
Al-Amir

MEXICAN
Acapulco's Gold
Casa-U-Betcha
Chez Jose
La Casa de Rios
Macheesmo Mouse
Maya's Tacqueria
Who-Song and Larry's
   Cantina

MIDDLE EASTERN
Abou Karim
Al Amir
Marrakesh

MILKSHAKES
Carnival
Coffee People Immediate
   Care Center
Fat City Cafe
Pharmacy Fountain

MOROCCAN
Marrakesh

NORTHWEST CUISINE
Albertina's
Atwater's
Esplanade at RiverPlace
   (Alexis Hotel)
Gazebo Gallery-Restaurant
Hall Street Bar & Grill
The Heathman Restaurant
   and Bar
Paisley's
Ron Paul Catering and
   Charcuterie
Tabor Hill Cafe

ONION RINGS
The Ringside

OUTDOOR DINING
Crepe Faire
Gazebo Gallery-Restaurant

Hall Street Bar & Grill
Hamburger Mary's
Hidden House
Humphrey Yogart
Harborside Restaurant
McCalls
Seafood Mama

PIZZA
American Dream Pizza
B. Moloch/The Heathman
   Bakery & Pub
Bridgeport Brew Pub
Escape from New York
   Pizza
Hot Lips Pizza
Vista Springs Cafe

PRIVATE ROOMS
Atwater's
Chen's China Clipper
Chen's Dynasty
Hidden House
Jake's Famous Crawfish
Koji Osakaya Japanese
   Fish House
Trios

SALVADORAN
El Palenque

SEAFOOD
Benjamin's
Boulevard Cafe
Chen's China Clipper
Couch Street Fish House
Formosa Harbor
Genoa Restaurant
Grant House
Hall Street Bar & Grill
Harborside Restaurant
The Heathman Restaurant
   and Bar
Jake's Famous Crawfish
McCormick & Schmick's
   Seafood Restaurant
McCormick's Fish House
   and Bar
Opus Too
Remo's Ristorante Italiano
Rich's Restaurant
Salty's on the Columbia
Seafood Mama
Tabor Hill Cafe
Trios

Winterborne

SMOKING: ALL
Vat & Tonsure

SMOKING: NON
Bridgeport Brew Pub
Broadway Cafe
Humphrey Yogart
Winterborne

SODA FOUNTAIN
Pharmacy Fountain
Zell's: An American Cafe

SOUP/SALAD/SANDWICH
Albertina's
Anne Hughes Coffee Room
Ashley's
Benji's
Broadway Cafe
Hawthorne Street Cafe
Humphrey Yogart
La Patisserie
Metropolis Cafe
Panini
Papa Haydn

STEAK
Cafe des Amis
Hall Street Bar & Grill
London Grill
(Westin Benson)
The Ringside

SUSHI
Bush Garden
Fuji
Ginza

TAKEOUT ONLY
Dan's West Coast Bento
Doris' Cafe

THAI
Bangkok Kitchen
Lamthong
Pattaya
Tara Thai House
Thai Villa
Thanh Thao

VEGETARIAN/NATURAL FOODS
*see also Indian, Middle
    Eastern, and all Asian
    categories*
Berbati
Old Wives' Tale

VIEW
Atwater's
Harborside Restaurant
McCalls
Salty's on the Columbia
Who-Song and Larry's
    Cantina

VIETNAMESE
Thanh Thao
Yen Ha

WINE BAR
Westmoreland Wine and
    Bistro

INDEX: LOCATION

RESTAURANTS

The Original Pancake
  House
Piccolo Mondo
Stanich Ten-Till-One
  Tavern

LAKE OSWEGO
Gazebo Gallery-Restaurant
Giant Drive-In
The Old Country Inn
Riccardo's Restaurant &
  Espresso Bar
Thai Villa

LAURELHURST
American Dream Pizza

LLOYD CENTER/IRVINGTON
Albertina's
Metropolis Cafe

MILWAUKIE
Buster's Smokehouse
  Texas-Style Bar-Be-Que

MULTNOMAH
Dragoon's Deli
Fat City Cafe
Marco's Cafe and Espresso
  Bar

NORTH PORTLAND
see Faloma, Swan Island

NORTHEAST PORTLAND
see Airport, Lloyd
  Center/Irvington, Rose
  City, Alameda

NORTHWEST
see also Chinatown, Old
  Town/Skidmore, Pearl
  District
Acapulco's Gold
Besaw's
Briggs and Crampton
Cafe des Amis
Caffe Fresco
Cajun Cafe and Bistro
Casa-U-Betcha
Coffee People Immediate
  Care Center
Dan's West Coast Bento
Delphina's

Escape from New York
  Pizza
Foothill Broiler
Ginza
L'Auberge
Marrakesh
Paisley's
Papa Haydn
Pharmacy Fountain
The Ringside
Ron Paul Catering and
  Charcuterie
Seafood Mama
Thirty-One Northwest
Trios

OLD TOWN/SKIDMORE
Alexis
Berbati
Bijou Cafe
Chang's Mongolian Grill
Couch Street Fish House
Dragoon's Deli
Johnny's Greek Villa
La Patisserie
Lotsa Pasta
McCormick & Schmick's
  Seafood Restaurant
Obi
Opus Too
Uogashi

PEARL DISTRICT
Anne Hughes Coffee Room
Bridgeport Brew Pub
Remo's Ristorante Italiano

PORTLAND HEIGHTS
Goose Hollow Inn
Vista Springs Cafe

RALEIGH HILLS
Hot Lips Pizza

RIVERPLACE
Esplanade at RiverPlace
  (Alexis Hotel)
Harborside Restaurant
McCalls

ROSE CITY
Yen Ha
Sumida's

SE DIVISION
Ichidai
Indigine

SE POWELL
Pattaya

SELLWOOD
El Palenque

SOUTHEAST
see Arleta, Brooklyn, East
  Portland, Hawthorne,
  Laurelhurst, Sellwood,
  SE Division, SE Powell,
  Terwilliger Blvd, and
  Woodstock

SOUTHWEST
see Downtown,
  Burlingame, Cedar
  Mill, Johns Landing/SW
  Macadam Ave, Mult-
  nomah, Portland
  Heights, Raleigh Hills,
  RiverPlace, SW Barnes
  Rd, and West Slope

SW BARNES ROAD
Hands On Cafe

SWAN ISLAND
Hot Lips Pizza

TERWILLIGER BLVD/
DUNIWAY PARK
Carnival

TIGARD
L'Ecurie

TUALATIN
Rich's Restaurant

VANCOUVER, WA
Grant House
Hidden House
Pinot Ganache
Who-Song and Larry's
  Cantina

WEST SLOPE
Yen Ha

TOP 152 RESTAURANTS

Abou Karim

221 SW Pine St, 223-5058 (map:I5)
Moderate; beer and wine; AE, V, MC, DC; local checks only
Lunch Mon-Fri, dinner Mon-Sat

Portland's most established Middle Eastern restaurant, Abou Karim has built itself more than a pillar of pita. With its wide range of kebabs, vivid grilled chicken and lamb dishes, and a particularly addictive baba ghanouj, the restaurant consistently manages to fill its newly expanded quarters.

One unique feature is a menu worked out with the American Heart Association, with some items listed as particularly low in fat and cholesterol. It would be a mistake, however, to hold that health-consciousness against the restaurant; most of the dishes strike an admirable balance between art and arteries.

Acapulco's Gold

2610 NW Vaughn St, 220-0283 (map:FF6)
Inexpensive; full bar; MC, V; local checks only

12700 NW Cornell St, 644-5224 (map:FF9)
Inexpensive; beer and wine; MC, V; local checks only
Lunch Mon-Sat, dinner every day

Just plain Mexican food, but this place is perennially popular, with standees waiting for a table most every night. Burritos are a good bet—the Burrito Juarez is a satisfying pad of massive tortilla, stringy cheese, chicken, and pork, drizzled generously with sour cream. Bars on the windows, scruffy tile floors, and Mexican murals on the wall lend a dusty cantina atmosphere. The restaurant of the same name in Multnomah Village, related at one time, isn't anymore.

Al-Amir

223 SW Stark St, 274-0010 (map:I4)
Inexpensive; full bar; AE, MC, V; local checks only
Lunch, dinner Mon-Sat

The Bishop's House, complete with crosses and crenelations, seems an unlikely place to serve baba ghanouj. But Al-Amir, a solid Middle Eastern restaurant with both range and consistency, has finally conquered the original building. In addition to pungent kebabs, the menu includes kharouf muammar, a huge pile of moist, faintly sweet lamb chunks; and dujaj musahab, a charcoal-grilled chicken breast in lemon and olive oil. Holding everything together are pools of creamy hummus and baba ghanouj. Prices are reasonable, and a little Lebanese beer can make the light through the stained glass windows shine even more brightly.

Albertina's

424 NE 22nd Ave, 231-0216 (map:FF5)
Inexpensive; beer and wine; MC, V; checks OK
Lunch Mon-Fri

This establishment should be honored for good karma alone. Except for the head chef and kitchen manager, all help in the former orphanage is volunteer. Revenues are used to support the Albertina Kerr Center for the Treatment of Physically and Emotionally Disturbed Children. The lunch also happens to be good: on a recent visit we sampled a refreshing tomato and cucumber sorbet, sherried beef with mushrooms, and dessert. You'll need a reservation (two seatings daily). Next door in the Economy Jar you'll find heirloom jewelry and china sets to pass down through your own family. A gift shop and a thrift shop as well.

Alexis
215 W Burnside,
224-8577 (map:I5)
Moderate; full bar; AE,
DC, MC, V;
local checks only
Lunch Mon-Fri, dinner
every day

No place in Portland is quite like Alexis—a temple of good times that has evolved over the last nine years into something far beyond a little Greek eatery. The environment is a worthy evocation of Old Athens. Seven nights a week, members of the Alexis Bakourous family and their loyal staff patrol the premises with a professionalism all too rare on the West Coast. They welcome you exuberantly, like a long-lost relative from their native Filiatra on the Peloponnesus. The bear hug is the house greeting, lightning service the house pace, and loud laughter the house music. Expect the staff to move to the same beat, occasionally belting out a spontaneous *Opa!!* There's never a dearth of action, from lawyers' conventions to Old World folk dancing to Aurelia, the region's hottest Middle Eastern dancer. The food is authentic and of consistent quality. Some think you won't find better calamari this side of the Aegean, and the bronzed oregano chicken is full of robust flavors. Complete dinners give you the most for your buck, but regulars also find the makings of a meal in the appetizers. Plan to dip into everything with Portland's finest house bread—the crusty wedges are essential for scooping up the lusty drippings.

American Dream Pizza
4620 NE Glisan St,
230-0699 (map:GG4)
Inexpensive; beer and
wine; MC, V; checks OK
Lunch Mon-Sat, dinner
every day
5020 NE 82nd Ave,
255-4360 (map:EE3)
Lunch Mon-Fri, dinner
every day

KIDS This is a by-the-slice place with a difference. They make up each slice individually, even going to the trouble of heating slices with anchovies in a separate oven, if you insist. Pizza toppings also decorate the house salad. Half the business is take-out, but it's worth eating in. Glisan Street decor consists largely of pizza boxes decorated in crayon by patrons (who have also been known to scribble on the paper tablecloths) and a driftwood mobile of Converse shoes. Over a dozen Oregon and Northwest brews on tap.

Anne Hughes Coffee Room
(in Powell's Books)
1005 W Burnside,
228-4651 (map:J2)

In 1985, the coffee room was just Anne Hughes' cart stashed among Powell's aisles. Two years later, Anne kicked off her wheels; now tabletops fill the ever-familiar literary arena. Nobody's thinking about the food here;

*Inexpensive; no alcohol;
no credit cards; checks OK
Breakfast, lunch,
dinner every day*

they are all either reading or writing (deadline camaraderie), so the tension level hovers at medium anxiety. The sandwiches (usually turkey, ham, or a vegetarian version on focaccia bread) are the only things made on the premises, but the soups and cookies are decent, too. Of course the coffee's good and abundant.

Ashley's
*436 N Main St, Gresham,
669-7748
Inexpensive; beer and
wine; AE, MC, V; local
checks only
Lunch, dinner every day,
brunch Sun*

The great convenience of Ashley's is that if you don't want to go all the way to Gresham for its desserts, there's a good chance they'll come to you: Ashley's supplies them to a number of other local restaurants. The European-inspired desserts, especially fruit tarts and cheesecakes, are impressive, the fruit retaining its flavor while never overpowering the delicate crusts. The rest of the menu, largely sandwiches, salads, and fairly predictable entrees, is competently prepared. But a visit is rewarded by the building itself, a carefully maintained old church where you might find yourself sitting just beneath the pulpit or next to a big pillar. When the light through a stained glass window hits the whipped cream, the effect is spiritual.

Atwater's
*111 SW 5th Ave,
275-3600 (map:J4)
Expensive; full bar; AE,
DC, MC, V; no checks
Dinner every day,
brunch Sun*

Five years ago, Atwater's appeared atop the US BanCorp Tower in a swirl of rolling vistas and culinary confusion. Recently, with the arrival of chef George Poston, the restaurant has begun to have menus to match its mountain views. The menu changes every season but always relies on Northwest seafood, game, wild mushrooms, and fruit, although the original fascination with cranberries has ebbed. The six-course formal dinner is $35, but the three-course version for $24.50 is a bargain. The all-you-can-eat Sunday buffet has been a particular hit, tables groaning with a vast assortment of traditional and contemporary items, chefs whipping up omelets, and only a few steam-table perennials. The star is the space itself, with an etched-glass wine cellar in the middle of the peach-tone dining room and hundreds of miles of Oregon and Washington stretching out beyond the windows.

B. Moloch/The Heathman Bakery and Pub
*901 SW Salmon St,
227-5700 (map:G2)
Moderate; beer and wine;
AE, MC, V;
local checks only*

This offshoot of The Heathman Restaurant and Bar is the brainchild of chef Greg Higgins. He designed everything, from the modestly priced bistro menu to the industrial-chic decor. One of the big attractions here is a 25-ton wood-burning brick oven, embellished with a copper hood and old Dutch tiles, where some of the city's best pizzas and breads are born. A seafood cal-

*Breakfast, lunch, dinner
every day*

zone, stuffed with smoked mussels, shrimp, and plenty of ricotta, was wonderful. Salmon, peppered ham, and sun-dried tomatoes are cured in a cold-smoker in back of the massive baking furnace. There's a take-out counter for on-the-go types, and if leisure is in order, the micro-brew bar (Widmer Brewery) has some of the region's finest malt happenings on tap. The breakfast menu is an homage to culinary creativity: hazelnut and stout (yes, as in beer) waffles with marionberry syrup, and Eggs in Purgatory (eggs stirred in marinara sauce and spiked with the pub's homemade Italian sausage). With stuff like that, you can expect lines.

Bangkok Kitchen
*2534 SE Belmont St,
236-7349 (map:GG4)
Inexpensive; beer and
wine; no credit cards;
checks OK
Lunch Mon-Fri, dinner
Mon-Sat*

Outstanding food makes up for the dearth of decor. The setting here is kitschy cafe, but authentic Thai offerings and the wacky good humor of owner-chef Srichan Miller and her family draws a loyal coterie of fans. They come for the heat treatment—the array of searing house soups, peanut sauces, and salads of fresh shrimp and lime. One of the popular specials is a whole fried fish covered in a feverish chile paste and deeply sauteed peppers, all decorated with basil leaves and other artful trimmings. If you want good food at decent prices, this is the ticket—though the reluctant service can sometimes ruin the meal.

Benjamin's
*1211 SW 5th Ave (2nd
floor), 223-8103
(map:F2)
Moderate; full bar; AE,
DC, MC, V; checks OK
Lunch Mon-Fri, dinner
every day*

Benji's
*1211 SW 5th Ave (1st
floor), 221-1534
(map:F3)
Beer and wine; AE, DC,
MC, V; checks OK
Breakfast, lunch Mon-Fri*

The Portland outpost of an established Seattle restaurant, Benjamin's (on the second floor of the PacWest Building) both benefits and suffers from its office-building location: jammed at lunch, it keeps a lower profile at dinnertime. But the lunch crowds know something: the restaurant's consistently successful with fresh seafood and has a wide-ranging menu (from burgers to yakisoba to a massive sesame chicken salad) and a dramatic, open layout. Benjamin's may not be the most imaginative restaurant in town, but it's consistent and professional.

Downstairs, at breakfast, lunch, and late into the afternoon, Benji's fills up the building's lobby with a huge sandwich, salad, and espresso operation. Order the chicken-breast burgers and the three-salad sampler, and try to figure out which lunchers come from City Hall across the street, from *The Oregonian* on the next block, or from the law firms upstairs.

Berbati
19 SW 2nd Ave, 226-2122

Although it lives in the same Old Town neighborhood as a couple of higher-octane Greek eateries, this unassum-

(map:J6)
Moderate; full bar; AE,
DC, MC, V; local checks
only
Dinner Mon-Sat

ing establishment easily holds its own. A quiet store-front blossoms into a huge back room, nicely furnished with Hellenic simplicity. Service here is leisurely, if not laid back, so you have plenty of time to savor your retsina and sample some creamy, garlicky tzatziki. Scoop it up with some of the warm, wholesome house bread. Entrees range from simple fish and herbs with Berbati's signature lemon-basted roast potatoes to a finely blended pastitsio—lamb, pasta, cheese, tomatoes, and cream sauce combined in a Greek lasagne.

Besaw's
2301 NW Savier St,
228-3764 (map:FF6)
Inexpensive; beer and
wine; AE, MC, V; local
checks only
Breakfast, lunch, dinner
every day

Three in the morning is a good time to have a hot roast beef sandwich. Tucked away in an old frame building on the edge of a residential neighborhood in far northwest Portland, the cozy all-wood Besaw's is open 24 hours a day. The menu begins with a long write-up on the history of the place (since 1903), but it pays to cut right to the food, which means breakfasts, omelets, sandwiches, and hamburgers. Orders are large and geared more to pleasing the palate than the eye. Standbys like ham and beans and corned beef hash share the menu with shrimp salad and an omelet filled with marionberries, hazelnuts, and cream cheese. Whatever you order, make sure it comes with a side of sassy sour-cream-and-onion French fries. At press time, they were installing an espresso machine—they have big plans for their new employee, Mr. Caffeine.

Bijou Cafe
132 SW 3rd Ave,
222-3187 (map:J5)
Inexpensive; beer and
wine; no credit cards;
checks OK
Breakfast, lunch every day

It's lost a little of its cult status, but the lines stretching out onto the sidewalk on Saturday morning still testify to the Bijou's early-morning power. Grilled cinnamon bread, specialty muffins, and oatmeal with helpful garnishes lead the list, and this is still one of only two places in Portland that can scramble an egg. The sandwiches and salads might not make your day, but the burgers are solid—try the one with cheese, ham, and egg—and the milk shakes are top of the line. Breakfasts are served long past the time some people start thinking about lunch.

BJ's Brazilian Restaurant
7019 SE Milwaukie Ave,
236-9629 (map:II5)
Moderate; beer and wine;
MC, V; checks OK

Portland's first Brazilian restaurant offers reasonably good, moderately priced versions of specialties such as bacalhoada (dried codfish) and feijoada (a black-bean and pork stew). Chicken dishes, such as one baked in dark beer and red palm oil—we're a long way from Kentucky Fried—are also admirable, along with appetizers of small, deep-fried meat pies called pastels. In the low-

Lunch Mon-Sat, dinner every day

key storefront atmosphere, decorated with little more than a poster on the wall, everything comes with rice, a grain dish called farofa, and a mixture of chopped cilantro and red pepper that can and should be spooned on everything in sight. Even with a huge bottle of an intense dark Brazilian beer call Xin gu, you haven't spent $40.

Boulevard Cafe
7958 SW Barbur Blvd,
245-9954 (map:II6)
Inexpensive; beer and
wine; AE, DC, MC, V;
local checks only
Breakfast, lunch, dinner
every day

A roadside restaurant with good food, neighborhood families, and spillovers from the Lewis and Clark dining halls, and a dash of dazzle every now and then: a breakfast with fresh-fruit pancakes, a dinner of tender Oregon rabbit. Indeed, dinner may be the Boulevard's finest hour. It starts with chewy homemade focaccia, and tortellini dusted with rosemary. Best to order the pasta and seafood—there are always one or two specials posted. Lately we've noticed some minor problems having to do with inexpert staff, out-of-stock wines, and inconsistent desserts. But that rarely detracts from the no-nonsense satisfaction of the place.

Brasserie Montmartre
626 SW Park Ave,
224-5552 (map:F1)
Moderate; full bar; AE,
DC, MC, V; checks ok
Lunch Mon-Fri, dinner
every day, brunch Sun

This is a place where spiked heels compete with spiked hair. It's also one of the only spots in town for late-night eats: on weekends you can graze until 3am. Hot local jazz (no cover) is also a plus. A few of the pastas are in the same league as the operation's ambitions—linguine with pesto and scallops, for example—but the salmon with lingonberry sauce is the real triumph here. There are some decent desserts: try the chocolate gateau with almonds and currants. The setting is artsy/decadent Paris of the '30s, which might have a bad influence on the less-than-model service.

Bridgeport Brew Pub
1313 NW Marshall St,
241-7179 (map:N1)
Inexpensive; beer and
wine; MC, V;
local checks only

½

KIDS This place is a cave—part of an old warehouse—but that comes with being a brew pub. Some think the malt-flavored-crust pizza is the best in Portland, others favor the unusual (though short) list of toppings (feta, eggplant, yellow peppers, Fred Carlo's chorizo, and olives). You can see the brewery from the pub, but by law kids are not allowed to peek at the beer-making process, so there's a large room set aside for families (until 8:30pm). No smoking.

Briggs and Crampton
1902 NW 24th Ave,
223-8690 (map:FF7)
Expensive; beer and wine;

A small event like lunch takes on grand proportions here. There appears to be nothing like it outside Portland, and people are flying in from afar to see what all the buzz is about. But they'd better have a reservation *be-*

MC, V; checks OK
Lunch Tues–Fri
(by reservation only)

fore they buy a plane ticket: reservations are taken once every three months (45 dates—aka tables—are available) and they book up in a matter of hours. It is, however, worth the difficulty. Nancy Briggs and Juanita Crampton's one-table restaurant acts as a playground for their true passion—catering; in fact, they claim to have never prepared the same meal twice (tough to verify, though!). Wintery fare may include a curried apple and potato soup and perhaps quail stuffed with wild rice sided with fresh pear chutney. Summers bring a lighter touch, employing locally grown vegetables, edible flowers, fresh herbs, and often seafood. Choose a special person and take the afternoon off.

Bread and Ink Cafe

3610 SE Hawthorne
Blvd, 239-4756
(map:GG5)
Inexpensive; beer and
wine; MC, V; checks OK
Breakfast, lunch, dinner
Mon-Sat, brunch Sun

Considering the Hawthorne area's boom over the last decade, you might almost call Bread and Ink a neighborhood restaurant that created its neighborhood around it. The idiosyncratic menu boasts everything from the city's best homemade blintzes to a wild salad (with some 17 greens and flowers) to burgers in which the condiments—mayo, mustard, ketchup—are made right on the premises. Blackboard specials venture successfully into neo-American, Mediterranean, and Mexican specialties. Any place where lunch can consist of spring rolls, chicken enchiladas, and a sublime Italian cassata for dessert—before things get more ambitious at dinner —has both nerve and style. Not surprisingly, there's a large and loyal clientele. Wonderful homemade cookies and silken chocolate pots de creme are mainstays of the dessert selection. For breakfast there are delicious, billowing omelets, assorted homemade breads, and great coffee. On Sunday, bring *The New York Times* and settle in for a soul-satisfying four-course Jewish-style brunch.

Bush Garden

900 SW Morrison St,
226-7181 (map:H2)
Moderate; full bar; AE,
DC, MC, V; no checks
Lunch Mon-Fri, dinner
every day

Some of the city's best practitioners of sushi art pass through this kitchen. Chefs here have turned out versions of sushi and sashimi not found elsewhere: a brilliant flounder sushi dressed with chiles, sake, and soy sauce, for example; or mackerel with jelly-textured kombu and toasted sesame seeds. When they're available, try the hand-rolled maki containing small bouquets of radish sprouts and salmon-skin shavings. Regular Japanese fare is offered in tatami rooms; however, some of those entrees have been thoroughly stripped of authentic character. Others, such as tea on rice and jellyfish salad, are so authentic they can only be meant for the Japanese business crowd. You figure it out.

Buster's Smokehouse Texas-Style Bar-Be-Que
17883 SE McLoughlin Blvd, Milwaukie, 652-1076 (map:II5)

1355 E Burnside, Gresham, 667-4811 (map:FF1)
Inexpensive; beer and wine; MC, V; local checks only
Lunch, dinner every day

One deep whiff as you come in tells you all you need to know about Buster's, where huge wood-smoke ovens leave their mark on both the meat and the atmosphere. Brisket, chicken, beef and pork ribs, and links all pass through the cooker and come out estimably pink and juicy. The pungent barbecue sauce helps considerably, and beer is the beverage of choice. Accompaniments are simple: fries, slaw, barbecue beans, and, for the daredevil, stuffed jalapeno peppers. Pecan pie is a solid finish. Equal emphasis on barbecue essentials at both the original Milwaukie location and the newer Gresham branch.

Cafe des Amis
1987 NW Kearney St, 295-648 (map:FF5)
Moderate; full bar; AE, MC, V; checks OK
Dinner Mon-Sat

The now-upscale Cafe des Amis has dimmed a bit from its beginnings as a down-home French cafe, but it still produces mostly satisfying meals that are surprisingly reasonable. The fragrant soups and hearty stews of provincial France and the Spanish Pyrenees are still around, and the duck terrine with pistachios and the chicken-liver pate redolent of figs and port still glisten. Look for mussels in a marvelous soup enriched with curry and cream. Add a salad with toasted walnuts, a basket of terrific oven-fresh French rolls, and one of the many bottles of good wine, and you have the makings of a light but satisfying meal. Recent entrees included quail in a honey-lime duck reduction, and a fillet of salmon, sauteed and then poached, in a sauce of creme fraiche and shallots. Chef Dennis Baker also makes the best steak in town, a buttery, two-inch-thick fillet in a sauce that alchemizes port and garlic. The dessert tray always merits serious consideration, and you can rely on the serving staff to assess the day's offerings candidly.

Caffe Fresco
2387 NW Thurman St, 243-3247 (map:FF6)
Inexpensive; no alcohol; no credit cards; local checks only
Breakfast, lunch every day, brunch Sun

On the fringe of northwest Portland's industrial zone, this mini-cafe serves breakfast "until it is gone." And that doesn't take long, given the simple morning offerings: muffins and scones (which should be tried with the lemon curd spread), quiche and granola, and a hearty "breakfast pudding" that's concocted of oats, dates, currants, and other fruit in a bread custard. Lunch is less memorable: uninspired dolmathes or perhaps a savory spanakopita-like turnover that combines spinach, ricotta, and tomatoes in phyllo. An expanse of tall windows over Thurman Street makes Caffe Fresco a good place to people-watch.

Cajun Cafe and Bistro

2074 NW Lovejoy St,
227-0227 (map:FF5)
Moderate; full bar; AE,
DC, MC, V; no checks
Lunch Mon-Fri, dinner
every day

★½

After a period of nonstop blackening, the Cajun Cafe has headed down the Santa Fe trail, and from recent reports they may have gone too far. Solid renditions of jambalaya and crawfish etouffee are now joined by a mediocre "terminator" green chile and black bean cake with salsa fresca and goat cheese. The changes have been accomplished without loss of the original Cajun core, with enough heat to justify repeated applications of Dixie beer and Cajun martinis. Still, only some of the additions maintain the balance of earthiness and sophistication. The kitchen occasionally strays from the two cuisines—the leg of lamb in a ginger-hoisin marinade and the grilled venison with wild mushrooms, hazelnuts, and tarragon may be hard to place, but they're easy to eat. The servers are reliable and competent guides who won't let you venture too far from New Orleans.

Carnival

2805 Sam Jackson Rd,
227-4244 (map:HH6)
Inexpensive; no alcohol;
no credit cards; local
checks only
Lunch, dinner Mon-Sat

KIDS If you have children in Portland, you probably know Carnival like you know your pediatrician. The major choice here is whether you want the quarter-pound or half-pound burger, and whether you can keep the kids calm during the few minutes between watching your burger hit the grill and seeing it appear at the cash register. You can stall by debating which kind of milk shake everybody wants.

Casa-U-Betcha

612 NW 21st Ave,
227-3887 (map:FF4)
Moderate; full bar; AE,
MC, V; no checks
Lunch Mon-Fri, dinner
every day

★½

Welcome to Portland's first taco club. This wild and crazy eatery has become one of northwest Portland's most "happening" restaurants. One of the reasons is the interior, best described as hardware sci-fi. Galvanized stovepipe doubles for industrial-art cacti, sprouting from glitzy Formica banquettes and metal-topped tables beneath an electric orange sunset of corrugated Fiberglas deck roofing. The bar is a psychedelicized tile affair, invariably inhabited by punks and preppies. The cumin jalapeno cheesecake is only one example of the restaurant's neo-Mex cuisine. Specials are ambitious, if not always successful. Regular stabs at Brazilian and Chilean cooking by chef John Huyck reveal an understanding that "south of the border" need not be restricted to Tijuana. A Seattle branch opened recently (2212 First Avenue).

Chang's Mongolian Grill

1 SW 3rd Ave, 243-1991
(map:J4)
Inexpensive; beer and

If you'd like to prepare your own meal but can't be troubled to stock a cupboard full of esoteric ingredients, this is the place. You move along a buffet stocked with fresh, uncooked fixings—meats, seafoods, and vegetables, plus a full range of seasonings, oils, and spices—

*wine; MC, V; no checks
Lunch, dinner every day*

½

and select whatever combination your mood dictates. Your creation is then stir-fried to perfection atop a half-ton convex grill manned by two cooks. Back at the table you enclose your concoction, burrito-style, in thin Chinese pancake wrappers. You're the boss here, which means the experience probably won't be disappointing. All this in a setting exhibiting an outstanding specimen of restaurant art: a 3-D depiction of warring Mongol horsemen galloping through fiery fluorescent lights across a neon blue sky.

Chang's Yangtze
*921 SW Morrison St,
241-0218 (map:I2)
Moderate; full bar; MC,
V; local checks only
Lunch Mon-Sat, dinner
every day*

Chi-wei Chang, who also owns Chang's Mongolian Grill, has been a mover and shaker in Portland's Oriental cooking scene for more than a decade. He figured out years ago that Sinophiles expect fiery sauces, authentic ingredients, and exotic touches. This is the fare at the Yangtze, a stylish but casual little place with a hot-and-cool interior of pink, turquoise, and red. The menu includes favorites from the six major culinary regions of China, and the chicken dishes—especially the onion chicken and the five-flavored chicken—are considered the best around. Pass up the routine appetizers and concentrate on the house specials. Also not to be missed is sesame beef on crisp white noodles—a stunning blend of chile heat and high flavor.

Chen's China Clipper
*6750 SW Beaverton-
Hillsdale Hwy, 292-4898
(map:HH7)
Moderate; full bar; AE,
DC, MC, V; checks OK
Lunch every day*

In the middle of 1988 chef Chi-siung Chen jumped his Portland ship. Leaving downtown for the suburbs, he opened a restaurant specializing intensely in seafood (note the giant papier-mache fish hanging from the ceiling), including 28 different shrimp dishes. The results are sometimes uneven but often brilliant, and usually well worth getting your feet wet for. Shanghai Harbor Crab, a whole Dungeness in a hoisin sauce flecked with ginger and scallions, is a good example of the place at its best. Chiang siu—whole crispy fish and scallops in a nest, Hunan-style—demonstrates how effectively Northwestern seafood and Far Eastern inspiration can blend. Be warned: you're going to pay more than you might expect for Chinese food, and when Chen himself is not in the kitchen, standards dip toward the waterline.

Chen's Dynasty
*622 SW Washington St,
248-9491 (map:I3)
Moderate; full bar; AE,
MC, V; no checks*

The 12-page menu must be one of the most complete anywhere this side of the People's Republic—you could explore culinary China here for years without repetition. Several dishes are rarities for these parts: sweet and pungent fish with honey-roasted pine nuts; squid cut to

Lunch Mon-Sat, dinner
every day

look like clusters of flowers and perfumed with Sichuan peppercorns; and pheasant Hunan-style. Standbys such as kung pao shrimp and General Tsao's Chicken are usually treated with respect. The decor dispels the notion that Chinese restaurants must look like the sets for Fu Manchu movies. Among the nice touches is a rendering of the Great Wall that winds from the doorway to the dining room entrance, festooned with soft cotton serpents.

Chez Jose

8502 SW Terwilliger
Blvd, 244-0007 (map:JJ6)
Inexpensive; full bar; MC,
V; local checks only
Lunch Mon-Sat, dinner
every day

½

First off, there's all the iguana kitsch you would expect in a place with a rhyming biethnic name. There are also a bunch of faux marble pillars and lively rock music from a radio. The proximity to Lewis and Clark College explains a lot about some of the waiters—and customers. There is a short menu of the usual Mexican dishes, including a salady tostada, enchiladas, and a Mexican chicken soup that's worth catching a cold for (but where does the "chez" come in?). An outstanding green-pepper salsa (sweet and hot).

Coffee People Immediate Care Center

817 NW 23rd Ave,
226-3064 (map:JJ6)
Inexpensive; no alcohol;
no credit cards; checks OK
Dessert every day

No, it's not an extension of nearby Good Samaritan Hospital but a coffee and pastry place providing fixes for a lot of late-night caffeine addicts. This narrow turquoise and green storefront is an outgrowth of the coffee-bean business in an old house across 23rd Avenue. A lengthy menu of coffee drinks, tea and hot chocolate options, and Eugene's Prince Puckler's ice cream. The 16 milk shakes include one flavored with freshly ground peanut butter. Or perhaps an espresso float to accompany the cookies, muffins, and sweet rolls provided by a trio of local bakeries. Try Black Tiger, a coffee with 30 percent added caffeine; after a jolt like that you may really need immediate care.

Couch Street Fish House

105 NW 3rd Ave,
223-6173 (map:K5)
Expensive; full bar; AE,
MC, V; checks OK
Dinner every day

Old World tradition envelops this place like a cloak. Waiters in formal dress bring warm hand towels before the meal and, much later, whipped cream and brown sugar with your coffee. Several of them converge on your heavily linened table to whisk the covers off all the entrees in one swift movement. The tradition also means a commitment to lovely presentation, which makes this the kind of place to go on an expense account. Food is not adventurous (Horst Mager keeps a tight rein on his chefs), but it is well prepared, especially the appetizers (including a memorable ravioli stuffed with foie gras) and desserts. Sauces are near perfect. If you're going to splurge here anyway, go ahead and start things off with the utterly fresh Columbia River sturgeon caviar—a dangerously expensive addiction.

Crepe Faire
133 SW 2nd Ave,
227-3365 (map:I5)
Moderate; full bar; AE,
DC, MC, V; checks ok
Breakfast, lunch, dinner
Mon-Sat

 ★½

This gracious establishment, with large arched windows, exposed brick, and crimson and gray tones, is one of the few places in town that continues to take the almost-vanished crepe genre seriously. Ironically, except for some permutations on the dessert list, crepes are among the least interesting option here. Breakfast features impressive muffins, the spinach and mushroom gateau is always around, and evening brings out a stylish green-peppercorn chicken and a good beef fillet with even better pommes frites. Chocolate chestnut torte is a grand finale, and the wine list is one of the better and more reasonably priced in Portland. Crepe Faire is a place for romantic tete-a-tetes, high-minded dealings, or just a good, leisurely meal with attentive service, especially at the sidewalk tables on nice days.

Dan's West Coast Bento
2340 NW Westover Rd,
227-1779 (map:FF7)
Inexpensive; no alcohol;
no credit cards; no checks
Lunch Mon-Fri

 ★

The smartest lunch buy in town. After a stint in the Far East, Big Dan decided to create a yakitori bento (lunch box) restaurant. Open only for lunch, this enterprise offers a wonderful menu: skewers of barbecued beef, chicken, lamb, or seafood served on brown or white rice, sauced with a simultaneously sweet and spicy yakitori concoction that's delightful. Complement that with hum bao, pot-stickers, or steamed pork pastries, and add a side of fiery kimchi, and lunch takes on bountiful and flavorful dimensions rarely seen in America. DWCB number two is coming soon.

Dave's Delicatessen
1110 SW 3rd Ave,
222-5461 (map:G4)
Inexpensive; beer and
wine; no credit cards, local
checks only
Breakfast, lunch, early
dinner Mon-Sat

The original owners, who knew everybody who ever ate here, are gone now, but Dave's stands as it's always stood, dispensing pastrami on the ground floor of the Multnomah County Hall of Justice. Given its extensive legal clientele, it can claim to be the place where the torts meet the schmaltz. The sandwiches are huge, the Russian dressing is passable, and what you think of the corned beef and pastrami will probably depend on whether you've ever eaten the stuff east of the Hudson River. If you haven't, it's fine, and if you have, there's always the turkey sandwich—and lots of lawyers.

Delphina's
2112 NW Kearney St,
221-1195 (map:FF5)

When owners Michael Cronan and Tory Hedgpeth opened this Italian eatery a decade ago—borrowing Cronan's grandmother's name and recipes and Hedg-

Moderate; full bar; AE, DC, MC, V; no checks Lunch Mon-Fri, dinner every day

peth's pasta know-how—the neighborhood was less than highfalutin *and* the clientele was prone to writing rubber checks. A risky venture that has since paid off, as (eventually) has the faithful clientele.

Under the hands of chef Joy Graham the restaurant usually turns out well-crafted meals in the Northern Italian vein (chicken in a mustard cream sauce over homemade linguine, a wonderful pasta al pesto). And whether ordering a pasta dish (which can at times can be uneven in quality) or one of the specialitas della casa (Oregon rabbit, perhaps), be sure to request the dark greens tossed with walnuts and chunks of Gorgonzola and dressed with walnut oil and sherry vinegar. But perhaps the underlying reason for Delphina's long-lasting success is the pizza—a well-crusted affair boasting unusual toppings. The restaurant also offers a commendable wine list. Regardless of what you order, the dark wood, high booths, and remarkable art (mostly by Portland artists) create an atmosphere that has tempted more than a few locals (who by now may have added a few more zeros to their income) to make Delphina's their living room.

Doris' Cafe
3240 N Williams St, 287-9249 (map:EE5) Inexpensive; no alcohol; MC, V; local checks only Lunch, dinner Tues-Sat

A hickory-burning brick pit and two hinged oil drums outside produce serious beef and pork ribs, with a sauce that is more sweet than angry. If you've sworn off barbecue, fried chicken is lovely, fresh, and gently complex. Desserts vary, but the buttery pound cake and the mousselike sweet potato pie should not be missed. Most take their food to go, but if you decide to stay, get comfortable: nothing's going to come too quickly.

Dragoon's Deli
50 SW 2nd Ave (New Market Village), 223-4711 (map:J5)

6651 SW Capitol Hwy, 244-0111 (map:II7) Inexpensive; no alcohol; no credit cards; local checks only Breakfast, lunch, dinner Sun-Fri

½

For Easterners who were raised on knishes, bagels, mouth-stretching corned beef sandwiches, and egg creams (and who bemoan the lack thereof in Portland), Dragoon's is the next best thing—complete with a dispenser of fresh horseradish. All the meats are Hebrew National. The beef franks are top dog here; but there's also New York chopped liver, Philadelphia whitefish salad, and New York light corn rye bread. It doesn't look much different from the other New Market stands, but one bite might just put you back home in the Big Apple. The other branch, in the Mittleman Jewish Community Center, is larger, sells more meat products, and offers seating.

All places in this book are recommended; even "no stars" are worth knowing about.

Eddie Lee's

409 SW 2nd Ave,
228-1874 (map:I5)
Inexpensive; full bar; AE,
DC, MC, V; checks OK
Lunch Mon-Fri, dinner
Mon-Sat

All too often, restaurants open impressively and then taper off. Eddie Lee's opened impressively and keeps getting better. From a solid premiere in 1987 with stunning sandwiches such as roast pork loin with fruit mustard and sweet onion relish on focaccia, and lighter entrees such as Portuguese mussels with chorizo, the restaurant has extended its hours and broadened its menu. There was a brief (and outstanding) attempt at breakfast—but no more. Now nighttime means grilled duck breast with smoked tea butter, pasta with black beans and prawns, or bouillabaisse. The setting—two small dining rooms crowded with director's chairs across a lobby from one another—not only makes the late-night effect more dramatic, it keeps prices down. The fun here is not only in consuming an impressive meal but in seeing the latest items the kitchen has come up with.

El Palenque

8324 SE 17th Ave,
231-5140 (map:II5)
Inexpensive; beer and
wine; MC, V; checks OK
Lunch, dinner Tues-Sun

Salvadoran in Sellwood, we heard. When we arrived for lunch at this tinsel-draped restaurant, we found only mediocre huevos rancheros, enchiladas, and chile rellenos. Central American samplings, it turns out, only appear on the dinner and weekend menus—but they do (and should) make exceptions at lunch. Ask for Salvadoran and nowhere else in Portland will you begin your meal so gently as with orchata (a lovely drink of rice, milk, sugar, and a dash of cinnamon). Savor sublime pupupas (two plump corn tortillas with loroco—an aromatic flower—and cheese) pepped up with a lively sauce and cabbage marinated in vinegar, or Platanos con Frijoles y Crema (a wonderful marriage of plantains, beans, and cream). Salvadoran Cuisine 101 is taught by sincere waitpeople anxious to introduce you to the tastes of their native country.

Escape from New York Pizza

913 SW Alder St,
226-4129 (map:I2)
Inexpensive; beer only; no
credit cards;
local checks only
Lunch, dinner Mon-Sat
622 NW 23rd Ave,
227-5423 (map:FF6)
Lunch, dinner every day

The name comes from a movie—it's not an invitation to Chicago-pizza fans. And the place might more accurately be called Escape *to* New York Pizza, because the combination here of thin crust, spicy tomato sauce, and a massive mozzarella layer is as close to a Big Apple pie as anything in the state.

For those diners who insist on eating on the premises, each branch has its own ambience: teenage punk on Alder (drawing from Pioneer Courthouse Square and Lincoln High School), and laid-back in the northwest, fitting nicely into the rest of the neighborhood.

Esplanade at RiverPlace (Alexis Hotel)

*1510 SW Harbor Wy,
295-6166 (map:E4)
Expensive; full bar; AE,
DC, MC, V; checks OK
Breakfast, dinner every
day, lunch Mon-Fri,
brunch Sun*

From high-price, low-success beginnings, Esplanade continues to improve, although it still has a way to go. The strengths are still there: a lovely room, a wide-angle view of the Willamette, and a formality of service that can convince you that something special is going on. As for the food, instead of silly amalgamations created solely for looks, there now seems to be an honest attempt to create something actually edible. Soups such as lobster bisque and apple-broccoli are outstanding, and salads—especially the endive and Stilton with apple slices and calvados vinaigrette—are impressive and imaginative. Appetizers and entrees are less consistent, but a fine meal is certainly possible here. Service is attentive without being intrusive. The fixed-price Sunday brunch, which includes an appetizer platter, breads and brioche, your choice of entree, and a selection from the dessert tray, is far superior to all-you-can-eat offerings at the same price.

Fat City Cafe

*7820 SW Capitol Hwy,
245-5457 (map:II7)
Inexpensive; no alcohol;
no credit cards; local
checks only
Breakfast, lunch Mon-Sat*

Fat City was already famous for its massive cinnamon rolls when Portland Mayor Bud Clark fired his police chief there in 1987. Now the history looms as large as the pancakes. Nothing very subtle, but on Saturday morning lines still run out the door of this storefront in Multnomah Village. The ham comes in slabs, the eggs over easy actually are over easy, and the biscuits are soft enough to cushion a firing. Lunchtime means the basics, and the old-time soda counter offers milk shakes worthy of it.

Fong Chong

*301 NW 4th Ave,
220-0235 (map:K5)
Inexpensive; full bar; no
credit cards; checks OK;
Lunch, dinner every day*

The setting—a cacophony of Chinese and Caucasian voices, clattering teacups, and clicking chopsticks—is far from sedate. From 11am to 3pm daily, young waiters scurry from table to table, hawking their handmade morsels on miniature saucers. Welcome to Portland's finest dim sum parlor, where an array of steamed buns and savory dumplings is dispatched with gusto. Come here in an adventurous spirit; dishes are inexpensive enough for you to discard the occasional one that fails to please. Order by simply pointing at what looks interesting. At night, Fong Chong is transformed into a quiet Cantonese eatery, with average preparations and a few surprises.

Foothill Broiler

*33 NW 23rd Pl, 223-0287
(map:FF6)
Inexpensive; no alcohol;*

KIDS This is a step-up-from-a-cafeteria kind of place to have a hamburger and a piece of pie. The grill does patties in three sizes, with or without cheese, and offers good French fries or baked beans alongside. The cooks

no credit cards; local checks only
Breakfast, lunch Mon-Sat, dinner Mon-Fri

will even grill a tuna sandwich if that's the way you like it. The cafeteria line takes you past stalwarts like Jell-O with fruit and cottage cheese en route to some fine layer cakes, cheesecakes, and pies. Tilework and framed prints raise the interior from the merely cafeterian to the stylish. Expect long lines at mealtimes.

Formosa Harbor
1130 SW 11th Ave,
228-4144 (map:G1)
Inexpensive; no alcohol;
MC, V; no checks
Lunch Mon-Fri, dinner Mon-Sat

KIDS Billed as a seafood restaurant, this small, unassuming establishment does a fine job with meat dishes, too, including a robust General Tsao's Chicken, Sichuan beef, and twice-cooked pork. The lunch boom makes reservations advisable. Of special note is fried shrimp with tomato chile pepper sauce, tender chunks of seafood that are tangy, slightly sweet, spicy. The pace slows and the menu grows in the evenings; this remains one of the best bargain dinners. Service is eager and friendly, and the owners' children are sometimes seen in the evening doing their homework at a corner table.

Fuji
2878 SE Gladstone St,
233-0577 (map:HH4)
Inexpensive; beer and wine; MC, V; no checks
Lunch Tues-Fri, dinner Tues-Sat

Fuji is, hands down, Portland's favorite sushi bar. There are those who eat here once a week just to challenge chef Fujio Handa's resourcefulness. Handa regularly departs from Old School rules of sushi making to whip up creative concoctions (incorporating Western ingredients) that would make natives of Tokyo blush—and ask for more. The sharp black and white geometric decor has flair, though the regular menu doesn't (our tempura udon had tough prawns, and the gyoza were greasy). But sushi is why you are here.

Gazebo Gallery-Restaurant
11 SW Mt Jefferson Tce,
Lake Oswego,
635-2506 (map:KK7)
Moderate; beer and wine;
AE, MC, V; checks OK
Lunch Tues-Sat, dinner Thurs-Sat

This is where Lake Oswegoans go for a (usually) lovely lunch. The glassed-in gazebo architecture and wrought-iron furniture provide a calm atmosphere, with the feel of a greenhouse. Dishes are prepared with fresh seasonal ingredients, from a vegetarian enchilada to cioppino to veal Marsala with wild mushrooms. A circular staircase leads up to the gallery.

Genoa
2832 SE Belmont St,
238-1464 (map:GG5)
Expensive; wine only; AE,
DC, MC, V; checks OK
Dinner Mon-Sat

For the most ambitious meal in town, Genoa is the clear winner—provided you like an intimate atmosphere, Northern Italian food made with care and skill, and meals that span hours without running out of imagination.

There's no view to act as drawing card: the windowless dining room is without much illumination, and it can be a couple of courses before you even know who you're dining with. By then, however, you may hardly care; saffron-inflected fish soup, seafood ravioli, or spinach dumplings overshadow all other thoughts. Of the seven courses—appetizer, soup, pasta, fish, entree, dessert, and fruit—not all will be spectacular, but a couple will certainly be, and the rest will be very good. The only choice of the evening comes with the entree, when you're offered dishes such as pork tenderloin in a tomato and Marsala sauce or veal scallops in Madeira and morels. You can also choose dessert from a trayful of tortes and gelati, but there's really only one showstopper: boccone dolce, a baroque layering of meringue, chocolate, berries, and whipped cream. Some diners have been known to sob audibly over it.

Tearful outbursts and other special situations are well handled by knowledgeable staff, who carefully describe the food and know the well-thought-out wine list. Theatergoers will be pleased with the abridged version of dinner (antipasto, pasta, entree, dessert) served at 5:30pm and 6pm and then again at 10pm and 10:30pm.

Giant Drive-In

15840 SW Boones Ferry Rd, Lake Oswego, 636-0255 (map:LL7) Inexpensive; no alcohol; no cards; checks OK Lunch, dinner every day

KIDS This old drive-in, all 900 square feet of it, is, as Spencer Tracy would say, "cherse." There are some 30 specialty burgers with things like soy sauce and pineapple on them, but the basic burger is the perfect amalgam of meat, veggies, sauce, and bun. The Filler holds ham, bacon, and that all-important Dagwood ingredient, an egg. Order the skinny and crisp fries and a real ice cream milk shake: it's like dying and waking up in 1955. Burgers come in adults and children's sizes, but any child over the age of 7 will be able to down an adult version—it's that good.

Ginza

730 NW 21st Ave, 223-7881 (map:FF6) Moderate; full bar; MC, V; local checks only Lunch Tues-Fri, dinner Tues-Sat

Ginza recently expanded both its size and the range of its sushi bar, and both have turned out fine. Private tatami rooms now line the walls, and the sushi bar does particularly interesting things with hamachi and salmon skin; even the basic assortment seems a bit more imaginative than most. Other strong dishes, particularly welcome at lunch, when sushi is not available, include pungent gyoza and salt-broiled mackerel that manages to be oily and crunchy and tasty all at once. The TV set near the sushi bar shows what appear to be Japanese commercials.

Goose Hollow Inn

1927 SW Jefferson St, 228-7010 (map:GG6)

Best known as the home of the beer that made Bud Clark mayor, the Goose also produces a small but consistent menu of some of the best bar food in the owner's

Inexpensive; beer and wine; no credit cards; local checks only Lunch, dinner every day

constituency. The Reuben, the roast beef on a soft roll, and the Tuesday crab salad are deservedly popular, and all are assisted by the products of local microbreweries. Friendly, heavy on the regulars, and popular with local political and media types, the Goose is likely to have an unlimited term of office.

Grand Cafe American Restaurant

832 SE Grand Ave, 230-1166 (map:G9) Lunch Mon-Fri, dinner Mon-Sat Moderate; full bar; AE, DC, MC, V; checks OK

If you were to put an American cafe in Paris, this is what it would look like. Small tables, booths, and a grand piano make it a good destination for dinner for two. Chef Chris McCune handles a menu that spans US cuisine, from seafood to Cajun, and seems to have an affinity for nuts —and somehow it works (even hazelnuts in the clam chowder). It's the kind of place where you can come early to nibble on an appetizer of smoked seafood or stay late—desserts go well while the pianist tickles the ivories from 6pm–11pm.

Grant House

1101 Officers' Row, Vancouver, WA, (206) 696-9699 (map:BB5) Expensive; full bar; AE, DC, MC, V; checks OK Lunch Mon-Fri, dinner Mon-Sat, brunch Sunday

Grandly lit and festooned with nearly as many flags as the UN, the Grant House makes you want to salute. Formerly the home of Fort Vancouver's commanding officers, the renovated mansion opened in late 1988 as an expensive eatery boasting an extensive, award-winning wine list as well as heavily-sauced entrees that have received accolades from Portland and beyond. Alas, recent visits indicate that to stray from staples is to risk a journey into mediocrity. Are they resting on their too-impressive beginnings?

The setting is elegant enough—stateliness with an edge of stiffness—and the meal begins with a dainty puff of salmon mousse. The ravioli appetizer is the Grant House at its best: lobster- and salmon-stuffed pouches topped with a delicate pesto sauce that left us nearly swooning. Unfortunately, we didn't stay starry-eyed for long. Even Popeye would shake his head at the spinach salad flambe: this time, anyway, the dressing seemed just too sweet for the greens. To eat well here, stick with the simpler entrees: grilled Columbia River salmon, pine nut–smothered sturgeon, or roasted duck. Forget their attempts at sophistication. The waiter-endorsed baked chicken en croute (stuffed with chestnuts and wrapped in a pastry) was boring at best. The shrimp, scallop, and salmon linguine was lacking many signs of sealife. In short, what's good at the Grant is excellent, but what's not....Upstairs in the lounge, there's often a blazing fire before which, in 1853, Ulysses S. Grant doubtless lingered with a glass of port.

RESTAURANTS

The Grapery
4190 SW Cedar Hills Blvd, Beaverton, 646-1437 (map:GG9) Moderate; beer and wine; AE, MC, V; checks OK Lunch Mon-Fri, dinner Mon-Sat

Until Fred Meyer began its wine steward program, the Grapery was the best wine store in Beaverton. Now, locals hate to admit, it's the best wine store that's also a restaurant. Diners may choose from 350 wines (a half-dozen or so by the glass). While the menu has no ethnic focus, owner Craig Peck sometimes whips up an Oriental stir-fry for fun; he has also hosted some fine wine-tasting dinners. As of press time, Peck had put the establishment up for sale—but under the condition that the buyer maintain it essentially as it was.

Greek Deli and Grocery
1740 E Burnside, 232-0274 (map:FF5) Inexpensive; beer and wine; MC, V; checks OK Lunch, dinner Mon-Sat

The quintessential "great find": the city's most gregarious grocery store, home of the best souvlaki and gyros in town and purveyor of perfect pistachios (imported from the family farm in Greece). The owners are characteristically Greek, warm and welcoming. Where else can you get a guided tour of aisles packed with Aegean specialties? It's also the only spot in Portland where you can take a break from shopping and dive into authentic ethnic eats dished up from the operation's small deli. A fun place full of surprises.

Hall Street Bar & Grill
3775 SW Hall Blvd, Beaverton, 641-6161 (map:HH9) Moderate; full bar; AE, MC, V; checks OK Lunch Mon-Sat, dinner every day

With high vaulted ceilings and oak floors, Hall Street looks and acts like a typical fern bar. The difference is in the food, featuring rock salt–roasted prime rib and mesquite-grilled steaks from Nebraska cows. An inventive daily menu includes another half-dozen entree selections, mostly nouveau fish prepared with ingredients like lime, ginger, basil, hazelnuts, and/or avocado salsa. A recent wine list (usually a dozen Northwest and California wines) offered three different nouveaux Beaujolais. A superb burnt creme with a hard sugar crust leads the list of strong desserts. Service is personable.

Hamburger Mary's
840 SW Park Ave, 223-0900 (map:G2) Inexpensive; beer and wine; AE, MC, V; no checks Breakfast, lunch, dinner every day

The name's a bit misleading. We come not just for the burgers, but for the omelets, for which the diner gets to choose from a long list of ingredients. Ditto the baked potatoes. Burgers come oozing with melted cheese. We're talking comfort food here, folks, eaten in a dark-wood shell while it's raining outside. It's a silly, late-'60s spot, a frenzied kitsch collection that includes fringed lampshades and baby bottles for creamers. The coffee is excellent.

Hands On Cafe
8245 NW Barnes Rd, 297-1480 (map:GG9)

At this rustic little dining room, which operates under the auspices of the Oregon School of Arts and Crafts, you can dine off handmade pottery as carefully crafted as

Inexpensive; no alcohol; no credit cards; checks OK Lunch Mon-Fri, dinner Mon-Thurs, brunch Sun

the artworks from the adjoining school. The ever-changing lunch menu is low on selection but high on innovation: Basque bean and pumpkin potage, fresh tomato and pesto tart, Kenyan chicken stew, and pear custard tart are typical offerings. The place really lights up—and fills up—for Sunday brunch, when the inspiration can range from the Pacific Northwest to New Orleans to Peru. Good sticky cinnamon rolls, fresh fruit, and French bread come with your choice of entrees. Expect to wait, but there are certainly things to look at while you do.

Harborside Restaurant

0309 SW Montgomery St, 220-1865 (map:C5) Moderate; full bar; AE, DC, MC, V; local checks only Lunch, dinner every day, Sunday brunch

Portland's RiverPlace promenade draws huge crowds of strollers eager to see the Willamette up close, and Harborside seems designed to have something for each one of them. The riparian outpost of the McCormick & Schmick empire has a menu that runs not only from salads to burgers to grilled salmon with fettucine, but from Oregon to Italy to Greece to Louisiana to Jamaica. Since not even airline food successfully stretches that far, the key is to stick close to home, with the local seafood that swims through the entire M&S food chain. Desserts are also solid, and the restaurant is set up so that virtually every table overlooks the marina. After dinner, you can tack over to the teeming, rocking Shanghai Lounge next door, where younger singles train for the big leagues at Jake's.

Hawthorne Street Cafe

3354 SE Hawthorne Blvd, 232-4982 (map:GG4) Inexpensive; beer and wine; MC, V; checks OK Breakfast, lunch Tues-Sun

KIDS The '60s are alive in an old house on Hawthorne Boulevard. The Hawthorne Street Cafe revives the term "mellow," which—considering how many of the people who used it now have children—is a timely reappearance. Breakfasts here are sizable, with huge, imaginative omelets lapped by piles of fried potatoes and home-baked coffee cake and muffins, or the mandatory granola alternative. Sandwiches are large and overflowing, but a lot of the laid-back clientele seem to have breakfast whatever time it is. Terrific coffee cake. The service is invariably cheerful, even if it's not exactly at breakneck pace.

The Heathman Restaurant and Bar

1009 SW Broadway, 241-4100 (map:G2) Expensive; full bar; AE, DC, MC, V; checks OK

This is the local leader in the Pacific Northwest cuisine movement. Since taking over the kitchen in 1985, chef George Tate has helped turn this once ho-hum eatery into a showcase of regional excellence: a stately place with a marble-top bar, big leather chairs, and a wall of Andy Warhol paintings. Under Tate's guidance, native

*Breakfast, lunch, dinner
every day*

bounty has become more the specialty of the house; local seafood, game, and seasonal produce are some of the highlights. A dinner menu might feature Chinook salmon sharpened with Sichuan spices. On another night, quail comes in a nest of fresh rosemary, and sturgeon is delivered in a fire of Thai curry.

Breakfast is served in an elegant setting, with great attention to taste and detail. Eggs Benedict takes on a Northwest flavor with smoked salmon replacing the ham; waffles come with a hint of malt and a mound of seasonal fruit; and cornmeal cakes with fresh blueberry compote take griddle food to new heights. The bar, a rich, glinting affair of marble and brass, features tapas and a fine selection of Portland's best microbrews.

Helvetia Tavern
Helvetia Rd, Hillsboro,
647-5286
*Inexpensive; beer and
wine; no credit cards;
no checks*
Lunch, dinner every day

Polished sports cars and motorcycles share space in the parking lot of this joint, where locals and highway travelers pack the premises and there's much chumminess between staff and patrons. Hamburgers and fries are the establishment's raison d'etre—beyond these options, proceed at your own risk. Burgers are topped with lightly sauteed onions, crisp lettuce, and tomatoes, and finished with a mayonnaise sauce—a decent old-fashioned burger. The fries are terrific, long and lean with skins intact, and heaped into a mound that covers half the plate like a golden haystack. There's Bingo on Wednesdays.

Hidden House
100 W 13th St,
Vancouver, WA,
(206) 696-2847
(map:BB5)
Moderate; beer and wine;
AE, MC, V; checks OK
*Lunch Mon-Fri, dinner
Tues-Sun*

The Hiddens, a leading family in these parts since 1870, made their money in a brick factory. This handsome house (of brick, of course) was constructed in 1885 in the stylish manner of the day; after fourteen years in the restaurant business the Hidden House, with Susan Courtney and her staff carefully cooking, has become a reliable place for an intimate dinner. You are offered an interesting combination of freshly made goods, small-city standards (pasta prima vera and scampi and tenderloin), and unusual gourmet dishes—getting lighter with the times. For lunch, the smoked salmon pasta with spinach and pinenuts in a sweet cream sauce or the shrimp Louie with a ginger lime dressing are popular. At dinner you are presented with very fresh seafood (salmon, halibut, mahi mahi) draped with a different sauce each night. Demand has kept such silly items on the menu as tender veal Rothschild (topped with shrimp, cream cheese, herbs, and green onions). Not all reports have been favorable from Vancouver's venerable establishment, but we admire what they're trying to do—and the range of clientele who seem to return for their homemade soups, breads made exclusively from unbleached flour, and natural, unprocessed cheeses. There's a porch for outside dining in the summer, and gas fireplaces in some of the rooms come winter.

Hot Lips Pizza

1909 SW 6th Ave (and branches), 224-0311 (map:C1)
Inexpensive; beer and wine; no credit cards; local checks only

These days, everyone is putting sun-dried tomatoes on pizza. Hot Lips does it with Montrachet or blue cheese, roma tomato, Romano cheese and fresh garlic, and how about good old pepperoni? Patrons can choose from about 40 toppings in designing pies with lots of cheese and just enough homemade sauce. Hot Lips also does enough business in by-the-slice sales that it can usually offer four or five varieties, at least at the PSU store. Other branches: downtown (222 SW Washington Street, 222-5477), Raleigh Hills (4825 SW 76th Avenue, 297-8424), Swan Island (4703 N Lagoon Street, 286-1038).

Huber's

411 SW 3rd Ave, 228-5686 (map:H4)
Moderate; full bar; AE, DC, MC, V; checks OK
Dinner Mon-Sat

Mahogany-paneled Huber's, established in 1879, continues to feel like a hub-of-the-city restaurant, in that people line up expectantly for the 5 o'clock dinner opening. The menu's as manly as the dark, woody place itself, working in the narrow range between baked ham and roast turkey (with a few fish selections). But while we salute Huber's for its concern with cholesterol (the substitutes were perfectly fine), really, turkey without mashed potatoes and gravy is like Adam without Eve. The line is probably shorter for the meal than for the after-dinner show starring the flaming Spanish coffee.

Humphrey Yogart

737 SW Salmon St, 228-7413 (map:G2)
Inexpensive; no alcohol; no credit cards; local checks only
Lunch, dinner every day

KIDS For a quick lunch, a bite at dinnertime, or, especially, coffee and low-calorie desserts, this bright, pleasing eating spot satisfies. Soups, salads, and sandwiches are well made from fresh ingredients and have imaginative touches (thinly sliced lamb with feta and chopped black olives, for instance). The yogurt dishes, both low- and non-fat, come with several mix-in ingredients for do-it-yourself customizing. Counter staff are pleasant and courteous, which in itself is a real treat. No smoking.

Hunan

515 SW Broadway, 224-8063 (map:I3)
Moderate; full bar; MC,

Visit Hunan if you want to get acquainted with some of the more fervid aspects of Chinese cooking. Despite an occasional misfire, it's one of the most consistently on-target Chinese eateries in town. Among the standouts: Hunan beef, Lake T'ung T'ing Shrimp, and minced

V; local checks only
Lunch, dinner Mon-Sat

Sichuan chicken wrapped in pancakes. The restaurant's versions of the spicy standards—General Tsao's Chicken, twice-cooked pork, chicken in tangy sauce—are pungent and massively popular. Service comes in one mode: fast and impersonal.

Ichidai
3384 SE Division St,
233-2179 (map:GG4)
Inexpensive; beer and
wine; MC, V; no checks
Lunch Tues-Fri, dinner
Tues-Sun

Outside, Ichidai still looks like the fast-food joint it was in a former life. Inside, it's a rare treat: a casual Japanese restaurant where you won't spend a fortune. The atmosphere is simple and tasteful, yet relaxed (staff and clientele wear jeans). Start with an artful tray of sashimi: mouth-watering octopus, snapper, tuna, mackerel dressed with cucumber and seaweed garnishes and green dabs of wasabe. Tough to go wrong with the teriyaki dinner or the seafood nabe (vegetables and seafood in a clear, fragrant broth).

Indigine
3725 SE Division St,
238-1470 (map:GG4)
Moderate; beer and wine;
MC, V; checks OK
Dinner Tues-Sat

The regulars who fill this small, unpretentious eatery are a casually dressed group for whom eating out is serious business. They put great stock in the wizardry of owner-chef Millie Howe, whose maverick style and obsession with quality guarantee that nothing here will be routine or prepackaged. For example, when Howe serves brunch—once a month—she makes the bagels as well as the cream cheese, and cures the lox. Saturdays are reserved for a blowout East Indian feast. The four-course extravaganza starts with something unexpected, perhaps mango mousse and homemade goat cheese in phyllo. There's a choice of entrees, typically a searing rabbit vindaloo, lamb curry, seafood curry, or a collection of vegetarian options. It's not unusual to find a stunning selection of Howe's chutneys on the side. Weeknight suppers have Latin American, European, or Pacific Northwest overtones: roast chicken stuffed beneath its skin with wildly garlicky pesto; a lovely salad basket overflowing with greens; and seafood enchiladas with hot chiles and cream. While there are numerous dessert offerings, Howe's pies are hard to beat.

Jake's Famous Crawfish
401 SW 12th Ave,
226-1419 (map:J1)
Moderate; full bar; AE,
DC, MC, V; checks OK

The length of its daily fresh list keeps this brass and mahogany Portland landmark on top of the Portland seafood restaurant list. No other local establishment of any kind can compete with it for style, atmosphere, and non-stop social scene. The faithful—and on some nights, one suspects, the unfaithful—pack the bar. In the dining room, the reservationless don't seem to mind the hour's wait for one of the coveted tables; they know their

Lunch Mon-Fri, dinner every day

patience will be rewarded with some of the best seafood in the city and a grand old time. For sure satisfaction, order from the fresh sheet—local crawfish are available May through September, and every August Jake's takes on a New Orleans restaurant in a crawfish cookoff. Items on the regular menu, as well as some of the stabs at Cajun, can be inconsistent. But when the restaurant is hot (the bouillabaisse, packed with fish and fennel, is one example), it's hot. The ultrarich truffle cake leads the desserts, but the peach-and-pear crisp has loyal supporters.

Jarra's Ethiopian Restaurant
607 SE Morrison St,
230-8990 (map:H3)
Inexpensive; beer and
wine; MC, V;
local checks only
Lunch Wed only, dinner
Mon-Sat

Nothing, neither those four-alarm Texas chiles nor those palate-flogging peppers from Thailand, packs the wallop of this kitchen's wat stews. Made of chicken, lamb, or beef, they are deep red, oily, and packed with pepper after-kicks. Full dinners come with assorted stewed meats and vegetables, all permeated with vibrant spices and mounded on injera—the spongy Ethiopian bread that doubles as plate and fork. The variety is not extensive, but this is the area's unequaled heat champ. Be sure to take time to chat with the friendly owners, Petros Jarra and Ainalem Sultessa, who will explain the origins of the food, give you an Abyssinian history lesson, and debate Ethiopian politics. Take it all in with plenty of cold beer, the logical beverage with this cuisine.

Johnny's Greek Villa
200 NW 3rd Ave,
227-1096 (map:K5)
Inexpensive; full bar; MC,
V; checks OK
Lunch, dinner Mon-Sat

Nothing's outstanding in this simple Old Town restaurant—but there haven't been many complaints, either. Johnny's blue-checkered Greek Villa is a good place to start for simple Greek cooking—moussaka (heavy with eggplant, lamb, and myzithra), horgiatiki salad (a toss of tomato, cucumber, onion, olives, and Feta), and great dolmathes. It all comes sided with overcooked fasolakia (green beans) and lukewarm orzo. Service is pleasantly brusque—and the check may just be verbal, $15 (for two).

Kashmir
1705 NE Couch St,
238-3934 (map:FF5)
Moderate; no alcohol; AE,
MC, V; checks OK
Dinner Tues-Sat

Teetotalism doesn't stand in the way of deep, purring contentment at the Pakistani-owned Kashmir restaurant: the melon smoothie will make you forget all the chateau-bottled delights you tried at the previous restaurant. When rents went up downtown, Kashmir moved into this turn-of-the-century house (formerly Thyme Garden). The lights are low and the air is colored with tinkling, rambling-creek sounds of the East. A five-course dinner ($18.95) is generously portioned with crispy vegetable samosas with hot dip, a tangy cucumber and tomato salad alert with cilantro, a feather-light popadum, two chewy Frisbees of chapati, raita (yogurt with cucumbers, tomatoes, and spices), basmati rice, an entree of terrific lamb korma or chicken liver curry, and a rice pudding. Close the meal with a milky tea spiced with cardamom.

Koji Osakaya Japanese Fish House
7007 SW Macadam Ave,
293-1066 (map:II6)
Moderate; full bar; AE,
DC, MC, V; no checks
Lunch Mon-Fri, dinner
every day

High on atmosphere, low on frills, and with enough noise to drown out a fraternity party, this is the Japanese answer to the neighborhood tavern. Koji's is also where you come to catch up on the latest in sumo wrestling— Nippon's most popular sport is broadcast on a television perched above the sushi bar. Sushi fans pack the 23-seat raw-fish counter to watch dueling behemoths ritualize the physics of overfed flesh. Most of the standard sushi preparations can be had here, as well as a few rarities such as the pungent plum-mint rolls. It's a busy place, and service can be, shall we say, leisurely.

Kyoto
506 SW 4th Ave,
274-7004 (map:I4)
Moderate; beer and wine;
AE, MC, V; local
checks only
Lunch, dinner Mon-Sat

Squeezed into a small storefront is a fair amount of Japanese imagination. Kyoto does the Japanese standards —teriyaki, sukiyaki—but does them and several other dishes with a flair of its own. The made-at-table sukiyaki, for example, comes with the authentic touch of a bowl of raw egg for dipping, and the waitress also whips up a tableside dipping sauce for the gyoza. And this must be the only restaurant around offering a Japanese breakfast (though it doesn't open until 11am).

The sushi choice is not wide, but each dish is served on a carved wooden boat, with wasabe near the mainmast and pickled ginger in the forecastle. At Kyoto, you can both see and taste the effort.

L'Auberge
2601 NW Vaughn St,
223-3302 (map:FF7)
Expensive; full bar; AE,
DC, MC, V;
local checks only
Dinner every day

Those who think French restaurants are stuffy should wander into the bar on Sunday nights. In a setting known for stylish informality, an innovative, eclectic menu, and—Sunday nights only—free screenings of classic movies, you'll discover terrific cheeseburgers and what might be the best barbecued ribs this side of the Mississippi. Welcome to L'Auberge's bar, a softly lit den of elegant rusticity and upscale hipness, with a well-stoked hearth in winter, a homey outdoor dining deck in summer, and, in all seasons, a witty, personable staff. The bar is easily the most relaxing and attractive retreat in town. Changing every two weeks, the bar menu is replete with great finds, such as grilled swordfish with cilantro pesto and a salad of wild edible greens cultivated on a farm in southern Oregon.

The sunken, split-level dining room downstairs takes a more serious approach. Execution is fairly understated—this is not a place to look for the shock of the new—and the dinners are among the most expensive in town. But L'Auberge, which celebrated its 20th birthday in 1989, is distinguished by consistently high standards. Three- or six-course dinners are offered six nights a week in a country-inn atmosphere highlighted with contemporary touches. The kitchen emphasizes fresh local ingredients: entrees usually include game birds, veal, beef, or fresh fish. Options run from grilled quail with prune custard to rack of lamb marinated in pomegranate juice. Service is highly informed, the wine list astutely compiled.

L'Ecurie
12386 SW Main St,
Tigard, 620-5101
(map:KK9)
Moderate; full bar; AE,
DC, MC, V;
local checks only
Lunch Tues-Fri, dinner
Tues-Sat

Tiny L'Ecurie does not stray from French tradition for the sake of fashion: there's an emphasis on beef, lamb, and poultry, with enough butter and cream in some dishes to keep you insulated through a cold and drizzly winter. The smooth, rich scalloped potatoes with each entree are a fine meal in themselves. A superb and reasonably priced wine list. Traditions carry on into dessert: a chocolate mousse or plateau a fromages. A welcome refuge from Tigard's fast-food joints.

La Casa de Rios
4343 SE Hawthorne
Blvd, 234-2038
(map:GG4)
Inexpensive; beer and
wine; MC, V; checks OK
Lunch, dinner every day

This funky place is about the size of a double-wide house trailer, if you don't count the back room, and at dinnertime there is usually a small line of people in team jackets standing in the rain waiting for a seat in that dark red-and-black interior. They come for tostadas buried under a mile of shredded lettuce, plump tamales, cheesy enchiladas in red or green sauce, and a good selection of Mexican beers. Dinners include foil-wrapped flour (made on the premises) or corn tortillas for dipping.

La Patisserie
208 NW Couch St,
248-9898 (map:K5)
Inexpensive; beer and
wine; MC, V; no checks
Breakfast, lunch, dinner
every day

This second-floor patisserie recently changed hands. It appears, however, that much of the flavor and content will remain true to the original intent. Breakfast is busy and honest, lunch or dinner a light soup-and-sandwich affair. They do well with coffee drinks (a deadly espresso shake) and desserts. Still, what is most attractive is the atmosphere of artists, thinkers, and talkers. The windows offer wonderful street views. We hope the competent new owners (formerly of Jazz de Opus) are already busy with improvements; they may want to start by training the staff.

Lamthong
12406 SW Broadway, Beaverton, 646-3350 (map:HH9)
Inexpensive; beer and wine; MC, V; no checks
Lunch Mon-Fri, dinner every day

Lamthong II
213 SW Broadway, 223-4214 (map:C1)
Inexpensive; beer and wine; MC, V; no checks
Lunch Mon-Fri, dinner every day

Burlap walls, soft lights capped with straw hats, charming miniature wooden Thai houses stationed over each table, cerise silk menus with engaging misspellings, a winning young waiter straight out of *The King and I* in a long white linen jacket, red velvet breeches, and white stockings: this apparently simple storefront restaurant has got it beautifully right. Crisp noodles are lovely; take a mouthful with the spicy beef served hot (in both senses) and curled into a lettuce leaf resembling Hiroshige's wave. Perhaps a flawless beef curry (the specialty of the house, laced with threads of fresh coconut) or a creamy seafood extravaganza plump with moist shrimp, scallops, crab, fish, and a lively whip of lemon grass. Wine's a buck a glass, but your palate (fiery from curry) might prefer a Tsingtao beer.

London Grill (Westin Benson)
SW Broadway at Oak St, 295-4110 (map:J3)
Expensive; full bar; AE, DC, MC, V;
local checks only
Breakfast, lunch, dinner every day

There was a time years ago when the London Grill was *the* place to go for a consistently fine meal in Portland. To some Portlanders it still is, for the Grill oozes tradition in its ambience, its service, its wine list (one of the best in town), and its menu. It is the dark, plush domain where anniversaries are celebrated and deals are made over a proven Caesar salad and steak Diane (both prepared at the table without a slip). Gradually, new flavors such as carpaccio of fresh ahi with a papaya chutney and lobster enchiladas are taking their places on the menu alongside the traditional oyster cocktail and snails in herb butter. Here one can experience a delightful range of less-familiar flavors and get exceptional value as well. Whether you stick with the trieds or dip into the new, you'll find most well executed.

Lotsa Pasta
16 NW Broadway, 227-2782 (map:J3)
Inexpensive; full bar; AE, MC, V; no checks
Lunch Mon-Fri, dinner every day

Lotsa pasta for not so lotsa dough. You know the restaurant: order mountains of pasta (perhaps the ricotta and spinach tortellini with a creamy mushroom and pancetta sauce, or the pollo piccata) and get a small antipasto plate, soup (clam chowder was good), green salad with a Gorgonzola dressing, and mediocre garlic bread. The decor's bare essentials, but what do you want when two can leave stuffed for under $25.

The facts in this edition were correct at presstime, but places close, chefs depart, hours change. It's best to call ahead.

Macheesmo Mouse

723 SW Salmon St (and branches), 228-3491 (map:G2)
Inexpensive; beer and wine; no credit cards; checks OK
Lunch, dinner every day

The concept is dynamite: a futuristic fast-food outlet with a health-conscious menu. Judging by the number of branches that have opened up around the Northwest in the past year or so, Macheesmo is doing something right. The menu still stays inside cheese-chicken-black-bean-tortilla territory, but they've added a few enchiladas, a dinner option (where you can get salad and a side dish), and a kids' menu. The patrons come for the quality, if not the hip neo-industrial decor, and offerings are geared to the fast-lane crowd—low-fat, high-protein stuff made to wolf down with confidence in its nutritional high octane. There are a number of other outlets, but Salmon Street is best.

Main Street Restaurant

120 N Main St, Gresham, 661-7877
Moderate; beer and wine; AE, MC, V; checks OK
Breakfast, lunch Mon-Sat, dinner Wed-Sat, brunch Sun

Smack in the middle of Portland's most conservative suburb, this progressive little operation has somehow managed not only to survive but to thrive. The ambience is artsy, and the setting is a hybrid of California commune mercantile and New York City loft: big storefront windows, exposed brick, and high ceilings decorated with braided garlic, wicker baskets, and fresh flowers. Dinner offers predictable appetizers and pasta, with a few ambitious projects like chicken en croute—a boneless breast baked in herbed cream sauce and tucked into phyllo dough. There's also a nice variation on Oregon quail.

Marco Polo Garden

19 NW 5th Ave, 222-1090 (map:J4)
Moderate; full bar; MC, V; no checks
Lunch Mon-Fri, dinner every day

While Chinese food is plentiful in Portland, good Chinese food has historically been the domain of only a few restaurants. Marco Polo Gardens does a fair job on some dishes and a good job on others: excellent pot-stickers, soups, sauteed green beans, superior sesame beef. In sum, stick with the Northern Chinese offerings. While not all dishes are standouts, this is a much better restaurant than some local reviewers would like you to believe.

Marco's Cafe and Espresso Bar

7910 SW 35th Ave, 245-0199 (map:II7)
Inexpensive; beer and wine; MC, V; checks OK
Breakfast, lunch Tues-Sun, dinner Tues-Sat

In a sunny space in Multnomah Village, Marco's is actually two restaurants, and for Multnomah they're both impressive. Mornings and noontimes come solid lunches and breakfasts, especially a continental breakfast featuring home-baked croissants, Black Forest ham, fresh orange juice, and cappuccino. Evenings, Marco's turns into an imaginative and accomplished dinner operation, with menus changing nightly to include chicken breasts and pork medallions, for example, with inspirations ranging from Italy to Thailand. Ownership has recently changed, and although the former owners were also the chefs, Jerry Phipps seems to be handling the line well. So far, the differences are minimal.

Marrakesh

121 NW 23rd Ave,
248-9442 (map:FF7)
Moderate; beer and wine;
AE, MC, V; checks OK
Dinner Tues-Sun

The traditional code of Moroccan hospitality demands that a host treat all guest with graciousness and concern. Ben H. Alaoui, who opened Portland's first Moroccan restaurant a few months ago, guarantees that your meal will begin with the customary finger-washing ceremony and end with the sprinkling of rose water over your hands. In between, you will experience—without the benefit of utensils—a cuisine that seems a reflection of the lushness and fertility of the Maghreb itself. Alaoui's formula worked in Seattle, and so far it seems to be working here. You sit on cushions along a tapestried wall and begin with harira Marrakshia, the cumin-and-coriander lentil soup of North Africa and the Middle East. The meal continues through a Moroccan eggplant salad and a Bastella Royale (a dry chicken and nut mixture covered with phyllo dusted with powdered sugar). Then you choose your entree (you can let the chef choose for you, but when we did the four of us were confronted with three chicken dishes and a lamb). The couscous and honey-prune chicken was almost too sweet, and the special (with carrots and peas) lackadaisical. Try instead the lamb with eggplant or the braised hare in a rich cumin and paprika sauce. Or visit with a large group and order the mechoui, Morocco's famous roast lamb (three days' notice required)—but don't expect any special treatment. A sweetened mint tea and a warm fruit mash seem to cleanse at the end of the meal. For $12.95 you get a lot of food, though pay attention when ordering and reordering wine: the price rises quickly. Marrakesh tries hard for authenticity in the service department—but it's a poor act.

Maya's Tacqueria

1000 SW Morrison St,
226-1946 (map:H1)
Inexpensive; beer and
wine; no credit cards;
local checks only
Lunch, dinner every day

With atmosphere kept to an absolute minimum, Maya's herds its diners down a cafeteria line offering half-a-dozen kinds of burritos, tacos, and enchiladas. The strength is in the number of options available—not that many places can offer you a chile verde taco or a chicken mole enchilada—and all vividly flavored. Chile rellenos are also worth a try, and a handful of icy Mexican beers keeps everything flowing. It's hard to spend much money, or much time, but the down-home tastes keep the crowds returning. Another opens in spring 1990: Santa Fe (831 NW 23rd Avenue).

McCalls
1020 SW Front Ave,
248-9710 (map:F5)
Moderate; full bar; AE,
MC, V; local checks only
Lunch Mon-Fri, dinner
Thurs-Sat

In what used to be the Visitors Information Center, and what claims to be the first plywood building ever, is McCalls. This brand-new restaurant (only feet from the Willamette River, in the middle of Tom McCall Waterfront Park) has a lot going for it, including views, good salads, and an impressive bar. The dinner entrees may not be quite up to the estimable desserts, but the place is gaining a following, especially at lunch. Finding them open is another problem: at press time, McCalls will only be open regularly May 15–October 15. Other days, look to the sky: if the sun's cooking, they may be too.

McCormick's Fish House and Bar
9945 SW Beaverton-
Hillsdale Hwy,
Beaverton, 643-1322
(map:HH9)
Moderate; full bar; AE,
DC, MC, V; checks OK
Lunch Mon-Fri, dinner
every day

This secondary version of McCormick and Schmick's downtown operation lacks the fine touches of its progenitor. The seafood dishes are solid, if low on risk: poached salmon and sauteed scallops are the kinds of basics that work in the 'burbs. But the bar, like its cousin in the big city, is an occasion for good business anytime.

McCormick & Schmick's Seafood Restaurant
235 SW 1st Ave, 224-7522
(map:I5)
Moderate; full bar; AE,
DC, MC, V; checks OK
Lunch Mon-Fri, dinner
every day

We try, we try, but we seldom get past the appetizers. The house oyster arrangement combines half-a-dozen species from various waters, which says something about priorities here. There are at least two dozen seafood possibilities, as well as the fresh list—and that's just to start. We'll return to sample Pacific yellowfin tuna, Columbia River sturgeon, and Alaska prawns. And for all of its attention to food that swims, M&S's also manages to dish up great cheeseburgers and golden fries.

Metropolis Cafe
2015 NE Broadway,
281-7701 (map:FF5)
Moderate; beer and wine;
MC, V; checks OK
Breakfast Sat-Sun,
lunch, dinner Mon-Sat

This successful neighborhood cafe (with a metropolitan feel) follows some basic guidelines: fresh, quality ingredients; simple preparations; service as important as the product; and reasonable prices. Pasta dishes are well tempered and lamb dishes are vibrant, especially the Moroccan-inspired one. Full-bodied soups, salads of varied presentations, and light breakfast omelets.

Nick's Famous Coney Island Food
3746 SE Hawthorne
Blvd, 235-4024

A craving for a Coney dog can really only be satisfied in one very run-down place on the southern shores of Long Island. But for 34 years, Nick (now Frank) has been grilling dogs that give Coney Island a run for its money

(map:GG4)
Inexpensive; beer and
wine; no credit cards;
checks OK
Lunch, dinner every day

(and not much money, at that). Three bucks will get you, the Trail Blazers, and sometimes the mayor, an oversized wiener drowned in chili and onions. Sportscasters tell it like it is on the TV, and Frank bellows from behind the bar about how it should have been.

O'Connor's
529 SW 4th Ave,
228-0854 (map:H4)
Inexpensive; full bar;
MC, V; local checks only
Breakfast, lunch, dinner
every day

There's not much at O'Connor's that you won't find elsewhere, but you won't find many places handling an inexpensive, basic American menu so reliably. This is what Denny's might be if Denny's menu were done right. Here, the American and local basics—burgers, clam chowder, fried-oyster club sandwiches—are done consistently well, making the place a small local landmark. One thing that other places don't have is Eggs O'Connor, a poached egg covered with chicken, bacon, asparagus, tomato, and Mornay sauce. It's enchanting, but how many different kinds of cholesterol can your aorta handle at once?

Obi
101 NW 2nd Ave,
226-3826 (map:J5)
Moderate; full bar; AE,
DC, MC, V; no checks
Lunch Mon-Fri, dinner
Mon-Sat

The most striking innovations come in the maki section, where wild new combinations of gleamingly fresh seafood, vegetables, and Northwest mushrooms come wrapped in seaweed under names like Oregon Roll, Crazy Roll, and Rock 'n' Roll. Fish appears not just in the usual configurations but in items such as Tiger Eyes—teardrop-shaped squid with a center of salmon and scallion. It's hard to pick a favorite, but let's just say that Rock 'n' Roll is here to stay.

The Old Country Inn
148 SW "B" St, Lake
Oswego, 636-7500
(map:KK6)
Moderate; full bar; AE,
DC, MC, V; checks OK
Lunch Tues-Fri, dinner
Tues-Sat

This Victorian house is by no means in a verdant setting, being exactly one block behind the downtown Lake Oswego gas station. But get past the blacktop and into Hans and Rosemarie Heyer's European inn, and you'll be very comfortable. Rosemarie takes care of the front, Hans is in the kitchen, and the waitpersons are efficient and quick-witted. The menu is Swiss, German, and Austrian: sauteed veal with chanterelles and sherry, sweetbreads with shallots and capers, rack of lamb dusted with Parmesan. All generously accompanied by soup (homemade split pea) *and* salad. No cabbage, though. Dessert might be a cappuccino mousse cake or a frozen Grand Marnier souffle. Bring a sweater—it's a bit too airy on cold nights.

Old Wives' Tale
1300 E Burnside,
238-0470 (map:FF5)

KIDS When Holly Hart opened Old Wives' Tale, the restaurant doubled as a feminist gathering place—a back room where men and women met for heated discus-

Inexpensive; beer and wine; MC, V; checks OK Lunch Mon-Sat, dinner every day, brunch Sunday

sions, with an indestructible playroom for the kids. A decade (and many issues) later, the playroom's still around but now food's the talk in the remodeled back room. At press time, the worn-out Old Wives' Tale was getting a facelift (lightening up the decor a bit, sprucing up the bathrooms, and opening a second dining room). The food is primarily vegetarian (spanakopita, carrot cashew burgers), but throws in a few hot pastrami sandwiches or chicken enchiladas for the unconverted. The children's menu is utterly practical (turkey frank without the bun, half a PB&J) and meets parental approval.

Opus Too
33 NW 2nd Ave, 222-6077 (map:J6) Moderate; full bar; AE, DC, MC, V; no checks Lunch Mon-Sat, dinner every day

The combination here is fish and fire; grilled seafood is so expertly done at this small operation that it has earned a devoted following even among the area's most diligent dieters. Great slabs of fresh seafood come away from the mesquite-fueled flames dripping with any of the restaurant's eight sauces, from Bernaise to beurre rouge. The decor is urban cool—tile floor, dark-wood booths, and a long swivel-chair bar overlooking the open kitchen and grills. The exuberant environment is complemented by a respectable wine list, some fine desserts, and piles of flavorful fettucine. A terrific sourdough bread is part of the deal.

The Original Pancake House
8600 SW Barbur Blvd, 246-9007 (map:HH6) Inexpensive; no alcohol; no credit cards; checks OK Breakfast, lunch Wed-Sun

The name says it all. This landmark operation does its sourdough flapjacks from scratch, nearly 20 species of them—from wine-spiked cherry to wheat germ to a behemoth apple variety with sticky cinnamon glaze. A good bet is the ultrathin, egg-rich Dutch baby, dusted with powdered sugar and served with fresh lemon (essential to its overall flavor). Drawbacks are a painfully long wait for seating (bring a copy of *War and Peace* if you're thinking of weekend breakfast), a 90-decibel interior, and the town's weakest coffee. Once you're seated, the service is rushed and aloof.

Paisley's
1204 NW 21st Ave, 243-2403 (map:FF6) Moderate; beer and wine; AE, MC, V; checks OK Dinner Tues-Sat

There are those in Portland who wonder how Paisley's has fared since Linda Faes (now of Panini) sold in 1989. They needn't worry, the place is in capable hands. Dinner has been added to the restaurant that once celebrated desserts—perhaps a savory beef tenderloin marinated in an herbed red wine sauce or salmon sauteed in a port-lime sauce. And impressive entrees are crowned with a stunning finale: chocolate souffle (expect a 20-minute wait). Twosomes drop in after 8pm for an espresso, pot de creme, and to bask in Paisley's sweet and quiet pleasantries.

Panini

620 SW 9th Ave,
224-6001 (map:I2)
Inexpensive; beer and
wine; no credit cards; local
checks only
Breakfast, lunch, early
dinner Mon-Sat

One reviewer claims that if you were to write a book about a cafe, Panini is the one you should write about. Linda Faes and Richard Ford opened Portland's first panini bar a year and a half ago. In size, it's just a hole-in-the-sidewalk; in spirit, however, it's chic and molto Italiano—where the counter help more than remember your name, they remember that you like your latte with a dash of cinnamon and just a little foam. Three-bite–sized panini of anything from roast beef with homemade mayonnaise to pesto, fresh mozzarella, and tomato. Or drop by for a late afternoon tiramisu. On warm days, have a soothing lemon mousse at a sidewalk table. At press time the breakfast menu was being rewritten to include more substantial morning foods, such as Italian casseroles and waffles.

Papa Haydn

5829 SE Milwaukie Ave,
232-9440 (map:II5)
Inexpensive; beer and
wine; AE, MC, V;
local checks only
Lunch, dinner Tues-Sat

701 NW 23rd Ave,
228-7317 (map:FF6)
Inexpensive; beer and
wine; AE, MC, V;
local checks only
Lunch, dinner Tues-Sat,
brunch Sun

This chocolate empire continues to expand: there's pasta, good chicken dishes, and imaginative sandwiches, with the northwestern outpost more serious-minded than the original in southeast Portland. But the core is still the display of towering, intense desserts, led by the Autumn Meringue—layers of chocolate mousse and baked meringue festooned with chocolate leaves—and the boccone dolce, a mountain of whipped cream, meringue, chocolate, and fresh berries. There are also subtler temptations, including a shocking purple blackberry ice and dense shortbread cookies. The northwest location has decent wine and beer lists and a full bar. The clientele there tends toward the upscale, while the southeast owes more to the cerebral Reed College crowd, but both have lines running out the door.

Pattaya

8729 SE Powell Blvd,
774-0369 (map:HH3)
Inexpensive; MC, V;
checks OK
Lunch Tues-Fri, dinner
Tues-Sun

Plainly packaged in a small, nondescript house on Powell Boulevard, this family-run Thai restaurant unfolds unexpected delights: a limey tom yum soup with lemon grass, straw mushrooms, and shrimp; a garlicky Pad Kratiem; and a peppy squid yum with green onions, mint leaves, and cucumber spiced hot and cooled with lemon.

Perry's on Fremont

2401 NE Fremont St,
287-3655 (map:EE7)
Inexpensive; beer and
wine; AE, MC, V;

Three years ago, Hamburger Patti's grew out of its former neighborhood. A year ago, it grew out of its name. Now it's settled into both the ambience of youthful Fremont and a lighter menu: chicken enchilada casserole and a Northwest Cobb salad, and a few specials, such as a tangy lemon chicken breast salad or a Gar-

checks OK
Lunch, dinner Mon-Sun

denburger (no meat but all the trimmings). An enticing dessert list, as always, but, whoa, where'd the carrot cake go?

Pharmacy Fountain

2334 W Burnside,
224-9226 (map:FF7)
Inexpensive; no alcohol;
no credit cards; local
checks only
Breakfast, lunch Mon-Sat

The swiveling barstools, yellow Formica countertops, and smiling, gray-haired ladies seem incongruous with the updated look of the Uptown Shopping Center. This old soda fountain inside the Uptown Pharmacy provides some respite from the northwest's tonier shops. And sure enough, almost every seat in the long, narrow eatery is taken by folks who know the waitresses by name (and even notice if they're losing weight) and who order a light omelet and hash browns for breakfast, half a grilled meatloaf sandwich and a cup of tomato soup for lunch, or maybe just share a late afternoon milk shake. Don't even think to ask for an espresso.

Phnom Penh Express

4604 SE Hawthorne
Blvd, 232-8608
(map:GG4)
Inexpensive; beer and
wine; MC, V; checks OK
Lunch, dinner Tues-Sun

A high ceiling, bare walls, and a few pots of fake flowers give this Cambodian restaurant on Hawthorne Boulevard a rather hollow appeal; however, when the food arrives at your table and titillating smells permeate the air, the barren room takes on a more exotic atmosphere.

A plea from a local restaurant reviewer for Phnom Penh Express to ditch the Chinese and Thai portions of its menu was successful. A native of Cambodia, Pong Chan has learned to prepare the food she knows best. Now with only one cuisine represented, a wrong choice will be tough to find, and if you need a recommendation, trust the staff to lead you confidently to number 39 (an outstanding tender chicken with thin, crisp slivers of onion, green pepper, and lemon grass in a nutty hot chile sauce). Or number 9. Or 22. Or 23.

Piccolo Mondo

5331 SW Macadam Ave
(Johns Landing),
248-9300 (map:II6)
Moderate; full bar;
MC, V; checks OK
Lunch Mon-Sat, dinner
every day

Piccolo Mondo means "small world" in Italian, and this spot at Johns Landing is truly its own small world. In addition to wonderful bread and Americanized Italian offerings, Piccolo Mondo has light lunch entrees to return for: marinated calamari salad, tortellini salad, and antipasto platters. Hot pasta dishes include chicken and black olives in cream sauce, and some interesting treatments of fish and shellfish. You can get a half order of pasta with salad and bread—a good idea, since dessert is a necessity.

Pinot Ganache

1004 Washington St,

Passersby are bound to see ecstatic expressions as diners taste the salmon and spinach dill mousse: this

Vancouver, WA,
(206) 695-7786
(map:BB5)
Moderate; beer and wine;
AE, MC, V;
local checks only
Lunch, dinner Mon-Sat

 ★★

handsome, modernistic bistro sits uncurtained on a corner in what's not the chic-est part of the world— downtown Vancouver. There are moments, mind you (say, on a rainy night), when you'd welcome a warming curtain between you, the strolling public, and the flashing neon Lucky Beer sign in the distance. An alternative hors d'oeuvre to the mousse, the chicken satay beats that served in many a Thai restaurant in the Northwest—plump and moist, its peanut sauce is stingingly spicy. Unfortunately, the dinners don't stand up to the starters. The best thing about this sterile restaurant with high ceilings and black simulated-marble tables is that it's open late; although the kitchen closes at 9pm, you can get any light dish till 11. The after-movie crowd drops in for the made-on-the-premises cakes, plus coffee or wine from an excellently varied list.

Plainfield's Mayur
852 SW 21st Ave,
223-2995 (map:GG5)
Moderate; full bar; AE,
DC, MC, V; no checks
Dinner every day

 ★½

This is the only spot in Portland with an authentic tandoor oven. The style is basically Mogul, with an emphasis on subtle flavors and aromatic spices. The setting is sparse and somewhat formal: bone china, crystal, candles, and linen-covered tables. Portions are small and tariffs a bit steeper than one usually expects for this cuisine. For starters, bypass the traditional offerings for something unusual, such as tomato coconut soup. The tandoori dishes—roasted prawns in tandoori jhinga, for one—are outstanding.

Produce Row Cafe
204 SE Oak St,
232-8355 (map:GG5)
Inexpensive; beer and
wine; no credit cards; local
checks only
Lunch, dinner every day

Not so much a cafe as a tavern that draws the local Ultimate Frisbee crowd and others who come to devour the House Special sandwich—a gooey tangle of steak, cheese, and grilled onions—and quaff a beer imported from just about anywhere on earth. It's especially popular in the summer, when the spacious walled deck opens to the sky and fills with hungry bargain seekers who know that a large sandwich feeds three.

Remo's Ristorante Italiano
1425 NW Glisan St,
221-1150 (map:L1)
Moderate; full bar; AE,
MC, V; local checks only
Dinner every day

 ★

Snazzy. With a bar that hosts some wonderful musicians and serves good food and decent drinks. The dining room has a pleasingly informal elegance to it. Service, too, can be commendable. Too bad, then, that entrees are so bland and the pastas so disappointing. A smoked-salmon fettuccine had wonderful salmon buried under a sticky tangle of noodles; cannelloni and chicken linguine suffered likewise. The exception was the non-Italian dish: roast pork medallions. You'll do best if you stay downstairs for the music and the bar food.

Riccardo's Restaurant & Espresso Bar

16035 SW Boones Ferry Rd, Lake Oswego, 636-4104 (map:JJ6) Moderate; beer and wine; DC, MC, V; checks OK Continental breakfast, lunch Mon-Fri, dinner Mon-Sat

It's not a fancy place with checkered tablecloths and all, but it has sophisticated dishes (olives stuffed with a five-meat pate, fried mussels in a garlicky herb sauce) for those who care, and ordinary ones (spaghetti, lasagne) for those who don't. Such are the ingredients of a good family restaurant. Richard Spaccarelli's so proud of his Italian wine list he'll pour you a taste before you decide.

Rich's Restaurant

18810 SW Boones Ferry Rd, Tualatin, 692-1460 (map:MM9) Moderate; full bar; AE, DC, MC, V; no checks Lunch Mon-Fri, dinner every day, brunch Sun

Rich's Restaurant (aka Rich's Kitchen) is one of the few noteworthy restaurants in the Tualatin area. Given a closer-to-the-competition location, its value would most likely diminish; however, mealtimes in this old converted firehouse are busy times. Ignore the attempts at Frenchness: they do best with the simpler seafood preparations; salmon can be broiled to perfection, and grilled skewers of seafood can be amazingly pleasing. A kinder attitude toward customers would do much to improve the place. Reservations are a good idea.

Rimsky-Korsakoffee House

707 SE 12th Ave, 232-2640 (map:GG5) Inexpensive; no alcohol; no credit cards; local checks only Dessert every day

No signs tell you you're here. That's the way Goody Cable, an assembler of interesting people, provocative thoughts, and good coffee, wants it. Come if you're in the know—but not if you're in a hurry. Inside this big red house on the corner of SE 12th Avenue and Alder Street young Portland thinkers, actors, and writers meet to exchange ideas and listen to the music of whoever's lined up for the evening. Enjoy a chocolate pot de creme or the favored mocha fudge cake. A dozen different espresso variations.

The Ringside

2165 W Burnside, 223-1513 (map:GG7) Moderate; full bar; AE, DC, MC, V; no checks Dinner every day

The mythically juicy steaks here might not bowl over those beef connoisseurs in Kansas, but in this territory they're hard to beat; for texture, color, flavor, and character, they're everything you could want from a hunk of steer. The degree of cooking is as ordered and deviations are few. Still, it's the plump but light, slightly salty onion rings, made with Walla Walla Sweets, that single-handedly made the Ringside famous—an order is essential. The menu has recently expanded into ocean fare; other house specialties include crackling fried chicken and nicely charred burgers. Appetizers and salads are limited, although the marinated herring deserves attention; the desserts do not. You may have French fries or cottage cheese with your entree, but the baked potato is best. It has a crisp skin and a firm, piping-hot interior begging for sour cream and chives. The black-jacketed and bow-tied waiters are eminently professional, even when 30-odd musicians from the Northwest Chamber Music Festival flock in for a late-night summer meal.

Ristorante Medici
2924 E Burnside,
232-9022 (map:GG4)
Moderate; full bar; AE,
MC, V; checks OK
Dinner Tues-Sun

Northern Italian cuisine in Portland took a great leap forward in 1988 when Nick Medici decided to depose his Duchess of Burnside restaurant and reopen it with the family name and the family recipes. The resulting new menu was a stunning victory for family values and a considerable expansion of Portland options. A meal beginning with polenta cups filled with toasted pine nuts and Gorgonzola; continuing with a thick veal T-bone marinated in olive oil, herbs, and balsamic vinegar; and ending with a fresh cherry cake doused with Frangelico would be a triumph anywhere. We have seen some inconsistency recently—meals verging on average, sandy mussels. Gentle, helpful service, 40 Oregon pinot noirs, and a view of Burnside complete the experience.

Ron Paul Catering and Charcuterie
2310 NW Everett St,
223-2121 (map:GG6)
Moderate; beer and wine;
MC, V; checks OK
Breakfast, lunch, dinner
every day

For such a small operation, Ron Paul's packs in the options; you can eat indoors, outdoors, or get the goods to go. Located inside this smart-looking northwest place (part produce stand, part flower shop, part eatery), Ron Paul turns out a range of distinctive dishes: individualized pizzas, great barbecued chicken, a spicy Moroccan orzo salad with dates, and some of the best specialty breads in town (try the rich, dark walnut wheat). Desserts, from the rhubarb pie with phyllo crust to the ultrarich Black Angus Cookies to the carrot cake with ricotta and raisins, rank high. Quality control here is an obvious priority: the kitchen cures the salmon, smokes the sausages, and mixes the pates. On Friday nights the counter becomes a tapas bar with an array of Spanish appetizers, and on Fridays and Saturdays during the summer a mesquite grill is fired up outside. If you're looking for a morning spot, you won't find better coffee or rum-glazed bran muffins anywhere. Bring a sweater—the concrete floors and glass walls keep the place cool.

Salty's on the Columbia
3839 NE Marine Dr,
288-4444 (map:CC4)
Moderate; full bar; AE,
DC, MC, V; checks OK

Salty's on the Columbia washed in on a wave of doubt created by the mediocre performance of Salty's on the Willamette. But this operation is not only on a more exciting river, it has a considerably more exciting menu, served up with consistency and style. There is a daily

*Lunch Mon-Sat, dinner
every day, brunch Sun*

fresh list of about 20 items, but the regular menu is even more impressive, including cioppino, and catfish fried in cornmeal batter. The restaurant is usually jammed, both the dining room downstairs and the upper deck lounge, for the view as well as the food.

Seafood Mama
*721 NW 21st Ave,
222-4121 (map:FF7)
Moderate; full bar; AE,
MC, V; no checks
Lunch, dinner Mon-Sat*

Nothin' fancy, just good fish. Every city needs an inexpensive seafood restaurant. This is Portland's. The key here is to stay simple—start with the smoked seafood platter and then dip into a cauldron of cioppino, or perhaps a melodious heap of seafood medley. At press time they had expanded into the space next door, thus adding a nonsmoking section. The nautical barroom extends out to the garden during the summer. There are a number of microbrews on hand—which go well with the beer-battered halibut and nightly live jazz piano.

Stanich Ten-Till-One Tavern
*4915 NE Fremont St,
281-2322 (map:EE4)
Inexpensive; beer and
wine; no credit cards; local
checks only
Lunch, dinner Mon-Sat*

Stanich's West
*5627 SW Kelly St,
246-5040 (map:FF4)
Inexpensive; beer and
wine; no credit cards; local
checks only
Lunch, dinner Mon-Sat*

The menu at this sports bar begins and ends between two buns. The standout is the hamburger—big, juicy, tasty. Its only failing is that the bun usually gives out before the insides. The World's Greatest Hamburger adds cheese, ham, bacon, and an egg. Wash it down with a Henry's or a Bridgeport Ale, on tap. Kids are allowed at both locations. The eastside has the pool table, but the westside establishment is particularly homey, a comfortable place to get in out of the rain.

Sumida's
*6744 NE Sandy Blvd,
287-9162 (map:FF3)
Moderate; beer and wine;
MC, V; no checks
Dinner Wed-Sun*

Etsuo Sumida is nothing less than the patron saint of Portland's sushi scene, and his restaurant is where you come to indulge your raw-fish fetish. Just watching this master's virtuoso knifework is an experience: he's the Toshiro Mifune of seafood carving. Everything in this cozy neighborhood eatery is impeccably fresh, from tuna to uni with quail eggs. Sumida is also an expert at sushi rice preparation: proper vinegared rice must be sticky enough inside to hold fish, avocado, and such, but easy to handle on the outside. This difficult balance is something of a litmus test for true sushi chefs, rare in the Northwest. Most of the grilled seafood is reliable here, for those whose taste for the raw is limited, and the tempura and teriyaki chicken are well executed.

RESTAURANTS

Sweet Basil

3401 SE Belmont,
231-1570 (map:GG4)
Moderate; beer and wine;
MC, V; no checks
Breakfast, lunch every
day, dinner Wed-Sat

Breakfasts are a hit—and miss—here. When they're on, they're really on. We've heard only raves about their specials: blueberry blintzes with lemon sauce and mint, gingerbread waffles, with apples and fresh whipped cream, eggs Benedict topped with outstanding hollandaise sauce, lemon pancakes with raspberry sauce. Unfortunately, we've also encountered unripe fruit and molasses-tasting syrup on our waffle, an inexcusibly cold poached egg and cheese (from the menu), and forgetful service. Your turn.

Tabor Hill Cafe

3766 SE Hawthorne
Blvd, 230-1231
(map:GG4)
Moderate; beer and wine;
MC, V; checks OK
Breakfast, lunch, dinner
Thurs-Tues

For the past three years, Tabor Hill Cafe has satisfied more than its Hawthorne neighbors with honest chile, chicken, blue cheese, or bacon omelets. Getting a table on weekends has become next to impossible. Lunch is inspired soups, fat sandwiches, and billowing salads. Dinners consist of Northwest ingredients prepared with sophistication but no pomp. An attractive nook that's gaining, and deserving, a lot of local respect. Scrumptious desserts.

Taj Mahal

1135 SW Morrison St,
223-9240 (map:I1)
Inexpensive; beer and
wine; AE, MC, V;
checks OK
Lunch Mon-Sat, dinner
every day

Small and informal, with lights that are just too bright for its space. In fact, the best improvement they could make would be to install a dimmer switch. The food, however, is spiced just right. East Indian favorites include the samosas with a piquant cilantro chutney, biriyani (a curried chicken over an almond and cardamom rice), and a memorable chicken tandoori (though they don't use the authentic clay ovens). The poori—usually a light, fluffy, deep-fried Indian bread—has been greasy on occasion. All in all, a good deal for the money—which isn't much.

Tara Thai House

4545 SW Watson Ave,
Beaverton, 626-2758
(map:HH9)
Inexpensive; beer and
wine; MC, V; checks OK
Lunch Mon-Fri, dinner
Tues-Sat

This is perhaps the only restaurant in Portland's large contingent of Southeast Asian operations that regularly serves Laotian dishes. In her artistically arranged specials, owner-chef Lavanny Phommaneth fuses local ingredients with native techniques and flavorings: fresh salmon spiked with red or green curry paste, clams graced with a pungent Thai chile sauce. Another standout is ho mok kai—steamed chicken shredded in coconut sauce and laced with fresh basil. Portions are somewhat small, and service is somewhat friendly.

Thai Villa

340 N 1st St, Lake
Oswego, 635-6164
(map:KK6)

Hidden away in a corner of a municipal parking lot next to the Lake Oswego fire station is a Thai restaurant with few matches but a lot of fire. Thai Villa specializes in pungent soups served swirling in a moat around a pillar

Inexpensive; beer and wine; MC, V; checks OK
Lunch Mon-Fri, dinner every day

Thanh Thao
4005 SE Hawthorne Blvd, 238-6232 (map:GG4)
Inexpensive; beer and wine; AE, MC, V; checks OK
Lunch, dinner Wed-Mon

Thanh Thao II
8355 SE Powell Blvd, 775-0306 (map:HH3)
Inexpensive; beer and wine; AE, MC, V; checks OK
Lunch, dinner every day

Thirty-One Northwest
31 NW 23rd Pl, 223-0106 (map:GG7)
Moderate; full bar; AE, MC, V; checks OK
Lunch Mon-Fri, dinner Mon-Sat

Trios Fresh Grill
333 NW 23rd Ave, 221-0333 (map:FF7)
Moderate; full bar; AE, DC, MC, V; local checks only
Lunch, dinner Mon-Sat, brunch Sun

unrated

of flame, and a wide range of seafood dishes. The spicing is up to you, but the highest level of heat is called "volcano," and they're not kidding. The chef is also handy with basil, garlic, and subtle hints of sweetness, and the prices are reasonable, especially on a cost-per-tingle basis.

In an area fast becoming something of a Little Vietnam, this is the favorite Vietnamese spot not only for those from the southeast (Portland, that is). The friendly Nguyen family can tell you everything you need to know about the Vietnamese or Thai food. A bowl of vegetable curry (crisp broccoli, snow peas, and sprouts in a creamy curry broth with fresh pineapple and cilantro) warms the body. You'll find some ordinary dishes here (like cashew chicken), but all are generous. Try the muc xao thap camp (squid sauteed with pineapple, tomato, mushroom, and celery) or the dau hu chua ngot (sweet-and-sour tofu) for a delicately steamed and sauced dinner. Thanh Thao's popularity led to the 1988 opening of a second place on Powell Boulevard.

After a roller coaster of owners, chefs, and menus, things seem to have finally gelled. Thirty-One Northwest has emerged as a quietly elegant place to enjoy a moderately priced meal. Flavors rely on fresh local ingredients and Pacific Rim and Mexican influences. Dungeness crab fajitas, at once spicy and crabby; tiger prawns in a zingy Indonesian sauce; a fairly wide selection of lighter seafood fare (grilled salmon with green peppercorns and a mustard sauce). At times we prefer to stick with the inventive appetizers and a glass of wine, or lunch on a Caesar salad with flank steak. Regrettably, the wine list is not what it once was, but there are a few good choices.

Riding the grill-and-bistro craze, suave Trios promises a great deal more than it has yet delivered. At this writing it's still on a shakedown cruise, and while the sailing is not always clear, the place somehow makes you feel... elegant. Lamb, salmon, chicken, prawns, pork, and steak each come grilled with their own glaze or marinade or herbed butter, but sides such as rosemary-laced red potatoes and tart, fresh-braised kale come a la cart. The chicken is the winner among the main dishes, an exceptionally soul-satisfying and tender grilled bird. But others, like the lamb, can be overcooked, and the portions (especially the fish) sometimes meager. Overall, there's an eagerness to please, they've mastered desserts, and service is crisp and attentive. Perhaps when menu adjustments are made and more attention is given to producing deeper flavors, Trios will turn the corner.

Uncle Chen
529 SW 3rd Ave,
248-1199 (map:I5)
Inexpensive; full bar; AE,
MC, V; no checks
8775 SW Cascade Ave
(Cascade Plaza),
Beaverton, 646-6429
(map:HH9)
Lunch, dinner every day

Even though original chef Chi-siung Chen has long since departed for greener woks, this remains one of the prettiest Chinese restaurants in the city. A front room with bright banners fluttering from the ceiling gives way to a gardenlike back room framed by a two-story brick wall. Have a cocktail before ordering from the modest (by Chinese restaurant standards) Northern Chinese menu, which includes the signature broccoli with tangy sauce and a fine crisp-fried duck.

Uogashi
107 NW Couch St,
242-1848 (map:K6)
Moderate; full bar; AE,
DC, MC, V; no checks
Lunch Mon-Sat, dinner
every day

Uogashi is one of the more strikingly designed Japanese restaurants in Portland, with huge ceremonial kimonos and a courtyard effect in the dining room. It also has the most active bar scene, with live jazz in the early evening and karaoke singing late at night. The food is not particularly innovative, but it is solidly prepared, with a few unusual seafood flourishes. Sushi is fresh, and the restaurant is comfortable and pleasant.

Vat & Tonsure
822 SW Park Ave,
227-1845 (map:G2)
Inexpensive; beer and
wine; no credit cards;
checks OK
Lunch, dinner Mon-Sat

The original inspiration for this kind of place was the coffeehouse of the '50s and '60s—a setting for earnest and thoughtful conversation. But that era is gone, and now intelligent discourse is best enjoyed where the food and spirits are in sync with the sophistication of American dining in the '70s and '80s. V&T is such a place. The high-backed wooden booths on the upper and lower decks of this split-level eatery are filled with cerebral and arty types (and, not surprisingly, plenty of smoke) that wax philosophical to a background of classical music. Owner Mike Quinn runs the bar and offers one of the town's most complete wine cellars. His wife, Rose-Marie Barbeau, handles the kitchen, turning out some fine stuffed Cornish hens, sauteed prawns, and lamb chops. Service can be slightly aloof with newcomers, but advice, once obtained, is reliable.

Vietnam's Pearl
1037 SW Morrison St,
241-4740 (map:I1)

Portland's first Vietnamese restaurant is now one of nearly a dozen. It's also been surpassed in quality, in part due to the fact that Quang Nguyen, the original

Inexpensive; beer and wine; AE, MC, V; local checks only Lunch, dinner Mon-Sat

owner, sold it—though he bought it back when he couldn't bear to watch it slip. The place looks tidier now, and if you're downtown the Pearl is a comfortable, quiet meeting spot. The Imperial Rolls are properly crisp, a common dish of ginger chicken surprisingly flavorful. The Vietnamese specialty of sweet and salty shrimp, though generous, lacks zip. Things do seem to be picking up a bit—but sometimes it's tough to regain lost ground.

Vista Springs Cafe

2440 SW Vista, 222-2811 (map:GG6) Inexpensive; beer and wine; AE, MC, V; checks OK Lunch, dinner every day

KIDS Oddly situated in Portland Heights, this small cafe and pizzeria has cultivated a bustling clientele of pizza fiends and converts. The proverbial pie has rarely tasted like this: pesto and artichoke, feta and Kalamata olives, Fred Carlo sausage and Italian cheeses. Three by-the-slice selections can be supplemented with an adequate salad. Round it all out with a bowl of ice cream. Nice folks here, led by gentle Ben.

Western Culinary Institute

1316 SW 13th Ave, 223-2245 (map:GG7) Moderate; beer and wine; MC, V; checks OK Lunch, dinner Mon-Fri

If your sense of adventure extends to offering yourself as a guinea pig to students in the culinary arts, it is possible to enjoy a seven-course dinner for under $20 or a five-course lunch for under $8, wine not included, at the Western Culinary Institute (now owned by Phillips Colleges Inc). Meals are prepared and served by eager-to-please students in this fully accredited school. Emphasis used to be on classical cuisine, Escoffier in particular, but recently there has been a shift toward more Northwestern influences. A Thursday night buffet ($14) has an international theme and offers as many as 40 different dishes. The menu changes daily, and the food is often (but not always) good. For the price, the odds are in your favor.

Westmoreland Wine and Bistro

7015 SW Milwaukie Ave, 236-6457 (map:II5) Moderate; beer and wine; MC, V; checks OK Lunch Tues-Sat, dinner Thurs-Sat

A quiet escape from a predatory world. Here's a bistro and wine shop with an informal atmosphere and crack service. Friday-night wine-tasting dinners (reservations required) are a bargain and have adeptly planned food and wine pairings. The menu for other nights changes weekly but tends toward somewhat inventive ethnic creations. Wines are available from the retail wine supply, and a modest corkage fee allows one a wonderful wine for a very reasonable price. Coffees are excellent, too; have one with dessert.

Portland Best Places *lists all the finest establishments throughout Portland, north to Vancouver, Washington, south to West Linn, west to Beaverton, and east to Gresham.*

Who-Song and Larry's Cantina

111 E Columbia Wy,
Vancouver, WA,
(206) 695-1198
(map:BB5)
Moderate; full bar; AE,
DC, MC, V; no checks
Lunch, dinner every day

If you've wondered, wandering around downtown Vancouver, where all the *people* were, you'll find them here. The entire basketball team is packing in enchiladas right next to you; families are enthusiastically descending on the large buffet; there's lots of chat to make you feel part of a large, homey party. Jolly menu patter is a bit of a delusion: Larry, in his 80s, is actually back East, and his Mexican partner, Who-Song, is no longer living—the place is yet another link in the vast El Torito chain. Mexican buffet ($4.95) is no great shakes (tired taco shells, etc.), but there are great margaritas and swift service (free chips and salsa before you draw a breath). A jolly little bar away from the hubbub lets you nibble nachos with your Corona and watch the grain boats force the Vancouver-Portland bridge to open up.

Winterborne

3520 NE 42nd Ave,
249-8486 (map:FF4)
Moderate; beer and wine;
AE, MC, V; checks OK
Dinner Wed-Sat,
brunch Sun

★½

A sense of '60s solemnity still seems to pervade Portland's first nonsmoking restaurant. For years it has been quietly turning out some of the most respectable fish dishes in town. No pretensions to elegance here— there's not a pastry wagon or a maitre d' in sight. Instead, plain dishware, dim lights, classical music, and a few lithographs set the tone. Chef-owner Dwight Bacon's menu is small, and entrees are complemented by fresh whole-wheat bread, a simple salad, and fragrant fish soup. None of the half-dozen main courses are overwhelmed by their simple sauces. Pan-fried oysters with homemade tartar sauce make an excellent starter. For dessert try the thick, bittersweet chocolate mousse.

Yacob's Rainbow

11793 Beaverton-
Hillsdale Hwy (Beaverton
Town Square),
Beaverton, 641-7090
(map:HH9)
Inexpensive; beer and
wine; no credit cards;
checks OK
Lunch, dinner Mon-Sat

½

If you take your meal as the Ethiopians do, your fingers will be rather yellow when you leave. Across the expansive Fred Meyer parking lot, a few steps from Kobos Coffee, is Beaverton's first (the area's third) Ethiopian restaurant. The usual wats are on the menu, but they're not quite as high voltage as others we've encountered. The service, provided by the owner's wife, is gentle and sweet, and the prices are modest. Scoop up the yedoro wat chicken (drenched in lemon, red peppers, onion, garlic, cinnamon, and ginger) with a triangle of injera—a thin, porous bread. Or skip it, and let your fingers wallow in a sambusa (a cuminy lentil stew in a sweet, paperthin pastry shell). A daily special—chicken marinated in

Wondering about our standards? We rate establishments on value, performance measured against the place's goals, uniqueness, enjoyability, loyalty of clientele, cleanliness, excellence and ambition of the cooking, and professionalism of the service. For an explanation of the star system, see How To Use This Book.

fresh lemon juice and sauteed with red pepper sauce, honey, and the appropriate Abyssinian spices—came with chopped carrots, yellow peppers, and potatoes for $4.95. It'll be better when they decorate the almost bare walls a little. Maybe they could finish the meal with a serving of t'ej.

Yen Ha (west)
8640 SW Canyon Rd,
292-0616 (map:HH9)
Moderate; full bar; AE,
MC, V; checks OK
Lunch, dinner every day

Talented Vietnamese chef Bach Tuyet has moved her popular operation to the suburbs. Her new purple-labyrinth digs are spacious enough to feed most of the large community of West Slope. The food is still the same great fare that wowed *The New Yorker*'s food essayist Calvin Trillin on a recent Portland visit. While there's much to recommend, the classic is bo noung vi. For this amazing do-it-yourself dish, you plunge slivers of marinated beef into a pool of hot oil on a stove placed on your table. Once cooked to taste, the beef is wrapped with assorted fresh greens and mint in a pliable, edible rice skin. A frisky anchovy sauce is the finishing touch, bringing out all of the succulent package's exotic flavor. There is also a wonderful shrimp salad garnished with crushed peanuts, and a wide selection of chef's specials. Try the wonton soup, full of plump dumplings and Vietnamese herbs.

Yen Ha
6820 NE Sandy Blvd,
287-3698 (map:FF3)
Inexpensive; beer and
wine; MC, V; checks OK
Lunch Tues-Fri, dinner
Tues-Sun

Last year, Duck Van Tran inherited the original Yen Ha from his celebrated culinary cousin, Bach Tuyet (now stationed on Canyon Road), and he's made it his own: Yen Ha east is a bustling Vietnamese cafe with an innovative kitchen. Try the superb soups, the succulent salt-fried Dungeness crab in tangy sauce, or the hot pot with seafood, vegetables, and Asian exotica. This is a menu worth exploring, and service is better than in most Vietnamese operations.

Zell's: An American Cafe
1300 SE Morrison St,
239-0196 (map:GG5)
Inexpensive; beer and
wine; AE, MC, V;
checks OK
Breakfast, lunch every day

Now *this* is breakfast! Smoked sturgeon omelet, spring Chinook salmon and scrambled eggs, huckleberry pancakes, home-baked scones and two jams. The powerful coffee and fresh-squeezed orange juice are the kinds of touches that make getting up in the morning worthwhile. This establishment boasts one of the few soda fountains around that isn't a campy imitation of the originals: Zell's is a converted '50s drugstore whose owners wisely spared the fountain counter from the remodeler's saw. Finally, if you can't resist recklessly sweet things in the morning, try the German pancakes with apples.

Zen

910 SW Salmon St,
222-3056 (map:G3)
Expensive; full bar; AE,
DC, MC; local checks only
Lunch Mon-Fri, dinner
Mon-Sat

The oldest Japanese restaurant around, Zen still sets the standard for the basic Japanese repertoire. Beef and seafood dishes are strongest, and a dish of spicy grilled beef (yakinuku) is a highlight. The sushi bar is more of an afterthought. Zen is the only restaurant around offering kaiseki, the formal, multicourse (arrange-in-advance) Japanese banquet. The chef manages to fulfill both the artistic and culinary challenges it provides, but come sometime when you've got nothing planned for later on.

NIGHTLIFE CONTENTS

NIGHTLIFE

BAR INDEX: TYPE

ANACHRONISM
Alibi
Ye Olde Towne Crier

CLASSIC PORTLAND
Delphina's
The Heathman Hotel
Huber's
Jake's Famous Crawfish
L'Auberge
McCormick and Schmick's
The Ringside
Vat & Tonsure
Westin Benson

DRINKS WITH A VIEW
Atwater's
Cal's at Johns Landing
Salty's on the Columbia
Salty's on the Willamette

HAPPY HOUR
Atwater's
Digger O'Dells
Huber's
Jake's Famous Crawfish
McCormick and Schmick's
Seafood Restaurant
Veritable Quandary
Virginia Cafe
Westin Benson

LATE NIGHT
Cassidy's
Hung Far Low
Jazz de Opus

OYSTER BARS
Digger O'Dells
Jake's Famous Crawfish

PIANO BARS
Cal's at Johns Landing

Digger O'Dells
The Heathman Hotel
McCormick and Schmick's
Oak Street Restaurant
Salty's on the Columbia
Wilf's

SINGLES
Casa-U-Betcha
Hall Street Bar and Grill
Virginia Cafe

SPORTS BAR
East Bank Saloon

WINE BARS
Bacchus Wine Bar
Delphina's
The Grapery
Thirty-One Northwest
Vat & Tonsure

BAR INDEX: LOCATION

BEAVERTON
The Grapery
Hall Street Bar and Grill

DOWNTOWN
Atwater's
Cassidy's
The Heathman Hotel
Huber's
Jake's Famous Crawfish
O'Connors
Vat & Tonsure
Veritable Quandary
Virginia Cafe
Westin Benson

EAST PORTLAND
Digger O'Dells
East Bank Saloon

FALOMA
Salty's on the Columbia

HILLSBORO
Rock Creek

JOHNS LANDING
Cal's at Johns Landing

NORTH PORTLAND
Alibi

NORTHWEST
Casa-U-Betcha
Delphina's

L'Auberge
The Ringside
Thirty-One Northwest

OLD TOWN
Alexis
Bacchus Wine Bar
Hung Far Low
Jazz de Opus
McCormick and Schmick's
Oak Street Restaurant
Wilf's

SELLWOOD
Salty's on the Willamette

SOUTHEAST
Ye Olde Towne Crier

BARS

Alexis
215 W Burnside,
224-8577 (map:J5)

Small and windowless, with cushions on wooden benches, the back bar at Alexis is the sort of place former Portlanders rush to the minute they return to the Rose City. A magnet for food critics and city commissioners with a fondness for ouzo, festive Greek music, golden-fried calamari, and feverish belly dancing, weekends.

The Alibi
4024 N Interstate Ave,
287-5335 (map:EE6)

On a classic neon strip on Interstate Avenue, a few blocks up from the lit-up palms, you'll find this spot flashing in red. Inside, fishnets hang overhead, shells adorn the lamps, and Hawaiian girls luau the night away on the walls. Upstairs there's a pool table.

Atwater's
111 SW 5th Ave, 30th
floor, 275-3600 (map:J5)

Even people deathly afraid of heights—and big bills—find it worthwhile to ascend to the 30th floor of the US BanCorp Tower. There, at least during the week, you can land a window table with a view of bridges and skyscrapers that's enough to convince even a hard-core Seattleite that Portland is indeed a city. Surprisingly, drinking in this contemporary living-room–style lounge doesn't cost much more than it would at ground level.

Bacchus Wine Bar Cafe
34 NW 1st Ave,
224-WINE (map:K6)

Portland native Joseph Balogh (formerly of Tigard's L'Ecurie) installed Portland's first cruvinet (wine dispenser) seven years ago in the Blagen Block building. He now pours two dozen wines by the glass (most are French, yet two pinot noirs and two chardonnays are Oregon's own) and sells plenty more by the bottle to the well-heeled. Weekends, sip and chat to the music of a guitarist.

Casa-U-Betcha
612 NW 21st Ave,
222-4833 (map:FF6)

They come for the cute bartenders, black bean nachos, and the occasional bingo nights. Carloads empty into this perma-filled tiled bar, where the chips are free and the crowd is cool. If you run out of pretty people to look at, you can always check out the wall of mirrors.

Cal's at Johns Landing
5310 SW Macadam Ave,
241-2971 (map:HH6)

Cal's is a class act, from its summer barbecues on the deck to the sounds of the piano in the high-ceilinged, cozy bar come winter. Oh sure, there are other places at Johns Landing with views of boats cutting through choppy waters, but Cal's is one of the few that doesn't make its waitresses prance around in silly outfits.

▼
BARS

Cassidy's
*1331 SW Washington St,
223-0054 (map:J1)*

When most dance floors are empty and the happy hours end, feet start stampeding toward Cassidy's—the place for a last-call drink. You can knock 'em back until 2:30am. Still, no one seems to care about finishing their drinks as they scan the late-night pack in search of a meaningful encounter.

Delphina's
*2112 NW Kearney St,
221-1195 (map:FF6)*

Inside a former northwest district warehouse, the festively casual Delphina's bar (adorned with upside-down colanders) attracts a steady stream of Portland's most successful entrepreneurs and starving artists alike. Many wander in after 10pm to take advantage of the bar menu: a slice of pizza ($1.50) or the outstanding insalata di pesce.

Digger O'Dells
*532 SE Grand Ave,
238-6996 (map:GG5)*

The Henry Barber block is a century old, but this woody eastside bar (owned by the Burns Brothers of West Coast truck stop fame) just celebrated its 10th anniversary. Digger O'Dells, named after a famous undertaker (the building used to be a mortuary), has managed to stay comfortably clear of the tonier downtown crowd. Hide out behind the piano bar (Wednesday–Sunday) or come any time you get a craving for freshly schucked oysters or thick, crunchy onion rings.

East Bank Saloon
*727 SE Grand Ave,
231-1659 (map:GG5)*

The East Bank is sports fans' first choice, with games broadcast from TVs in every corner. The noise level can get pretty high, especially when teams swarm in after a game for a brewski, a burger, and a chat with the pretty waitresses.

The Grapery
*4190 SW Cedar Hills
Blvd, Beaverton,
646-1437 (map:GG9)*

Even if you're not comfortable in mini-malls, you'll settle easily into Craig Peck's low-key Beaverton wine bar. Peck has been an avid wine student for over a decade, and his expertise shows in the 300 or so well-chosen wines (beers, too) that line the walls of his shop/bar/restaurant. Bottle prices are retail (and reasonable), with no extra corkage fee. The lights are too bright for intimacy, but it's a great place to launch the night.

Hall Street Bar & Grill
*3775 SW Hall Blvd,
Beaverton, 641-6161
(map:HH9)*

One of Beaverton's swankiest—and roomiest—spots. Patrons spill out (by choice) onto the back patio, where overhead space heaters attenuate the effects of Oregon's weather. Others choose the upholstered comfort of the lounge for a margarita made with fresh-squeezed lime and served in a shaker. A dozen wines by the glass and more than 30 beers.

NIGHTLIFE

Heathman Hotel
*SW Broadway and
Salmon St,
241-4100 (map:G2)*

One of Portland's classiest bars is really three: there's the cool ambience of the Marble Bar, where the symphony crowds rendezvous after the show and executives convene for lunch; the high-ceilinged Lobby Lounge, as formal as a Tudor drawing room, with a fire blazing in the hearth and Daryl Kaufmann at the piano five nights a week; and upstairs, the Mezzanine Bar, where industrial art decorates the walls. In any of the three, you feel majestic—even if on a budget—and the spicy Thai shrimp appetizer alone is worth begging for, though the management prefers charge cards or cash.

Huber's
*411 SW 3rd Ave,
228-5686 (map:H5)*

Waiter Alex Berez and his knock-'em-dead Spanish coffee have become a star team in Portland's oldest bar. Inside this oft-crowded mahogany-trimmed room, Alex and his pals swirl flaming 151, Kahlua, and Triple Sec with the drama of fire eaters. Expect a wait, especially when there's a nip in the air.

Hung Far Low
*112 NW 4th Ave,
223-8686 (map:L5)*

The strong, cheap drinks have little to do with the fact that you can barely make out who's sitting across from you in this infamous Chinatown bar. A clandestine air hangs over the place, as though the walls might mysteriously open onto secret tunnels to...where? Drinking ends at 2:30am, but barbecued pork in a lethal mustard sauce can be had until 3am. A sister restaurant is next door, with some of the brightest lights west of Newark.

Jake's Famous Crawfish
*401 SW 12th Ave,
226-1419 (map:I1)*

The calendar on the wall counts down the days before St. Paddy's, when the place becomes the most densely populated square footage in the city. The other 364 days of the year, this 1892 soda fountain is an after-work watering hole with eight kinds of oysters on the half shell. Women might prefer an escort to get them past the horn-rimmed wildlife in the bar.

Jazz de Opus
*33 NW 2nd Ave,
222-6077 (map:J6)*

Most everything is low here—from the love seats to the lighting to the waitress kneeling at your side. Tempting smells from the mesquite grill next door at Opus Too waft through this hobbit-hole, and the darkness and background jazz set a your-place-or-mine kind of mood for glassy-eyed couples—though some don't get any farther than the couch in the back room.

L'Auberge
*2601 NW Vaughn St,
223-3302 (map:FF6)*

Understated elegance is the lure here, in a bar on the premises of one of the city's finest French restaurants. In winter, settle into plush fireside seats; in summer, the patio out back is pleasant. And comfort isn't the only draw: try the pate of breast of chicken or the veal appetizer once, and you won't think twice about the price. Free movies and popcorn (you buy the beer and the burgers) on Sunday nights.

McCormick and Schmick's
235 SW 1st Ave, 224-7522
(map:H5)

The piano bar here has always been a popular after-work stop for architects and advertising execs. Ever since the astoundingly low-priced bar menu was added, the brass-and-oak bar has been packed at all hours. Thick Cajun burgers and fettuccine primavera can feed the hungry (1pm–2:30pm, 4pm–7pm, and after 9:30) for $1.95, though you may need pencil and paper to converse during these times.

O'Connor's
529 SW 4th Ave,
228-0854 (map:H3)

O'Connors likes to boast that it's where folks from Montana meet the rest of the world. Indeed, there is a rustic element here, but we're not sure Montanans would like the reference. Ceiling tiles may drop at any given moment (usually the result of an overflowing tub upstairs), and it's filled with characters, from music execs on the make to old-timers who still reminisce about the days when bars were men-only. A cafe off to one side, and a pool hall off to the other.

The Ringside
2165 W Burnside,
223-1513 (map:FF6)

Sure, the steaks are thick and juicy, but it's those plump, lightly battered Walla Walla Sweet onion rings that gave the venerable Ringside its name. The bar, which fits about three comfortably, somehow manages to accommodate 30.

Rock Creek Restaurant and Bar
Old Cornelius Pass Rd,
Hillsboro, 645-3822

Way out in the boonies of Hillsboro is Rock Creek, occupying an old farmhouse rich in dark wood and high ceilings and scattered with antiques. Outside dining in the summer, though you don't really come here to eat.

Salty's on the Columbia
3839 NE Marine Dr,
288-4444 (map:CC4)

Salty's on the Willamette
513 SE Marion St,
239-8900 (map:JJ5)

Tropical plants towering overhead, strange art clinging to the walls, a view of boats, and a sketch of Vancouver. At Salty's on the Columbia, the marine air stings your cheek and the drink prices sting your wallet. All's soothed by the piano. The original Sellwood branch has the same menu and similar view, but of a different river.

Thirty-One Northwest
31 NW 23rd Pl, 223-0106
(map:FF7)

This bar can't seem to shake its airport-lounge appeal; however, it's a respectable wine bar (but not wine exclusively) with an ample assortment of Oregon bottlings. Tapas include grilled chicken in peanut sauce and

Montrachet cheese baked with spreadable garlic cloves. After 9pm, the music from the Dandelion Pub downstairs vibrates through the floor and shakes the tables, effectively killing the tender mood.

Vat and Tonsure
822 SW Park Ave,
227-1845 (map:G2)

You'll either fit in here or you won't—and the waiters will be happy to let you know which is the case. Stark wooden booths, simple fare (perhaps Cornish hens and lamb chops), and opera blaring in the background are characteristic of one of Portland's most delightful (if you pass the staff's inspection) and cerebral bars. Mike Quinn runs the bar, and his extensive wine list is some of the best reading in town.

Veritable Quandary
1220 SW 1st Ave,
227-7342 (map:E4)

The narrow linear design of this downtown exposed-brick and dark-wood bar encourages body contact. By day, you rub up against corporate types who lunch on whole baked trout and seafood stew. By night, a jazzy, darkly dressed crowd moves in and transforms V.Q. into a sultry late-night spot.

Virginia Cafe
725 SW Park Ave,
227-0033 (map:H2)

The V.C. is almost a guarantee for laughs, and like the dollar drinks (Thursdays and Saturdays), it quickly grows addictive. Comfy in a beat-up-couch sort of way, though at times it's nearly impossible to wrestle your way into one of the wooden booths. Nevertheless, the crowd is young, arty, and fun-loving.

Westin Benson Hotel
309 SW Broadway,
228-9611 (map:I3)

The opulent Benson lobby lounge is dark, lined with imported Russian walnut and furnished with sinkingly comfortable black leather chairs. Rarely crowded and always ideal for an after-dinner drink, it offers an extensive selection of wines by the glass and liqueurs. Downstairs in the tiny London Grill bar, your ears may catch the playing of a harpist. Off to the corner is Trader Vic's, the Tiki-style chain known for its rum concoctions.

Wilf's
800 NW 6th Ave (Union
Station), 223-0070
(map:M4)

Wilf's—in the train station, of all places—seems out of a different era: red velvet wallpaper and tunes from the '40s and '50s that Jim Schroeder coaxes out of the ivories as if they were written yesterday.

Ye Olde Town Crier
4515 SE 41st Ave,
774-1822 (map:HH4)

Decorated in colonial style, this friendly hideaway sparkles with four fireplaces, woodcuts on the wall, and a candlelit warmth—a romantic spot. It's not crowded, and that's part of its charm.

PUBS AND TAVERNS

Accuardi's Old Town Pizza Company
226 NW Davis St,
222-9999 (map:K6)

Oh-so-comfortable, and eclectically furnished with what look like samples from virtually every store in town. A favorite spot for beer and thick, spicy pizza (try the chanterelle and sun-dried–tomato combination). With so much charm, you may wish you could rent it out as your living room—some patrons almost do.

B. Moloch/The Heathman Bakery and Pub
901 SW Salmon St,
227-5700 (map:G1)

A half-dozen sardonic portraits—originals from its 19th-century caricaturist namesake—smirk from the walls of this boisterous restaurant-cum-microbrewery. With its utterly fresh Widmer brews and carefully drafted North-west wine list, B. Moloch doesn't need many other lures. But its proximity to the South Park Blocks (the Schnitz, the Oregon Art Institute, and the PCPA) al-most guarantees a crowd.

Bridgeport Brew Pub
1313 NW Marshall St,
241-7179 (map:O1)

Portland's first microbrewery, in a cleaned-up Pearl Dis-trict warehouse, is often filled with young folks (but not too young) indulging their addiction to Bridgeport Ale. A devotion to the chorizo (from Fred Carlo) and artichoke pizza is, for some, equally strong. Oddly, they don't sell Coke and such—just Soho Naturals—but then, there's really only one thing you're supposed to be drinking at Bridgeport. Kids are allowed in the "family room."

Cornelius Pass Roadhouse and Brewery
Route 5 (off Hwy 26 at Cornelius Pass Rd),
Hillsboro, 640-6174

If only Cornelius were right around the corner. This 1866 clapboard farmhouse affords customers a tavern warmth they won't find elsewhere these days, and two dozen McMenamin micros on tap. Settle into one of the four softly lit rooms or, on languid eves, on the balcony or at a picnic table on the sprawling lawn. Word is there's talk of tearing it down to put in an industrial park—however, the third-floor ghosts might object.

Fulton Pub and Brewery
0618 SW Nebraska St,
246-9530 (map:I16)

Chinese kites are suspended overhead, and there's a flower-trimmed beergarden out back. This is but one of the 20 McMenamin pubs; all are different, from the Mis-sion Pub, with its free top-rate movies, to McMenamin's Tavern and Pool, the Northwest's famed pool hall. Still, all share McPub burgers (the Communication Break-down burger's heavy on the onions) and brews (includ-ing a six-glass beer sampler—almost 18 ounces—from unfiltered Terminator Stout to raspberry Ruby Ale). An-other common denominator is the friendly service.

Goose Hollow Inn
1927 SW Jefferson St,
228-7010 (map:GG6)

For decades, the Goose was a hotbed of political debate. And since its owner, Mayor J.E. "Bud" Clark, handed the tavern to wife Sigrid, it's been no less a social institution. Join the hundreds before you and surreptitiously carve your initials into the dark wooden booths, or sink your teeth into one of the thick Reuben sandwiches that have made this place as much a classic as the "Expose Yourself to Art" poster on the wall. Safe, too: it's Portland's first tavern with a condom dispenser in the women's room.

Helvetia Tavern
Route 1, Box 669,
Hillsboro, 647-5286

A legendary country tavern, legendary in part for its voluminous hat collection, in part for the two-fisted burgers, and in part for the camaraderie between staff and patrons. Perhaps the biggest draw—and certainly the reason that the volume level soars—is the Wednesday night bingo games.

Hillsdale Brewery and Public House
1505 SW Sunset Blvd,
246-3938 (map:HH6)

KIDS Until October 1985, an old law left over from Prohibition days declared brew pubs illegal. Shortly after it was repealed, the McMenamin brothers opened Portland's first brew pub just off Capitol Highway in Hillsdale. It's formulaic McMenamin, with civilized burgers (an egg on top), gigantic orders of fries, and generous seven-days-a-week hours; but at this one, kids are invited.

Mission Theater and Pub
1624 NW Glisan St,
223-4031 (map:FF6)

See Movies in the Arts chapter.

Pal's Shanty
4630 NE Sandy Blvd,
288-9732 (map:FF4)

Beats us why folks rave about this Sandy Boulevard stop. The pub swims with hungry souls who have eyes only for the buckets of clams or the shrimp cocktails (and stomachs large enough to finish the heaping portions). Wash it all down with a beer while the friendly waitresses apologize for the lack of coffee, tea, or milk on the premises.

Portland Brew Pub
1339 NW Flanders St,
222-7150 (map:L1)

Six microbrews, from the good-for-newcomers Portland Ale to the aromatic, spiced Winter Ale, are brewed and poured at this tiny, cordial pub. Live music some Friday and Saturday nights (although the musician's balcony won't hold more than one guitarist), but absolutely no smoking. Don't forget your ID.

Send us your feedback and tips on the report form at the back of this book.

Produce Row Cafe
204 SE Oak St, 232-8355 (map:GG5)

Even a remodel didn't change Produce Row, which has been the same (give or take a few hundred beers) since it opened 16 years ago. Next door to the fruit and produce warehouses underneath Martin Luther King Jr. Boulevard (formerly Union Avenue), the Row takes in a steady flow of newcomers and regulars for its 200 bottled beers, 27 draughts (mostly micros), and fresh cider. A friendly spot for all, from punks to Mom and Pop; kids are welcome (except at the pool table) until 9pm.

Stanich's Ten-Till-One Tavern
4915 NE Fremont St, 281-2322 (map:FF4)

Stanich's West
5627 SW Kelly St (Johns Landing), 246-5040 (map:II6)

On the outside, this dive resembles most other eastside neighborhood tavs. Inside, the walls of sports banners, menus that introduce the staff by name, and a darn good burger set it apart. An Empire State Building of a hamburger is constructed with ham, bacon, egg, and representatives of nearly every other type of food. Mouth-stretching exercises are advised. The Johns Landing Stanich's offers the same swell atmosphere and food.

NIGHTCLUB INDEX: MUSIC/TYPE

ACOUSTIC
Buffalo Gap
Demetri's Cafe and Bar
East Avenue Tavern
Great Blue Heron Cafe

ALL AGES (SOMETIMES)
Pine Street Tavern
Starry Night

ALTERNATIVE
Blue Gallery
Pine Street Tavern
Satyricon

CELTIC
Dublin Pub and Restaurant

COMEDY
Last Laugh

COUNTRY
The Drum
Jubitz Truck Stop

GAY
Embers

JAZZ
Belmont's
Belmont's
Cafe Vivo
DJ's Village Jazz
The Hobbit
Museum After Hours
    (Portland Art Museum)
Remo's Ristorante Italiano
Uogashi

KARAOKE SINGING
Uogashi

LATE NIGHT
Brasserie Montmartre
Buffalo Gap
The Drum

LATIN JAZZ
Museum After Hours
    (Portland Art Museum)

LIVE 6 To 7 NIGHTS
Belmont's
Key Largo
Parchman Farm

NO COVER

Brasserie Montmartre
DJ's Village Jazz
Parchman Farm
Remo's Ristorante Italiano

REGGAE/AFRICAN
Reggae-African Club

RHYTHM/BLUES
Belmont's
Cafe Vivo
Dandelion
Dublin Pub and Restaurant
Great Blue Heron Cafe
Key Largo
Museum After Hours
    (Portland Art Museum)
White Eagle

ROCK
Dandelion
Day for Night
Demetri's Cafe and Bar
Key Largo
Satyricon

TOP 40s
Dakota
Shanghai Lounge

NIGHTCLUB INDEX: LOCATION

NIGHTCLUBS

Belmont's
3357 SE Belmont St,
232-1998 (map:GG5)

Belmont's has a sort of split personality. It's actually three very different bars: a fern bar, a '50s bar, and a pool hall. Once the tunes are turned up, there's no question that it's a hot spot for rock, blues, or R&B on any night (music is free on weeknights). The slickest dance floor in town—great for splits and jetes.

Blue Gallery
222 NW 10th Ave,
274-0177 (map:K2)

Art, music, and beer blend well up front where the young, the chic, and the bummed-out lean at the bar. In back, where the blues blares, the Blue Gallery has the atmosphere of a garage, with alternative—some might say experimental—music to match. Tone Dogs, Nemo, or, er, Sweaty Nipples may play Thursday through Saturday. No cover charge on First Thursdays.

Brasserie Montmartre
626 SW Park Ave,
224-5552 (map:I2)

A fancy-sounding name but truly a very casual joint, affectionately known as "The Bra." It's not only packed during most of its business hours, people have been known to line up outside and wait for its 11:30am opening. Some head to the high-ceilinged establishment for the nightly jazz (free); some go for the paper-covered tables and the jar of crayons; some dribble in late at night for the scrambled eggs with smoked salmon (until 3am, weekends).

Buffalo Gap
*6835 SW Macadam Ave,
244-7111 (map:II6)*

Upstairs in this unpretentious tavern, the sounds of acoustic guitars warm chilly nights; in the summer, the festivities expand onto the back patio. Beer drinkers from Lewis and Clark mingle with local night owls; Buffalo Gap is open until 2:30am, with a satisfying munchie menu.

Cafe Vivo
*555 SW Oak St, 228-8486
(map:J4)*

On the bottom floor of the rose-colored US BanCorp Tower sits this tony club. It's the only place where you can regularly catch the upbeat jazz of the Tom Grant Band as well as the occasional R&B romp of Lloyd Jones' Struggle. There's a surplus of yuppies and young women on weekends.

DJ's Village Jazz
*500 SW 1st St, Lake Oswego, 636-2024
(map:KK6)*

For the Lake Oswego jazz lover, this bar is just the thing. During the week the music is piped into the intimate setting, which still retains a neighborhood feel, but on the weekends there are live bands. No surprises in the music (it's often Rebecca Kilgore and Quartet), but the raves over the Steak Oswego were unexpected.

Dakota Cafe
*239 SW Broadway,
241-4151 (map:J3)*

Something's always happening at the Dakota; you just have to push past the drunken frat boys to find it. It's usually in back—music, that is, seven nights a week (cover charge Fridays and Saturdays). Some nights it's disco, others it's dance-inspired rock or R&B by the Carleton Jackson Band.

Dandelion Pub
*31 NW 23rd Pl, 223-0099
(map:FF6)*

Some of the state's (dare we say the world's?) best R&B finds its way to this Northwest beer joint. The smoky gloom lifts to the sweet wailing of Curtis Salgado's harmonica or the bluesy rhythms of the Paul Delay Band. There's dancing, but only the slim have a chance of finding a place to squeeze in.

Day for Night
*135 NW 5th Ave,
243-2556 (map:K4)*

Housed in what used to be a Cajun restaurant, this brand-new club is spiced with a smorgasbord of music, dancing, and late-night noshing. Irregular cover charges—some nights it's just plain on the house.

Demetri's Cafe and Bar
*824 SW 1st Ave, 295-1012
(map:G5)*

Formerly Aldo's, Portland's hottest singles bar, Demetri's has had a tough act to follow. They got off to a slow start, but now business is picking up—and so are the patrons. Upholstered comfort, with soft rock playing at night, and live music on weekends. There's a dance floor for bumping and thumping.

The Drum
14601 SE Division St,
760-1400 (map:GG1)

The dance floor is rarely empty at the Drum, where swing and two-step dancers hoard the floor until 4am—the unabashed join in. Dancers with two left feet may want to play pool. *The Oregonian* named the Drum Portland's best country music club; we quite agree. Cover on weekends only.

Dublin Pub and Restaurant
3104 SE Belmont St,
230-8817 (map:GG4)

6821 Beaverton-Hillsdale
Hwy, 297-2889
(map:HH7)

When neighbors complained of the noise from the original Dublin Pub on the eastside, the owners snatched up a spacious spot in Raleigh Hills, thus assuring that the bagpipe would live on in the Portland metro area. The pipes—and Celtic balladeers—sound during the early eves. Later on, there's rock and blues guitar. The Belmont address is now acoustic music only.

East Avenue Tavern
727 E Burnside,
236-6900 (map:J3)

Nothing more than a friendly tavern with good beer (a dozen microbrews on tap), and nothing less than the city's finest acoustic, folk, and Celtic music—some of which you can actually dance to.

Embers
110 NW Broadway,
222-3082 (map:I3)

The pulsing lights and throbbing beat are two clues that you've reached Embers, Portland's premier gay disco. The bar closes at 2:30, but dancing doesn't stop until 4 on Fridays and Saturdays.

Great Blue Heron Cafe
203 SE Grand Ave,
238-1115 (map:GG5)

Save the political discussions for downstairs. Upstairs, where listening—not talking—is encouraged, is reserved for music (blues to acoustic guitar) and the occasional poetry reading. For a tavern, there are an awful lot of Meliors on the tables. Good pizza and now a basic breakfast menu, too.

The Hobbit
4420 SE 39th Ave,
771-0742 (map:HH4)

Laid-back and dimly lit, the Hobbit is *the* traditional jazz nook. Finger-snapping jazz aficionados and dabblers alike enjoy the tunes—often played by the Mel Brown Sextet with Leroy Vinnegar. An appealing way to finish the night.

The Jubitz Truck Stop
10210 N Vancouver Wy,
283-1111 (map:CC6)

There's more testosterone pumping through this truck stop than on a battlefield, but the dance floor—lined with lit-up tailgates—offers burly drivers, cowboys, and others an outlet for their hormones and relief from highway stress. Live country-western bands play seven nights a week. If that's not entertainment enough, you'll find pool tables and video games off to the side. Handily, there's a motel and weigh station next door.

Key Largo
31 NW 1st Ave, 223-9919
(map:J6)

It's tropical, and the boys are, well, cute. Dancing tunes run in the rock and R&B vein. For once, there's room to move. It's at its finest in the summer, when the college crowd is in full starlight swing on the back patio.

The Last Laugh
426 NW 6th Ave,
295-2844 (map:L4)

All the intimacy of an auditorium, and a two-drink minimum; you often can't hear the jokes if you're sitting in the back. Nonetheless, it's Portland's pick for comedy. When owner Joe Torres is feeling bullish his comedians can be some of the nation's finest. Unfortunately, that's not usually the case.

Museum After Hours
(Oregon Art Institute)
1219 SW Park Ave,
226-2811 (map:F1)

On Wednesday eves during the cool-weather months the Portland Art Museum lets down its hair and warms up with hot jazz (Andre Kiteau Trio), blues (Taj Mahal), Latin jazz (Salcocho), and a cappella (The Bobs) letting loose in the museum's sculpture court. Wind down after work (5:30–7:30) and roam the museum with a glass of wine and the music. Tickets are $3.50 for nonmembers, $2 for members; benefit concerts slightly higher.

Parchman Farm
1204 SE Clay St,
235-7831 (map:FF5)

The Farm runs close behind Jazz de Opus as Portland's nook for late-night romance: the lighting's soft, the mood subtle. An acoustic guitar duo blends with the deep pulse of a stand-up bass to keep the heart alive. No cover, full bar.

Pine Street Theater
221 SE 9th Ave, 235-0027
(map:GG5)

Usually all ages are allowed here, and they mix admirably. There's a huge dance floor, video games, an espresso bar, and—for ID-bearers—a wine and beer bar. Music ranges from thrash to folk, so call ahead, especially if you prefer one extreme over the other.

Reggae-African Club
(Red Sea Restaurant)
318 SW 3rd Ave,
241-5450 (map:I5)

The dance floor must have been an afterthought: a meandering hallway connects the Ethiopian restaurant to the city's smallest dance spot. That's OK: the reggae is played to a full house. Stiff drinks.

Remo's
1425 NW Glisan St,
221-1150 (map:L1)

No cover, ever, in the rakish bar of this Pearl District restaurant. We've come to count on Remo's for keen jazz every night. Appetizers are cheapest before 7pm and after 10.

Satyricon
125 NW 6th Ave,
243-2380 (map:K4)

If you need an injection of underground music (Hell Cows and Coffin Break), don black and head for Satyricon: weird art, blacklights, and killer souvlaki. There's an endless spattering of what could be award-winning graffiti on the bathroom walls.

Shanghai Lounge
0309 SW Montgomery St,
220-1865 (map:B5)

"Shanghaiing" is a good word for the come-ons of the young, single corporate escapees. The dance floor is spacious and the entertainment primarily Top 40. You can always turn your back to the drunken courting and let your gaze drift down the Willamette. Full bar.

Starry Night
8 NW 6th Ave, 227-0071
(map:J4)

Once a two-story Apostolic Faith church, Starry Night presently books some of Portland's biggest acts (Leon Russell, Karla Bonoff, Holly Near). It's smoky, boozy, and noisy with heavy metal, folk, and comedy acts (some shows are for all ages). Whether you dance or not, be prepared to sweat. NW 6th Avenue is a seamy street: pay attention between your car and the club.

Uogashi
107 NW Couch St,
242-1848 (map:K6)

See Restaurants chapter.

White Eagle Cafe and Saloon
836 N Russell St,
282-6810 (map:FF5)

The Eagle nests amid the smokestacks of the decidedly industrial Lower Albina district. Half the customers come from the other side of town, a few from other parts of the country (Matt Dillon was once sighted here). The sultry R&B of the Terry Robb Band or the Razorbacks (rockin' each Wednesday) lures large crowds. No music Sundays or Tuesdays.

▼

THE ARTS CONTENTS

THE ARTS

ART IN PUBLIC PLACES

Portland's public art can be found everywhere, outdoors and in, thanks to the government Percent for Art program and the patronage of the private enterprise sector. Virtually every City of Portland office building, lobby, and park boasts its signature mural, sculpture, painting, relief, or fountain. More than 30 pieces (from Simon Benson drinking fountains to stunning murals) add interest and color to Portland's landscape. The best way to tour the art landmarks is to begin at the Metropolitan Center for Public Art, in the Portland Building (1120 SW Fifth Avenue, 796-5111, map:F3), itself a controversial landmark (the first major work by architect Michael Graves, described with every imaginable adjective from "brilliant" to "hideous"). There you can pick up a free brochure that will guide you on a downtown walking tour.

Kneeling above the entrance to the Portland Building is Raymond Kaskey's monumental statue *Portlandia*. In 1985 this piece, the nation's second-largest hammered-copper sculpture (the Statue of Liberty is the first), was barged down the Willamette River, trucked through downtown, and hoisted to a ledge three stories up. Most Portlanders have forgotten that *Portlandia* is meant to be a descendant of Lady Commerce, the figure on the city seal. Her nicknames (Copper Goddess, Queen Kong) have been bestowed with affection.

Directly across the street from *Portlandia* is Don Wilson's abstract limestone sculpture *Interlocking Forms*. Nearby is City Hall (1220 SW Fifth Avenue, map:F3), whose east courtyard contains the oldest of Portland's artworks, petroglyphs carved into basalt rock over the Columbia River in the 16th century. One of the city's most familiar landmarks is the bronze *Elk* of Roland Perry, set in the fountain on Main between SW Third and SW Fourth (map:F3) that once served as a watering trough for both horses and humans and now is a traffic divider. Inside the Justice Center (between SW Second and SW Third, and Madison and Main, map:F4) is a fine 19th-century Kwakiutl carving of an eagle and an array of contemporary pieces. At the entrance are Walter Dusenbery's untitled travertine sculptures representing the various paths to justice. Near them is a wall of stained-glass windows by Ed Carpenter.

The true centerpiece of downtown art is Pioneer Courthouse Square (map:H3), a gathering place for Portlanders at every hour of the day. The amphitheater-style design of the square is well suited to people-watching. Just before noon the *Weather Machine*, a shiny sphere atop a 25-foot pole, plays a musical fanfare and sends forth one of three creatures, depending on the day's weather. When it's clear, you'll see the sun figure Helia; on stormy days, a dragon; and on gray, drizzly days, a great blue heron. Equally popular is the bronze sculpture by Seward Johnson, *Allow Me*, a life-sized replica of a gracious businessman with an umbrella, undoubtedly the most photographed piece of art in the city.

Across the square is the purple ceramic tile fountain and waterfall of Will Martin, which dampens, so to speak, the noise of the surrounding streets. At Yamhill and Morrison streets, behind the historic Pioneer Courthouse building, look for Georgia Gerber's delightful bronze animals gathered around small pools of water (map:G3).

The Fifth and Sixth Avenue Transit Mall (map:F3) is lined with sculptures, including Kathleen McCullough's limestone cat (a children's favorite) and Norman Taylor's notorious *Kvinneakt*, the nude that Portlanders know as Mayor Bud Clark's accomplice in the "Expose Yourself to Art" poster. Another amiable bronze woman is *Rebecca at the Well*, a graceful sculpture and (now dry) fountain placed in the South Park Blocks in 1926 (SW Salmon and SW Main streets, map:G1).

Portland's best privately financed artwork is set inside the Pacific First Federal Center (SW Broadway between Taylor and Yamhill, map:G2): Larry Kirkland's suspended woven panels cascade into the lobby, catching the changing light throughout the day. A little-known and hard-to-find sculpture, *Electronic Poet*, flashes lines of poetry from a building arcade (SW Morrison between 9th and 10th, map:H2). To the south, in front of the Civic Auditorium, is the *Ira Keller Fountain*, better known as the "Forecourt Fountain," a cool resting place in the middle of downtown; it's a full city block of waterfalls and pools built specifically with summer splashing in mind.

Not listed in the Center for Public Art's walking tour is the Sculpture Mall on the north side of the Oregon Art Institute (1219 SW Park Ave, map:F1). Look for the Barbara Hepworth sculpture *Dual Form*, and works by Lee Kelly and Clement Meadmore. In Old Town stands the bronze and granite 1888 *Skidmore Fountain* (SW First Avenue and Ankeny Street, map:J6); two bronze caryatids hold above their heads a bowl that overflows into the fountain. One of the newest and most popular fountains is the ever-changing *Salmon Street Springs*, in Waterfront Park where SW Front Avenue and SW Salmon Street meet.

A modern application of trompe l'oeil effects can be seen from the South Park Blocks between SW Madison and SW Jefferson streets. The new Richard Haas murals on the south and west walls of the Oregon Historical Center depict figures from Oregon history: Lewis and Clark, Sacajawea, fur traders, and pioneers who journeyed westward on the Oregon Trail.

Finally, keen eyes might catch sight of the Zoo Bus #63, painted in kaleidoscopic colors by Scott McIntire.

CLASSICAL MUSIC

Chamber Music Northwest
Reed College, SE Wood-stock Blvd (map:II4), and Catlin Gable School, SW Barnes Rd, 223-3202 (map:GG9)

"Chamber Music Northwest" is a bit of a misnomer. One of the finest chamber groups in the country, it relies on imported New York musicians for a varied, month-long series of programs in early summer. A nucleus of players from the Chamber Music Society of Lincoln Center is supplemented by other first-rank freelancers, about two dozen in all, to offer works from the 18th century to the present. Performances range from solo recitals to works such as Copland's *Appalachian Spring* or Stravinsky's *L'Histoire du Soldat*. The breadth and variety of the programs improve each year. Particularly when challenged with an unusual piece, these musicians can rise well above the typically under-rehearsed but slick festival standard.

Oregon Repertory Singers
227-3929

Fifteen years of innovative concerts have given Gilbert Seeley's 40-voice ensemble a reputation for creative programming. Representing the United States at an international choral festival in Austria in 1987, the Singers walked off with all the top prizes. Seeley can be counted on for supple work with orchestras (Haydn's *Creation*, Bach's B-minor Mass, Mozart's *Coronation* Mass) and for lyrical readings of neglected classics such as Frank Martin's *Mass*. Premieres of new works by American and European composers are often programmed with pieces from the 16th century, in revealing combinations. Call for location.

Oregon Symphony Orchestra
Arlene Schnitzer Concert Hall, 1037 SW Broadway, 248-4496 (map:G2)

The Symphony has come a long way under conductor James DePreist. Once a mere community ensemble, it is now a respected orchestra with three CDs under its belt, a budget larger than the Seattle Symphony's, and 90 percent audience attendance. DePreist is especially effective at whipping the orchestra into a fine frenzy with the late Romantic and early modern repertoire—Rachmaninoff, Ravel, Richard Strauss. Celebrity soloists and a variety of ancillary programs—family concerts, pops concerts—fill out the 39-week season.

Portland Baroque Orchestra
224-7908

One of the youngest baroque orchestras in the country is finding its place near the top. Under conductor Ton Koopman, the Dutch superstar harpsichordist, this 20-piece group tackles everything from Monteverdi to Schubert, on period instruments. Its annual choral presentations of the *Messiah* breathe new life into Handel's glorious warhorse. All concerts are brisk and fresh and played with absolutely first-rate ensemble phrasing. Most performances are in the Trinity Episcopal Church (147 NW 19th, map:FF6); call to confirm.

DANCE

Arte Flamenco Dance Company
647-5202

KIDS Flamenco: a form of folk art that without Jose Solano (and his small troupe of family and friends) would otherwise seldom be seen in Portland. Flamenco dancing is presented as it should be—up close (in taverns and other intimate city spaces) and, when possible, with all ages of family members participating on both sides of the stage. If you chance upon an afternoon performance when all ages are invited, do as the Solanos do: bring the entire family.

Contemporary Dance Season
Lincoln Performance Hall, Portland State University, 725-3131 (map:D1)

This yearly series of performances by cutting-edge modern dance companies is imported from Los Angeles, San Francisco, and New York by Portland State University. The dance department and, more specifically, dance professor Nancy Matschek deserve a lot of credit for bringing acts to Portland that might otherwise never appear here.

Do Jump Movement Theatre
1515 SE 37th Ave, 231-1232 (map:GG5)

Vigorous, athletic works are the trademark of the resident dance company of Echo Theatre. Do Jump is pure entertainment; critics use words like "zany" and "fearless" to describe their signature visual comedy. Novel props such as trapezes, along with a penchant for innovative costuming, enhance this gymnastic group's high-wired stunts.

Oregon Ballet Theatre
1119 SW Park Ave, 227-6867 (map:G1)

Thanks to the recent merger of Ballet Oregon and Pacific Ballet Theatre, this new entity is now considered *the* ballet company of Portland. With that privilege—and that of sharing major tenant status at Civic Auditorium with Portland Opera—comes the responsibility of meeting the city's ballet needs. To that end, the troupe of approximately 25 dancers performs both classical and off-the-wall modern works. Although artistic director James Canfield and his associate, Dennis Spaight, make significant choreographic contributions, OBT has expressed a commitment to exhibiting the works of up-and-coming choreographers from around the country.

Oslund and Company/Dance
236-3265

Artistic director and choreographer Mary Oslund Van Liew is the primary creative force behind these quirky yet technically polished performances. Local critics rave about her shows, which linger somewhere between postmodern and new dance. Oslund Van Liew's husband, Mike Van Liew, along with others, composes and performs original music for many of the company's productions, and the troupe is apt to employ the services of local musicians, poets, visual artists, or filmmakers for any given show—wherever it may be.

GALLERIES

FREE Portland's art and craft galleries have flourished in recent years, particularly since the inception of **First Thursdays**. Some two dozen galleries stay open late on the first Thursday of each month to welcome visitors to their new shows, and many serve refreshments. The Portland Art Museum joins in with free admission, beginning at 4pm.

Galleries can be found in every corner of the city and suburbs, but many cluster around two areas: downtown and in the Pearl District. Downtown, many galleries line the streets of the Yamhill and Skidmore historic districts, between SW Front and SW Third avenues. The Pearl District, once an aging northwest Portland industrial center north of Burnside between NW 10th and NW 14th, is steadily turning warehouses and storefronts into galleries, artists' lofts, and art-oriented businesses. (See also Major Attractions in the Exploring chapter.)

ART GALLERIES

Argus Fine Arts Corp
840 SW 1st Ave, 224-2735
(map:F5)
Mon-Sat

Primarily a dealership for collectors of limited-edition prints and those interested in owning something by one of the century's tried and true: Miro, Chagall, Hundertwasser, Calder. The tiny, high-ceilinged space is not well suited to browsing; the best way to view the collection is to stand in the center of the room and turn in a circle. There is an upstairs space with a larger inventory, but an appointment is required. Posted hours don't always apply—call ahead.

The Art Gym
Marylhurst College, 10
miles south of Portland on
Hwy 43, Marylhurst,
636-8141 (map:MM5)
Tues-Sat

Once a gymnasium, this 3,000-square-foot space at Marylhurst College is now a well-respected showcase (and testing ground) for the work of the Northwest's rising stars and established artists. Christine Bourdette, Ronna Neuenschwander, Lee Kelly, Lucinda Parker, Mark Calderon, Tad Savinar, and Mel Katz have all shown here. The Art Gym (on the second floor of the B.P. John Administration Building) occasionally mounts major retrospectives, but there is always a place here for the experimental. Juried group and alumni shows and student thesis presentations round out the year of exhibits.

Augen Gallery
817 SW 2nd Ave,
224-8182 (map:F4)
Mon-Sat

As one of the largest and most comprehensive galleries in Portland, Augen caters to the tastes and budgets of a diverse clientele—from works by renowned 20th-century American artists to those by contemporary artists with regional reputations. Monthly exhibits featuring one or more artists occupy the central space on the main floor. Works by regular gallery artists are generally shown downstairs, among them the perhaps-too-pretty prints of Thomas McKnight and the disturbing acrylic paintings of Bill Brewer. Augen plans to open an upstairs space for sculpture, compensating a little for the relative scarcity of sculpture in Portland galleries.

Blackfish Gallery
420 NW 9th Ave,
224-2634 (map:K2)
Wed-Sun

Over the last decade, Blackfish has gained a loyal following among Portlanders and has become a fixture on the First Thursday circuit. Now housed in the Pearl District, at the sign of the aging and smudged wooden fish, Blackfish remains a local artists' cooperative, primarily displaying the latest works of its 20-some members in monthly shows. Media are as varied as styles, running from figurative sculpture to abstract painting.

Blue Sky Gallery and Nine Gallery
1231 NW Hoyt St,
225-0210 (Map:L1)
Tues-Sat

These two galleries share a space in the Pearl District. Blue Sky, which opened in 1975, displays outstanding contemporary and historical photography. The contemporary selections often show considerable wit, in distinct contrast with the seriousness of more traditional photography. It is places like Blue Sky that have expanded our notions of what photography can be. The Nine Gallery, in an adjoining room, is a cooperative run by nine local artists, working in a variety of media.

Butters Gallery Ltd
312 NW 10th Ave,
248-9378 (map:K2)
Tues-Sat

This small new Pearl District gallery made an impressive debut. Monthly exhibits feature works by regionally and nationally prominent artists, yet you'll often catch glimpses of emerging talents, too, such as Harry Widman, Tom Cramer, and Ted Katz. Butters' first annual print show was a mix of gallery artists and international names such as Robert Motherwell, Jasper Johns, Frank Stella, and Claes Oldenburg. A handful of these works can still be found in Butters' inventory.

Elizabeth Leach Gallery
207 SW Pine St, 224-0521
(map:I5)
Mon-Sat

This airy space in the historic Hazeltine Building is well suited to large-scale sculpture, of which all too little is seen in Portland galleries. But the excellent exhibits here are equally strong in two-dimensional works. Don't be surprised if the genial Elizabeth Leach remembers you and your likes and dislikes after your first visit. She speaks sensibly and knowledgeably about the artists she represents, and she wants you to know who they are too. (The bountiful art in the Heathman Hotel is a fine example of Leach's consulting expertise.)

Gango Gallery
205 SW 1st Ave, 222-3850
(map:I5)
Mon-Sat

Gango should get the Most Improved award: it's recently taken a turn toward fresh and technically accomplished Northwest contemporary artists. The latest shows have been of consistently high quality, in a wide range of media and styles. Gone now are the decorator arts, Gango's former stock in trade, and all but gone are the displays by artists who allow their works to be mass-produced for greeting cards and posters. The posters remain, however, in the adjacent Poster Gallery, which serves as the entrance to Gango and seems to get more business.

Hoffman Gallery
Oregon School of Arts and Crafts, 8245 SW Barnes Rd, 297-5544 (map:GG9)
Every day

In every corner of the Oregon School of Arts and Crafts —on the grounds, in the modern but rustic structures, in each classroom—there is eye-pleasing design and detail. Functional yet aesthetically pleasing forms remind us that art need not be slid under glass and hung on a wall. A streamlined steel sculpture sits on a rooftop; landscaped garden paths lead to a sculpture patio.

The Hoffman Gallery is entered through an elaborate swirling wrought-iron gate. Featured artists are primarily from the Northwest, working in various combinations of fiber arts, ceramics, glass, metal, and wood. Among the latest of the gallery's diverse offerings have been group shows of Pilchuck School glass and Hmong stitchery. The adjacent sales gallery displays and sells superbly crafted gifts. Before leaving OSAC, stop at the Hands On Cafe for coffee (in a handmade ceramic cup) and lunch beside the sculpted steel fireplace. And your visit's incomplete without a look at the restroom.

Image Gallery
1026 SW Morrison St, 224-9629 (map:H1)
Tues-Sat

The small and eclectic Image Gallery contains many little delights and real finds. Since 1961 it's been one of Portland's few sources of folk and tribal arts of West Africa and Latin America. But on a recent visit, a fine old Louis Bunce oil painting was spotted tucked away on a high shelf, and scattered here and there were several of Amanda Snyder's paintings, among traditional carved masks from the Ivory Coast and antelope headdresses from Mali. Latin American folk art has included terracotta figurines and fanciful polychrome wooden masks from Guerrero, Mexico.

Jamison/Thomas Galleries
1313 NW Glisan St, 222-0063 (map:L1)
Tues-Sat

If the eclectic bunch of contemporary West Coast artists shown at this outstanding gallery have anything in common, it is vision. It is sometimes hard to remember that Jamison and Thomas started out in the early '80s representing self-taught and other non-mainstream artists, whose works were mixed in with the tribal and folk arts formerly in abundance here. (And William Jamison can probably be credited with introducing the term "outsider art" to Portland.) Now such artists have become familiar names in the Northwest. Gregory Grenon, for his oil on Plexiglas paintings of those endearing and dyspeptic females; Stuart Buehler, for his inspired and wacky mixed-media work; Stan Peterson, for his delightful polychrome carvings; Wague, for his animal-decorated ceramics. Some have exhibited in the gallery's New York branch (at 588 Broadway), which opened in 1986, for a change bringing the best of the West to the East. Jamison/Thomas continues to take risks in its choice of exhibits, and for that reason in the new Pearl District location it can be counted on to present shows that are powerful and challenging, sophisticated and witty.

Laura Russo Gallery
805 NW 21st Ave,
226-2754 (map:FF6)
Mon-Sat

Laura Russo maintains a strong commitment to artists from the Northwest, and she has earned a solid reputation for representing some of the most respected. Russo does not shy away from the controversial and experimental in the work of new gallery artists. One of the most extraordinary of her recent exhibits was a group of constructions by Jim Clausnitzer, whose paint, wood, tricot, and cast-sand pieces give new meaning to the term "mixed media." This handsome, bright gallery is one of only a handful with space enough to display large-scale works.

Littman Gallery and White Gallery
Portland State University,
725-4452 (map:D1)
Mon-Fri

The Littman Gallery, in the Smith Memorial Center at PSU, has earned an excellent reputation in the region and has long been a regular stop for gallery-goers from outside the university as well as within. Down the corridor from the Littman is the space known as the White Gallery, where primarily two-dimensional works are displayed. In recent years, some of the most engaging and memorable photographic exhibits in town have been at one or the other of these galleries.

Maveety Gallery
842 SW 1st Ave, 224-9442
(map:G5)
Tues-Sat

Formerly the Lawrence Gallery, the Maveety maintains a sizable inventory of paintings, ceramics, glass, and sculpture. The ceramists offer the most original and exciting work, in both handmade decorative vessels and in sculptural pieces using clay and various minerals. The plentiful landscape paintings at Maveety seem less vital and more conventional than those elsewhere in town.

Photographic Image Gallery
208 SW 1st Ave, 224-3543
(map:I5)
Mon-Sat

This is the place to go for fine prints of such masters as Ansel Adams, Imogen Cunningham, Minor White, and Edward S. Curtis. Exhibits rotate monthly, featuring contemporary photographers from all around the country, including Portland's own Ray Atkeson. There is a small but excellent selection of books and cards as well.

Quartersaw Gallery
528 NW 12th Ave,
223-2264 (map:L1)
Tues-Sat

Always willing to take a chance on the untried, this vital little gallery has created a forum for those just getting a start in the local arts market. Paintings dominate the shows, which emphasize the figurative, in styles from the relatively representational to the relatively abstract. Small-scale pieces are effectively displayed in the tiny front gallery, while the two back rooms are reserved for larger works.

Pulliam/Nugent Gallery
522 NW 12th Ave,
228-6665 (map:L1)
Tues-Sun

At press time, Portland's youngest gallery had moved to a new spot on NW 12th Avenue and one step closer to becoming a real force among regional exhibitors of contemporary art. The diversity and quality of selections are often stimulating and rewarding. Owners Rod Pulliam and Tim Nugent prefer figurative, expressionistic works from Northwest artists. The staff is accommodating yet unobtrusive, and will gladly show you additional works from stock by those artists you admire.

CRAFT GALLERIES

Contemporary Crafts Gallery
3934 SW Corbett Ave,
223-2654 (map:HH6)
Tues-Sun

The oldest nonprofit gallery in the nation (established 1937), with a longstanding reputation in Portland for its well-wrought works, is perched on a hillside in an old south Portland neighborhood in a building that affords spectacular city views from its decks and windows. Many of the shows here remind us that the line between craft and art is often hard to fix. The fabulous annual international glass shows, featuring premium sculptural and decorative pieces, rival those of any gallery anywhere. The ceramics, always in abundant supply, go way, way beyond the functional and into the artful.

Quintana Galleries
139 NW 2nd Ave,
223-1729 (map:K6)
Mon-Sat

Northwest Coast tribes—Haida, Kwakiutl, Tlingit—are well represented here in the stylized carved masks, storage vessels, and totems. Less consistent in quality are the paintings of Western subjects and the soapstone and alabaster carvings from various areas, which range from the charming and inventive to the commercial and sentimental. Relatively new to Quintana are Inuit prints from Hudson Bay, depicting scenes from a way of life that is perhaps vanishing. Exquisite Pueblo pottery from Arizona and New Mexico are featured in Quintana's annual fall Southwest Indian Market.

Map locators refer to the fold-out map included in this book. Single letters refer to the Downtown Portland map; double letters refer to the Greater Portland map on the other side.

The Real Mother Goose
901 SW Yamhill St (and branches), 223-9510 (map:H2)
Mon-Sat

A fairy tale shop with singular art pieces best described as the objects artists make to pay rent; the monthly exhibits are the stuff that satifies the artists' souls. Jewelry designer and goldsmith on staff to design wedding rings and custom baubles. A popular stop for holiday shoppers and travelers seeking out choice Northwest gifts—with a price range that has an appeal for both those on a budget and those not.

The furniture gallery at the spacious downtown store carries contemporary pieces, in creative blends of fine and sometimes exotic woods. All are made with the kind of quality people expect to last for generations. Mother Goose is no longer strictly downtown: two other locations include Washington Square (620-2243) and the Portland International Airport (284-9929), where the selection is limited, but prices are the same and the shops are open every day.

Vox Furniture
530 NW 12th Ave, 224-6821 (map:L1)
Mon-Sat

Vox defies categorization. Is it more a furniture store or a gallery? Are those whimsical and stylish creations art or craft, contemporary or postmodern? Here you'll find artistically rendered lamps, desks, chairs, and tables— one-of-kind pieces by local designer-artisans as well as manufactured pieces from international sources. An unusual assemblage of materials: wood, paint, galvanized steel, marble, vinyl, cowhide, papier-mache, and what have you.

LITERATURE

In the beginning, there was Powell's—open 365 days a year and rumored to have broken up marriages of people who spent too much time in its endless aisles. More than 15 years after one of the nation's largest literary institutions (soon to be *the* largest) opened its doors, Portland boasts no less than 109 independent new-book shops and probably just as many, if not more, dealers in used and rare books, all for roughly 600,000 residents. No less staggering is the fact that almost 50 percent of Portland's residents hold active library cards.

It's no surprise, then, that books are big news here. Portland Arts and Lectures director Julie Mancini and the best-selling authors who speak at the Schnitzer Concert Hall are continually wowed by the overwhelming response to the five-year-old lecture series—John McPhee drew an audience of 2,000, for example. Why this voracious hunger for the written word? Locals reason it's probably due to the city's two dozen universities and colleges, or the strong resident-author community. Or perhaps it's the weather, the sort that doesn't exactly make you want to head for the tennis court.

For obvious reasons, bookstores are very supportive of Portland's print fetish.

LITERATURE

Of all the local stores, **Powell's** (1005 W Burnside, 228-4651, map:J2) is especially influential: it underwrites dozens of literary projects and events, from book-talk programs on KBOO-FM to films at the Northwest Film and Video Center (recently it funded a five-part Gabriel Garcia Marquez series); donates books to word-hungry kids in north Portland; and supports once-a-week readings (September–June) in its **Anne Hughes Coffee Room**, a familiar address to aspiring writers. Other stores contribute to the city's literary life in smaller but no less important ways, including autograph parties at **Catbird Seat** (913 SW Broadway, 222-5817, map:F2); an excellent 12-page newsletter from **Conant & Conant** (5201 NE Sandy Boulevard, 287-8462, map:FF4); and the busy bookstore and regional scholarly-and-trade–book press of the **Oregon Historical Society** (1230 SW Park Ave, 222-1741, map:F2), one of the nation's finest historical societies.

With the increasing number of readers comes record-setting lecture attendance. The **Portland Arts and Lectures Series** (241-0543), created in 1984 to bring authors who might otherwise bypass the city on their way to Seattle, now attracts Schnitzer-sized crowds to hear Garrison Keillor, John Updike, or maybe Joyce Carol Oates, and has become a vital booking for national tours (series tickets, $65). Smaller, less formal lectures are held next door in the First Congregational Church. The **Science, Technology, and Society Lecture Series** (725-4788) presents writers and thinkers of a more scientific nature, from Carl Sagan to Stephen J. Gould. Equally lofty thoughts (with a smaller crowd) are shared during Goody Cable (of Rimsky Korsakoffee House) and Joanna Knapps' (of Powell's) **Creativity in the Terms of Our Survival** talks. Call Powell's for more information. **Multnomah County Library** (221-7724) also has its own lecture series. **Open-mike readings** are regularly scheduled at local establishments such as Delilah's (243-3324), the Blue Heron Cafe (238-1115), and Satyricon (243-2380). Check calendar listings in the local newspapers.

Twice a year, bookworms (sellers, publishers, writers, and readers) surface en masse for the **Northwest Writers LitEruption** (222-2944). LitEruption, which was started in 1988, is held in March at the Masonic Temple but spills over into the South Park Blocks. In September, a book fair (mostly readings) is a small but vital part of the Labor Day performing and fine arts celebration, **Artquake** (227-2787). (See also Calendar chapter.)

Behind all the book hullabaloo are a number of remarkable writer support groups. For $25 a year, professional Oregon writers can exchange tips on taxes, pay, risky publications, fair editors, and even health insurance, through **Northwest Writers Incorporated** (222-2954). A good writing group with its own meeting place in Rockaway is the **Oregon Writers' Colony** (PO Box 15200, Portland, OR 97215). **Mountain Writers' Series** (26000 SE Stark St, Gresham, 667-7496), at the Mount Hood Community College, is one of the largest reading series in the country, offering readings, workshops, and lectures by Pulitzer Prize winners and other notable writers. And not only Lewis and Clark students take advantage of the **NW Writing Institute** (293-2757), with its growing list of courses and workshops. The **Oregon Institute of Literary Arts** (223-3604) encourages writers by bequeathing awards and grants to outstanding Oregon authors.

Looking for a particular place? Check the index at the back of this book for individual restaurants, nightclubs, lodgings, shops, attractions, and more.

MOVIES

For a city of its size, Portland has a considerable number of movie screens (reputedly, more per capita than any other medium-sized American city), but not much in the way of art film venues or novelty film houses. Yet what few alternative cinemas there are happen to be well managed, providing a pleasing variety of films that the studio-bound theaters fail to book. For a complete movie listing check the entertainment section of *The Oregonian* or the film reviews in *Willamette Week*.

Cinema 21
616 NW 21st Ave (at Hoyt St), 223-4515 (map:FF6)

Portland's best cinema is one of a dying breed—the single-screen movie house. This large, repertory-style theater (with a huge calendar that comes out about every three months) is equipped with a balcony, a cry room, and rocking-chair seats. Films range from outrageously bad B-movies (usually running for a day or two) to longer runs of recent art house releases and an occasional premiere.

Clinton Street Theatre
2522 SE Clinton St, 238-8899 (map:GG5)

Risks are taken at this collectively run theater, and the space is sometimes barely filled. Yet college students return again and again—maybe it's the treats at the snack bar they're after. *The Rocky Horror Picture Show* has played every Friday and Saturday night for the past several years, with no sign of quitting.

The Guild
829 SW 9th Ave, 248-6964 (map:H2)

This quirky venue in the heart of downtown shows a mix of foreign films, rock documentaries, and hipsters like *Do the Right Thing*.

KOIN Center Cinemas
SW 3rd Ave and Clay St, 243-3515 (map:E3)

Smack in the middle of downtown, it's more eclectic than Portland itself: Hollywood releases, foreign films, and art house movies appear on KOIN's six screens.

L'Auberge Restaurant
2601 NW Vaughn St, 223-3302 (map:FF6)

Every Sunday night, this intimate French restaurant changes its mood to informal (and its menu to burgers) and shows a classic film in its bar to a crowd of hushed eaters. Free popcorn after the movie begins.

Lloyd Cinemas
1510 NE Multnomah Blvd, 248-6938 (map:FF5)

With 10 screens, Lloyd Cinemas is the biggest movie site in the city. It is one of many theaters owned by the ACT III theater chain (the largest in the state after buying out the former Luxury Theaters). The films are traditional Hollywood fare, yet the building is remarkable for features such as a long, neon-lit interior boulevard. A coffee bar too? It must be the '90s.

All places in this book are recommended; even "no stars" are worth knowing about.

Mission Theatre and Pub
1624 NW Glisan St,
223-4031 (map:GG6)

A pint of beer (and maybe a Communication Breakdown burger) is your ticket to recent 16-millimeter releases in this beloved brewery housed in an old union hall with a horseshoe-shaped balcony. The free movies can be hard to hear at times, though if they're especially good the place remains more or less quiet.

The Movie House
1220 SW Taylor St,
222-4595 (map:I1)

Once a great space for foreign films, the Movie House has become a theater without much of a personality and with only the occasional exceptional film. Upstairs, board games and card tables are thrown together in the lobby, with an outdoor balcony for summer. The congenial staff makes up for the hard, close seats.

Northwest Film and Video Center
1219 SW Park Ave,
221-1156 (map:F1)

A steady menu of art films, independent features, and documentaries, with guest filmmakers showing their recent work. This nonprofit corporation also presents the annual Portland International Film Festival, which shows more than 50 new films from over 20 countries.

MUSEUMS

American Advertising Museum
9 NW 2nd Ave,
AAM-0000 (map:K6)
Wed-Sun

See Major Attractions in the Exploring chapter.

Carousel Courtyard and International Museum of Carousel Art
830 NE Holladay St,
between 7th and 9th,
235-2252 (map:FF5)
Every day (Fri-Mon in winter)

KIDS During the late 1800s, carousels were built at the end of streetcar lines in places called "trolley parks." So it's fitting that Duane and Carol Perron built the Carousel Courtyard right on the MAX light rail line (get off at Seventh Avenue). Today's "light rail park" sports a wide, landscaped plaza with a gazebo, benches, picnic tables, and, of course, an outdoor carousel. This 1895 model by master craftsman Charles Looff is a beauty, with its magnificent prancing horses, a sea serpent, a bear, and other creatures. And Carol Perron's initial passion for a carousel horse has turned into a save-the-carousels crusade. The restoration area of the museum contains enough animals to complete up to 17 carousels —which the staff hopes to do someday. Due largely to the Perrons' efforts, Portland has become fabled as the "city of carousels," with seven of them placed throughout the city (five were bought and restored by the museum). Contact the Visitors and Convention Bureau (26 SW Salmon Street, 275-9750) for a listing of the whereabouts of all the carousels.

On weekends, the Carousel Company puts on some of the best children's theater in town at the Carousel Theater. Museum admission, including a ride, is $1. Call ahead; carousels don't like rain.

Children's Museum
3037 SW 2nd Ave,
248-4587 (map:HH6)
Tues-Sun

KIDS This museum is not really a museum; it's a simple play and learning center for children up to age 10. The "Please Touch" exhibit includes a kid-sized grocery store with shopping baskets, canned goods, and a check-out line. Other displays include "H₂OH!" (explaining how water works), a tiny African village to explore, and a Baby Room for toddlers. The basement Clayshop opens in the fall for kids who like to get their hands into modeling clay (Wednesdays only). Birthday parties can be scheduled at the museum, which will present a Clayshop program or a multicultural presentation from its Customs House series. Admission donation is $3 for adults, $2.50 for children. A move to relocate to the eastside near the Carousel Courtyard is presently under active consideration.

Oregon Art Institute
(Portland Art Museum)
1219 SW Park Ave,
226-2811 (map:F2)
Tues-Sun

See Major Attractions in the Exploring chapter.

Oregon Historical Center
1230 SW Park Ave,
222-1741 (map: F2)
Mon-Sat

FREE KIDS The Oregon Historical Center, in the South Park Blocks, is both a museum and the home of the Oregon Historical Society's excellent research library and press. In April 1989 the society inaugurated its new wing (formerly part of the Sovereign Hotel building) with an exhibit of a century of Oregon fashions. A permanent display tells the story of Oregon's Indians, European and American exploration, and the growth of its communities. Paintings, artifacts, and photographs illustrate Oregon's political history and the settling of the Northwest. Boat building is currently under way at the SW Park Avenue entrance, where builders and their students are creating replicas of the jolly boat from the Columbia Rediva that explored the mouth of the Columbia in May 1792. New shows are mounted throughout the year—a recent exhibit of Oregonian cartoonist Art Bimrose shed new light on the state's—and the nation's—history. The bookshop offers Oregon Historical Society Press books and many others, on subjects from antiques

MUSEUMS

to logging, from Portland bridges to Oregon sightseeing. There is also a fine selection of fiction and nonfiction by such renowned Oregon authors as Barry Lopez, Ken Kesey, and Craig Lesley. Outside, the south and west walls are adorned with stunning trompe l'oeil murals, designed by Richard Haas and painted in 1989, which depict a bit of Oregon history. There is no admission charge to the museum.

Oregon Museum of Science and Industry
4015 SW Canyon Rd (Washington Park), 222-2828 (map:GG7) Every day

KIDS On rainy Portland afternoons, there's no place like OMSI for kids. Poke around in an old airplane, play a game on a computer, learn about weather forecasting and the Earth's crust. A favorite is the Space Wing, with its Gemini capsule and interactive exhibits such as Mission Control Center. The numerous hands-on exhibits are popular with parents, too. These explore the five senses, teach the functioning of the human heart, investigate the forces of the universe. Facts from physics, chemistry, and biology are taught at the "Up and Atom" stage. At the Kendall Planetarium there are regular shows on the stars, planets, and galaxies, and an occasional light show to display the wonders of laser imagery. Traveling exhibits on science and technology come regularly as well. Planning is now under way for OMSI's 1992 expansion, in a new southeast location near the Marquam Bridge. The present building gets quite crowded on weekends, so it pays to come early. Admission is $4.25 for adults and $2.75 for children 3–17 and seniors. Members are admitted free.

World Forestry Center
4033 SW Canyon Rd, (Washington Park), 228-1367 (map:GG7) Every day

KIDS The talking tree inside the World Forestry Center in Washington Park is strictly for children: the 20-foot-high fir tells them (literally) about its natural functions. The exhibits focus primarily on logging and the processing and manufacturing of wood products by Oregon's timber industry. The Tropical Rain Forest Exhibit deals more with forest products—wood, spices, coffee—than with forest ecology. New to the center is a monumental tiger sculpture carved from a 1,000-year-old tree for the 1988 Summer Olympics in Seoul. The Jesup Wood Collection, cross-sections of scores of tree species, is displayed both indoors and out. Fighting forest fires is another big theme. Periodic shows feature Oregon woodworkers, carvers, and wooden toys. Admission is $3 for adults, $2 for students 6–18 and seniors. Members and children under 6 are free.

The carousel in front of the center, a historic landmark, is not restricted to young riders (open only during the dry seasons). Nearby is the now dormant steam engine "Peggy," used from 1909 to 1950 to haul logs from the forests to the mills.

OPERA

Portland Opera
222 SW Clay St (Civic Auditorium), 241-1802 (map:D3)

It's the only operatic game in town. Instead of trying to carve out a niche of its own—like Seattle, Boston, Santa Fe, or St. Louis—Portland Opera settles for performances of time-tested productions with second-line singers. Nevertheless, opera addicts abound; the three shows of each of the season's four or five operas are always sold out.

THEATER

Portland theater is astonishingly active: there are more companies than in Seattle, and the population is only half as large. Perhaps because of the competition from **Oregon Shakespeare Festival Portland** (248-6309), an offshoot of the famous Ashland extravaganza, the city's other resident troupes work harder than ever. The result for the theatergoer is a profusion of good shows, from musicals and light comedies at Portland Civic to the offbeat and experimental at IFCC and Storefront to solid repertoire at New Rose, Portland Rep, Artists Rep, Oregon Shakespeare Festival Portland, and Columbia. The best actors in town are likely to appear on any of these stages, and most companies' seasons continue through the summer.

Columbia Theater Company
2021 SE Hawthorne Blvd, 232-7005 (map:GG5)

The Columbia's offerings range from the excellent to the terrible, so it's always best to read the reviews before buying a ticket. Recent successes include *The Lion in Winter* and *Monday After the Miracle*, two very different kinds of plays. *Knock Knock*, a wacky comedy, was also well received. Don't expect posh surroundings. However, you might very well see some of Portland's finest actors on this modest stage.

IFCC Theatre
5340 N Interstate Ave, 243-7930 (map:EE6)

The Interstate Firehouse Cultural Center doesn't do a lot of plays. Still, two of Portland's biggest recent hits have been IFCC productions: *The Colored Museum* and *Tea*. This group focuses on multiracial or all-black shows, and in this respect it fills a void in Portland. The small theater is comfortable, and the level of commitment and enthusiasm is without peer in this theater community. A little jewel in the crown.

Oregon Shakespeare Festival Portland
1111 SW Broadway,
248-4496 (map:G2)
Intermediate Theatre,
Portland Center for the
Performing Arts

When Ashland's prestigious spring, summer, and autumn festival opened a Portland branch in 1988, the quality of Portland theater rose immediately. The Portland (and, of course, Ashland) festival continues its long tradition of blending talented actors, exacting directors, and very high production values (fine sets, costumes, lights, and music) into outstanding performances. The result is a rewarding repertoire that ranges from classic to contemporary, tragedy to farce, naturalistic to weirdo-eclectic.

Portland Repertory Theater
25 SW Salmon St,
224-4491 (map:F5)

The city's oldest Equity company draws an audience that likes confident performances—with no surprises. The repertoire at Mark Allen's company includes English (and American) drawing-room comedies, contemporary "theme" plays (about politics, growing old), and classics like *Bus Stop*, but not much in the way of classical theater: no Shakespeare, Moliere, Shaw, Ibsen, or Chekhov. Still, the work is solid here, sometimes even inspired, though it's in a determinedly naturalistic tradition. The 230-seat theater is intimate, the most appealing spot in town to see a play, and the word is out. Don't wait too long—the entire season is 92 percent subscribed.

Storefront Theatre
1111 SW Broadway
(Dolores Winningstad
Theatre, Portland Center
for the Performing Arts),
224-4001 (map:G2)

For years, Storefront was Portland's most adventurous theater company, staging avant-garde political plays, original satirical musical revues, and other crazy things that no other theater would touch with a 10-foot stage hook. Storefront has mellowed a little with age, and in doing so it's become more reliable. Even so, it's still committed to the unusual. Last season's production of Yeats' *Cuchulian Cycle* attracted national attention. Every season features a premiere or two: recent winners include *Woza Albert!*, a powerful fable about South African politics; and *Illuminati*, a wacko religious sendup. There are seldom any misses nowadays. Shows also at 6 SW Third Avenue.

Artists Repertory Theatre
1111 SW 10th Ave (Wilson
Center, YWCA),
242-2400 (map:G1)

Here's proof that it's the actors and directors who make ART work. There's neither space nor budget to do much Shakespeare here (the company is run by the actors), though there's no fear of the classics. Modern plays, on the other hand, are its meat and potatoes. The quality at ART is consistently good; disappointments are rare. This may be the best place to see what Portland's flourishing small-theater world is all about.

THE ARTS

New Rose Theatre
904 SW Main St,
222-2487 (map:G1)

Not nearly as consistent as Artists Rep, New Rose nevertheless pulls off some dandy productions, such as 1988's *A Christmas Carol* and 1989's *Travesties.* You might check the reviews, however, before buying tickets. The leading actors are as strong here as anywhere else in town (in fact, they're often the same people), but the company isn't deep—supporting roles can be amateur turns.

Portland Civic Theatre
1530 SW Yamhill St,
226-3048 (map:GG6)

Portland's oldest theater company is not only a theater, it's also a theater school for kids and adults. In 1988, due to increasing competition (it wasn't that long ago that this was the only theater in town), PCT went to an almost–all-musical format. On the main stage, and in the 125-seat Blue Room, it put on such confections as *Oklahoma, The Fantasticks,* and *Hair* (with ratings from excellent to terrible, in that order). An annual Christmas *Peter Pan* pays a lot of the bills. When Bill Dobson directs and Jon Newton conducts the orchestra, PCT's shows often soar.

SHOPPING CONTENTS

SHOPPING

SHOPPING AREAS

DOWNTOWN

See Major Attractions in Exploring chapter.

NEIGHBORHOODS

Along NW 23rd Avenue north to about NW Pettygrove Street in **northwest Portland** (map:FF7) is the window-shopping center for chic apparel, arty gifts, and housewares, along with a selfish share of the city's good restaurants. (See Northwest Portland in Major Attractions in the Exploring chapter.) Down toward the river is the restored **Skidmore/Old Town** (between Front and Fourth from SW Oak to NW Glisan streets; map:H5-L5), which has a few good shops but especially more galleries and Greek restaurants than elsewhere. On weekends, Skidmore livens with the Saturday Market (see Major Attractions in the Exploring chapter). Southwest of town is the quiet **Multnomah Village** (just off SW Multnomah Boulevard on SW Capitol Hill Highway; map:II7), with a quaint, small-town personality revolving around a home-cooking cafe, an excellent bookstore, and over half-a-dozen antique shops. Alongside the Willamette is **The Water Tower** at Johns Landing (between Ross Island and Sellwood bridges on SW Macadam Avenue; open every day and weekday evenings; map:II5), with three stories of discerning shops, including imported and specialty-size clothing shops and jewelers—once the only place to shop in town. Cross the Sellwood Bridge into the city's southeast corner, **Sellwood** (SE Tacoma Street and SE 13th Avenue; map:II5), inundated with country antiques (see Daytrips in the Outings chapter). **Hawthorne** (SE Hawthorne Boulevard between SE 35th and SE 45th avenues; map:GG5) has that thrown-together look—great for browsing. Scavengers spend hours pawing through secondhand-record shops and vintage clothiers, recently joined by an Italian specialty shop, an excellent cookbook store, and natural-fiber boutiques (see Major Attractions in Exploring chapter). Spurred on by the success of Holladay's Market and more recently the Lloyd Center overhaul (not to mention the new convention center), **NE Broadway** (NE Broadway St from NE Seventh Avenue and east; map:FF5) is experiencing a renaissance of its own, with lots of new home accessory shops, a good wine shop, a women's bookstore, a perfume shop, and even a brew pub.

SUBURBAN MALLS

The country's first major mall, the **Lloyd Center** (east across the Broadway Bridge bordered by NE Broadway to NE Multnomah and NE Ninth to 16th avenues; open weekdays until 9pm, Saturdays until 6pm, and Sundays until 5pm, map:FF5), is now trying to reestablish itself as Oregon's largest mall—by summer 1991. A $100 million renovation includes a glass roof over the entire mall (including the ice rink), adding three levels with 60 new shops (for a total of 175), spiffing up the existing anchor stores (Meier and Frank, Nordstrom, Lamonts), and adding a fourth anchor store, which at press time was unchosen. Its proximity to downtown (connected by MAX light rail), as well as the new Oregon Convention Center (NE Martin Luther King Jr. Boulevard and Holladay Street) and the nearby addition of the Lloyd Cinema complex, Carousel Courtyard, and International Museum of Carousel Art (at the NE Seventh Avenue MAX station), should all help give this formerly faltering mall a new life.

The west side is sprawling with malls, led by **Beaverton Town Square** (off SW Canyon Road and SW Beaverton-Hillsdale Highway off Highway 217; open weekdays until 9pm, Saturdays until 6pm, Sundays until 5pm; map:HH9), marked by its clocktower and the recently remodelled **Beaverton Mall** (take SW Walker Road exit off Highway 217; open weekdays until 9pm, Saturdays until 6pm, Sundays until 5pm; map:HH9). Between Beaverton and Tigard is **Washington Square** and **Square Too** (just off Highway 217; open Monday–Saturday until 9pm and Sundays until 6pm; map:II9). East across the river lie **Mall 205** (take the SE Stark Street exit off I-205; open weekdays until 9pm and weekends until 6pm; map:GG3) and the booming **Clackamas Town Center** (take the Sunnyside Road exit from I-205; open weekdays until 9pm and weekends until 6pm; map:KK3) right smack in the middle of high-tech–ville. Up north is **Jantzen Beach Mall** (just off I-5 at Jantzen Beach; open weekdays until 9pm and weekends until 6pm; map:BB6), which stands out from the crowd with a 72-horse merry-go-round in the center of the mall (50 cents per ride).

ACCESSORIES AND LUGGAGE

de la Salandra
220 SW Ankeny St,
226-6168 (map:J6)
Tues-Sun

"Wearable art" (most made on the premises), which here can just as easily mean exotic fantasy pieces as well-tailored suiting and New York–chic shoes. One-of-a-kind garments in one-of-a-kind sizes.

de nada
555 SW Taylor St,
223-0361 (map:F5)
Tues-Sat

Owner Christi Cawood personally travels to mountain villages in Mexico to buy what is now trendily known as "naive art"; most pieces come from the Nahua Indians— except for the wrought-iron furniture and lighting.

John Helmer Haberdasher Inc.
969 SW Broadway,
223-4976 (map:G2)
Mon-Sat

Tried-and-true men's clothing since the 1920s; however, the real substance here is hats, and lots of 'em. A good place for classic umbrellas and gentlemen's attire (ascots, suspenders, gloves). Custom orders taken, and three generations of experienced help. Hints, for those who ask, on knotting a bow tie.

Pen & Paper
510 SW Third Ave,
223-3345 (map:I4)
Mon-Fri

Most people in Portland deliberately avoid ostentatious displays of wealth—except for the $500 fountain pen. Whether it's the discreet luxury of a pen or the obsession Portlanders have with literacy, this two-year-old shop is thriving (with clocks, crystal inkwells, and desk sets, too) on its downtown street corner.

Portland Luggage
1003 SW Washington St,
226-3255 (map:I2)
Mon-Sat

10120 SW Washington
Square Blvd, 639-2131
(map:JJ9)
Every day

A few years short of its 50th anniversary, competitively priced Portland Luggage can best be described as a purist's delight, with fine leather luggage and business cases. None of the exotic gifts that most luggage stores seem to carry.

Sunbow Gallery
206 SW Stark St,
221-0258 (map:H5)
Every day

See Imports in this chapter.

Dazzle
704 NW 23rd Ave,
224-1294 (map:FF7)
Every day

V Claire
121 NW 23rd Ave,
222-2033 (map:FF6)
Every day

A table set with dishes from V Claire always reflects good taste. And it's these tabletop items that will be passed on to future generations. A reassuring sense of heartwarming holidays to come and special moments about to happen pervades this store.

ANTIQUES

Give antique-lovers a free afternoon and a handful of good shops to poke through, and it doesn't really matter if they bag their intended prey—it's the thrill of the hunt that counts. As the increasing number of antique malls, colonies, and villages indicates (at press time two more—one on NE Broadway and one out in Gresham—had just entered the scene), dealers who cluster together provide especially appealing hunting grounds.

In Portland, the biggest such browsers' mecca is **Old Sellwood Antique Row**, where about two dozen antique stores—plus a generous leavening of country and gift shops—line a 12-block stretch of SE 13th Avenue. See Major Attractions in Exploring chapter.

Another popular territory, southwest Portland's **Multnomah Village**, has the look of a small-town Main Street—which is just what it was until Portland swallowed it up many years ago. Today there are 10 vintage stores within a sedate two-and-a-half-block stretch of Capitol Highway (map:II7).

A warehouse district (north of Burnside between NW 18th and Broadway) is presently being gentrified into lofts and art galleries. Dubbed with the image-enhancing moniker the **Pearl District**, the area is also home to four large antique furniture shops. Northwest 23rd Avenue and downtown Portland contain other notable concentrations of collectibles.

In addition, Portland is home to a handful of flea markets, frequent estate sales, and several annual antique shows. **Gramstad's Antique and Collectible Market** (2701 NW Vaughn Street, 777-6200, map:FF6), held once a month with 300 or so tables, is jammed with all sorts of finds. The granddaddy of them all, however, is Don Wirfs' accurately named America's Largest Antique and Collectible Sales (Expo Center, 282-0877, map:CC6). For one weekend each in March, in July, and in October, 1,200 US dealers fill six indoor acres at the Expo Center (wear walking shoes). In December, at Portland's Convention Center, a fourth Wirfs show joins the lineup. Dickering is the order of the day.

Darwin's Little Brother's Place
7919 SE 13th Ave,
231-1101 (map:II5)
Wed-Sun

The owner's brother, Darwin Otto, runs the nearby Etc. Antiques. However, Greg Otto and his partner, Doris Messier, specialize in what could be called Ralph Lauren rustic: old wicker, Adirondack chairs, and log furniture upholstered with Indian-motif Pendleton blankets. Vintage wicker repair; designer-style prices, too.

1874 House
8070 SE 13th Ave,
233-1874 (map:II5)
Tues-Sat

See Hardware section in this chapter.

End of the Trail
5937 N Greeley St,
283-0419 (map:EE6)
Every day

It's almost a mini-mall in itself: behind the unprepossessing storefront is a warren of 14 rooms. There's no furniture for sale—and much stock has several decades to go before it qualifies as antique—but if it's collectable (marbles, swords, postcards, straight-edge razors) it'll be at the End of the Trail.

The General Store
7987 SE 13th Ave,
233-1321 (map:II5)
Mon-Sat

Tough to miss, as it's attached to a vintage red caboose. Margie Waite's been in the antique business now for 17 years, and her selection (her refinishing techniques, too) shows it: Victorian and turn-of-the-century walnut, mahogany, and oak furniture.

Hippo Hardware and Trading Company
201 SE 12th Ave,
231-1444 (map:GG5)
Mon-Sat

See Hardware section in this chapter.

Jack Heath Antiques
1606, 1612, and 1700
NW 23rd Ave, 222-4663
(map:FF6)
Wed-Sun

The purposely English-sounding name is a bit misleading. Jack and Heather Reinhart aren't from England, and though much of their merchandise *is* Victorian (usually dark woods such as mahogany or walnut), most hails from Portland consignments. Heather's got a fine eye for redecorating, and skilled hands for reupholstering.

▼ ANTIQUES

Jerry Lamb Interiors and Antiques
1323 NW 23rd Ave,
227-6077 (map:FF6)
Tues-Sat

Interior designer Jerry Lamb's showroom displays Oriental antiques, especially porcelains. Embroidery and woodblock prints come from China or Japan, and hundreds of porcelain pieces—Imari, blue and white Canton, celadon, and Rose Medallion—are stocked.

The New Antique Village Mall Inc
1969 NE 42nd Ave,
288-1051 (map:FF4)
Every day

Antique malls seem, oddly, to be the wave of the future. Northeast Portland's Hollywood neighborhood holds the city's largest. More than 60 dealers have banded together to fill 9,000 square feet with collectibles. The friendly staff (they always have coffee brewing) will help you find anything from Depression glass and plastic radios to Victorian furniture.

Partners in Time
1313 W Burnside,
228-6299 (map:J1)
Every day

Both antique and new European pine pieces are stocked in this Pearl District spot. Oriental rugs of all ages.

Pine Design Antique Imports
1308 NW Everett St,
227-3368 (map:K1)
Tues-Sat

The stock of one of the West Coast's largest importers of antique country pine furniture comes primarily from Denmark (circa 1850s–1880s). Pine armoires and tables to pre-1940 Royal Copenhagen porcelain.

Portland Antique Company
1314 and 1211 NW Glisan St, 223-0999 (map:L1)
Every day

35,000 square feet of floor space makes this one of the Northwest's biggest antique retailers. A 40-foot container of furniture (from England and Europe) is unloaded here weekly. Sturdy English oak tables, armoires, and dressers predominate at 1314 Glisan Street, and prices are reasonable. Down the street, prices are augmented to match the more ornate European styles.

Rejuvenation House Parts Company
901 N Skidmore St,
249-2038 (map:EE5)
Mon-Sat

See Hardware in this chapter.

Richard Rife French Antique Imports
300 NW 13th Ave,
294-0276 (map:K1)
Tues-Sat

In 1966, Richard Rife established his business in Portland, and for the last six years he has specialized in fine French furniture, garnering a reputation for quality and knowledgeability. Nearly every French era is represented, with emphasis on Louis XV and XVI. Prices reflect the high caliber of the merchandise.

The facts in this edition were correct at presstime, but places close, chefs depart, hours change. It's best to call ahead.

Sellwood Peddler Attic Goodies
8065 SE 13th Ave,
235-0946 (map:II5)
Every day

A little bit of everything is crammed into this space, with emphasis on what some dealers call "girl stuff": glassware, china, sterling flatware, jewelry, and quilts. There's also a fair amount of furniture. And a tool room...for the boys.

Welch's
700 and 1004 N Killingsworth St, 228-3637
(map:EE5)
Sat only

In what could be defined as a permanent estate sale, these two stores turn over a surprising amount of merchandise in a frenzy each Saturday, unintentionally creating addicts. Many dealers shop for their stock here—antique furniture, rugs, collectible kitchenware, tools—because of the ever-changing inventory and reasonable prices. A word to the wise: if you like it, buy it.

APPAREL

Citterio
711 SW 10th Ave,
227-5005 (map:H2)
Every day

True Soho in Portland: dark racks of pleated pants, oversized jackets, and unisex rayon coats. Citterio leads Portlanders into a sophisticated, inner-city style. Some think they are ready for it, others don't.

Easy Street
16337 SW Bryant Rd,
Lake Oswego, 636-6547
(map:MM7)
Mon-Sat

A large enough selection of glitz-and-glamour evening dresses to last through this holiday and the next. Working into its 13th year, Easy Street knows how to dress you up for special occasions.

El Mundo for Men
904 NW 23rd Ave,
274-9477 (map:FF6)
Every day

Casual wear that won't break the bank. We only had the opportunity to shop at the Cannon Beach and Seaside stores until 1988, when El Mundo for Men decided to make it easier on natural-fiber fans and open a store in northwest Portland. Some dressier items and upbeat accessories (sharp hats, bolo ties) have been added for the metropolitan market.

El Mundo for Women
3556 SE Hawthorne Blvd, 239-4605
(map:GG4)
Every day

A familiar doorway on Hawthorne Boulevard, El Mundo for Women sells comfort in the form of Mishi pants and tops, colorful cotton and rayon dresses, and an eclectic assortment of blouses and sweaters. Offbeat jewelry to match. Recently, El Mundo opened a Seaside branch; the flagship store is in Cannon Beach.

Elizabeth Street
715 NW 23rd Ave,
243-2456 (map:FF6)
Every day

Just down the avenue from its old location, Elizabeth Street's roomy new shop is even more varied and cutting-edge than before; it's a MUST for the image-conscious, who check in regularly to track down the latest trend. Today it's cool cotton lingerie and feminine undershirts, or cranberry-colored rayon trousers tucked into beaded cowboy boots from Morocco. Tomorrow?

The Eye of Ra
*5331 SW Macadam Ave
(Johns Landing),
224-4292 (map:HH6)
Every day*

There seems to be an onslaught of import stores boasting ethnic clothing and jewelry. However, the Eye is not riding the tribal bandwagon. It's been in the business for 15 years now, and the selection of imported clothing, urban folkware, and jewelry shows depth. Reasonable prices and frequent sales.

Gattozzi's
*110 SW Yamhill
(Yamhill Marketplace),
228-7810 (map:G4)
Every day*

Some places it's the clothes that sell you, others it's the attentive staff. Here it's both. Carol Riegler buys comfort clothes for her devotees and genuinely cares about how they look on them. Her selection's small but nicely balanced. Wrap up in her signature cotton terrycloth bathrobes.

Helen's of Course
*9875 SW Beaverton-
Hillsdale Hwy,
Beaverton, 643-8402
(map:HH9)
Mon-Sat*

There was a time when any big party displayed a good representation of clothes from Helen's. Owner Helen Gell is still there on a daily basis, wearing her slippers and entertaining all who come through the door. However, Helen's no longer holds the exclusive on the city's show-stealing dresses. Sales help is pushy, and prices (like the shop) are definitely in Portland's outer limits.

Jeffrey Michael
*915 SW Broadway (and
branches), 224-0374
(map:G2)
Every day*

Somewhere between Nordstrom and Mario's sits Jeffrey Michael, with flattering sweaters and sport coats. Suits? Most European labels, including Hugo Boss and Giorgio Armani. An in-store tailor caters to the local businessman. Branches at Lloyd Center and Washington Square.

Jessica Jane
*8235 SE 13th Ave,
231-2767 (map:I5)
Every day*

Jessica Jane is sort of the Laura Ashley of the '90s. Owner Jessica McKinley's garments are charmingly basic: dyed cotton outfits, private-label box dresses (she's raising the waistline this year), and cotton tights. There's just enough space left in her intimate Sellwood shop for a few pairs of shoes, preferably flats. A second store, Maternity Jane's (724 NW 23rd Ave, 228-5778), has a, well, expanded version of the Jessica Jane look.

If you've found a place around town that you think is a Best Place, send in the report form at the back of the book. If you're unhappy with one of the places, please let us know why. We depend on reader input.

John Helmer Haberdasher
969 SW Broadway,
223-4976 (map:G2)
Mon-Sat

See Accessories and Luggage in this chapter.

Klopfenstein's
1010 SW 6th Ave (and
branches), 226-4701
(map:G2)
Mon-Sat

Pure tradition. Attorneys, accountants, and business-men will find what they want in quality, prices, and tradi-tion (pinstripe suits, buttondown shirts, and myriad ties) —but no surprises.

La Paloma
6316 SW Capitol Hwy
(Hillsdale Shopping
Center), 246-3417
(map:II6)
Mon-Sat

In the Hillsdale Shopping Center lies one of the best finds for natural-fiber clothing, imaginative accessories, silver jewelry from Southeast Asia, Mishi 100 percent cotton separates (with socks dyed to match), sweaters, and Indonesian batik and ikat clothing. The long-established confidence in free-flowing fashions rubs off on you. Call for easy directions.

Laura Ashley
419 SW Morrison St,
224-0703 (map:H3)
Mon-Sat

Laura Ashley invented the look that defines the type: demure and country elegant. At the four-year-old Port-land outpost you shop for the signature floral print ap-parel (and furniture). Recently, it's broken through the garden theme by introducing a more diverse lineup of executive wear and party collections.

The Mercantile
735 SW Park Ave,
223-6649 (map:H2)
Mon-Sat

2362 SW Burnside,
227-7882 (map:FF7)
Mon-Sat

Victoria Taylor and Dottie Johnson have consolidated three shops—the preppy Merc, the savvy Victoria's, and the tailored Mercantile—under one name. They're trying to display the same soft sportswear look through-out. Even so, the Park Avenue store remains the dres-siest (some Dior and Victor Costa). The Burnside loca-tion is more personal, though the selection is smaller.

Middy's
0315 SW Montgomery St
(The RiverPlace),
223-3224
Every day

Middy's boutique has become known for its assortment of costume jewelry and watches. There are touches of country in the clothing and accessories at this very femi-nine shop. Enviable sweaters by Susan Bristol, Sala-minder, and Eagle's Eye.

M. Willock
860 SW Broadway,
226-3405 (map:G2)
Mon-Sat

Located just across from the downtown Hilton, M. Wil-lock has invested in lighthearted yet practical vest-ments: Ciaosport, Haulber, and Geiger. It's been around for 12 years; so will your purchases.

Mario's
921 SW Morrison St

Now a Portland tradition, Mario's stands at the cutting edge of men's fashion. European-style suits, elaborate

(Galleria), 227-3477
(map:H2)
Every day

sweaters, low-vamp shoes, and fine cotton shirts are all found (expensively priced) at Mario's. If you stumble upon the biannual sale, you've run into a good thing.

Mario's for Women
811 SW Morrison St,
241-8111 (map: H2)
Every day

Mario's sister ship has as much an eye on European designer fashions as the men's store. If tomorrow's look isn't here yet, it's on its way: DKNY, Ventillo, and Tahari, to name a few. What's a month's rent? Or so the staff seems to think.

Norm Thompson
1805 NW Thurman St,
221-0764 (map:FF6)

Portland International
Airport, 249-0170
(map:CC3)
Every day

The refined country look gained mail-order fame through Portland's own Norm Thompson, now privileged with two retail locations. Those mail-order customers don't know what they're missing. Armloads of Scottish wools and English cashmeres, plus enviable suede coats and Rockport and Bally shoes for men and women. Prices at both stores are the same, although there is complimentary wine and cheese at the larger Thurman Street store. Excellent, understanding service with free shipping during the holidays and gift wrapping year-round.

Phillip Stewart
1202 SW 19th St,
226-3589 (map:GG6)
Mon-Sat

We're not sure why, in the heart of Goose Hollow, Phillip Stewart has become a bonafide Portland tradition. It's an upscale and expensive men's store. Perhaps it's the more than 200 choices of fabric for custom shirts that regulars (who get obvious preference here) have come to expect.

The Portland Pendleton Shop
SW 4th Ave between
Salmon and Taylor St,
242-0037 (map:F2)
Mon-Sat

Believe it or not, Pendleton has dusted off its look and charged into the '80s (just in time for the '90s). The shop in the Standard Insurance Building offers the most complete collection of Pendleton clothing anywhere in Oregon, including new petite sizes, skirt-and-shirt matchables, and summer silk and rayon combinations. Of course, it wouldn't be Pendleton without the wool chemises and blankets, endearingly familiar to virtually every Northwesterner.

Shea & Company
21 S State St,
Lake Oswego, 635-7603
(map:KK6)
Mon-Sat

Long split riding skirts (people don't really ride in these, though, do they?), countless Mara Shirtline blouses, and gabardine suits from the Toussaint and Mr. Jaxx lines are nicely displayed with a town & country look. Marlene Shea's spendy store in the Village Shopping Center transforms country into elegance with a European flair.

Looking for a particular place? Check the index at the back of this book for individual restaurants, nightclubs, lodgings, shops, attractions, and more.

Sidney's
921 SW Morrison St
(Galleria), 222-6120
(map:H2)
Every day

You'd never expect to find something this good up on the slow-paced third floor of the Galleria, but Sidney's has merit. It offers hand-painted or artist-embellished renditions of oversized jackets and one-of-a-kind separates, and is one of the two places in town to get the Australian outback oilcloth raincoat.

West End Ltd
22 NW 23rd Ave,
224-2600 (map:FF6)
Mon-Sat

West Hillers consider this *their* shop. Conversely, West End Ltd considers West Hillers *its* customers. So, there you have it. God forbid if anyone from, say, the northeast dares to consider any of these imaginative sweaters, day-to-night dresses, or 100 percent silk lingerie.

BAKERIES

B. Moloch/The Heathman Bakery and Pub
901 SW Salmon St,
227-5700 (map:G1)
Every day

They have a way with yeast: first in their beer, next in their bread. If you can't decide between the two, try their bier brot. This is more of a restaurant than a bakery, but that doesn't keep anyone from stopping in to pick up a loaf of very sour sourdough, Swedish rye, or pesto bread. For breakfast there might be oat and cheese bannock or sweet corn buns.

Beaverton Bakery
12375 SW Broadway,
Beaverton, 646-7136
(map:HH9)

8775 Cascade Ave (Cascade Plaza), Beaverton,
646-7816 (map:JJ9)
Every day

Beautiful (and tasty) wedding cakes are what BB is best known for. Too bad: the crusty monastery whole-wheat loaf, onion-cheese Fagasa bread, and apple-cinnamon loaves are addictive staples. There's no shortage of butter, and the prices reflect it. Lines are often long at the larger Broadway store.

Bowers Bakery and Deli
3545 SE Hawthorne Blvd, 231-0017
(map:GG5)
Tues-Sat

A friendly place with just two tables. So most take Sarah and Dave's oat bran and muffins, creamhorns, and, OK, maybe one deluxe raspberry and peanut butter brownie to go. The huge loaves of bread are sold by the pound.

Broadway Bakery
1924 SW Broadway,
243-1924 (map:D1)
Mon-Sat

Next door to PSU, this bakery with its own bistro upstairs has serious intentions. In this first year of business, the cases aren't brimming yet, but what it does have is good: eat-alone breads (sourdough rye, focaccia, French) and superior muffins (don't miss the apple). Sweets are for the late afternoon: the ubiquitous chocolate truffle torte or a rich tiramisu.

Delphina's Bakery
807 NW 21st Ave,
221-1044 (map:FF6)
Every day

Delphina's notorious crusty-chewy sourdough, garlic, and focaccia breads are widely available in Portland area groceries. You can buy the same breads—and more—at the retail bakery, down the street from Delphina's Restaurant (these days the bakery operates independently). Specialty breads include chocolate, Swedish cardamom braid, hazelnut rye, and others. Try a Gorgonzola focaccia round for lunch (seating is available) or meet a friend here for coffee and biscotti (orange, hazelnut, or anise). Day-old baked goods are sold weekdays at Delphina's Thrift Store, 3310 NW Yeon Street, 221-1829.

Gabriel's Bakery
2272 NW Kearney St,
227-4712 (map:FF6)
Mon-Sat

No shortage of temptations for the residents of northwest Portland, and the staff at Good Samaritan Hospital ensures that. Physicians appreciate the fact that 15 breads lack eggs and fats, but in truth the almond blackberry and almond raspberry muffins sell out first.

The German Bakery
10528 NE Sandy Blvd,
252-1881 (map:FF2)
Tues-Sat

This is the only place in town to find traditional German breads (light, medium, and dark rye, and a sourdough boule), butter cookies, and pastries. Sit at one of the several tables and sample some desserts: creamhorns, Black Forest and Bienenstich cakes, and German tea cookies.

Goldberg's Bakery, Deli, and Catering
4516 SW Vermont St,
246-4201 (map:GG6)
Tues-Sat

Goldberg's might not make it in New York, but the light and dark rye bread, half-a-dozen bagel varieties, bialys, challah, French bread, and the ubiquitous iced cinnamon roll satisfy kosher cravings. A decent deli, too.

Great Harvest Bread Company
837 SW 2nd Ave,
224-8583 (map:F4)

11633 SW Beaverton-Hillsdale Hwy (Beaverton Town Square),
Beaverton, 641-3373
(map:HH9)
Mon-Sat

Breads of substance, character, and a healthy amount of fiber are harvested daily at this Montana-based franchise. There are always free samples of almost the whole crop. In the morning, long lines form for no-cholesterol bran muffins or, maybe just this once, a large, sweet, gooey cinnamon roll.

Helen Bernhard Bakery
1717 NE Broadway,
287-1251 (map:FF5)
Mon-Sat

Thick-crusted sourdough is Bernhard's signature loaf, and with good reason: the sourdough starter is 66 years old. The Bernhard bakery (owned by the Bernhard family until a year ago), like the starter, dates back to 1924. It's pure American tradition—dinner rolls, donuts, cookies, pies, and wedding cakes.

JaCiva's Chocolates and Pastries
4733 SE Hawthorne Blvd, 234-8115 (map:GG4) Mon-Sat

Behind the retail area, Jack Elmer, Swiss-trained chocolatier and pastry chef, and his wife, Iva Sue, craft fine Swiss chocolates sold across the country. For the shop they bake exquisitely decorated cakes (a chocolate mousse dome) and billowing eclairs. Brides, bring your fork: a new wing is being added strictly for sampling wedding cakes.

Le Four a Bois
12320 SW Broadway (and branches), Beaverton, 626-0299 (map:HH9) Mon-Sat

It's one of the few places in town that really knows how to make croissants—flaky and buttery. As you would expect a la campagne, cases are prettied with delicate almond and fresh fruit tartlets straight from the Beaverton ovens (8618 SW Hall Boulevard, Beaverton, 641-4954, map:JJ9). The wood-burning oven at their original Broadway store produces hard-crusted baguettes and four-grain breads. At the Northwest branch, however, you'll find no ovens, just goods (921 NW 23rd Avenue, 274-9039, map:FF6).

Papa Haydn
5829 SE Milwaukie Ave, 232-9440 (map:HH5) Mon-Sat

701 NW 23rd Ave, 228-7317 (map:FF7) Every day

See Restaurants chapter.

Le Panier Very French Bakery
71 SW 2nd Ave (and branches), 241-3524 (map:J6) Every day

Le Panier could hold its own on the banks of the Seine. Plenty of newspapers, great coffee, and almond croissants entice lingerers long into the morning. When evening comes, customers return for a slice of decadent chocolate opera cake. Other branches at Yamhill Marketplace (Taylor Street and Second Avenue, 241-5613, map:G5) and—take-out only—Clackamas Town Center (659-5587, map:JJ3).

Portland Bagel Bakery & Delicatessen
222 SW 4th Ave, 242-2435 (map:I5) Sun-Fri

Crusty, dense, and chewy: Portland's best attempt at New York–style bagels, from onion to pumpernickel. But you'll probably only find an oat bran bagel on the West Coast. The bakery can get smoky at times, but it's fun to watch the bagel machine at work behind big windows.

Ron Paul Catering & Charcuterie
2310 NW Everett St (Everett Street Market),

To some, Ron Paul is a shrine of decadence; to others, who refuse to pay the high prices, it's a nemesis. The extraordinary dome-puff eclairs have been known to convert even the most frugal. Three to five daily breads

223-2121 (map:FF6)
Every day

may include buttermilk Cheddar, or Indian naan (a cara-melized onion, yogurt, and cardamom version).

Sunnyside Up Bakery
3568 SE Hawthorne
Blvd, 233-9405
(map:GG4)
Tues-Sun

It's always Sunnyside Up at this friendly over-the-counter spot. The oatmeal bread—textured with sun-flower seeds and cracked wheat—is definitely the best offering. You can see and smell the breads as they're made, but if you want to sit and gnaw you'll have to buy them at the cafe next door.

Three Lions' Bakery & Cafe
1138 SW Morrison St,
224-9039 (map:I2)
Mon-Sat

Bakers here are hip to the growing health consciousness and therefore offer a couple of light desserts. It's best, however, to walk in boldly and go for the nuts, butter, and cream. Croissants of all sorts are standouts, as are the scones, focaccia bread, and beautiful cakes often seen at other restaurants around town. No smoking at any of the dozen tables, but there's outside seating dur-ing the summer.

BOOKS AND MAGAZINES

A Woman's Place Bookstore
1431 NE Broadway,
284-1110 (map:FF5)
Every day

A Woman's Place is as much an emotional shelter as an outlet for feminist literature (and surprisingly nice to men). Lending library for women who can't afford to buy books...or coffee (it's free here).

Annie Bloom's Books
7834 SW Capitol Hwy,
246-0053 (map:II7)
Every day

Some bookstores serve Portland neighborhoods the way pubs serve English villages. Just try the armchairs in Annie Bloom's—inviting as Grandma's lap, with toys for the kids.

Beaverton Book Company
11773 SW Beaverton-Hillsdale Hwy,
Beaverton, 644-7666
(map:HH9)
Every day

A independently-owned bookstore in a mall is a rare find these days. John and LeeAnn Earlenbaugh's eight-year-old all-purpose bookstore services Beaverton well—with mall hours.

Book Barn for Children
4570 SW Watson St,
Beaverton, 641-2276
(map:HH9)
Mon-Sat

Most cities have one children's bookstore if they're lucky; Portland has five. This good-sized downtown Beaverton store carries books for elementary through high school readers. As part of the summer reading club, kids get 25 cents in credit for each book read, up to 20. One room is devoted to instructional resources.

Look for the **FREE**—it means this attraction or event is free of charge.

Book Port Books at RiverPlace
0315 SW Montgomery St,
Suite 340, 228-2665
(map:C5)
Every day

When it first opened four years ago, the Book Port's customers were waterfront tourists. As time passed, locals discovered the breadth of titles and good customer service. Will search for out-of-print books.

Cameron's Books and Magazines
336 SW 3rd Ave,
228-2391 (map:H4)
Mon-Sat

Portland's oldest used-book store, but old magazines account for most of the trade. Vintage glossies are kept well organized in the back room to keep them in good condition. A hodgepodge collection at very good prices.

Catalyst
437 NW 23rd Ave,
221-4224 (map:FF6)
Every day

Owned by a pair of the most energetic sisters you'll ever meet, this two-year-old general bookstore is growing rapidly. Their new well-lighted space emphasizes learning, travel, and children. In fact, at press time, plans were in the works for adding parenting classes and travel packages.

Catbird Seat Bookstore
913 SW Broadway,
222-5817 (map:G2)
Every day

This small general bookstore bustles with helpful employees, and the stock reflects the tastes of its opinionated buyers. Lately, Catbird Seat has developed a strong concentration of self-help and recovery titles (the store even publishes its own catalogs, "Helping Books" and "Helping Books for Children").

Conant&Conant Booksellers
5201 NE Sandy Blvd,
287-8462 (map:FF4)
Mon-Sat

Selling University Press books exclusively, owners Roy and Rebecca Conant aim to prove, contrary to myth, that such presses offer accessible, even exciting volumes. The bimonthly newsletter, *Bibliofile*, is among the best in town.

Future Dreams
1800 E Burnside,
231-8311 (map:FF5)

10508 NE Halsey St,
255-5245 (map:EE2)
Every day

The stuff of future dreams is one part sci-fi and one part comic art. New and used magazines, books, and comics range from favorites to esoteric, hard-to-find titles. There is also a reservation service for new volumes.

Ginger and Pickles Bookstore for Children
425 SW 2nd Ave, Lake
Oswego, 636-5438
(map:KK6)
Mon-Sat

Here, in one of Portland's well-off suburbs, Ginger and Pickles targets kids from precocious newborns to confused teens. The staff knows kids and their reading habits—pop-ups to history. A play area for those who think they've read it all.

Inspectors for the Best Places *series accept no free meals or accommodations; the book has no sponsors or advertisers.*

Great Northwest Bookstore
1018 SW Salmon St,
223-8098 (map:G1)
Every day

Any subject west of the Mississippi is fair game for these used-book shelves: Western Americana, out-of-print books, and antiquarian titles. A good selection of general books, too.

Hawthorne Boulevard Books
3129 SE Hawthorne
Blvd, 236-3211
(map:GG5)
Tues-Sun

Roger and Ilse Roberts invite the public into their Hawthorne home to browse their used and antiquarian books. They're particularly fond of classic literature and American history. A fireplace (when lit) makes it tough to leave.

House of Titles Ltd
5331 SW Macadam Ave
(Johns Landing),
228-0290 (map:II6)
Every day

Regular customers know this primarily–gift-book shop is not limited to coffee-table editions of Monet and Georgia O'Keeffe, but extends to in-depth photographic treatments of, say, endangered wildlife. A respectable sampling of general books.

Ladd's Editions Book Store
1864 SE Hawthorne
Blvd, 236-4628
(map:GG5)
Every day

Next to the Ladd's Addition neighborhood, Ladd's Editions is one of the few eastside bookstores to carry *new* books. Maureen Moreland and Dori Rosenblum's store carries a little bit of everything, revealing an educational, multicultural bent.

Laughing Horse Books
1322 NW 23rd Ave,
227-5440 (map:FF6)
Every day

Progressive politically and environmentally oriented publications and programs are the focus of this bookstore-coffeehouse collective. Twice-monthly meetings focus on social change—health care in Guatemala, war tax resistance, and rain-forest protection struggles. Bumper stickers to, er, change the world.

Looking Glass Bookstore
318 SW Taylor St,
227-4760 (map:G3)
Mon-Sat

The name originated in Looking Glass, Oregon. First a wholesaler of underground comic books, then a politically oriented bookseller. Now these owners try hard to emphasize books that others don't (Eastern philosophy, sci-fi, metaphysics).

Murder by the Book
3729 SE Hawthorne
Blvd, 232-9995
(map:GG4)

7828 SW Capitol Hwy,
293-6507 (map:II7)
Every day

The genius loci of Murder by the Book manifests itself as a trinity: Mystery, Thriller, and Spy Fiction. Look for Kate Fanslar in Cherchez la Femme and over 50 Northwest mystery writers in On the Homefront (many signings, too). New and used volumes to buy, sell, barter, and kill for (so to speak). At press time the Hawthorne shop was just about to acquire a new address on the same street.

Look for **FREE**—*it means this attraction or event is free of charge.*

SHOPPING

New Renaissance Bookshop
1338 NW 23rd Ave,
224-4929 (map:FF7)
Every day

The bottom floor of this Victorian is devoted to books and paraphernalia that help people take that next spiritual step, whether it be recovery, growth, business prosperity, or self-transformation. The top floor houses a gallery space by day and a classroom by night for visiting authors, psychics, and astrologers.

The Nor'Wester Bookshop
318 SW Washington St,
228-2747 (map:H4)
Every day

This shop tends to carry gently offbeat titles in architecture and design, crafts and art how-to, and food and wine. At press time they had just moved to a larger Washington Street location.

Old Oregon Book Store
1128 SW Alder St,
227-2742 (map:I1)
Mon-Sat

Not just another well-thumbed used-book store. There's plenty to learn from owner Preston McMann, one of the most knowledgeable Portlanders in the vintage book business—especially history. That is, if you catch him on a good day.

Oregon Historical Society Book Shop
On Broadway at SW Madison St, 222-1741 (map:F2)
Mon-Sat

A vital component of Oregon's literary scene, OHS offers a fine selection of regional history, perhaps the best in the state, including some titles of their own. Upstairs, the Society's extensive photo library offers reproductions of historical photographs.

Packrat Book Emporium
333 S State St, Lake Oswego, 635-8673 (map:LL5)
Every day

Packrat's growth from used paperbacks to general books reflects the happy fate of appreciated booksellers in Portland, and its best-selling subjects—self-help and recovery, business and investment—pretty much sum up the 1980s. Customers can listen to acoustic instrumental cassettes before buying.

Pegasus Books
4390 SW Lloyd St, Beaverton (and branches), 643-4222 (map:HH9)
Every day

By dropping the dubious-sounding "fantasy" from their name and remodeling the NE Sandy Boulevard store (284-4693, map:FF4), Pegasus Books brought a 95 percent increase in their sci-fi business—in one month. Now, their second Milwaukie store has an all-new, totally hip name: It Came From Outer Space (786-0865, map:JJ5), or try the original Milwaukie store at Main Street and Monroe Avenue(652-2752, map:JJ5). Videos are the big seller at their Division Street location (233-0768, map:HH5).

Periodicals Paradise
3415 SE Belmont St, 236-8370 (map:GG4)
Every day

The Fred Meyer of used-magazine stores, with over 50,000 issues available at any given time. Issues published within the past year sell for 80 percent off the cover price.

**Portland Audubon
Society Bookstore**
*5151 NW Cornell Rd,
292-6855 (map:FF7)
Tues-Sun*

Next door to a wildlife hospital at the bird sanctuary near Forest Park is Audubon's resource center. Inside, there's the cool odor of birdseed, and a treasure trove for naturalists particularly fond of the Northwest: field guides, natural history books, binoculars, and all.

Powell's Books Inc
*1005 W Burnside (and
branches), 228-4651
(map:J2)
Every day*

Some say Powell's *is* Portland. Now the granddaddy of a number of thriving local branches, Powell's is probably the biggest bookstore west of the Mississippi —and definitely will be by the time its expansion is complete in August 1990. Just inside the door, the tireless counterstaff is busy buying used books. A million volumes of used and new books fill nearly a city block at the main Burnside store, and the quirky, intelligent staff seems to know the whereabouts of every single one. Daunting in size, the store even provides maps to guide bibliomaniacs through the 50 sections, from Automotives to Zen. Upstairs is the heart of the store: the rare book room. Over 3,500 precious books are stashed here (the most expensive is a $10,000 fourth-edition Shakespeare, the oldest dates to 1597). Here you can find the only person in town to give rare-book appraisals at no charge. In the southwest corner of the store is the Anne Hughes Coffee Room, where bibliophiles linger and once a week authors read and do signings.

Powell's offspring each have their own specialty. Around the corner, Powell's Technical Books (32 NW 11th Avenue at Couch Street, 228-3906) deals in computer, electronics, and engineering books. Powell's Books in Cascade Plaza (Beaverton, 643-3131) has an excellent newborn branch across the way, Powell's for Kids. Tiny by comparison, Powell's at PDX's Oregon Market (249-1950) offers mostly new volumes.

Powell's Books for Cooks
*3735 SE Hawthorne
Blvd, 235-3802
(map:GG4)
Every day*

Inside Pastaworks, Books for Cooks is the only store of its kind on the West Coast. Sure, cookbooks are the thing here, but you'll find some entertaining and gardening books, too. Regular demonstrations by noted cookbook authors.

Powell's Travel Store
*SW Sixth Ave and Yamhill
St, 228-1108 (map:H3)
Every day*

The minute you walk in, you'll want to be somewhere else than underneath the bricks of Pioneer Courthouse Square. Powell's Travel Books guide you to faraway (and not so faraway) places. The staff knows where they're going; ask while you sip a latte and they'll tell you where they've been.

KIDS means it's a good place to bring kids.

Portland State University Bookstore
1880 SW 6th Ave,
226-3631 (map:C1)
Mon-Sat

Not just for students, the cooperatively run PSU Bookstore has been the major supplier of textbooks for 40 years; however, the stock of children's, computer, business, fiction, and reference books attracts even Ivy League alumni.

Reed College Bookstore
3203 SE Woodstock Blvd,
777-7287 (map:HH4)
Mon-Sat (Mon-Fri, when school's out)

Heavily academic, and no wonder—it's right in the middle of this liberal arts campus. The buyers here know they can't compete with general stores, so instead they fatten their shelves with humanities and a surprisingly substantial natural sciences collection.

Rich's Cigar Store
801 SW Alder St,
228-1700 (map:I2)

706 NW 23rd Ave,
227-6907 (map:FF6)
Every day

One hundred years ago, Rich's was just another newsstand/tobacco-seller in Portland. Now it's one of the few left, carrying a huge and thorough selection of magazines, foreign newspapers and magazines, and, yes, tobacco. The recently opened northwest store still feels like the new kid on the block.

Skidmore Village Children's Books
50 SW 3rd Ave, 222-5076 (map:J5)

NW Miller between 1st and 2nd, Gresham, 661-5887
Every day

The oldest children's bookstore in Portland just opened the youngest children's bookstore in Gresham. The owner's understanding of kids is lovingly displayed in the titles she (a grandparent herself) selects. Her daughter runs the Gresham store.

Stiles for Relaxation
4505 NE Tillamook St,
281-6789 (map:EE4)
Every day

Portland's answer to stress. Oralee Stiles and Marzenda Stiles McCombs' 10-year-old store emphasizes physical, mental, and spiritual improvements, and the merchandise is a means toward those ends. Phone for thought? Call 288-3420, ext. 281, for book reviews and a daily meditation.

Title Wave Bookstore
216 NE Knott St,
294-3243 (map:FF5)
Mon-Sat

Ever wonder where old library books end up? Over 20,000 volumes from the Multnomah County Library sell for bargain prices here at the old Albina Library. The volunteer staff organizes the books (including encyclopedia sets) by—what else?—the Dewey decimal system.

Twenty-Third Avenue Books
1015 NW 23rd Ave,
224-5097 (map:FF6)
Every day

Bob Maull's friendly demeanor is part of what makes this northwest store so appealing. Just what a bookstore should be—small, comfortable, with a strong sense of its authors.

US Government Bookstore
*1305 SW 1st Ave
(Jefferson-Columbia
Square), 221-6217
(map:E3)
Mon-Fri*

One hundred percent government issue with books on subjects from aviation to natural resources. The year-old store gets a lot of traffic from lawyers and business-people, but it's a fascinating place for civilians, too.

CAMERAS

Camera World
*500 SW 5th Ave,
222-0008 (map:I3)
Mon-Sat*

A huge selection for all your camera needs, with the best prices around. It's probably a good idea to know what you want before you go in, since salespeople are eager to sell you anything. Products are all on the high end of quality, and a mail-order system is available for out-of-towners or those too busy to come in.

Citizens Photo
*709 SE 7th Ave, 232-8501
(map:FF5)
Every day*

Not always well stocked with lighting and equipment, but when they've got it, it's quality. Each salesman has a specialty and, in fact, may tell you so ad nauseum. Not the cheapest, either, but the equipment's top-notch.

Timers
*1601 Broadway,
Vancouver, WA
(206) 696-0859
(map:AA6)
Mon-Sat*

Timers customers range from the novice to the professional who'll cross the river in search of chemicals and camera equipment. A very friendly staff with lots of advice; also a print and blueprint shop.

CANDIES AND CHOCOLATES

Candy Basket
*4036 SE 82nd Ave
(Eastport Plaza),
771-3393 (map:HH3)*

*6663 SW Beaverton-
Hillsdale Hwy, 292-4516
(map:HH7)
Every day*

Since 1977, Dick Fuhr has been perfecting the art of candy making and has come up with some extremely delectable confections. He has the usual oddities, such as caramel cars in 20 different models—or pick up a chocolate remote control or a user-friendly floppy disk.

JaCiva's Chocolates and Pastries
*4733 SW Hawthorne
Blvd, 234-8115
(map:GG8)
Mon-Sat*

American-born, Swiss-trained Jack Elmer and his wife, Iva Sue (hence JaCiva), opened this Hawthorne Boulevard sweetshop three years ago. With their own recipes they create chocolates that Grandma would envy. Cakes and pastries, too. At press time, an entire room was being added strictly for wedding cake samples.

Rococo Chocolates
*405 NW 23rd Ave,
248-9040 (map:GG6)
Every day*

The main philosophy of Rococo (located inside Roberto's) is, if you can't do something well, don't do it at all. And they seem to be sticking by this rule to the truffle. They use nothing but the finest ingredients, and you can taste the creamy difference. You pay for it, too.

CHILDREN'S CLOTHING

Bambini's Children's Boutique
*16353 SW Bryant Rd,
Lake Oswego, 635-7661
(map:KK6)
Mon-Sat*

A fun (and expensive) place to outfit your little bambini, newborn to preteen, with clothing as whimsical as the youngsters themselves. It's the only store around stocking Maine Madhatter sweaters and Tickle Me for girls or Tackle Me for boys. Mini-accessories, too.

Benetton 012
*96445 SW Washington
Sq, Tigard, 620-0440
(map:KK9)
Every day*

This children's version of the *molto di moda* adult chain is housed in the same store as an adult branch, under separate ownership. Clothes are fun, if criminally pricey: 100 percent wool or cotton, mix-and-match, unisex clothing by Italian designers.

Hanna Andersson
*327 NW 10th Ave,
242-0920 (map:L2)
Mon-Sat*

Most people know this Swedish-designed all-cotton clothing through Hanna Andersson's national catalog; however, Portlanders delight in their easy access to the company's only outlet. Quality clothes and a bundle of coats, hats, and mittens.

Lads 'n' Lassies
*12000 SE 82nd Ave
(Clackamas Town
Center), 652-1628
(map:FF7)
Every day*

A big store for little britches: the Beazely family has created an empire for children's clothes, from its embryonic stages in the Clackamas Town Center to its third and newest on NW 23rd Avenue. It's more than just beautiful infant-to-preteen clothes—the sales staff will treat your daughter like she's Gloria Vanderbilt's. The toy and book department rivals those of fine toy stores, as does the doll collection. Nursery furnishings on the upper floor, and a play area with a television tuned in to kids. Other Portland-area branches include: Northwest (30 NW 23rd Place, 223-0400) and Beaverton Town Square (11651 SW Beaverton-Hillsdale Highway, Beaverton, 626-6578).

Mako
*732 NW 23rd Ave,
274-9081 (map:FF7)
Every day*

We used to see Mako at the Saturday Market. Now, we find her in an under-the-groundfloor store on NW 23rd Avenue. Only about 10 percent of her stock is Mako-designed sweats and T-shirts, but they're all made from natural fibers. Fanciful sock collection.

Mrs. Tiggywinkles
*5331 SW Macadam Ave
(Johns Landing),
227-7084 (map:HH6)
Every day*

Everything here (from the sweaters to the Halloween costumes to the wooden rocking hippos) is handmade, and Sue and Jill Winegar do a lot of it themselves. If you want a modification, use a special material, or yearn for a Raggedy Ann with purple hair, they'll make it to order—and it always appears promptly when promised.

Natalie Rose de Paris
606 SW Broadway,
228-5765 (map:H2)
Mon-Sat

Very European children's clothing (through size 10) is featured at this downtown Portland store: Absorba, Petit Bateau, Dan Jean, Jean Bourget. Even a few pairs of Italian shoes. *Tres chic,* but also *tres cher.*

Room to Grow
2700 NW 185th St
(Tanasbourne Mall),
645-6221
Every day

What used to be two stores (Little Kingdom for clothes, Room to Grow for furnishings) is now one—with an emphasis on nursery goods. Clothing (through size 4) is primarily standard sleep- and playwear. A move across the street is planned for September 1990.

Second Generation
4029 SE Hawthorne
Blvd, 233-8130
(map:GG4)
Mon-Sat

100 percent cotton clothing seems to be what parents want these days. At Second Generation that's what they get—up to size 8 for boys and girls. Moms-to-be can pick up secondhand maternity clothing here, too.

Youngland
2121 W Burnside,
227-1414 (map:FF7)
Mon-Sat

For 36 years, Youngland has been a Portland landmark for children's clothing. In fact, they were doing so well that in 1987 they opted to move from their prime Uptown Shopping Center location to a larger space on W Burnside. Unfortunately, it hasn't been as busy since, but for kid stuff (strollers to shoes, and clothing to girls' size 14, boys 20), it's still tops. Stow the youngsters in the play area with its imaginative toys and quiet book corner. A remarkable shop (with its own charge account) and patient staff—a true tribute to owner Norman Mannheimer Sr.

COFFEES AND TEAS

Kobos
540 SW Broadway (and
branches), 228-4251
(map:H2)
Every day

Need coffee in a flash? Kobos does their own roasting and now has six locations around the Portland area. An extensive line of everything: glassware, cookware, gadgets, and of course coffees (Kenya, Sumatra, even macadamia nut fudge). An espresso bar is in service at each location.

Coffee People
803 NW 23rd Ave,
221-0235 (map:FF7)

1200 NE Broadway,
284-4359 (map:FF5)
Every day

If the name doesn't give it away, the wonderful espresso concoctions will: these people know coffee. And with their Immediate Care Center across NW 23rd Avenue, it's snowballed into a sinful empire of decadence. A delightful staff always ready to answer your coffee questions and help you choose from 60 varieties of beans.

Send us your feedback and tips on the report form at the back of this book.

Starbucks
Pioneer Courthouse Square, 2nd Ave and Taylor St, 223-2488 (map:H2)
Mon-Sun

Portland is quickly catching up to Seattle's infatuation with the caffe latte—with some help from Starbucks. The Seattle-based company has found its way into the bloodstream of Portland coffee lovers. Downtowners descend upon the place for a shot of espresso, calming classical music, and a refuge from the crowds in its front yard, Pioneer Courthouse Square.

Coffee Merchant
1637 NE Broadway (and branches), 284-9209 (map:FF6)
Mon-Sat

You can't buy a cup of coffee here; they *give* it to you. Four brews are always hot for sampling. An unequaled assortment of beans comes roasted or unroasted (a number of people prefer it that way). Dave McCammon and his staff have created a relaxed environment for sipping, perusing cookbooks, or selecting your weekly bean. Other locations: 3562 SE Hawthorne Boulevard, 230-1222, and Hillsdale Shopping Center, 244-4822.

Italia d'Oro Espresso
413 SW Morrison St, 228-1137 (map:G9)
Mon-Sat

Portland's own Boyd's coffee has recently branched out to become part of the espresso craze that's hit this city. The coffees are respectable but not exceptional. The espresso house doubles as a gift shop offering beans, candies, and coffee supplies to its customers.

DEPARTMENT STORES

Fred Meyer
3030 NE Weidler St (and branches), 232-8844 (map: FF4)
Every day

It was 1908 when Fred G. Meyer began business at SW Fifth Avenue and Yamhill Street with seven departments and a firm philosophy: create satisfied customers, earn their patronage, provide for profitable growth, and enrich the lives of Fred Meyer employees. Today that business has grown to over 112 stores nationwide, including the famous "one-stop shopping" stores, the newest located in the Hollywood district.

In addition to this expansion, the original seven departments have grown to over 25 specialty areas, and the new superstores include everything from a Chinese Express, a wine steward, and a jewelry shop to a deli, children's clothing, and fresh produce. The company has perfected the idea of one-stop shopping and has turned going to the grocery or clothing or hardware store into a fun experience. The "dairy area" has a wall decorated with the backsides of cows whose tails swing.

But above all, the key to Fred Meyer's success seems to be that it has stuck to the founder's original philosophy. Employees are friendly and helpful, the prices are competitive and fair, and the selection is nothing less than expansive. Portland's version of the corner store.

Meier & Frank
621 SW 5th Ave,
223-0512 (map:H3)
Every day

A grand Portland tradition began on SW 5th Avenue and Morrison Street in 1857 by the Meier & Frank families. It's now eight big stores owned by May department stores out of St. Louis. The original store comprises ten floors on a downtown block and offers a full complement of services: a beauty salon, a bridal registry, picture framing, jewelry repair, a travel agency. It's the "everyman's" department store in town, specializing in good-looking, moderately priced merchandise, from fine china to men's and women's fashions—and a lot of it. Quality seems to be slipping a bit of late, but it's still a good bet (with good prices) for sheets and towels, linens, mattresses, and a variety of electronics. But wait for the sales, which seem to occur almost every week. You can find Baccarat crystal at the Washington Square store only.

Nordstrom
701 SW Broadway,
224-6666 (map:H2)
Every day

After 18 years of hard work, this Seattle prodigy has Portlanders convinced it's something they can't live without. Much of this developing success is owed to Nordstrom's famous emphasis on service. The "Ask Me, I Know" booth, located on the main floor, provides visitors with maps and brochures in eight languages. An extremely helpful sales staff is very knowledgeable about current fashions and the merchandise they're selling, and they dress to emphasize the point.

Nordstrom started business as a shoe store in Seattle, and shoes are still its specialty at all locations. There is a tremendous range of styles as well as prices, and an impressive stock of hard-to-find sizes. Women's fashions are displayed in a series of five very well defined departments, ranging from sophisticated to playful and everything in between. Men can be outfitted to Nordstrom Ivy League specifications in three distinctively different shops.

Keep an eye out for the famous sales, the anniversary in July and the half-yearly both for women (June and November) and for men (June and January), notorious for great deals and outrageous crowds. The downtown location was Oregon's first, followed by the Lloyd Center site, which is now being remodeled to double the original square footage. Completion is planned for fall 1990.

All places in this book are recommended; even "no stars" are worth knowing about.

Saks Fifth Avenue
850 SW 5th Ave (Pioneer Place), no phone at press time (map:G4)

In September 1990, the Northwest will get its introduction to this distinguished New York–based department store when the 47th branch opens in downtown Portland. Discriminating shoppers are said to be curbing their clothes-buying in anticipation of the fall opening. Saks has become synonymous with fashionable, gracious living—known for luxury clothing (including two of their own lines, Real Clothes and The Works), spacious aisles, and elaborate shopping services such as multilingual consultants and executive service (for the professional with limited time).

DISCOUNT AND FACTORY OUTLETS

Act II Exclusive Resale Boutique
1139 SW Morrison St, 227-7969 (map:I1)
Tues-Sat

The labels in this high-brow store scream of the kind of good taste that gets noticed in society columns, from European elegance to art funk (prices $5–$400). This store pays the highest prices in town for discarded top-of-the-line clothes.

American Cancer Society Discovery Shops
1730 NE 40th Ave (and branches), 287-0053 (map:FF4)
Mon-Sat

Here you can buy The Limited leftovers in good conscience, as well as other new and barely-used clothing. Proceeds from the four shops go to the American Cancer Society. The Hollywood neighborhood location, with primarily new clothes (NE 40th Avenue), is the trendiest. The Gresham store (200 NE Second Avenue, Gresham, 669-0431) sells mostly used clothes culled from donations by discriminating, fashion-conscious volunteers. The northwest (274-9908) and Tigard (684-9060) stores are mixed.

Barbara Johnson Clothing Outlet
2020 8th Ave (Willamette Mall), West Linn, 657-5152
Fri-Sat (open other days for sales only)

About five times a year (February, June, September, November, April), Barbara Johnson announces the arrival of fresh merchandise (Lanz, J.G. Hook, Evelyn Pearson) and stays open for five to 10 days running. You'll find well-known brands two seasons *ahead* of the retail stores.

Bits & Pieces Factory Outlet
1420 NW Lovejoy St, 222-3847 (map:FF6)
Every day

Layton Home Fashions has made one good factory store out of what had become three mediocre outlets. The remaining store (designated a historical landmark) hunts for promotional offerings from mills like Cannon and occasionally gets raided itself by buyers from closeout giants like T.J. Maxx, Marshall's, and Ross. Discounts of 30 to 60 percent off retail.

DISCOUNT AND FACTORY OUTLETS

CC Exchange
506 NW 23rd Ave,
227-1477 (map:FF6)
Tues-Sat

One of the newest clothing shops in the city, CC Exchange has quickly become one of the most popular—we don't really know why. Descend the unassuming staircase to Camille Stevens' tiny, overstuffed store, where about half the designer-label merchandise is used, half is new, and nothing is that cheap.

Champion Factory Outlet
3552 SE 122nd Ave,
761-5150 (map:HH2)
Every day

Champion makes the heaviest cotton sweats on the market. Here is the most rugged of no-nonsense sportswear at no-nonsense prices. One of four factory stores in the state, this outlet offers seconds, irregulars, overruns, misprints, and some first quality. A plethora of collegiate logos available.

**Columbia Knit Factory
Outlet Store**
5100 SE Harney Dr,
777-7385 (map:II4)
Mon-Sat

The company sews built-to-last rugby shirts for famous national mail-order catalogs. In addition, the store offers some cotton and wool sweaters, and special cotton shorts and pants found nowhere else.

**Columbia Sportswear
Factory Outlet**
8128 SE 13th Ave,
238-0118 (map:II5)

*3 Monroe Pkwy, Lake
Oswego, 636-6593
(map:KK8)*
Every day

Columbia's Sellwood outlet is a favorite of those who think the best thing about Portland is leaving it behind on the weekends. Trucks deliver irregulars, closeouts, and overstocks of ski, hunting, running, and hiking gear fresh from the factory several times a week. Columbia's own gear is 30 percent below retail; miscellaneous others are discounted by 10 percent. The new Lake Oswego outlet is three times larger than the rest.

Cracker Barrel Outlet Store
1830 NW 19th Ave,
223-5409 (map:FF6)
*Tues-Sat (Every day
Nov-Dec)*

At the edge of the fashionably bohemian Pearl District, you'll find Norm Thompson samples, leftovers, and mail-order returns at 25 to 50 percent off. Also products from such spinoffs as Early Winters, Cravings by Mail, The Primary Layer, Columbia Harbor, and Solutions. Call Friday about the weekend 75 percent off special.

Danner Factory Outlet Store
12722 NE Airport Wy,
251-1111 (map:EE2)
Mon-Sat

Danner is boots: hunting, military, work, and hiking. First-quality sell for brand-new prices; irregulars are 40 percent off—no guarantee to be waterproof. Especially busy at hunting season. Sorry, but Inga the dog stays with the store.

Dehen Outlet Store
404 NW 10th Ave,
796-0725 (map:L2)
Mon-Sat

Dehen could outfit a soda pop commercial with its all-American line—at a fraction of retail. In real life, the company supplies L. L. Bean and many colleges and universities with casual, feel-good sportswear. The northwest store concentrates on upper-end cotton mer-

3551 SE Division St,
234-9382 (map:GG5)
Tues-Sat

chandise, while the Division Street branch focuses on cheerleading clothes, acrylic sweaters, and letter jackets (custom or not).

Kutters: An Outlet Store
104 SW 2nd Ave,
228-4858 (map:I5)
Every day

Every waiter in Portland knows Kutters; at $10, it's the best deal in town on a man's white dress shirt. For women, the off-price boutique carries a fast-moving selection of overruns, experimental designer lines, and brands only a seasoned traveler would recognize (labels are snipped). Regular customers pitch in on the occasional 5pm glass-of-wine happy hour, bringing in their own favorite vintages or bread and pate.

Nike Union Square Factory Store
3044 NE Martin Luther King Jr. Blvd, 281-5901 (map:EE5)
Every day

There are the full-price Nike stores, the employee-only stores, and then there's the off-price Nike outlet. The outlet, however, is still a relative secret, partially due to its location—near a gang-affiliated neighborhood. Nike hasn't ignored this store or the depressed neighborhood: as its top-price, high-tech shoe shrines open across the country, its factory outlet has quietly doubled in size and appeal. Everything's guaranteed—even imperfect shoes.

Nordstrom Rack
401 SW Morrison St,
299-1815 (map:G4)
8930 SE Sunnyside Rd,

Clackamas, 654-5415
(map:KK3)
Every day

The Rack carries clearance merchandise from the Nordstrom stores at up to 70 percent off. But that's not why it's so good. Supplemental buying fills in hard-to-find sizes and styles with jaw-dropping prices. The downtown basement store fills—and feels— like a tightly packed submarine, while the Clackamas location lets shoppers see the light of day. Retail clerks maintain the Nordstrom smile.

Pendleton Woolen Mills Outlet Store
2 17th, Washougal, WA,
(206) 835-2131
Mon-Fri

Even 80 minutes west of Portland on the Washington side of the Columbia River, and aggressively downplayed by its parent company, this outlet is always crowded. Irresistible values (50 percent off) in this classic Northwest dress code. Deals on fabrics, too.

Sellwood Ladies Resale
8079 SE 13th Ave,
236-6842 (map:II5)
Tues-Sat

Every neighborhood has its better resale shop. This is Sellwood's. Fur coats can cost anywhere from $50 to $2,000, the hat selection is generous, you may even find a belly-dancing costume. Occasionally, samples or closeouts from retailers appear, maybe a batch of shoes.

Looking for a particular place? Check the index at the back of this book for individual restaurants, hotels, B&Bs, shops, bars, parks, museums, galleries, neighborhoods, messenger services, nightclubs, and more.

▼

William Temple House Thrift Shop
*2230 NW Glisan St,
222-3328 (map:FF6)
Mon-Sat*

A slick ad campaign featuring the state's political heavyweights draws discards from homes of the socially correct, which then go on sale to the people living closer to the river. It's easier to forgive the not-so-thrifty price tags knowing that sales are responsible for one-third of the budget of a private organization that counsels and clothes those in need.

FABRIC AND KNITTING SUPPLIES

Calico Corners
*8526 SW Terwilliger
Blvd, 244-6700 (map:II6)
Every day*

Probably the biggest selection of home fabrics in the city, ranging from mill-ends to designer bolts from the US and Europe. The store appeals to do-it-yourself home remodelers, but there's also custom sewing for those not familiar with the details of re-covering their own sofas.

Cheryl's Own Design Fabric Outlet
*12675 SW Broadway,
Beaverton, 641-7271
(map:HH9)
Mon-Sat*

COD, subtitled "The Sports Connection," caters exclusively to sports-oriented tailors at outlet prices. Manufacturers like Nike, Roffe, Duffel, and Patagonia supply the raw materials (where else will you find wool stretch ski-pant fabric or 100 percent cotton cloth for sweats?). Some blueprint patterns and factory-excess D-rings, ribbings, and zippers, but no tweed.

Daisy Kingdom Fabrics and Trims
*134 NW 8th Ave,
222-9033 (map:K4)*

*12000 SE 82nd Ave
(Clackamas Town Center), 652-7464 (map:JJ3)
Every day*

Over three-quarters of the two-story (NW Eighth Avenue) store's fabric supply comes from the million yards the wholesale division designs and prints for international distribution. A discount store is scheduled to open across the street (spring 1990). The Clackamas Town Center store focuses more on infant and nursery ready-made items. The mail-order catalog includes company skiwear patterns.

Josephine's Dry Goods
*921 SW Morrison St
(Galleria), 224-4202
(map:I2)
Every day*

Josephine's is the only fabric store in downtown Portland, and it appeals to the accomplished, upscale seamstress. A fine selection of elegant natural fibers, generous button selection, and Vogue, New Look, and Burda patterns come together at this fabric boutique.

June's Fabric Shop
*429 SW 1st St, Lake
Oswego, 636-5505
(map:KK6)
Mon-Sat*

June's carries a lot of dressy fabrics—lame, glitter, tapestries, cotton prints, silks, and linens. Thirty-one years old and still going strong, with a bridal department as well as jewelry, accessories, and sewing notions.

SHOPPING

Mill End Store
*8300 SE McLoughlin
Blvd, 236-1234 (map:II5)*

*12155 SW Broadway,
Beaverton, 646-3000
(map:HH9)*
Every day

Long-time Portland residents still refer to the McLoughlin store as Oregon Woolen Mills. The old woolen mill building stores 70,000 square feet of fabric on one floor, claimed to be America's biggest fabric display, rolling out bargain end-cuts of imported fabrics once $200 a yard. A side room offers budget goods.

Jantzen Fabric Outlet
*2012 NE Hoyt St (and
branches), 238-5396
(map:FF5)*
Every day

The best selection of Lycra, nylon, and cotton swimwear fabrics. Best deals are in fabric by the pound. Other nearby outlets are in Beaverton (649-4411), Hood River (1-386-2552), and Vancouver, WA (206-694-0311).

Knotting Chamber
*3257 SE Hawthorne Blvd
(map:GG5)
232-1043 (knitting),
232-1854 (needlework)*
Every day

This century-old lavender and white house is the needlework capital of the universe. Well, Portland anyway. Fourteen rooms devoted to knitting, cross-stitching, needlepoint, and custom framing paraphernalia let wide-eyed beginners as well as ambitious experts choose basic threads or hand-spun delicacies. Separate staffs on each floor answer specific questions (needlework downstairs, knitting upstairs) and teach classes. Washing, blocking, and framing a specialty.

Northwest Wools
*3524 SW Troy St,
244-5024 (map:II7)
Mon-Sat*

Skeins of wool, linen, cotton, silk, and mohair; carpet warp for weavers; spinning fibers for spinners. If you don't know how to knit or spin, there are classes in both. If you don't have the time, they'll do it for you.

Westover Wools
*2390 NW Thurman St,
227-0134 (map:FF6)
Mon-Sat*

What happens when you have all the pieces of a sweater and no clue how to put them all together? Westover Wools can help or even do it for you. Complete supplier for the knitter and weaver, including hand-dyed yarns (please, no acrylics) and Rigid Heddle looms. Professional knitters can write you out a pattern for reproducing a favorite sweater.

FLORISTS

Flowers by Dorcas
*525 SW Broadway,
227-6454 (map:H4)
Mon-Sat*

At a glance, Dorcas resembles an upscale gift store—and about 60 percent of its business is, in fact, just that. But gardeny flowers there are, generally arranged in a loose, natural style. Prices are not low, a fact that doesn't seem to faze Dorcas' carriage trade clientele, but the quality is evident.

Flowers Tommy Luke
625 SW Morrison St (and branches), 228-3131 (map:H4)
Mon-Sat

After more than 80 years on the same downtown block, this high-volume florist's shop is a Portland tradition, with designs from standard FTD to airier "English garden" arrangements. In addition, there are select gifts. Uptown there's one branch at 2405 W Burnside (in the Uptown Shopping Center, 228-3134), and another at 1701 SW Jefferson Street (228-3140).

Gifford-Doving Florists
704 SW Jefferson St (and branches), 222-9193 (map:F1)
Mon-Sat

Gifford-Doving (family-owned since 1938) stocks perhaps the best selection of cut flowers in town. And in the late afternoon, it is one of Portland's busiest florists. Several kinds of greens are usually on hand as well, making this a favorite source for do-it-yourself arrangers. Branches are at 2310 NW Everett Street (open every day) and at 811 SW Second Avenue and 200 SW Market Street (both Monday–Friday only).

Kristin Lee Florist
3507 SW Corbett Ave, 227-6460 (map:HH6)
Mon-Sat

Kristin Lee is a purist. No gifts, candles, or balloons—just cut flowers, some topiary and blooming plants, and simple vases. Her floral designs are similarly focused, with a fresh-from-the-garden naturalness.

Rainyday Flowers
110 SW Yamhill St, 248-9524 (map:G5)

8775 SW Cascade Ave, Beaverton, 641-7229 (map:JJ9)
Every day

Rainyday means tropical flowers and Hawaiian plants. Orchids, antheria, gardenia corsages, leis, and Venus'-flytraps are generally on hand, along with bonsai, cacti, and a wide range of less exotic cut flowers. The Cascade Plaza outlet stocks outdoor plants, garden ornaments, and furniture, as well.

Richard Calhoun Old Town Florist
403 NW 9th Ave, 223-1646 (map:K3)
Mon-Sat

Located in the artsy Pearl District, Richard Calhoun is known for his sophisticated contemporary Oriental arrangements. Staffers favor striking designs of tropical flowers and foliage; the silk flowers are equally dramatic. Calhoun moonlights as a design consultant for parties and weddings.

FURNITURE

Bader & Fox Sofa Factory
3400 SE 122nd St, 761-6135 (map:HH1)
Mon-Sat

The showroom is in the factory at this custom furniture shop, probably because most customers want chairs, couches, or sofa-beds redone to their specifications and with their chosen fabrics. A lot of people bring in pictures from magazines; Bader & Fox is happy to re-create these designs for you, one piece at a time.

SHOPPING

CC Stores
9955 SW Beaverton-
Hillsdale Hwy,
Beaverton, 644-3944
(map:HH9)
Every day

"CC" used to stand for Children's Country. CC's bottom floor now stands for Contemporary Concepts; the other floor still offers kids' furnishings, but the look is contemporary there, too. The high-tech–influenced European lines have clean lines in basic colors like white, black, and gray. Kits keep the price down.

The Joinery
1126 NE 28th Ave,
287-9439 (map:FF4)
Mon-Sat

One of the best fine handcrafted wood furniture showrooms in the city. The Joinery (member of the Guild of Oregon Woodworkers) makes bed frames for stores in the Pacific Coast states and, in a new export twist, recently began shipping futon frames to Japan.

Kinion Furniture Company
4307 NE Tillamook St,
287-2605 (map:EE4)
Mon-Sat

One of the newest entries in the custom furniture market, this small showroom (the workshop's in McMinnville) has been open less than a year. Customers wanting handcrafted furniture can choose from the 25 or so samples of solid hardwood pieces with subtle traditional details.

Leather Furniture Company
311 SW Alder St (and
branches), 224-0272
(map:H4)
Every day

Leather, of course, in such quantities that this store can offer consistently lower prices, higher quality, and more specialized product knowledge than any other furniture store in the area. Two more shops in Beaverton (6800 SW Beaverton-Hillsdale Highway, 297-1034; 9315 SW Beaverton-Hillsdale Highway, 292-1903) and a fourth outlet in the Clackamas Town Center (Clackamas Corner, 652-1027).

Lloyd's Interiors
1714 NE Broadway,
284-1185 (map:FF5)
Every day

Lloyd's Outlet
337 NE San Rafael St,
281-4268 (map:FF5)
Every day

With the best-designed pieces around, Lloyd's continues to stand apart from other furniture stores, and now mixes in classics from the 1950s and earlier. Primarily custom work and higher-quality furniture from around the world, but the warehouse outlet is geared to apartment dwellers and people moving into their first homes.

Northwest Futon Company
400 SW 2nd Ave,
242-0057 (map:H4)

3443 SE Hawthorne
Blvd, 235-0977
(map:GG5)
Every day

Customers of Northwest Futon tend to belong to the YMCA, shop at Nature's Fresh, ride mountain bikes, and sport a social conscience. Futon and mattress frames, custom futon cover fabrics, lighting, shoji screens, and tatami mats bolster the image. The cotton and wool futons here are relatively inexpensive, while still appealing to the thirtysomethings.

---

*Look for **FREE**—it means this attraction or event is free of charge.*

The Real Mother Goose
SW 9th Ave and Yamhill St (and branches), 223-9510 (map:H2) Mon-Sat

See Galleries in Art chapter.

Scan/Design
10760 SW Beaverton-Hillsdale Hwy, Beaverton, 644-4040 (map:HH9)

333 S State St, Lake Oswego, 636-7890 (map:KK6) Every day

Danish and Norwegian imports in teak and rosewood with timeless, clean Scandinavian lines. Scan/Design can furnish every room in the house, as well as the office.

Vox Furniture
530 NW 12th Ave, 224-6821 (map:L1) Mon-Sat

Its name Latin for "voice," Vox carries some of the most outspoken pieces in the city. Progressive local designers explore materials ranging from steel, aluminum, concrete, and glass to more whimsical painted wood. All are functional to some degree, and they tend to be the center of aesthetic attention both in a home and on First Thursday gallery walks.

GIFTS AND STATIONERY

Absolute Zero
838 NW 23rd Ave, 274-2249 (map:FF7) Every day

Absolute Zero is an aggressively trendy experience that takes impulse buying to just about its limit. Countless supplies for the throwaway generation—lots of cards, plastic bathroom accessories, bottle-cap earrings, T-shirts from local artists, and an eight-foot-long pink Cadillac pool float.

Alder Street Clock Shop
251 SW Alder St, 227-3651 (map:H4) Mon-Fri

With four decades of clock knowledge, the staff can advise you on the most, er, minute detail of your purchase. Music boxes and weather instruments here, too.

The Barn Owl Nursery
22999 SW Newland Rd, Wilsonville, 638-0387 (map:QQ9) Wed-Sat (closed Jan-Mar, Aug-Sep)

See Nurseries in this chapter.

Callin Novelty Shop
412 SW 4th Ave,

Behind-the-counter expert magicians can show you how to do pranks right. Callin's sells the props for jokesters of all ages. This store also has everything you ever

223-4821 (map:I5)
Mon-Sat

wanted to buy from the back pages of comic books: sea monkeys, magic rocks, X-ray specs.

The Cat's Meow
3538 SE Hawthorne
Blvd, 231-1341
(map:GG5)
Tues-Sun

The purrrfect store for the discriminating cat lover. Owner Pam Gibson ceded management of the premises to the beige-furred, blue-eyed Mr. Muddles long ago. Customers can paw through cat jewelry and kitty hammocks plus memorabilia of the city's most famous feline, Bob the KATU Weather Cat.

Claytrade
2332 NW Westover Rd,
224-0334 (map:FF6)
Every day

Claytrade began in Eugene as a cooperative business selling rough-hewn pots and mugs. Now also in northwest Portland, this aggressively whimsical store features impeccable craftsmanship, from the best-selling traditional stoneware bowls and elegant Italian-inspired platters to the wackier bright furnishings, witty plates, and technoromantic earrings. A third shop, Twist, will open in the new Pioneer Place in spring 1990.

Contemporary Crafts Gallery
3934 SW Corbett Ave,
223-2654 (map:HH6)
Tues-Sun

See Galleries in Arts chapter.

The Design Source
600 SW 10th Ave (The
Galleria), 223-3098
(map:H2)
Mon-Fri

Just knock on room 513; it's Portland's most secret gift shop. Alexandra Lynch shares the space with her husband, David, a freelance graphic artist. Ask to see Alexandra's cases brimming with jewelry from India, Guatemala, Thailand, China, and Africa. She sells the lower-priced local crafts you would buy for friends and family on a romp around the globe.

Itchy Fingers Gallery
1318 NW 23rd Ave,
222-5237 (map:FF7)
Tues-Sun

Itchy Fingers falls somewhere between a gallery and a gift shop. A fresh-from-California spot (the owner is, at least) with a gallery of sorcerer puppets, ceramics, paintings, and wall hangings. Who says it isn't art—drop by on First Thursday and see for yourself.

Jelly Bean—The Store
802 SW 10th Ave,
222-5888 (map:H1)
Mon-Sat

Don't be fooled by its candy-store name. Across from the Multnomah County Library, this card shop revels in its 20-year recipe of nine parts fun plus one part poor taste. A great selection of birthday cards hunkers down among trendy cultural commentary on T-shirts, political humor on buttons, sexual humor on cards in the "over 21" section (no minors allowed).

KIDS *means it's a good place to bring kids.*

▼

GIFTS AND STATIONERY

Julia Collection
1016 SW Morrison,
274-9308 (map:I1)
Mon-Sat

A glorious mishmash of everything from Russian lacquer boxes and brooches to dashing barrettes of bright leather dripping seed pearls and steel. African and Indonesian wall masks startle; a perfect model bicycle (in foot-high splendor) surprises. A good find: repro jewelry from, say, the Tang dynasty, for $12.

Lora Davis Ltd
25-1 NW 23rd Pl,
223-9030 (map:FF6)
Mon-Sat

Lora Davis' shop has gained a reputation as the place to find that perfect gift. These days tableware and linens are giving way to other interior niceties—but everything is interesting.

Made in Oregon Shops
7000 Airport Wy (and
branches), 282-7827
(map:CC3)
Every day

Where everything is made, caught, or grown in Oregon (smoked salmon, conversation-piece wooden slugs, Pendleton clothes, hazelnuts, wines, and, of course, myrtlewood). What do you expect from a store whose first venture (now seven branches) was at PDX? For a catalog, call (800) 828-9673, out of state; (800) 428-9673 in Oregon.

Plate du Jour
728 NW 23rd Ave,
248-0350;
(800) 782-1590 for bridal
registry (map:FF6)
Every day

See Home Accessories in this chapter.

Oregon Peace Institute
Peace Resource Center
SW 9th Ave and Alder St
(Galleria), 228-7422
(map:H2)
Every day

A necessary stop for the politically correct shopper. Over 20 peace groups thrive in the Rose City, and this store (with merchandise from most) gives peacemongers the chance to put their money where their mouths are: hopeful sweatshirt slogans, and basketfuls of the mandatory buttons and bumper stickers. For teachers, the education-oriented store offers much to enhance the curriculum. Staffed by volunteers, the Resource Center earns two-thirds of the Oregon Peace Institute's annual budget. The more scientifically inclined may prefer reading material from the Physicians for Social Responsibility office in suite 500 (274-2720), open two to three days a week.

The Perfume House
3328 SE Hawthorne
Blvd, 234-5375
(map:GG5)
Every day

The ultimate in olfactory stimulation: Chris Tsefelas' perfume house has been praised by the likes of Yves St. Laurent and Jean Patou as the finest in the world. You can sniff exquisite scents, from the rare Russian "Czarina" perfumes to "Corina" from the Patrician House, introduced at the 1962 Seattle World's Fair and considered one of the greatest perfumes ever created. Prices range from $2 for a sample-sized vial to $8,500 worth of L'Air d'Or.

The Real Mother Goose
SW 9th Ave and Yamhill
St (and branches),
223-9510 (map:H2)
Every day

See Galleries in Arts chapter.

Salutations
219 SW Ash St, 224-8248
(map:J5)
Every day

Salutations is Portland's best little card shop, located in an obscure space in Old Town a stone's throw from the Saturday Market. Whimsical owner Lu Ann Schreiber will occasionally paint chairs or tailor a bag to suit her passing fancy. The custom-designed bags are for sale, but usually they are given away to customers who make large purchases. Closed Sundays, January–March.

Sunbow Gallery
206 SW Stark St,
221-0258 (map:H5)
Every day

Dazzle
704 NW 23rd Ave,
224-1294 (map:FF7)
Every day

A ray of inspiration: Sunbow is always one step ahead of everyone else, with original creations and ethnic objects. Its newer northwest store, Dazzle, has walls that suggest the trendy southwestern style, but the wacky merchandise throws any sort of interior design plan into chaos. Free giftwrapping year-round.

V Claire
121 NW 23rd Ave,
222-2033 (map:FF6)
Every day

A table set with dishes from V Claire always reflects good taste. And it's these tabletop items that will be passed on to future generations. A reassuring sense of heartwarming holidays to come and special moments about to happen pervades this store.

Zoolooz
115 SW Ash St, 223-9320
(map:J6)
Every day

Still the place for a quick fix. Two levels of inexpensive goof—Marilyn Monroe T-shirts, anodized aluminum Slinkys, and saw-horse cows. An entire room of cards upstairs.

HARDWARE

1874 House
8070 SE 13th Ave,
233-1874 (map:II5)
Tues-Sat

Architectural remnants that most homeowners ripped out decades ago are found at 1874. A jumble of venerable light shades and fixtures, antique and reproduction hardware, old doors, windows, shutters, and mantels all wait to be reinstalled. Younger than much of its contents, this place has been around for over 20 years.

Hippo Hardware and Trading Company
207 Ash St, 231-1444 (map:I9)
Mon-Sat

Hippo is the place that fathers, tinkerers, and movie producers dream of: it's packed with architectural gems from mantels to vintage nuts and bolts. A potbelly stove and a wonderfully quirky staff keep you smiling as you paw through organized bins of clutter. If you can't find something, ask; if they don't have it they might just be able to splice, cut, or file something to fit.

Rejuvenation House Parts Company
901 N Skidmore St, 249-2038 (map:EE5)
Mon-Sat

This north Portland store has quietly built a nationwide catalog business for superior reproductions of turn-of-the-century and craftsman-style light fixtures—and there's even more in the store. The owner, Jim Kelly, offers a wealth of advice to do-it-yourselfers as well as licensed architects.

Uptown Hardware
27 NW 23rd Pl, 227-5375 (map:FF7)
Mon-Sat

The northwest district's favorite do-all shop. Bring 'em anything that's broken and they'll help you fix it. This 39-year-old family-owned business doesn't get into heavy machinery, but it does get into everything else. A knowledgeable, service-minded staff that's out to answer every need.

Wacky Willy's
417 SE 11th Ave, 234-6864 (map:J1)
Mon-Sat

A cross between a surplus store, a museum, and a joke shop, Wacky Willy's is a strange and zany place where you can find just about anything, from 27,000 pieces of Plexiglas to a hundred telephones from some office building that closed down. He unites the old and the new with a smile and a lot of advice. If you're looking for something you can't even describe you might just stumble upon it at Wacky Willy's.

WC Winks Hardware
903 NW Davis St, 227-5536 (map:K3)
Mon-Fri

We're not too sure that Jayne Kilkenny's father intended to stock 50,000 items when he opened this hardware store in 1909. But everything from 1,000 sizes of springs to 36 different wire sizes gives Winks a full house. An impressive assortment of outdated, odd, and funny types of things. No housewares, though.

HOME ACCESSORIES

Ann Sacks' Tile and Stone
500 NW 23rd Ave, 222-7125 (map:FF7)
Mon-Sat

Primarily a showroom for tiles from all over: many custom lines, some set designs (made to order), and imports from Italy, Spain, Portugal, and France. Ann Sacks is always on the lookout for designs which speak to an aesthetic not addressed elsewhere. Her own line includes villa-style floor tiles and colorful relief tiles.

The Arrangement
4210 NE Fremont Ave,
287-4440 (map:FF4)
Every day

Off the normal retail track, this friendly shop in the Alameda neighborhood overflows with ever-changing decorative items for your home. The staff will work with your colors, fabrics, photos, or whatever to create just the right wreath or table arrangement to fit your decor.

Embry & Co
4709 SW Beaverton-
Hillsdale Hwy, 244-1646
(map:HH7)
Mon-Sat

This shop is packed with folk art, antiques, furniture, and other homey treasures. The stock changes often since owner Embry Savage frequently returns from travels abroad with armloads of new merchandise.

The Gazebo Gallery–Restaurant
11 Mt Jefferson Tce, Lake
Oswego, 635-2506
(map:LL7)
Tues-Sat

You can poke around to your heart's desire in this restaurant-cum-gallery-cum-antique shop while you're waiting for lunch. You'll find baskets, pots and planters, lamps, various hand-thrown pottery pieces, and paintings, many of which were created by local artists. Proprietor Elizabeth Morrow's selection is as imaginative as she is.

Geri Miner Ltd
524 NW 23rd Ave,
242-2539 (map:FF6)
Mon-Sat

Three years on 23rd makes Geri Miner an old-timer in this part of town, especially for such merchandise as antique quilts and bent-willow furniture. Miner's one of the few with a full selection of MacKenzie-Childs Ltd pottery, and she can special order those pieces you might want to add to your collection. The staff offers distinctive gift wrapping, as well as free shipping.

Impulse Interiors
921 SW Morrison St
(Galleria), 227-1187
(map:I2)
Every day

If you don't like black, red, and white, stay clear of this high-tech '90s shop. Anything in hard lines and cool colors fits in here, from computer tables to tea kettles. Functional items with a whimsical bent.

Pier 1
5331 SW Macadam Ave
(and branches), 248-0359
(map:HH6)
Every day

Over the years, Pier 1 has consistently kept pace with the trends, offering the latest colors and styles at comfortable prices. The Portland stores are no exception. Recently, we've seen wicker furniture, chintz pillows, rag rugs, pottery lamps, and window shades. In the realm of tabletop accessories, it's tough to beat the selection of colorful, sturdy pottery and the wide assortment of placemats and flatware. Baskets have always been a strong point—if they don't have it, you probably don't need it.

Plate du Jour
728 NW 23rd Ave,
248-0350;

Strictly tabletop. Owner Cookie Yoelin knows how to find casual stoneware and elegant bone china and combine them in appealing displays. In business for only

(800) 782-1590 for bridal registry (map:FF6)
Every day

three years, it's a good spot to purchase wedding gifts. A complete selection of Fitz and Floyd dinnerware, along with Christian Dior, Limoges, and Dansk. If you can't find it, Cookie will gladly order it. Free gift wrap.

Storables
2405 W Burnside,
Uptown Shopping Center
(and branches), 221-4500
(map:FF6)
Every day

Storables got its start in 1981 by getting others organized. Closet organizers, shelving cut to order, bright-colored grids, and wire basket systems interlock to create order—or at least the appearance of it. Now with five Portland stores (and three in Seattle) it's come out of the closet and into the bedroom, kitchen, and living room.

Virginia Jacobs
2328 NW Westover Pl,
241-8436 (map:FF6)
Mon-Sat

Portland's finest bed and bath shop does a good job of exposing us hinterlanders to the finer things in life: crisp Palais Royal linens, plush Fieldcrest towels, white goose-down comforters, delicate soaps and scents. Or custom design your own look with their lightweight upholstery fabrics and other yard goods. Not for the budget conscious.

IMPORTS

Arthur W. Erickson Fine Arts
1030 SW Taylor St,
227-4710 (map:H1)
Mon-Fri

An astonishingly eclectic melange of whatever the owner happens to fancy: a fragment of Hittite sculpture ($35), a long, all-bead Sioux blanket band ($1,030). A 1,000-year-old clay whistle from South America is $48, and you'll find it hard to resist the impulse to buy a witty Japanese iron insect as a table decoration.

Designs of Scandinavia
2173 NE Broadway,
288-3045 (map:FF5)
Mon-Sat

Whimsical Scandinavian designs abound, from the 65-cent red wooden candlestick to a glorious handknit $170 Norwegian sweater, properly silver-buttoned, with all the traditional patterns in blue, cream, and gray. Lots of Iittala glass from Finland, sensible wooden trivets, greeting cards, lazy Susans in teak, and tartlet tins. Crowded and cosy, easy parking.

The Design Source
600 SW 10th Ave (The Galleria), 223-3098
(map:I2)
Mon-Fri
(by appointment only)

See Gifts in this chapter.

Inspectors for the Best Places series accept no free meals or accommodations; the book has no sponsors or advertisers.

SHOPPING

Eye of Ra
*5331 SW Macadam Ave
(Johns Landing),
224-4292 (map:II6)
Every day*

See Apparel in this chapter.

Image Gallery
*1026 SW Morrison St,
224-9629 (map:I1)
Mon-Sat*

Owner Beverly Shoemaker visits Mexican villages each year to ferret out the shop's fine folk art; etchings and paintings by Pacific Northwest artists share the space. There are lots of nooks and crannies in this three-room shop—plan to browse.

Kathleen Connolly Irish Shop
*725 SW 10th Ave,
228-4482 (map:H1)
Mon-Sat*

No fashion revolution in the Emerald Isle: this shop is resolutely traditional, selling tweed caps, Aran knits, blackthorn walking sticks, Waterford crystal. Best buys include gossamer Irish linen in gleaming black at $13–$20 a yard, and silver Kells chokers etched in brass, with matching earrings. Lyons tea is here, and to go with it, Scottish(!) oatcakes.

Julia's
*1016 SW Morrison St,
274-9308 (map:I1)
Mon-Sat*

See Gifts and Stationery in this chapter.

La Paloma
*6316 SW Capitol Hwy
(Hillsdale Shopping Center), 246-3417 (map:II6)
Mon-Sat*

See Apparel in this chapter.

Nelson's Antiques
*521 SW 11th Ave,
228-4436 (map:I2)
Mon-Sat*

Nothing screams or flashes, not even the prices, which are far lower than in Seattle or San Francisco. Chinese lacquered bamboo birdcages, fairylands of curving lines with wrought-iron handles, are $165, though a Sotheby's catalog in the shop prices them at $1,000.

Panca Sikha Inc
*818 SW 20th Ave,
228-8833 (map:H2)
Mon-Sat*

Panca Sikha means love, prosperity, and happiness in Burmese. Stun your all-American friends by displaying a gilt Buddha studded with bright stones ($141). Revel in the lushness of the southern Orient.

Scandia Imports
*10020 SW Beaverton-
Hillsdale Hwy, 643-2424*

Finnish Iittala glass, gleaming brown stoneware by Arabia, and heavy pewter candelabras from Denmark dazzle at surprisingly low prices. Homesick Scandina-

(map:HH9)
Mon-Sat

vians can buy birthday cards in their native languages, good Swedish mint pastilles, and enough candles for a hundred Santa Lucia nights.

Simpatico Mexico
515 SW Broadway,
223-1734 (map:I3)
Mon-Sat

A colorful gem in the midst of jewelers' row on Broadway. Mexican glass goblets that catch the light; sturdy Ecuadoran handknit sweaters in bold combinations; and hanger upon hanger of long cotton Josefa dresses that carry you gracefully from the beach to the fireside.

Wold's Loft Gallery
8775 SW Cascade Ave
(Cascade Plaza),
Beaverton, 646-2679
(map:JJ9)
Every day

This gallery is rich in Southwest Indian art and artisan work—great heavy turquoise and silver pendants, traditional pottery in terra cotta, Acoma pots from New Mexico in black and cream. The terra-cotta doll families make heartwarming children's gifts.

JEWELRY AND REPAIRS

Art a la Carte
525 SW Broadway,
221-0431 (map:H3)
Mon-Sat

Costume jewelry with punch. In addition to Portland's omnipresent three-tier drops of trader beads and old coins, this enchanting shop above Flowers by Dorcas has bold clip earrings from Greece and Mexico ($15–30) and many silvery barrettes ($12).

Collaboration
5200 SW Macadam Ave,
Suite 530, 242-4945
(map:HH6)
By appointment only

Seven artists work out of the same space on custom-designed jewelry. Each artist has a specialty, from wild electronic baubles to silver charm bracelets. Go with a dream and leave with a jewel.

Dan Marx
511 SW Broadway,
228-5090 (map:H3)
Mon-Sat

For 101 years Portlanders and their visitors have been buying from Dan Marx (the firm has *two* 800 numbers)—something must be right. Clean-lined jewelry, gorgeous stones, and the staff's quiet politeness set the timid at ease. 18-karat gold is used throughout this immaculate little shop, whose senior members came directly from Strasbourg.

Goldmark
1000 SW Taylor St,
224-3743 (map:H1)
Tues-Sat

There's nothing Cal Brockman of Goldmark likes better than to have a few ancestral stones tossed at him: he loves to create strong, dazzling—or perhaps tendrilly and delicate—pieces out of unworn jewelry.

Jewelers Four
14312 SW Allen Blvd,
Beaverton, 646-8700
(map:HH9)
Tues-Sat

Repairs are the strong suit here, where experienced jewelry designer John Snyder reigns as one of Portland's finest jewelers. In the Safeway plaza near Murray, he makes classic pieces on the spot.

Lapstar Two
4680 SW Hall Blvd,
Beaverton, 646-1718
(map:HH9)
Mon-Fri

Knowledgeable and pleasant staff cheerfully undertake repairs on all kinds of jewelry. They'll even steer you to a helpful gem shop for special needs. Traditional designs on display.

Jerome Margulis
801 SW Broadway,
227-1153 (map:G2)
Mon-Sat

Sleek, glossy, and very spacious. Neoclassic designs by David Margulis, such as a round lapis plaque pendant centered with a small, perfect diamond. Unusual pieces like the sculpted silver cat placed horizontally across a black suede wristband ($198). A family-owned business for 60 years, but it's hardly a traditional shop.

Silver Hammer
840 SW Broadway,
223-8940 (map:G3)
Tues-Sat

Custom designers Gary Swank and Curt Oldenstadt also work in gold and platinum—though silver is preferred. On-the-spot creations of bold earrings, necklaces like something from an Egyptian tomb, and handsome silver chains. Vintage watches here are an extra lure.

KITCHENWARE

Cloudtree and Sun
112 N Main St, Gresham,
666-8495
Every day

Today's home and kitchen standbys: Le Creuset, Chantal, Mikasa crystal, and squat Italian highball glasses. Individual gourmet goods rarely found elsewhere. Lots of taste and bustle, friendly (and free) gift wrapping. Cloudtree flows into the lively Main Street Cafe, where people pause, refresh, and shop on.

Cook's Corner
Beaverton Town Square,
Beaverton, 644-0100
(map:HH8)
Every day

Quite the crown jewel of Portland's cookware outlets. Temptations include French and Japanese white porcelain cookware, terra-cotta taco holders, even a slicer you clamp to a shelf for slenderizing your string beans. Lots of inexpensive gadgets tucked among the Le Creusets—a gift-giver's mecca.

Kitchen Kaboodle
8788 SW Hall Blvd (and
branches), 643-5491
(map:II9)
Every day

Here's a 15-year-old chain store that saw an eat-on-the-run trend and intelligently adapted to it, combining outstanding kitchenware (Krups, Gerber) with a generous selection of stunning tabletop wares.

Kobos Company
*5331 SW Macadam Ave
(and branches), 222-5226
(map:II6)
Every day*

David and Susan Kobos founded a coffee-roasting business in 1973; now the enterprise has grown to include
chefs' tools as well as coffee beans. There are several
branches, but the Johns Landing store has the largest
assortment of kitchenware, including a good selection of
knives. And when they dull, Kobos' knife-sharpening
service will restore their edge by hand.

LINGERIE

The Best Underneath
*3543 NE Broadway,
287-3218 (map:FF4)
Tues-Sat*

With its Oriental flair, the subtle smell of incense, and
walls covered in teal and rose, this shop will show you
how to pamper yourself Asian-style. Owner Pam Best
has managed to capture the mystique of the Orient and
blend it with a little practicality. A gift of a sachet goes to
each of her clients.

Jean-Marie Lingerie
*25-2 NW 23rd Pl,
224-4598 (map:FF7)
Mon-Sat*

Lingerie in this Uptown Shopping Center shop isn't lace
and frill, but rather silk and cotton done in modest elegance. Even those unfamiliar with such luxuries will feel
comfortable exploring a wide variety of European styles
offered here.

Zona
*2700 NW 185th Ave,
629-5865
Every day*

Zona, the owner, believes in carrying all price ranges as
well as all sizes, from petite to huge, in this expansive
shop. In addition, it's the only place around that does bra
fittings for women who have had a mastectomy.

MARKETS AND DELICATESSENS

Anzen Importers
*736 NE Martin Luther
King Jr Blvd, 233-5111
(map:FF5)*

*4021 SW 117th Ave,
Beaverton, 627-0913
(map:HH9)
Every day*

For all things Japanese—fish and nori for sushi, pickled
ginger, live geoduck, fresh yellowfin tuna, and octopus
—Anzen is the ticket. The Beaverton branch has more
elbow room, but both locations carry upwards of 10,000
items—prepared deli foods (sushi and bentos, among
them), plenty of packaged and canned goods, and a large
selection of sake and Asian beers.

Becerra's Spanish Food
*3022 NE Glisan St,
234-7785 (map:FF5)
Every day*

The groceries come from Mexico (canned cactus!),
Southern California, and South America, and Becerra's
customers come from as far away as Spokane. Mexican
white cheeses are a specialty, as is the store's own beef
and pork chorizo. Like many ethnic groceries, Becerra's
rents videotapes—in Spanish, of course.

Circus Produce
*110 SW Yamhill St
(Yamhill Marketplace),
222-1683 (map:G4)
Every day*

A glance at Circus' produce tells you that American eating habits must be changing: endive and escarole, chayote squash and purple potatoes, fresh figs and Florida starfruit. A prime downtown location keeps prices on the spendy side, and reports of limp vegetables steer us more toward the exotics that are tough to find elsewhere.

Comella & Son & Daughter
*6959 SW Garden Home
Rd, 245-5033 (map:II8)
Every day*

Store founder Frank Comella doesn't sit around in some back office. He's often arranging produce and handing out melon or maybe orange samples. The variety—from kohlrabi to taro root, deli sausages to fresh flowers— draws his customers. What's more, produce prices are good.

Corno Foods
*711 SE Union Ave,
232-3157 (map:GG5)
Every day*

A Portland institution (almost a museum) created by the late Jimmy Corno, now operated by his son. An incredible selection of produce and an active (though not always fully stocked) meat counter anchor the store. Prices can be quite attractive. Unfortunately, staff turnover and other problems have hurt the store's ability to delight as it used to. Still, it's a fun alternative to too-slick marketing elsewhere.

The Daily Grind
*4026 SE Hawthorne
Blvd, 233-5521
(map:GG4)
Sun-Fri*

What?! No chocolate, no meat, no white sugar, no coffee? This no-frills natural foods store proves the day doesn't have to be a grind without a caffeine fix. In the bakery, healthy ingredients go into tasty and inexpensive muffins and cinnamon rolls. A dozen breads include several salt- and wheat-free loaves. Much of the produce is organically grown, including that in the salad bar. Closes early on Friday.

Elephant's Delicatessen
*13 NW 23rd Ave,
224-3955 (map:FF6)
Mon-Sat*

Well-heeled food lovers can now Elephax their lunch order for a three-cheese on rye or smoked turkey on pumpernickel spread with homemade herb mayonnaise, to be delivered by noon. The newly expanded kitchen also bakes numerous breads, voluptuous desserts, and frozen take-home dinner entrees (seafood strudel or cannelloni marinara). Be decisive: service can be a bit impatient.

Fong Chong & Co.
*301 NW 4th Ave,
223-1777 (map:K4)
Every day*

This is one of Portland's busiest Chinese markets, perhaps because of the succulent roasted and barbecued pork and ribs and the Peking duck available for take-out, cooked at the adjoining Cantonese restaurant of the same name. Narrow aisles bulge with sacks of rice, teas, noodles, seasonings, and sauces from China, Hong Kong, and Taiwan.

Fong's Market
2929 SE Powell Blvd,
234-9656 (map:HH4)
Every day

A clean, well-lit place for Asian food. Stocked with foods fresh and packaged—from Vietnam, Thailand, Cambodia, Laos, Indonesia, and the Philippines. Chac Fong can recommend the best curry paste or ginger tea for your needs and explain, if you ask, how Chinese preserved eggs are made.

Food Front
2375 NW Thurman St,
222-5658 (map:FF6)
Every day

The bulk foods are for the health-conscious, and the trendier fare (Salumeria di Carlo sausages, Sichuan noodle salad, Vietnamese steamed buns, European chocolates) is for the socially conscious. The wines are priced conservatively, and there are always two choices in the produce department: organic or non.

Golden Leaf Bakery & Deli
1334 SE Hawthorne
Blvd, 231-9758
(map:GG5)
Mon-Sat

Even those without an everyday need for Lebanese spices, rose water, or thyme pickle will learn to frequent this Middle Eastern grocery. The hummus and baba ghanouj are addictive, especially when joined with Golden Loaf's own pocket bread. Manaiish, a crisp round flatbread topped with spices and sesame seeds, is a good alternative.

Greek Deli & Grocery
1740 E Burnside,
232-0274 (map:FF7)
Mon-Sat

See Restaurants chapter.

International Food Bazaar
915 SW 9th Ave,
228-1960 (map:H2)
Every day

You can smell this multicultural market from the sidewalk above. An amazing range of goods is sold here: ghee, teas, and lentils from India; olives and feta cheese from Greece; Pakistani and Indian basmati rice; halal meat and poultry for Moslems; and kosher pickles from Israel. Sit at one of the lunch tables and travel abroad vicariously.

Kruger's Specialty Produce
1200 NE Broadway
(Holladay's Market),
288-4236 (map:FF5)
Every day

A few exotics—edible flowers, baby bok choy, purple potatoes—are mixed among more familiar (and some organic) produce. Kruger's also sells bulk and packaged natural foods and gourmet items, from breakfast cereals to dried pasta. Unforgiving holiday prices, year-round.

If you've found a place around town that you think is a Best Place, send in the report form at the back of the book. If you're unhappy with one of the places, please let us know why. We depend on reader input.

Lair Hill Market
2823 SW 1st Ave,
227-4269 (map:HH6)
Mon-Sat

Copies of *Gourmet*, *The Wine Spectator*, and *Chocolatier* on this market's magazine rack give fair indication of what to expect here. The building is circa 1912, the refrigeration cases are from the '40s, but the select groceries and wines are yupscaled to the '90s. An espresso in one hand and Wisconsin Cheddar soup or vegetarian lasagne in the other is a common sight.

Lake Grove Market
16331 SW Bryant Rd,
Lake Oswego, 636-8457
(map:KK5)
Every day

This store is relatively new in the somewhat lacking Lake Grove business district, and is still establishing itself department by department. The seafood section holds promise and can be a reasonable source of fresh, well-priced seafood. This establishment clearly wants to do a great job—the spirit and dollars are there—now someone needs to think the task through.

**Martinotti's Cafe &
Delicatessen**
404 SW 10th Ave,
224-9028 (map:J2)
Mon-Sat

See Wines, Beers, and Spirits in this chapter.

**Mekong Oriental Foods
& Gifts**
1805 NE 39th Ave,
281-7108 (map:FF5)
Every day

Jasmine rice, Vietnamese, Thai, and Japanese noodles, curry pastes, a dozen different chile sauces, and fresh Thai basil (from Hawaii) are just some of what's available at this mostly Thai grocery. It's a tiny place; the helpful clerks know their inventory.

Nature's Fresh Northwest!
3449 NE 24th Ave (and
branches), 288-3414
(map:EE5)
Every day

In the beginning, Nature's was the place for nitty-gritty-sprouty bulk food and garden supplies. Today the line between health food and other food, including gourmet fare, has blurred. Nature's is hip to the changing times, offering an excellent range of common and less common produce, much of it organically grown, along with hormone- and nitrate-free meats, a sophistication of cheeses and wines, deli fare (Sichuan noodle salad to mushroom pate), and desserts as decadent as you dare. The remodeled (and finally spacious) northeast store has a deli, as does the large Beaverton store (4000 SW 117th Avenue, Beaverton, 646-3824, map:II5), with full-service meat and seafood counter, and Nature's Deli (333 S State Street, Lake Oswego, 635-3374, map: KK5). The original (5909 SW Corbett Street, 244-3934, map:HH6) does not.

If you are traveling in the Pacific Northwest, consult Northwest Best Places, *the only reliable guide to superior restaurants, lodgings, and attractions in Washington, Oregon, and British Columbia.*

MARKETS AND DELICATESSENS

Pastaworks
3735 SE Hawthorne
Blvd, 232-1010
(map:GG5)
Every day

As a whole, Pastaworks is all things Italian. And it's a good thing, too, considering the dearth of Italian restaurants in the city. Three businesses (Pastaworks, Powell's Books for Cooks, and Salumeria di Carlo—see Books section and Meats section in this chapter) share the most popular address in the Hawthorne district's good-food ghetto. An interesting assemblage of those elements that, combined, make for civilized lives: fresh pastas, pesto and chanterelle sauces, 35 kinds of olive oil, herbed vinegars, whole-bean coffees, take-home entrees (torta rustica, polenta), cookbooks, preservative-free sausages, Spanish cheeses—and what a wine section!

It's doubtful a better Italian wine selection exists west of the Mississippi, with some bottlings so esoteric as to escape mention even in Italian wine books. Don't hesitate to ask for help—you may need information from Don and Peter, the owners, about this collection, even if you think you know wines. Pay for purchases from any of the three shops at the front registers.

Pasta a la Carte
2309 NW Kearney St,
222-4879 (map:FF6)
Tues-Sat

One of Portland's original fresh-pasta outlets. Bundles of pasta keep company with the ever-popular tortellini and ravioli and their generous fillings. On any given day you might find corn ravioli with jalapeno filling or pumpkin ravioli stuffed with pumpkin and roasted hazelnuts. Sauces to match.

Sheridan Fruit Inc
409 SE Martin Luther
King Blvd, 235-9353
(map:GG5)
Every day

Founded in 1916, this is one of the last remnants of the city's old Produce Row. Sheridan, like its long-time rival Corno's down the street, is now much more than standard produce: bulk foods, a full-service meat counter, and local breads. Snip some fresh herbs.

Strohecker's
2855 SW Patton Rd,
223-7391 (map:GG7)
Every day

You *can* walk out of here with a carton of milk or a prescription, but this 87-year-old Portland institution is designed primarily for serious gastronomes—with ample cash. From orchids to British bangers, fresh Matsutake mushrooms to vintage wines (some with three-digit price tags), Strohecker's has it. An outstanding full-service meat and seafood department (domestic lamb, sport-caught fish, local beef) and a small showcase of Oregon products make West Hillers very proud to have Strohecker's as their neighborhood market. It's worth taking advantage of the valet parking—otherwise finding a slot can be a hassle.

Wizer's Oswego Foods
330 SW 1st St, Lake
Oswego, 636-1414
(map:KK5)
Every day

A second-generation food store, Wizer's does not smoke meats or prepare special recipe items, although they do a good job filling customers' special requests at the meat and seafood counter. A reputable wine cellar. See Wine, Beer, and Spirits in this chapter.

MEATS

Bill's Beef House Meats
18238 SE Division St,
Gresham, 665-9013
Mon-Sat

No lamb here; as the name states, it is (mostly) a beef house. An unassuming storefront opens onto a wide selection of well-trimmed beef and pork cuts. The store sells its own smoked meats and a variety of fresh sausages. Try the peppered bacon and dry-cured hams. A small poultry selection where fresh turkeys sans injections and hormone treatments are available.

Burlingame Grocery
8502 SW Terwilliger
Blvd, 246-0711
(map:HH6)
Every day

See Seafood in this chapter.

Edelweiss Sausage Company and Deli
3119 SE 12th Ave,
238-4411 (map:GG5)
Mon-Sat

This crowded, nose-pleasing store is famous for its German and other European foods and sundries, and for its wonderful meat and cheese case. Stacked chock-a-block are dozens of kinds of sausages (try the spicy beer kind), as well as such favorites as Black Forest hams and some of Portland's best bacons. Ask for a taste.

Fetzer's German Sausage and Deli
2485 SW Cedar Hills
Blvd, Beaverton,
641-6300 (map:HH8)
Mon-Sat

Ready for a picnic, a trip to the coast, or a ski weekend? Before you go, stop by Fetzer's for homemade German bratwurst, blood sausage, bauerschinken, weisswurst, Black Forest ham, smoked meats....The hams are excellent, the beef always slightly overcooked at this lively, stuffed-to-the-rafters store. Game processing and smoking available.

Gartner's Country Meat Market
7450 NE Killingsworth
St, 252-7801 (map:EE3)
Mon-Sat

OK, you want a red-meat market? This is *the* no-flourishes, serious-about-meat store. Busy but truly pleasant counter people staff a large, open preparation and display case area. Roasts, whole filets, steaks, chops, hams, and bacons fill the L-shaped meat case (no lamb, though). Smoky, aromatic smells spice the air,

---

Map locators refer to the fold-out map included in this book. Single letters refer to the Downtown Portland map; double letters refer to the Greater Portland map on the other side.

and meat saws whir in the background. Enthusiasm and pride imbue the store with a feeling of quality and value. They smoke their own hams and bacons, which are delicious. Try these guys.

Hartwig Retail Meat Market
2131 NW Kearney St,
226-3875 (map:FF7)
Mon-Sat

Gary Gilgan, manager/partner in this retail market, has been in the meat business since he was 15. His experience and expertise have allowed him to fashion a retail business of the highest quality. The trimmed-meat prices are measurably higher than elsewhere; however, the quality is unquestionably superb. Check out the sought-after bottlings and good values in the wine section, too.

Meating Place Meat Market and Smokehouse
3172 NW 185th Pl,
645-6811
Mon-Sat

An array of sports accoutrements on display invites browsing in this wonderful long, narrow meat store. Quality is good for red meats and poultry (specialties include smoked sausages and hams); the bacon (smoked on the premises) is a treat. The owner cheerfully accommodates requests and queries.

McFarland's Meats Inc
1200 NE Broadway
(Holladays Market),
284-3232 (map:FF5)
Mon-Sat

The proprietors are old hands at the meat business, and they are good at helping customers select and prepare meats for specific occasions. While prices are somewhat higher than those at supermarkets, the assistance can be of great value. Quality is good to excellent.

Nature's Fresh Northwest!
4000 SW 117th Ave,
Beaverton, 646-3824
(map:HH8)
Every day

See Markets and Delicatessens in this chapter.

Otto's Sausage Kitchen & Meat Market
4138 SE Woodstock Blvd,
771-6714 (map:II4)
Mon-Sat

The third generation of ownership can be seen on occasion, giggling behind the counter or munching on wieners. This solid, good-natured store is Germanic in spirit, with lots of smoked meats and homemade sausages. The smoked meats are delicious, the stuffed chicken breasts their own recipe, and the sausages are ground and stuffed in the back room. Don't pass up the hams, smoked and dry cured. An evenly balanced wine selection including good sparklies and excellent French choices. Good beers, too.

Phil's Uptown Meats
17 NW 23rd Pl (Uptown
Shopping Center),

Phil the Butcher looks like the Original Butcher. The good news is that Phil knows meats. This is a small, black-and-white-tiled shop, with white porcelain display

224-9541 *(map:FF7)*
Tues-Sat

cases, butcher blocks, fan-type butcher scales, and gorgeous quality meats and poultry with a small seafood selection. Also of interest is the domestic lamb—a rare commodity.

**Salumeria di Carlo
(Pastaworks)**
*3735 SE Hawthorne
Blvd, 232-1010
(map:GG4)
Mon-Sat*

As growth led to boom, the fare at Pastaworks expanded to include, among other things, the sausages of Fred Carlo, a Portlander of Sicilian descent who uses Carlo family recipes. Now an integral part of this fascinating store, Salumeria di Carlo presents prosciutto-style ham, marinated chicken, fresh sausages (such as chanterelle, Lyonnaise, rabbit, seafood, and chicken), and a fantastic boneless stuffed pig.

White's Country Meats
*1206 SE Orient Dr,
Gresham, 666-0967
Mon-Sat*

Gresham residents highly recommend this establishment: it's a straightforward, good-quality meat store with its own smokehouse and processing facilities. Fresh, honestly trimmed, reasonably priced meats. A variety of roasts, steaks, and ground meats are available; poultry and pork look better than at most other meat counters.

NURSERIES AND GARDEN CENTERS

The mild climate and fertile soil of the Willamette Valley allow Portlanders access to some of the best nurseries in the country. Nurseries that most gardeners know only through mail-order catalogs are just a short drive outside the city limits. Most notable include **Swan Island Dahlias** in Canby (995 NW 22nd Avenue, 1-266-7711), the nation's largest grower of dahlia bulbs; and **Northwoods Nursery** in Molalla (28696 South Cramer Road, 1-651-3737) for food-bearing plants, from hardy kiwis to persimmons. The businesses listed below provide some of the city's finest garden supplies.

Barn Owl Nursery
*22999 SW Newland Rd,
Wilsonville, 638-0387
(map:QQ9)
Wed-Sat (in season)*

One step inside the door and your nose knows: this is herb heaven. Dried herbs and herb soaps begin the list of fragrant gifts. What sets Barn Owl apart from scores of similar "country" boutiques is the fact that it's also a working nursery. Budding herbalists stroll through the acre of display gardens (April–July, October–November) and choose from over 100 herbs.

The Bovees Nursery
*1737 SW Coronado St,
244-9341 (map:KK5)*

Customers can wander under towering firs and among hundreds of types of rhododendrons in the display garden, examining neatly labeled mature samples of prospective purchases. The star rhodies and deciduous

Wed-Sun (closed Jan and mid-Aug to mid-Sept)

azaleas bloom nearly six months of the year, but trees, hardy perennials, and Northwest natives are also in abundance here.

Caprice Farms Nursery
15425 SW Pleasant Hill Rd, Sherwood, 625-7241 (map:PP8) Mon-Sat

Day lilies—for times when just yellow and orange won't do. There are nearly 80 varieties of these long-blooming beauties—blazing reds, shimmering whites, delicate lavenders—which dot the Rogers family's 4-acre nursery (mail-order catalogs available). Peony lovers should visit during Caprice's two open-house weekends in May, when 60 kinds of peonies bloom.

Dennis' 7 Dees Nursery and Landscaping
6025 SE Powell Blvd (and branches), 777-1421 (map:HH4) Every day

Years of appearing as the garden expert on local TV talk shows has made Dennis Snodgrass a familiar face in Portland; his real job, however, is running three garden centers and a florist shop. There's the standard array of gardening supplies alongside a smattering of plants ranging from trees to annuals. Three branches: Beaverton (10455 SW Barnes Road, 297-1058, map:GG9); Lake Oswego (1090 McVey Street, 636-4660, map:LL6); and NE Portland (6405 NE Glisan Street, 236-4712, map:GG3)—the last is a florist and gift shop only.

Dragonfly Gardens
2230 SE Hawthorne Blvd, 235-9150 (map:GG5) Every day

Dragonfly has built a loyal following by emphasizing unusual perennials and annuals—stocking not only blue, white, and purple delphiniums, for example, but rarer reddish-orange varieties as well. Herbs, indoor plants, and bonsai supplies, too. The staff is unusually well informed.

Drake's 7 Dees Nursery and Landscaping
16519 SE Star St, 255-9225 (map:GG1) Every day

Advice for gardeners, a telephone information line, and a regular newsletter are only a sampling of this southeast garden center's services. Plants and garden supplies are supplemented by more concrete Madonnas, deer, and birdbaths than you can shake a gnome at.

Gerber Gardens
15780 SW Boones Ferry Rd, Lake Oswego, 635-9414 (map:JJ6) Every day

Indoor offerings range from standard houseplants to palatial 3-foot-tall birdhouses; outdoors, a surprising number of plants pack the 1-acre lot, including hard-to-find blue poppies, weeping pines, and many dwarf conifers. Prices are sometimes a bit high, but bargain hunters will like the fall sales.

Kasch's Garden Center and Nursery
2500 SE Tacoma St (and

On the plus side: this well established chain has six Greater Portland locations and a broad range of garden goods. On the minus side: a sometimes spotty selection

*branches), 231-7711
(map:JJ5)
Every day*

at the smaller branch stores, and staffs whose expertise is far from consistent. Ornamental shrubs and spring bulbs are strong points. The main branch is best.

Kline Nursery Company

*Mailing address: PO Box 23161, Tigard, OR, 97223; 636-3923 (map:JJ8)
Tues-Sat (by appointment only)*

For more than 30 years, Kline has supplied Western gardens with ferns, lilies, Northwest native perennials, and—its specialty—10 varieties of cyclamen. At press time it was all being transplanted from Lake Oswego to new territory in Tigard; call first to verify the location. Sales are primarily wholesale (retail through the catalog), but interested individuals who call ahead may drop by and pick out their own plants (March–September).

Portland Nursery

*5050 SE Stark St, 231-5050 (map:GG4)
Every day*

Hands down, this is the city's finest nursery: an abundance of good-quality plants and supplies fills the 5-acre grounds. The perennials are especially bountiful, but many unusual trees and shrubs, witch hazels and Franklinia trees are stocked as well. The store's reputation owes much to its uniformly knowledgeable and helpful staff, ready to track down the answers to any questions they can't immediately answer themselves.

OUTDOOR GEAR

Andy & Bax Sporting Goods

*324 SE Grand Ave, 234-7538 (map:GG5)
Mon-Sat*

Andy & Bax is Portland's best rafting and whitewater resource. Heaps of personality, split three ways between rafting and whitewater equipment, piles of army and navy surplus, and family camping and cold-weather gear. The store also offers information on guides and beginner classes. Reasonable prices—some true bargains.

Athletic Department

*3255 SW Cedar Hills Blvd, Beaverton, 646-0691 (map:HH9)
Every day*

This was the original Nike store at the beginning of the running boom, when both runners and Nike were considered slightly demented. Then, when five years ago Nike turned its massive marketing attention to a full line of specialty stores, ex-Nike employee Danny Adams bought this shop. He hasn't changed it much. As far as he knows, it's the only non–Nike-owned Nike-only store in the country.

B&R Sportshoes

*2940 NE Alberta St, 281-5819 (map:EE5)
Every day*

B&R is now thirtysomething. It's a comfortable northeast Portland shop, but its barred windows suggest a slightly tough neighborhood. Good prices for kick-around clothes and discount athletic shoes for running, basketball, hiking, aerobics, court sports, and walking. Free Tootsie Roll with each purchase.

Beat Feet
2331 SW 6th Ave,
248-9820 (map:GG6)
Every day

The oldest running-only store has reclaimed its original name. At the foot of the popular Terwilliger Boulevard running route, and two blocks from Duniway Park's track. Tiny but well-stocked. Owner Jim Davis has stayed healthy running, and his store has an almost cult-like following.

Bicycle Repair Collective
4438 SE Belmont St,
233-0564 (map:GG4)
Mon-Sat

The Bicycle Repair Collective has only a handful of peers nationwide. It sells parts and accessories, rents work space, and gives classes on bike repair and maintenance. For $20 a year or $3 an hour, cyclists can tune their bikes and adjust their chains. A terrific resource.

The Bike Gallery
5329 NE Sandy Blvd,
281-9800 (map:EE4)
Every day
821 SW 11th Ave,
222-3821 (map:H1)
Mon-Sat

The Bike Gallery is to cycles what Nordstrom is to clothes. Begun as a small, family-run shop, it's now one of the country's finest bike dealers. All sales are guaranteed, so customer risk is minimal. Last year, the Bike Gallery bought Tailwind Outfitters (2625 SW Cedar Hills Blvd, 641-2580), adding a winter nordic-skiing season to the Beaverton store (moving nearer to Beaverton Mall). Its downtown store just moved, too, closer to the Multnomah County Library.

Bob's Bicycle Center
10950 SE Division St,
254-2663 (map:GG2)
Every day (closed Sunday
in winter)

Bob's started as a small BMX store and is now the largest single cycling shop in the Northwest. The stock of 2,000 bikes (now BMX to touring) clearly emphasizes family cycling. The service department is renowned for quality, as well as decent prices.

Cal Skate and Sport
213 NW Couch St,
223-0245 (map:K6)
Every day

Cal's is for kids. Primarily skateboards and surfboards, though a good place for snowboards and RollerBlades, too. A thriving mail-order business is conducted via Watts line.

Cascadden's Ski-Hike-Bike
1533 NW 24th Ave,
228-0945 (map:FF7)
Every day

Despite its trendy northwest address, Cascadden's is just enough off NW 23rd Avenue that parking's not a problem. It's a seasonal store: in winter, the shop specializes in servicing and selling alpine and nordic ski gear. In summer, the merchandise focuses on wacky clothes and comfortable gear for walking and hiking.

Countrysport
1201 SW Morrison St,
221-4545 (map:I1)
Mon-Sat

With the recent opening of Countrysport, Portland now has two specialty fly-fishing shops. The satellite store of a Seattle retailer, Countrysport bought the fly department from Oregon Mountain Community and expanded to 12th Avenue and Morrison Street. A great source for fishing friends of all levels.

Kaufmann's Streamborn Fly Shop
8861 SW Commercial St, Tigard, 639-7004 (map:KK9) Mon-Sat

Kaufmann's has been Portland's consummate fly shop for nearly 20 years. The knowledgeable staff can outfit you for fishing on the Clackamas or they can equip you for specialty fishing trips anywhere in the world. Besides one of the best selections of flies in the country, Kaufmann's offers fishing classes and fly-tying materials. Its catalog has made the store world-renowned.

The Mountain Shop
628 NE Broadway (and branches), 288-6768 (map:FF5) Every day

The Broadway branch of this store may well be the area's best downhill gear shop. It's certainly the most unabashed, with three floors of ski gear to help you perfect your style. The two other stores, at 17727 SW Boones Ferry Road in Lake Oswego (635-1170) and 9955 SW Beaverton-Hillsdale Highway in Beaverton (526-1032), are smaller.

Mrs. A's Surf Shop
2840 SE Powell Blvd, 235-7983 (map:HH5) Every day

Mrs. A's started in the Beach Boys days of long hair and long boards. Nowadays, all rad thrill-seeking water and cement action sports are covered by the merchandise and accessories here: snowboarding, boogie boarding, water-skiing, and sidewalk surfing—skateboarding, that is. Attitude-free shopping.

The Nike Store
920 SW 6th Ave, 241-2710 (map:G3)

7000 NE Airport Wy (Portland International Airport), 284-3558 (map:CC3) Every day

Nike is an attitude and an image, and the incredible new state-of-the-art downtown Portland store (in the former I. Magnin building) will open this summer to prove it. Interior designs were being kept secret as we went to press, but inside sources reveal that the 10,000-square-foot showcase will display the entire Nike line: all collections, all colors. The Portland space in PDX's retail row packs as much as it can into a small space. Runners can call the hotline for race information, 223-RUNS.

Northwest Fitness Supply Co
1338 NE Sandy Blvd, 231-1330 (map:FF5) Every day

Northwest Fitness might be the best all-around individual exercise store in the state. About half the place is devoted to dependable exercise equipment, from simple designs to the ultimate high-tech models. The other half includes a selection of athletic shoes for all paces. Outstanding women's fitness gear—swimwear, too.

Oregon Mountain Community
60 NW Davis St, 227-1038 (map:K6)

OMC is a two-season store: in winter, the popular Old Town outdoor store stocks up with skis; in summer, look for packs, tents, sleeping bags, and rock-climbing equipment. Other sorts of outdoor clothing and equip-

7000 NE Airport Wy
(Portland International
Airport), 287-1838
(map:CC3)
Every day

ment are available year-round. The sales staff has a tremendous amount of outdoor experience—they just need some coaxing.

Osborn & Ulland
3225 SW Cedar Hills
Blvd, Beaverton,
643-8457 (map:HH9)
Every day

Osborn & Ulland has long been a model of low-key consistency in prices and service. After two years in Lloyd Center, they've moved to the other side of town. A reliable, family-oriented place for ski gear (all kinds), golf, and racquet sports.

Pacesetter Athletics
4431 SE Woodstock Blvd,
777-3214 (map:HH4)

11355 SW Scholls Ferry
Rd, Beaverton, 643-4847
(map:HH9)
Mon-Sat

Some of the area's better athletes work in the store, so the merchandise reflects a slightly more technical bias than that of the typical running store. In addition to more than 115 models of running shoes, Pacesetter sponsors a 30-person racing team. A casual, helpful atmosphere for customers not as fast or knowledgeable as the staff.

Phidippides
333 S State St, Lake
Oswego, 635-3577
(map:KK6)
Every day

This small, service-oriented place owned and staffed by runners lets customers run in new shoes before they buy them. Like old-time podiatrists, staff will listen to your injury history, training program description, and personal preferences to fit you with shoes and clothing.

Play It Again Sports
9242 SW Beaverton-
Hillsdale Hwy, 292-4552
(map:HH8)
Tues-Sun

For moms and dads, Play It Again must be a great idea. This new store targets kids who are growing too fast to wear anything out and beginners who don't want to pay a fortune to try out a sport. New and used sports equipment (skis to backyard games). Its location next door to an ice-skating rink keeps the store stocked with hockey and ice-skating equipment—roller skates, too. Sell it back? If it's clean and in good repair, give it a try.

Rebel Skates
1100 NW 21st Ave,
274-0427 (map:FF7)
Every day

Rebel Skates opened in 1985, when skating was the preferred mode of transportation for a generation of Portland kids. The lingo here is hardcore skater-to-skater.

REI (Recreational Equipment Inc)
1798 Jantzen Beach Ctr,
283-1300 (map:BB7)
Every day

The nation's largest co-op (13 West Coast stores, just over two million members) will soon be opening a second Portland store in Tualatin for people in the southern metropolitan area. Until then, members and nonmembers brave the constant construction and changing traffic patterns of I-5 near the Jantzen Beach Shopping Center, to find clothes and equipment for mountaineering, backpacking, downhill and cross-country skiing, cycling, watersports, and walking. The store prides itself on well-priced, technically appropriate gear, though it seems to be slowly slipping into the outdoor fashion market as well. The staff is warm and helpful. A one-time $10 fee earns cash back on nonsale purchases.

RECORDS

Bird's Suite
3736 SE Hawthorne Blvd (and branches), 235-6224 (map:GG8)
Every day

Don Anderson has been running his used pop, classical, jazz, and R&B institution for 15 years now. In June 1989 he opened an exclusively jazz outlet called Birdland (1008 SW Taylor Street, 274-2738, map:GG5). Recent reports of disappointment in the original store's stock leave us wondering if Birdland is stealing the show. The second downtown location is next door at 1016 SW Taylor Street, 274-0690.

Crocodile
3623 SE Hawthorne Blvd, 238-1957 (map:GG7)

828 SW Park Ave, 222-4773 (map:H2)
Every day

Two very different stores owned by the same three men: at Hawthorne Boulevard the tune is classic jazz to Grateful Dead; at Park Avenue (in fact, its original name until 1987) it's music for those who want to wear black and be depressed. Pop music fans get the cold shoulder at both places. Used CDs.

Django
1111 SW Stark St, 227-4381 (map:GG5)
Every day

What started 16 years ago as an excuse to sit around a card table and absorb fine jazz is now Bob Dietsche's shop—which is so good, so large, and so popular that it's often well picked over. The solution? Go often. Django's (named after jazz guitarist Django Reinhardt) has posters and secondhand CDs, too.

Music Millennium
3158 E Burnside, 231-8926 (map:GG7)
801 NW 23rd Ave, 248-0163 (map:FF6)
Every day

Music Millennium is one of a dying breed of record store—the few vinyl holdouts that still hold star signings. On its 20th anniversary last year, Millennium installed a stage, where Randy Newman or Peter Case have been known to pop in for a free afternoon concert before big gigs in the city. The stock's complete and goes well beyond the regular Top 40 names seen in the mall stores. The larger Burnside store (with its classical annex next door) supports a bigger stock and a friendly, knowledgeable staff.

Looking for a particular place? Check the index at the back of this book for individual restaurants, hotels, B&Bs, shops, bars, parks, museums, galleries, neighborhoods, messenger services, nightclubs, and more.

Ooze
2190 W Burnside,
226-0249 (map:GG6)
Every day

Like its name, the atmosphere in this contemporary record shop is pretty laid back. The selection ranges from dance to industrial to "world" music. The shop maintains a close relationship with a Dutch record store, and as a result there are good imports.

Rockport
203 SW 9th Ave,
224-0660 (map:J3)
Every day

There's a full line of music offerings at this shop, but its claim to fame is the selection of blues recordings, said to be the largest in the Northwest. Thousands of used, new, and hard-to-find cuts ranging from original '50s hits to alternative music.

2nd Avenue Records
418 SW 2nd Ave,
222-3783 (map:H9)
Every day

The room is crammed with a wildly eclectic record selection; the music breaks the punk and new-wave barrier. This is the source for alternative rock fiends, with reggae to rap to speed metal. If you're having a tough time locating your pick, just ask; it's usually there—somewhere.

Turntable Mary
120 SW Stark St,
227-3933 (map:I5)
Every day

There's only one criterion Mary's music has to meet: 105 to 110 beats per minute—disco dance music. The staff knows all the dance club tunes and (for a price) will put together a tape that will keep a party on its feet.

SEAFOOD

Burlingame Grocery
8502 SW Terwilliger
Blvd, 246-0711
(map:HH6)
Every day

Under new ownership, this store has flourished in its wine, produce, meat, and seafood departments. Leland Nichols operates the meat and seafood sections, with long-term neighborhood experience in both. This man knows fish; he has spent much time and effort learning about species, habitats, feeding patterns, and processing, concomitantly developing excellent relationships with his suppliers. He's swimming in good advice and will gladly share it.

Fresh Fish Co
13619 NW Cornell Rd,
Beaverton, 646-9624
(map:HH9)
Every day

Tucked into the Sunset Mall, Fresh Fish is tough to find but worth seeking out. It looks and smells fresh, and the cases are stocked with a good variety of seasonal offerings. A loyal clientele returns for reasonable, even low, prices. A fresh board lists the day's offerings, with origins noted.

Green's Seafood Inc
6767 SW Macadam Ave,

It sure doesn't look like much, yet Green's Wholesale Seafood supplies many of Portland's restaurants with

246-8245 (map:HH6)
Mon-Fri

top-quality merchandise, so it stands to reason that the retail market is also of high quality. Only a small part of the inventory is on display, so be sure to ask for what you want. The counter people are most helpful, and special requests can frequently be handled.

Lake Grove Market
16331 SW Bryant Rd,
Lake Oswego, 636-8457
(map:KK7)

See Markets and Delicatessens in this chapter.

Newman's Fish Co
1200 NE Broadway (Holladay Market), 284-4537
(map:EE5)
Every day

Newman's is regarded as one of the finest seafood markets in Oregon. Knowledgeable, energetic, and pleasant, they strive to do an excellent job. The variety is noteworthy, and freshness is a given. Helping customers learn to buy and prepare fish is a primary concern of the owners of this well-run establishment. Notice the fresh whole salmon, the Oregon lox, the selection of various fish steaks, and the scampi (when available).

Troy's Seafood Markets
11130 SE Powell St (and branches), 760-2566
(map:HH2)
Mon-Sat

Troy's used to be a vigorous set of five seafood stores, clearly leading the market in sales and growth. Recently, that vigor has been sadly lacking in some outlets. Still, with care, good quality fish and shellfish are to be found, and prices are often reasonable. Do ask questions, and request freshly prepared cuts.

SHOES

Joseph
9865 SW Beaverton-Hillsdale Hwy,
Beaverton, 626-0705
(map:HH9)
Mon-Sat

Foot art by Escada, Ferragamo, and Petra is a rarity not only in Portland, but in the Northwest in general. This Tennessee-based company has eight shoe stores, and the next-closest is in Beverly Hills. Shoes—and prices—of the stars. The extra expense is not spent on the staff.

Moda
821 SW Morrison St,
227-6522 (map:H2)
Every day

Sandwiched between the two Mario's stores at Ninth Avenue and SW Morrison Street, Michael Jolley features "fast-forward footwear." With lines such as Paloma, Charles David, and Perry Ellis, the look is European but still affordable. Jolley recently added a good lineup of Donna Karan hosiery and a wide variety of socks. He's quite a character, with lots of enthusiasm (even during the construction of the light rail) for his shop and customers.

Multnomah Leather Shop
315 SW Pine St, 227-4887
(map:I5)
Tues-Sat

Owner Mark Casperson is a second-generation leather craftsman. Trained by his father, he makes wooden, custom-fitted clogs—a shoe that's slowly making a comeback. Everything's made to order here, from moccasins and gloves to briefcases and billfolds.

Nofziger's
1001 SW Morrison St,
226-6108 (map:H2)
Mon-Sat

The best spot for moderately priced, somewhat trendy shoes and boots has graduated from the Galleria to a new, larger location just across SW Morrison Street. The Nofzigers have been in the footwear business for over 30 years, and their helpful and attentive service shows it.

The Shoe Tree
45 S State St (Village Shopping Center), Lake Oswego, 636-5090 (map:KK5)
Mon-Sat

A good neighborhood shop for active women and children, with a well-rounded selection of walking, aerobics, and tennis shoes. A complete children's area displays just about anything you might need for those growing little feet, from socks to special orders.

SPECIALTY SIZE CLOTHING: LARGE/TALL/MATERNITY/PETITE

Donna Grande
507 SW Broadway,
222-1125 (map:I3)
Mon-Sat

The most stylish outfitter of large (size 12–24) women in Seattle has opened a Portland outpost. Donna Grande carries Jones New York and Paul Stanley suits, stunning rayon outfits from Finland, Judith Ann beaded dresses, and other designers' lines, with an emphasis on career dressing. Everything is upscale and flattering—even the staff makes you feel glamorous.

Fifth Avenue Maternity
524 SW Yamhill St,
223-3625 (map:G3)
Mon-Sat

Seattle's primo maternity shop is now found in Portland, too. Lydia Williams runs a very personalized operation with a willing staff to help you plan your wardrobe for the upcoming months—with suits, separates, and casual wear. Accessories from nursing bras to nightgowns, and a good selection of evening wear.

Maternity Jane
724 NW 23rd Ave,
228-5778 (map:FF7)
Mon-Sat

Jessica McKinley's second store (she also owns Jessica Jane's in Sellwood) focuses on helping expectant mothers feel good about being pregnant. Natural fibers are primarily featured. She carries atypical maternity items that look great on any shape. There's a sample selection of nursing bras and some of her own private-label designs. Attentive service.

The Oswego Woman
242 B Ave, Lake Oswego,
635-4326 (map:KK6)
Mon-Sat

Something is always on sale at Oswego Woman, where size 16–24 women can find evening wear and a special-order service. Also on hand are French Vanilla, Jones New York, and other better sportswear lines.

Petite Woman's Shoppe
5331 SW Macadam Ave
(The Water Tower),
241-8595 (map:II6)
Every day

In the Johns Landing area, petite women have a place to call their own. Adrienne Vittadini, Calvin Klein, and Jones New York are just a few of the lines of better sportswear and career clothing available here. Excellent customer service.

Renoir's Lady
5331 SW Macadam Ave
(Johns Landing),
295-0416 (map:HH6)
Every day

Fans of Renoir's in Johns Landing frequent the store to see what designer names are in stock. They pick out an outfit, then wait to buy it. Fortune hunters have been known to find their favorite Casadei dress on the clearance rack for a quarter of the price.

TOYS

Child's Play
907 NW 23rd Ave,
224-5586 (map:FF7)
Every day

A great selection of uncommon American and European toys. The store's been enlarged, but the good stuff still goes faster than we'd like. An immense selection of dolls (Ginny, Madame Alexander, and hard-to-find American Collection). Go often (and well before Christmas) to see Child's Play at its finest.

Christmas at the Zoo
118 NW 23rd Ave,
223-4048 (map:FF7)
Mon-Sat

A marvelous menagerie of stuffed animals of every imaginable—and not—species, including heroes of children's literature from Paddington Bear to Curious George. The Zoo captures Dakin, Gund, Avanti, and Steiff, among others. A small, year-round selection of Christmas ornaments.

City Kids
810 SW 2nd Ave (and
branches), 224-5784
(map:G4)
Every day

Collectors, young and old, of imported and American playthings, dolls, and stuffed animals admire this distinctive toy shop. The original Yamhill Market store spawned two others: Clackamas Town Center (12000 SE 82nd Avenue, 659-9464) and Portland International Airport (7000 NE Airport Way, 284-9612).

Endgames
200 SW Salmon St,
224-6917 (map:G4)

12000 SE 82nd Ave
(Clackamas Town
Center), 652-1434
(map:KK3) Mon-Sat

Teach your youngsters checkers or tri-level chess. A full store devoted to board games and puzzles—enough entertainment here to keep kids amused for 91 years.

Finnegan's Toys and Gifts
922 SW Yamhill St,
221-0306 (map:H2)
Every day

Not quite FAO Schwartz, but for Portland it's the next best thing. Part of this stimulating store is set aside for test drives of the windup cars, flip-over monkeys, and whatnot. Look for Ambi rattles, Playmobiles, dollhouses, and craft supplies, all amid the smiling hustle and bustle.

Learning World
3255 SW Cedar Hill Blvd,
Beaverton, 643-6538
(map:HH9)

8652 SE Sunnyside Rd,
Clackamas, 652-1955
(map:KK2)
Every day

The first of its kind in Portland for educational toys (craft supplies, chemistry sets, abaci, and flash cards), Learning World has managed to keep ahead of the competition. An interesting resource for teachers (discounts, too), with classroom supplies and materials.

Paint the Sky Kites
828 NW 23rd Ave,
222-5096 (map:FF7)
Tues-Sun

A rainbow of kites hang in midair in this colorful new spot in the revitalized northwest. Everything from windsocks to stunt kites.

Sweet Zoo
12000 SW 82nd Ave
(Clackamas Town
Center), 654-9567
(map:KK3)
Every day

Another stellar stuffed-animal house, with lots of people impersonators, too. Dolls of all sizes and origins.

Tammie's Hobbies
3645 SW Hall St,
Beaverton, 644-4535
(map:II9)
Every day

Tammie's is always abuzz with enthusiastic hobbyists. Nowhere else in town will you find German LGB electric train sets (and spare parts). Few outgrow the yearning for radio-controlled race cars, airplanes, and boats. Plus models of all sorts and a paint center.

Toy Bear
121 N Main St,
Gresham, 661-5310
Mon-Sat

Intelligently chosen stock across the street from the Main St. Deli in Gresham. Upper-end inventory has a bit of everything: science games, dolls, cars, puzzles, and so on. A small selection of Boy Scout, Girl Scout, and Camp Fire Girl particulars.

VINTAGE

Avalon Antiques
318 SW 9th Ave,
224-7156 (map:I3)
Mon-Sat

Scratchy music from the big band era plays in the background at the West Coast's first retro store. Crammed with clothes from the '20s through the '60s, Avalon is best known for its leather jacket collection and its dresses—worth clawing through a crowd for, though you rarely have to go to such extremes. The counters are filled with antique paraphernalia, from jewelry to cigarette cases.

Big Bang
616 SW Park Ave,
274-1741 (map:H3)

8960 SE Sunnyside Rd
(Clackamas Promenade),
693-2630 (map:KK3)
Every day

Big Bang: an explosion of men's and women's vintage clothes, a bundle of coats and dresses, and a kingdom of antique jewelry. Halloween is serious business here. The Clackamas Promenade store is new—same incredible inventory.

Grin 'n Wear It
3535 SE Hawthorne
Blvd, 232-8425
(map:GG5)
Tues-Sat

Sniff and shop. It's the best-smelling retro shop in Portland. Incense is nice, but we like the clothes: '30s to '60s, heavy on the skirts. Men's clothing, too.

Fashion Passion
616 NW 23rd Ave,
223-4373 (map:FF6)
Tues-Sun

What could be mistaken for a shoe box is really a store stuffed with class clothing reaching all the way back to the 1800s (but as recent as the 1950s). Dress up in beaded sweaters, party purses, and froufrou hats. Just want to play? Rent 'em.

Keep 'em Flying
510 NW 21st Ave,
221-0601 (map:FF6)
Mon-Sat

This vintage clothier is more austere than the rest. Perhaps that helps define it as one of the more elegant, too. Keep 'em Flying (the name is from the WWII slogan) resells only the finest men's and women's garments from the 1900s to the 1950s. Pocket watches, fine-quality shoes, and classic luggage can also be found here.

Ray's Ragtime
1021 SW Morrison St,
226-2616 (map:I2)
Mon-Sat

Hundreds of gowns, glittery party dresses, and military uniforms hang in this downtown shop. And more: groovy ties, collectible vases, and rhinestone baubles. Renoir's women would revel in this place.

WINES, BEERS, AND SPIRITS

Burlingame Grocery
8502 SW Terwilliger
Blvd, 246-0711
(map:HH6)
Every day

The beer selection is unrivaled. Owner Tom Calkin's philosophy is to include every available import. Great beers that once sold poorly in the Portland market are frequently available en masse at very attractive prices. The wine section is especially strong in Californias and Bordeaux, with once-a-month tastings.

Portland Best Places *lists all the finest establishments throughout Portland, north to Vancouver, Washington, south to West Linn, west to Beaverton, and east to Gresham.*

WINES, BEERS, AND SPIRITS

Cheshire Cat
1200 NE Broadway,
284-5226 (map:FF5)
Every day

Wine samples at the counter help consumers broaden their knowledge and make the right purchase. Ron Bronleewe, the owner, scurries back and forth between the stacked wooden cases of wine and a well-stocked cheese case to inform, sell, and chat.

Clear Creek Distillery
1430 NW 23rd Ave,
248-9470 (map:FF7)
Mon-Fri;
by appointment only

Nationally recognized food and wine connoisseurs have been touched by Stephen McCarthy's eaux de vie. And Portland is privy to his distillery located at the far end of NW 23rd Avenue. With fruit from his family's Hood River orchards, an absence of any additives whatsoever, and a large sparkling copper still, McCarthy creates an utterly pure and colorless pear brandy and an apple one that's lightly tinctured from two years in Limousin oak barrels. Both digestifs smack a smooth, fruity 80 proof. A resourceful man, McCarthy just released a batch of grappa—traditionally a peasant concoction made from the leftover fruit pulp—with overwhelming success. Framboise is next.

Fred Meyer Market Places
NE 33rd Ave and
Broadway (and others),
280-1300 (map:FF4)
Every day

Kudos to a chain that sees the logic in offering consumers much-needed assistance with wine selection. At all Portland-area superstore locations, wine stewards (independent, to a degree, from store to store) have been employed to choose stock. Drafted from the retail and wholesale wine trade, they all, so far, have good to excellent credentials. The stock is exceptional at the newer superstores; at the smaller branches, without designated wine stewards, it's barely adequate. Let's hope they allow the stewards time enough to actually assist customers and not simply to stock shelves.

The Grapery
4190 SW Cedar Hills
Blvd, Beaverton,
646-1437 (map: HH9)
Mon-Sat

See Nightlife chapter.

Great Wine Buys
1515 NE Broadway,
287-2897 (map:FF5)
Every day

Believing her clientele would respond best to personal recommendations, Rachel Starr has tasted thousands of wines and written tasting notes for them. Lots of beer, too. Retro furniture and wine racks stacked with an international cache of good-value, good-tasting wines. Try her own label Oregon wines, in samples at the tasting bar—don't be shy.

The facts in this edition were correct at presstime, but places close, chefs depart, hours change. It's best to call ahead.

Harris Wine Cellars Ltd
2300 NW Thurman St,
223-2222 (map:FF7)
Mon-Sat

For years, this was one of only two places in Portland where the wine drinker could actually talk with a knowledgeable wine person. Art Thomas, proprietor, is a soft-spoken man, well educated about wines. The shop in many ways seems a relic of the past, with old fixtures, labels from decades ago montaged for posterity, and rare and fine wines found nowhere else in this market. However, the vigor displayed by newer wine tradespeople is lacking here, and so are some of the current selections that make the new shops worthy of your visit. Still, there is much to be seen and learned at this venerable wine shop.

Hartwig Retail Meat Market
2131 NW Kearney St,
226-3875 (map:FF7)
Mon-Sat

See Meats in this chapter.

Martinotti's Cafe and Delicatessen
404 SW 10th Ave,
224-9028 (map:J2)
Mon-Sat

The Martinotti family has developed a decidedly Italian grocery of good tastes, good smells, and good products. See Armand for wine, Dixie for catering, and Frank for lunch and the latest in microbrews. The wine selection is incredibly rich in Burgundies and Bordeaux futures, ample in Italy, curiously spotty in the Northwest and California. Armand tastes before buying, when he can, so he knows his product.

Nelson Brothers Cheese and Wine
13599 NW Cornell Rd,
Beaverton, 643-1140
(map:HH9)
Mon-Sat

Good friends with several Oregon winemakers, Larry and Loren Nelson have been wine purveyors for over a decade. They are both conversant with the major producing areas and can offer good advice on food-wine affinities. The selection is small and closely managed. Ask, if you don't see what you want; they are happy to make special orders.

Pastaworks
3735 SE Hawthorne
Blvd, 232-1010
(map:GG4)
Every day

See Markets and Delicatessens in this chapter.

Strohecker's
2855 SW Patton Rd,
223-7341 (map:HH7)
Every day

This is one of the best wine selections in any store on the West Coast. The cellar, although grossly diminished from previous glory days, still has wines not found anywhere else except in private collections. Actually, this *is* the private collection of Wayne Strohecker, a remarkable man whose personal history is entwined with wine

WINES, BEERS, AND SPIRITS

and wine people. Although the day-to-day logistics of the business have been handed over to a wine steward, Wayne can frequently be found in the department, still happy to help and discuss. As for beer, Keith Strohecker has built a noteworthy inventory of well-selected local, domestic, and imported beers.

Westmoreland Bistro and Wine
7015 SE Milwaukie Ave,
236-6457 (map:HH5)
Tues-Sun

See Restaurants chapter.

Wine and Roses
61 SW 2nd Ave,
223-6060 (map:I5)
Mon-Sat

This downtown Portland shop has a character all its own—wry, spare, basic, and unpretentious. Close to Portland's Saturday Market, it is a natural stop in a day devoted to urban exploring. Tastings are held on a regular basis, and inventory's in step with new arrivals on the market and new discoveries by the owner.

Wizer's Oswego Foods
SW 1st Ave and "A" St,
Lake Oswego, 646-1414
(map:KK5)
Every day

Still one of the best selections of wine in southwest metropolitan Portland. Although not as robust as in past years, this wine department has a wide array of domestic and imported wines with a vast repertoire of sale items. And do explore the cellar—an inventory book should be available for perusal....Imagine *own*ing some of the rare sweethearts.

Woodstock Wine and Deli
4030 SE Woodstock Blvd,
777-2208 (map:HH4)
Mon-Sat

Gregg Fujino, proprietor, is one of Portland's most astute wine sellers. He takes seriously the tasks of tasting, cataloging, and researching his wares. He has a remarkable shelf selection and liberal supplies of wine by the case. Located near Reed College, this shop is a good place to lunch, browse, taste, and learn. Check out their beers, too.

LODGINGS CONTENTS

LODGINGS

HOTELS
DOWNTOWN

The Heathman Hotel
*1009 SW Broadway,
241-4100 (map:G2)
Expensive; AE, DC, MC,
V; checks OK*

This is *the* place to stay in town: afternoon tea each day, exquisite marble bar, elegant rooms, and one of Portland's finest restaurants (see Restaurants chapter). The Heathman is also a historic landmark, restored about a decade ago by the Stevenson family. One recent addition is the bar on the mezzanine, furnished with a limited dining area, near the Elizabeth Leach Mezzanine Gallery. The most notable feature of the interior is the generous use of Burmese teak paneling—the owner, Mark Stevenson, is a timber magnate. Small guest rooms are furnished with leather-and-rattan chairs, marble-topped bathroom pieces with brass fittings, chintz window shades, celadon lamps, and original prints and paintings. Colors are soft green, rose, and cream. Among the amenities are a choice of approximately 300 complimentary movies, European soaps, bathrobes, and a nightly turn-down service. One of the Heathman's nicest qualities is the service—its employees are low-key (a highly valued quality in Oregon—indeed, in all the Northwest) but meticulously attentive. Guests feel well taken care of but not fussed over. Inside rooms are best; the hotel is on downtown Portland's busiest street. Rooms start at $125 (double).

Imperial Hotel
*400 SW Broadway,
228-7221, (800) 452-
2323 (OR and WA)
(map:I3)
Inexpensive; AE, DC,
MC, V; checks OK*

While it's not exactly fit for a king, the Imperial is clean, economical (starting at $48 for two), and right downtown. The folks here make you feel good: they'll park your car for you at all hours and they'll even let you leave your baggage (locked) in the lobby for the afternoon—*after* you've checked out. If you don't smoke, make sure to ask for a nonsmoking room (floors 4, 5, and 6)—though even then there's sometimes a hint that someone has cheated.

Mallory Motor Hotel
*729 SW 15th Ave,
223-6311,
(800) 228-8657 (map:I1)
Inexpensive; AE, DC,
MC, V; checks OK*

★½

This place is an older establishment in every sense—from the massive hunks of ornate wooden lobby furniture to the clientele to the senior staff. It's also one of the best bargains in town, starting at $43 for a double and with vast suites going for $75. While rooms are spacious, they bear no resemblance to the hotel's more elaborate entrance. On the other hand, this is one of the few areas bordering downtown Portland that is genuinely quiet. Parking is easy to find and mostly meter-free, and several of the rooms have good views of the city or the west hills. The bar, a kind of bizarre hybrid of '50s dark-plushy and '60s eccentric-cutesy, is not the major attraction here. The irritating Muzak in every corner of the ground floor is a drawback. The flaws fade, however, next to simple, charming touches such as the small, lace-trimmed pillow with needle, thread, and buttons left in your room and the almost motherly service.

Marriott Hotel
1401 SW Front Ave,
226-7600 (map:D4)
Expensive; AE, DC, MC,
V; checks OK

This big, urban place looks like standard convention lodging in every big city in the country. Redeeming is its location overlooking the Willamette River. There are 503 rooms in the 14-story structure, and facilities include a 24-hour health club, an indoor pool, two restaurants, and two bars. This is the kind of operation where callers can expect a chirpy-voiced clerk to put them on hold for five minutes, then field rate queries in terms of "current, tomorrow, and weekend." Don't settle for the first price quoted—if you probe them you might just find you qualify for more moderate prices (ask about weekend, senior citizen, AAA, and other special rates).

Portland Hilton
921 SW 6th Ave,
226-1611 (map:G2)
Expensive; AE, DC, MC,
V; checks OK

This downtown hotel offers no surprises, unless leafless, tree-style columns and a small atrium above the bar in the lobby strike you as refreshing. However, the Hilton boasts a prime location, on the Portland Transit Mall. And if you are able to get a room on one of the upper floors, your stay will be enhanced by the magnificent view of the city and Mount Hood—at least on those days when the mountain cooperates by letting itself be seen. Plenty of facilities: two restaurants (one of which is Alexander's on the 23rd floor), banquet and meeting rooms, an outdoor swimming pool (seasonal), and a bare-essentials workout room.

Red Lion Inn at Portland Center
310 SW Lincoln St,
221-0450 (map:B2)
Moderate; AE, DC, MC,
V; checks OK

The southern portion of Portland's downtown has one of the few attractive urban renewal projects in America: handsome apartment towers by Skidmore Owings & Merrill set amid the sensitive landscaping and fountains of Lawrence Halprin. Staying at this motel enables you to be near these projects and have an easy stroll through them to the Civic Auditorium. Doubles begin at $99, and the 237 rooms are standard, but some look out onto a landscaped central courtyard with a pool (seasonal). Freeway access is handy.

RiverPlace Alexis Hotel
1510 SW Harbor Wy,
228-3233,
(800) 227-1333 (map:D4)
Expensive; AE, DC, MC,
V; checks OK

The Portland counterpart to Seattle's elegant Alexis Hotel is situated in Portland's showcase riverfront district. It features 10 chic condominiums, 74 rooms, specialty shops, two restaurants (one, the Patio, is summers only), scenic jogging paths, and an upscale bar. Inside are many distinguishing features: plush furnishings, postmodern colors, televisions concealed in armoires, complimentary sherry in the bar, smashing views of the river, and a lively night scene. The best rooms face the Willamette River or look north across the park lawns to the downtown cityscape. A jogging path, extending along the riverfront from the hotel's front door to downtown, is so popular with guests that hotel management has added to its complimentaries list the loan of jogging suits and athletic shoes. Use of the adjacent RiverPlace Athletic Club facilities is an extra $5.

The hotel restaurant, Esplanade, is strong in New American cuisine (see Restaurants chapter), and the bar is staffed by one of the most knowledgeable wine stewards around.

The Westin Benson
309 SW Broadway,
228-9611 (map:I3)
Expensive; AE, DC, MC,
V; checks OK

Simon Benson was a philanthropic lumber tycoon who in 1912–1913 built the Benson Hotel, giving orders to spare no expense. The creation was a noble 13-story affair of brick and marble (the latter has by now acquired a pale-green patina), with a palatial lobby featuring a stamped-tin ceiling, mammoth chandeliers, stately columns, a generous fireplace, and surrounding panels of carved Circassian walnut imported from Russia. For decades this was the only classy lodging in town. Competition brought an end to the Benson's exclusive status; however, in May 1990 the hotel is launching a major comeback with a 14-month renovation, one wing at a time. Beginning with the older north wing, where the rooms have generally been small and jammed with furniture, plans are to actually reduce the number of rooms, enlarging each. The newer portion of the building—the south wing, with more forgiving accommodations—will be open until the plumbing, wiring, and looks of the north wing are brought out of the 1890s. There are two pricey restaurants in the hotel, the London Grill (see Restaurants chapter) and Trader Vic's.

EASTSIDE

Red Lion at Lloyd Center
1000 NE Multnomah St,

Its daunting size (a map in the lobby directs you to the three restaurants) and proximity to the Lloyd Center,

281-6111,
(800) 547-8010
(map:FF5)
Expensive; AE, DC, MC,
V; checks OK

Memorial Coliseum, and the new Convention Center make this corporate hotel a good choice for eastside conventions or seminars. With 476 guest rooms, it's currently Oregon's largest hotel, with a number of well-organized meeting rooms, outdoor pool, workout room, and courtesy airport van. Reserve a west-facing room above the fifth floor for a view of Mount Hood.

JANTZEN BEACH

Columbia River Red Lion
1401 North Hayden
Island Dr, 283-2111
(map:CC6)
Moderate; AE, DC, MC,
V; checks OK

The Columbia River being one of the great waterways of the world and a mere 7 miles north of downtown Portland, you may wish to stay on its banks. This garish, rambling, 351-room motel (formerly the Thunderbird) is poised right at waterside. It offers a pool (seasonal) with a sun deck that virtually overhangs the river, and airport pickup. Nearby, there's the 27-hole Heron Lakes Golf Course (via a two-minute free shuttle), a jogging path, a cinema, and a health club. Honeymooners are everywhere (the eight suites are in high demand). A piano plays for a few evening hours in the dining room, Misty's.

AIRPORT

Execulodge
6221 NE 82nd Ave,
255-6511 (map:DD3)
Moderate; AE, DC, MC,
V; checks OK

A good spot for corporate gatherings but not the individual traveler. This large airport hotel (202 rooms) is often booked solid with meetings and conferences. The rooms are standard, as are the amenities—an outdoor pool (summer only), a lukewarm Jacuzzi, and a bare-bones workout room—which take a definite second place to conferences and receptions and the needs of the business traveler. Service is often in the training stages.

Sheraton Airport Hotel
8235 NE Airport Wy,
281-2500,
(800) 325-3535
(map:DD3)
Expensive; AE, DC, MC,
V; checks OK

For the traveling businessperson PDX's Sheraton tops the list. For one thing, it's located—literally—on the airport grounds (Fed Ex planes load up next door, and arrival and departure times are broadcast at the main entrance). Inside, amenities abound: everything from meeting rooms and a complete, complimentary business center (IBM computer, printer, fax machine, and secretarial services) to an indoor swimming pool, sauna, and workout room. Details down to hair-dryers in the women's room (we didn't check the men's). At press time, the 65 standard-size rooms were set for a facelift. The executive suites (pastels and wood furnishings) consider the personal needs of the businessperson with extra touches such as double phones, sitting areas, and pullout makeup mirrors in the bathrooms. We only wish they would give the hotel a quarter turn: Mount Hood stands tall to the east, but you'd never know it from the airport-facing rooms.

GREATER PORTLAND: BEAVERTON

Greenwood Inn
10700 SW Allen Blvd,
Beaverton, 643-7444
(map:HH8)
Moderate; AE, DC, MC,
V; checks OK

The best thing about this modern 254-room motel and convention complex is its location just off Highway 217, the freeway connecting the Sunset Highway in the northwest with the teeming southwest suburbs of Beaverton and Tigard. The rooms are nothing special, although they are well soundproofed, a few of the suites have Jacuzzis and kitchens, and some rooms are set aside for guests with pets. The courtyard and trapezoidal pool are quite pretty. One unusual feature for a motel is room service, including complimentary coffee and a choice of newspapers in the morning; place an order the night before with the wake-up operator. From 5pm to 6pm there are complimentary cocktails. The crashing sound of a fountain flanked by enormous palms nearly assaults you as you enter the Pavilion Bar and Grill. Inside, lights are soft, and service treads the delicate line between chummy and concerned. The food's absolutely OK without being remarkable.

GREATER PORTLAND: TIGARD

Embassy Suites Hotel
9000 SW Washington
Square Rd, Tigard,
644-4000 (map:JJ9)
Expensive; AE, DC, MC,
V; checks OK

This is the westside equivalent of the Marriott. The Embassy is Urban-Moderno, right down to its location, adjacent to the sprawling Washington Square shopping complex in Tigard, about 15 minutes' driving time from Portland. The only real recommendation for this monolithic structure is quick access to Oregon's "Silicon Valley" business district in the flat plains between Beaverton and Tigard. Complimentary full breakfast, athletic club use (five minutes away by complimentary limo), and shopping-mall limo service. The usual Denny's-gone-velvet restaurant and lounge found in all hotels of this genre. Double occupancy begins at $98.

GREATER PORTLAND: LAKE OSWEGO

Howard Johnson Plaza Hotel
14811 SW Kruse Oaks
Blvd, Lake Oswego,

Boy, Howard Johnson's gone a long way from its signature burnt orange of the '60s. At press time, this blue-and-tinted-glass six-story tower was on the verge of

624-8400,
(800) 654-2000
(map:KK8)
Moderate; AE, DC, MC,
V; checks OK

unrated

completion (so we were unable to rate it). It seems to fit in well with the new corporate parks sprouting up in the 'burbs but contrasts with the few remaining Lake Oswego farms near the intersection of I-5 and Highway 217. The rooms are standard, but we suggest you request one on the outside of the "v" lest you wake up staring at your neighbor across the way. The pool (half outdoors, half indoors) will be open all year.

INNS AND BED & BREAKFASTS

SOUTHWEST

General Hooker's B&B
125 SW Hooker St,
222-4435 (map:HH6)
Moderate; AE, MC, V;
checks OK

Happy Hooker, an Abyssinian cat, greets you at the door of this gracious Victorian B&B in a quiet southwest neighborhood. The General's house offers three rooms with handmade batik quilts and other homey touches, including a large wood stove, an eclectic library, hanging metal artwork by owner Lori Hall's mother, and a sun deck. There's a VCR in each room, and the building has central air conditioning. The best unit is the Rose Room, with a king-size bed, private entrance, and skylit bath. Kids can stay in the bunk room downstairs. Wine is served to guests nightly on the roof decks, and there is half-price use of the nearby Metro YMCA. Duniway Park track, Terwilliger Boulevard bike path, and the Lair Hill public tennis court are also within walking distance. Downtown is five minutes by car and also accessible by bus.

MacMaster House
1041 SW Vista Ave,
223-7362 (map:GG7)
Moderate; AE, MC, V;
checks OK

This colonial is two blocks from the largest municipal park in the country—the Washington Park–Forest Park complex, which incorporates Portland's renowned Rose Gardens and Hoyt Arboretum. From the outside, MacMaster is a restored B&B, with a massive portico set off by Doric columns, a spacious manse with seven fireplaces and leaded glass windows. Inside, things get a bit more bizarre: a wall painted with palm trees in one room, Greek columns in the next, erotic art in another. Still, if you can stand the odd decor, five spacious rooms have queen beds, cable TV, and share two baths (in need of some repair). Four have colonial fireplaces. Not all will feel comfortable in the safarilike sixth room (the three-room suite): bamboo canopied bed, zebra-skin rugs, and cowhide chair. Breakfast is served communally in the stately dining room.

▼

INNS AND BED & BREAKFASTS

Mumford Manor
1130 SW King Ave,
243-2443 (map:HH5)
Expensive; AE, MC, V;
checks OK

The Mumford is a fully restored Queen Anne from the turn of the century. The blue-shuttered, three-story beige structure is ideally located in the heart of the commercial triangle—walking distance from the business hub of downtown, the indulgence shops of the northwest district, and the sequestered beauty of Washington Park. The master suite is Victorian (if you don't count the electric towel warmer), done in reds and chintz, and with a fireplace. The three other rooms are equally stylish, from their designer wallpaper and goose-down pillows and comforters to the antique pedestal sinks in the bathrooms. There's a grand piano and fireplace for all in the living room and a game room downstairs where there's often a jigsaw puzzle in the works. A wholesome breakfast is served on fine china and crystal.

NORTHWEST

Heron Haus B&B
2545 NW Westover Rd,
274-1846 (map:FF7)
Expensive; MC, V;
checks OK

Located in the exclusive Northwest Hills overlooking Portland, this striking three-story home has locked horns with its neighbors over zoning particulars. At press time, its fate was undecided. Politics aside, you won't find more luxurious lodging. Built in 1904 for a local cranberry baron, Heron Haus maintains many original touches, including parquet flooring on the main level. Updated amenities, however, are no less pleasant: one of the five rooms has an elevated spa offering a view of the city below. Another has turn-of-the-century plumbing, featuring a seven-nozzle shower. This is a spacious operation for a B&B, 7,500 square feet. There's a living room with modern furniture, a handsome, well-stocked library, a TV room, an enclosed sun room, and an outside pool. If you're visiting in late summer, you'll get in on the harvest from a miniature orchard of pear, apple, and cherry trees. It's also two blocks from the city's most popular shopping district—where you might want to park your car so as not to bother the neighbors.

NORTH

John Palmer House
4314 N Mississippi Ave,
284-5893 (map:EE6)
Moderate; MC, V;
checks OK

With PDX's bed and breakfast inns closing left and right due to strict zoning laws, the John Palmer House—securely situated in a business district—is bound to be around for a while. At a glance, this Victorian manse is an impressively ornate place for a night's sleep: a canopied bed in the bridal suite and a gazebo with a Jacuzzi. Unfortunately, it's not all it's advertised to be (and the neighborhood's not a good spot for an evening stroll). First, your breakfast takes second place to those of $10-a-seat non-guests, and complimentary high tea is no longer complimentary. Second, stay clear of the poster room. Third, you'll sometimes be asked not to arrive before 6pm. You won't find the same elegance but you will find more peace (and cheaper prices) in one of Grandma's three guest rooms next door, where a chipper 91-year-old does her share of cooking, cleaning, and tour duty. All in all Mary, Richard, and David Sauter run a tight ship—it's just that there's too much going on (from catering to carriage rides) all the time.

NORTHEAST

**The Clinkerbrick House
Bed & Breakfast**
*2311 NE Schuyler St,
281-2533 (map:FF4)
Moderate; MC, V;
checks OK*

Bob and Peggie Irvine's overkilned-brick house is warm with plenty of pillows and colorful quilts. While the house is open to guests, it's really the upstairs that's yours. Privacy (for all parties involved) is encouraged with a key to the upstairs. A fourth room is billed as a common area for guests but is set up less for lingering than for a quick cup of tea. Our favorite room, oddly enough, is the smallest one, where the sun (when out) seems to shine brightest. No smoking.

Hartman's B&B
*2937 NE 20th Ave,
281-2182 (map:EE5)
Moderate; MC, V;
checks OK*

Katie and Chris Hartman opened their B&B a few years ahead of schedule. But now (though both fully employed elsewhere) they have settled marvelously into juggling the responsibilities of B&B owners. Of the three upstairs rooms, pick the spacious Art Deco one (the entire third floor), which is only $15 more than its two shared-bath partners. There's a cedar sauna in the basement and a gazebo-covered Jacuzzi in the back yard. Robes and, of course, breakfast provided.

Portland Guest House
*1720 NE 15th Ave,
282-1402 (map:FF5)
Inexpensive; AE, DC,
MC, V; checks OK*

What PGH lacks in grandeur, it makes up for in simplicity and class. Since owner Susan Gisvold doesn't live here, she runs it like a small hotel; she's usually around just long enough to advise you on Portland doings and bake a batch of cookies. The rest of the time, guests have full run of the parlor, dining room, and—dare she? —the fully stocked fridge. In the morning, Susan drops in to cook a fine breakfast of fresh fruit, chocolate chip scones, maybe even a basil omelet. With only four rooms (two with baths), privacy is seldom a problem. When the weather's warm, the garden's the spot. You'll

INNS AND BED & BREAKFASTS

probably sample Susan's fresh corn, tomatoes, pumpkins, and herbs come harvest time.

Portland's White House
1914 NE 22nd Ave,
287-7131 (map:FF5)
Moderate; MC, V;
checks OK

Another local timber baron, Robert F. Lytle, built what is now a popular B&B to last—it's constructed of solid Honduras mahogany. From the outside it's an imposing white mansion with all the trappings of Brahmin taste: fountain, carriage house, and a grand circular driveway. Inside are six roomy units, exquisite Oriental rugs, and other elegant appointments. The Canopy Room has a private bath, its own balcony, and a large canopied bed. Another room, equally romantic, has a vintage brass bed and delicate lace curtains. Tea time is quiet time, unless your visit coincides with a wedding (for which they're consistently booked three times a month).

SOUTHEAST

Eastmoreland Bed and Breakfast
6702 SE 29th Ave,
775-7023 (map:HH5)
Moderate; MC, V;
checks OK

Eastmoreland does more than just fill the need for more places to stay near Reed College. In a quiet neighborhood with beautiful older houses and magnificent flowering trees in spring, this three-story Colonial maintains five B&B rooms often filled with students' parents and young, hopeful applicants. There's a hot tub and VCR library, too. An attached cottage with a small kitchen area sleeps three. Patricia Ehrhart prepares an ample breakfast of fresh seafood and purchases only recycled paper products. No smoking, no young children.

HOSTELS

American Youth Hostel
SE Hawthorne Blvd at
30th Ave, 236-3380
(map:GG4)
Inexpensive; no credit
cards; no checks

Portland's only official youth hostel on secondhand Hawthorne Boulevard has all the familiar rules: closed between 9:30am and 5pm, bring your own linens (or rent theirs), midnight curfew. Shared showers, bunk beds (there's a sleeping porch for hot summer nights), laundry facilities, blankets, a kitchen, and two small living areas are the amenities—but then the member's cost is just $8 a night (nonmembers pay $12). No age limit. There's a volleyball net in the side yard.

YWCA
1111 SW 10th Ave,
223-6281 (map:GG6)
Inexpensive; AE, MC;
checks OK

In recent years the Y has seen a number of budget-conscious young Japanese travelers pass through its doors. There are only four basic rooms to let in the downtown center, but the price is thrifty. A week's advance registration is recommended. Maximum six-night stay.

EXPLORING CONTENTS

EXPLORING

MAJOR ATTRACTIONS
DOWNTOWN
Between the Willamette River and I-405,
SW Market and SW Stark streets (map:D2-D13)

Technically, downtown Portland lies south of W Burnside. Its southern border cuts the town off short just north of where I-405 slices across Portland State University and through the urban renewal area to the downtown's easternmost border, the Willamette River. Recent years have brought changes to these outlying areas (and more were proposed in the 1988 Central City Plan), but nowhere so formally as in the **retail core**, which was created by the 1972 Downtown Plan.

At the intersection of the downtown **Transit Mall** (Sixth Avenue northbound, Fifth Avenue southbound) and **MAX light rail** (Morrison Street westbound, Yamhill Street eastbound) lies Portland's living room—**Pioneer Courthouse Square** (PCS). In this Will Martin–designed, 45,000-brick square (believe it or not, it was once an eyesore of a parking garage), people watchers are drawn by presidential rallies, concerts (a recent performance by the Temptations attracted thousands), the small wintertime skating rink, or simply to watch the peculiar weather machine make its 24-hour forecast at noon. Underneath the bilevel square is the **Tri-Met Customer Service Office** (for information regarding the bus system or MAX, call 233-3511) and **public restrooms. Powell's Travel Store** and **Starbucks** are the only retail outlets granted Square addresses. Encircling the meeting place are two big department stores and a bank (**Meier & Frank** at SW Sixth Avenue and Morrison Street, **Nordstrom** on Broadway between Morrison and Yamhill streets, and **First Interstate** in the American Bank Building on SW Morrison Street between Sixth Avenue and Broadway), and of course the stout **Pioneer Courthouse**, with a refurbished post office on the main floor. Just west of PCS is the **Galleria**, a splendid, remodeled, five-story terra-cotta building with three floors of retail shops. A minimum $15 purchase at major downtown retailers buys two hours of **free parking** at most downtown public parking lots.

Portland's newest project, **Pioneer Place** (228-5800), centered at SW Fifth Avenue and Morrison Street, encompasses three city blocks anchored by the Pacific Northwest's first **Saks Fifth Avenue** (850 SW Fifth Avenue) scheduled to open in September 1990 on, of course, Fifth Avenue. Among the highly-touted retail shops scheduled to join the airy four-level pavilion by spring 1990 are those familiar to other Rouse development projects (Westlake Center in Seattle, South Street Seaport in New York City): the San Francisco–based cookware store Williams-Sonoma and established clothing shops such as Ann Taylor, Talbots, and Eddie Bauer. Tough competition for the comparably tiny **Yamhill Market Place** (SW Second Avenue and Yamhill Street) two blocks east.

A few blocks south are a couple of Portland's signature buildings. Michael Graves' controversial Art Deco **Portland Building**, on which **Portlandia**, one of the largest hammered-copper statues in the world, kneels. The columnar **First Interstate Bank Tower** (SW Fifth Avenue and Broadway) remains Portland's second-tallest building, with the lunch-only **Rene's Fifth Avenue** on the 21st floor—worth the view. And the bold brick **KOIN Center**, whose distinctive shape—like an upside-down, blue-tipped pen—has left its indelible mark on Portland's skyline. Inside are six cinemas, the upscale **KOIN Center Grill**—a busy spot especially after a movie, and offices for its namesake KOIN TV. Kitty-corner to KOIN are the 18-foot cascades of the **Ira Keller Fountain** (SW Third Avenue and Clay Street), designed specifically with summer kid-fun in mind. **Public restrooms** are located on the main floor of the Clay Street parking garage, between SW Third and SW Fourth avenues.

Another vital, but peaceful, component of Portland's downtown is the elm-lined oasis known as the **Park Blocks**. An 18-block stretch (harshly interrupted by seven that are privately owned) sandwiched between SW Park and Ninth avenues, it is reserved entirely for public use and public institutions such as the **Oregon Art Institute** (between SW Jefferson and SW Main streets), the **Oregon Historical Society** (between SW Jefferson and SW Madison streets), and the **Portland Center for the Performing Arts** and **Arlene Schnitzer Concert Hall** (between SW Madison and SW Salmon streets), and capped by **Portland State University**. (See Park Blocks in this section.)

RIVERPLACE/TOM McCALL WATERFRONT PARK

Along the Willamette River from the Marquam Bridge to the Steel Bridge (map:A5-L5)

Who says you can't just move an expressway? In the early '70s, Portlanders decided they didn't like the way the city had grown—an expressway called Harbor Drive impeded access to the otherwise scenic Willamette River. So the Portland Development Commission did what the locals asked for: it took the road away and replaced it with a showcase riverfront park, starting with **RiverPlace** (map:B5), the elegant **Alexis Hotel** (228-3233), the tony **RiverPlace Athletic Club** (221-1212), a sporty marina (with a great rowing club, the **RiverPlace Rowing Shop**, 223-5859), middle-income housing (theoretically), and a short promenade lined with a few specialty shops (including the respectable **Book Port**, 228-2665). At press time, an old Pacific Power and Light plant just south of this complex was being demolished to make way for RiverPlace II.

Today, the **Tom McCall Waterfront Park** (named for the governor credited with helping reclaim Oregon's rivers) has become indispensable. Its showpiece green lawns and exceedingly popular jogging paths are as playful (and popular) as the waters of the **Salmon Street Springs fountain** (1988) at the foot of SW Salmon. In the summer, it's rare to find a weekend when something (Rose Festival, park concerts, the Bite) isn't going on here (see the Calendar chapter).

The old visitors' center, in the country's first plywood building (smack in the middle of the park), is now **McCalls** (248-9710), a view restaurant off to an excellent start. The esplanade stretches approximately one mile north to the Burnside Bridge—that is, until the 100 newly planted Japanese cherry trees in **North Waterfront Park** take root (by the summer of 1990, we hope), which will extend the walkway to the Steel Bridge.

Wondering about our standards? We rate establishments on value, performance measured against the place's goals, uniqueness, enjoyability, loyalty of clientele, cleanliness, excellence and ambition of the cooking, and professionalism of the service. For an explanation of the star system, see How To Use This Book.

PARK BLOCKS/OREGON ART INSTITUTE

Along Park Ave: SW Jackson to SW Salmon streets,
then Burnside to NW Glisan St (map:C1-L2)

If Pioneer Courthouse Square is the heart of the city, the **Park Blocks** are its pulse: a calm, 25-block stretch from Oregon's urban **Portland State University** on the south end to NW Glisan Street. The entire elm-arched strip (minus seven blocks that in 1871 mistakenly ended up in private hands) is reserved for public use— including all the buildings on its perimeter.

The **South Park Blocks** end in a six-block pedestrians-only zone on the Portland State University campus, and for a few blocks beyond SW Market Street (the main artery into town from Highway 26 eastbound), student apartments mix with upscale condominiums.

Each block is earmarked with a sculpture or fountain. Tipped-over granite monoliths adorn the three-church block between SW Columbia and SW Jefferson streets. Check out the eye-tweaking outdoor murals on the **Oregon Historical Society's** new wing. (See also Museums in the Arts chapter.) Theodore Roosevelt and his horse guard the territory from here to the multifaceted **Oregon Art Institute** (1219 SW Park Avenue, 226-2811).

The Oregon Art Institute comprises the **Portland Art Museum**, the **Pacific Northwest College of Art**, the **Northwest Film and Video Center** (running film series in the museum's Berg Swann Auditorium), and the **Rental/Sales Gallery,** holed up at the Masonic Temple next door.

Designed by Portland's venerable architect Pietro Belluschi, the **Portland Art Museum** is a landmark structure on the South Park Blocks with rotating exhibits of classic to contemporary art. Its permanent holdings (Northwest Coast Indian art, tribal art of Cameroon, prehistoric Chinese artifacts, modern European and American sculpture and painting) span 35 centuries. The museum is open Tuesday through Sunday. **FREE** Admission is $3 for adults, but free on Thursdays from 4pm to 9pm. There are regular lectures and tours. A popular after-work jazz series, too (see the Nightlife chapter).

A somber statue of Abe Lincoln rests outside the current home of the **Northwest Film and Video Center,** the **Masonic Temple.** On the east side of the block is the **Portland Center for the Performing Arts** (1111 Park Avenue, 248-4496), connected at SW Main Street (this block is closed during concerts) to the larger **Arlene Schnitzer Concert Hall,** formerly the Paramount Theater. Purchase tickets for events at either location through the Performing Arts Center.

While the Park Blocks seem to end abruptly at SW Salmon Street (where the hip **B. Moloch/The Heathman Bakery and Pub,** cool **Humphrey Yogart,** and health-conscious **Macheesmo Mouse** occupy the high-demand retail space), in fact they're only half over. Skip over the ugly parking garages between SW Salmon and Washington streets to **O'Bryant Square** (named for Portland's first mayor, Hugh Donaldson O'Bryant), with a jet-engine-like fountain encircled by brick steps, a good spot to catch noontime concerts in summer. On the other side of Burnside are the **North Park Blocks.** Unlike their southern counterparts, many of the timeworn North Park Block buildings sport FOR SALE signs, and a stagnant swing set sits on the forgotten greenery in front of the **US Customs House.** Still, the Portland Development Commission's Union Station project (linking the train station to downtown), scheduled to break ground in January 1991, may mean better times for the North Park Blocks.

NORTHWEST PORTLAND

North of W Burnside between NW 18th and NW 27th avenues (map:FF7)

To most people, northwest Portland means the lively **NW 23rd Avenue,** which until recently was more funk than high fashion. In fact, the residential area beyond NW 23rd has been home to established Portland families inhabiting monumental Victorian mansions since the city's beginnings. Writers and entrepreneurs fringe the blocks just off the district's main street. Over the past few years, NW 23rd from W Burnside straight through to the more industrial area around Pettygrove Street has been revamped. The long-established Uptown Shopping Center has a new '80s look, while down the street many Victorian homes have been remodeled into small shopping enclaves. Wandering down NW 23rd Avenue (and don't miss

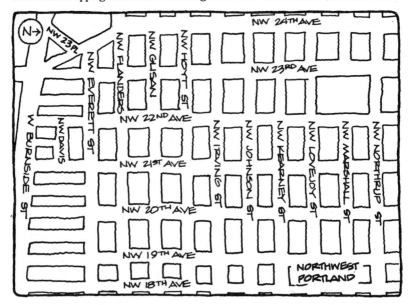

NW 21st) can easily make for an afternoon of browsing and an evening of good taste. **Parking** can be tough, so if you drive we suggest parking a few blocks off the avenue. Or take Tri-Met; call 233-3511.

Even though the **Uptown Shopping Center** (W Burnside and NW 23rd Avenue) is on the south side of Burnside, it's very much a part of northwest Portland. The **Town Pharmacy** (2334 W Burnside, 224-9226) has been an institution for 40 years (complete with soda fountain). Uptown spreads north of Burnside: **Elephant's Deli** (13 NW 23rd Place, 224-3955); **Phil's Uptown Meat Market** (17 NW 23rd Place, 224-9541); the district's utterly dependable **Uptown Hardware** (27 NW 23rd Place, 227-5375); **Foothill Broiler**, more like a cafeteria; and a new big store for little britches, **Lads and Lassies** (30 NW 23rd Place, 223-7811).

Just to the north are three other smart-looking shopping arcades. In the colorful concrete-and-glass **Everett Street Market,** the hedonistic **Ron Paul Charcuterie** (2310 NW Everett Street, 223-2121) shares a common area with a produce stand, a flower shop, and a yogurt shop. The **Nob Hill Exchange Building** houses Portland's first Moroccan restaurant, **Marrakesh** (121 NW 23rd Avenue, 248-9442), as well as **V Claire** (121 NW 23rd Avenue, 222-0233) for wedding gifts. Around the corner is a warm tangle of shops in the big clapboard **Westover Place**, where you'll find great coffee at **Kobos** (2340 NW Westover Road, 235-3331); one of the smartest lunch buys in town, **West Coast Bento** (2340 NW Westover Road, 227-1779); crisp white linens at **Virginia Jacobs** (4830 SW Scholls Ferry Road, 297-1882); and whimsically crafted things at **Claytrade** (2332 NW Westover Road, 224-0334).

Decadence is the name of the game on NW 23rd Avenue, and it comes in the form of a rococo chocolate mousse in an edible chocolate bowl at **Roberto's** (405 NW 23rd Avenue, 248-9040); a slice of pizza at **Escape from New York Pizza** (622 NW 23rd Avenue, 227-5423); a towering, intense autumn meringue at **Papa Haydn** (701 NW 23rd Avenue, 228-7317); or a molasses cookie from **Coffee People's Immediate Care Center** (806 NW 23rd Avenue, 226-3064), a sweet outpost of the **Coffee People** (803 NW 23rd Avenue, 221-0235) across the street. Its neighbor, **Macheesmo Mouse** (811 NW 23rd Avenue, 274-0500) is a more healthful cure for immediate needs. A wood-burning stove bakes excellent bread at **Le Four a Bois** (931 NW 23rd Avenue, 274-9039). Just across NW Pettygrove Street is the home of **Clear Creek Distillery** (1430 NW 23rd Avenue, 248-9470), which rivals European brandy makers with its pear and apple eaux de vie.

Indulgent storefronts, too: a stash of glassware and simple furnishings at **Kitchen Kaboodle** (NW 23rd Avenue and Flanders Street, 241-4040); the notoriously colorful **Benetton** (408 NW 23rd Avenue, 221-1131); and **Ann Sacks** (500 NW 23rd Avenue, 222-7125) handpainted tiles share the same old building on the corner of NW Glisan Street with **CC Exchange** (506 NW 23rd Avenue, 227-1477), an outlet for secondhand evening dresses. Attached is a fragrant frou-frou shop, **Geri Miner** (524 NW 23rd Avenue, 242-2539). At Irving Street, in its new location next door to Papa Haydn, is a dealer in cotton clothing for women, **Elizabeth Street** (908 NW 23rd Avenue, 243-2456), and down the street is **El Mundo for Men** (904 NW 23rd Avenue, 274-9477). Crystal and tablecloths adorn **Plate du Jour** (728 NW 23rd Avenue, 248-0350). Hip children's clothes hang downstairs at **Mako** (732 NW 23rd Avenue, 274-9081), and upstairs in the same building you'll find more than tops in **Sweaters** (728 NW 23rd Avenue, 226-0544). **Music Millennium** (801 NW

23rd Avenue, 248-0163) is to vinyl junkies what **Powell's Books** is to literary folk.

At NW Lovejoy Street, the **Good Samaritan Hospital** briefly interrupts this shopping-hound's street. Beyond, there's **Itchy Fingers Gallery** (1318 NW 23rd Avenue, 222-5237), with fresh-from-California art and gifts. At press time **Song of the Rose** (1328 NW 23rd Avenue, 224-0863) had opened its vegetarian doors to music from the neighboring new age bookstore, **New Renaissance** (1338 NW 23rd Avenue, 224-5097).

Parking's a tad easier on **NW 21st Avenue**, except at night, when there are crowds at Portland's favorite rocking-chair movie house, **Cinema 21** (616 NW 21st Avenue, 223-4515), and when restaurants here (and there are many) are busiest. Four bustling eateries between NW Lovejoy and Johnson streets jockey for position: **Ginza** (730 NW 21st Avenue, 223-7881), **Seafood Mama's** (721 NW 21st Avenue, 222-4121), **Delphina's** (2112 NW Kearney Street, 221-1195), and **Cajun Cafe** (2074 NW Lovejoy Street, 227-0227). A few blocks away is the region's first taco club, **Casa-U-Betcha** (612 NW 21st Avenue, 227-3887). Finish off the night with dessert from **Paisley's** (1204 NW 21st Avenue, 243-2403).

By day, volunteers run **The American Cancer Society's Discovery Store** (519 NW 21st Avenue, 274-9908), which doubles as a cancer information center and a select secondhand store (they do the weeding out for you). The extraordinary **Laura Russo Gallery** (805 NW 21st Avenue, 226-2754) maintains a strong commitment to Northwest artists. Before leaving the neighborhood, drop in for a draught at the **Blue Moon Tavern** (432 NW 21st Avenue, 223-3184), another McMenamin brew house.

AMERICAN ADVERTISING MUSEUM
9 NW 2nd Ave, AAM-0000 (map:J5)

KIDS FREE Who could forget Burma Shave signs, Will Vinton's California raisins, and Mobil's sign of the flying horse? All-American artifacts are preserved at AAM—the first museum of its kind in the world (conceived in '84, opened in '86). The print-and-broadcast advertising museum calls the 1890s former Erickson Saloon building its home—for now (it's quickly outgrowing its space). Time-line displays chart the development of advertising from the 15th century to the present. Memorable moments from radio days replay continuously, not just commercials but broadcasts that marked the course of history: FDR's final oath of office, CBS's Bob Trout announcing the end of World War II. Video recordings of the all-time best TV commercials keep your eyes glued to the tube as if you were watching *It's a Wonderful Life*. Periodic rotating exhibits bring Portland some of the best print-and-broadcast advertising around. Open Wednesday–Sunday. Admission is $1.50 for adults, kids are free.

PEARL DISTRICT
North of Burnside to Marshall Street between
NW 8th and NW 15th avenues (map:K2-N1)

Over the past six years, warehouses and wholesalers' storefronts in the aging industrial Northwest Triangle District have been taking on new lives. Empty spaces are slowly metamorphosing into clean-lined art galleries, antique showrooms, jazz

clubs, bookstores, and artists' lofts. And with the revitalization has come a new
name: the **Pearl District**. There's a long way to go before it's a real gem: unused
railroad tracks still crisscross streets, vacant buildings gape between pods of galleries, and loading docks stare emptily at the streets of this area that was once a
shipping hub.

The Pearl has become *the* place to gallery-browse, especially on the **First Thursday** of each month, when galleries stay open late with their new shows. Parking on
First Thursday can be tough, and blocks between gallery clusters can be dark—
wear walking shoes and bring a friend.

At press time the area boasted a total of 14 galleries, with a few more on the way.
(See Galleries in the Arts chapter.) Of particular interest are **Blackfish Gallery**
(420 NW Ninth Avenue, 224-2634), a local cooperative; two photography galleries,
Blue Sky and **Nine** (1231 NW Hoyt Street, 225-0210), which share a space; the impressive year-old **Butters Gallery** (312 NW 10th Avenue, 248-9378); the outstanding **Jamison/Thomas Gallery** (1313 NW Glisan Street, 222-0063), which
moved to the Pearl District as this book was going to press; the little **Quartersaw
Gallery** (528 NW 12th Avenue, 223-2264), always willing to take a chance on the
untried, with frequent success; and the **Pulliam/Nugent Gallery** (522 NW 12th Avenue, 228-6665), which in its new NW 12th Avenue space is one step closer to becoming a real force in regional contemporary art. Next door you'll find one-of-a-
kind furnishings at **Vox Furniture** (530 NW 12th Avenue, 224-6821).

FREE The art of beer making is not so much of a newcomer: pedestrians venturing
near NW 11th Avenue and Burnside have been greeted by the smell of hops since
Henry Weinhard moved his brewery here in 1904. Now **Blitz-Weinhard Brewing**

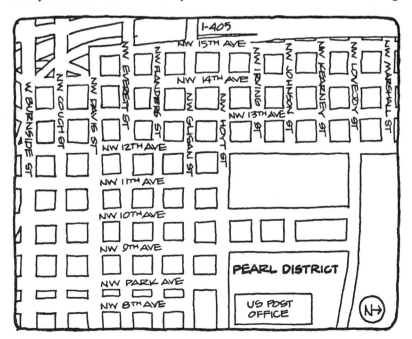

Company (1133 W Burnside, 222-4351) takes up five city blocks. Tours are followed by free samples. Lately, two microbreweries have moved in nearby: **Portland Brewing Company** (1339 NW Flanders Street, 222-7150) and **Bridgeport Brewing Company** (1313 NW Marshall Street, 241-7179).

Next door to Blitz-Weinhard, and almost as—pardon the pun—voluminous, is **Powell's Books** (1005 W Burnside, 228-4651). A visit to this literary institution is a tour in itself, so finish by resting your feet in the **Anne Hughes Coffee Room,** in the back of the store. For a pick-me-up caffe latte at the other end of the district, the jazzy **Giant Steps** (1208 NW Glisan Street, 226-2547), displaying art on loan from local galleries, is the spot to stop.

Nearby are two of the district's few retail outlets: Swedish-designed cotton kids' clothing from **Hanna Andersson** (327 NW 10th Avenue, 242-0920) and **Dehen Knitting Company** (404 NW 10th Avenue, 222-3871)—the place to buy that letter jacket you could only earn in high school.

SATURDAY MARKET
Under the Burnside Bridge at SW 1st Ave, 222-6072 (map:J6)

Seeing that Eugene had a thriving open-air Saturday market, a group of Portland artists decided their city needed one, too. Fifteen years ago they assembled the beginnings of what has become a major attraction for locals and visitors alike. Every Saturday and Sunday, March through December, 300 craft and food booths haphazardly cluster under the Burnside Bridge (for protection from Portland's notorious weather), to peddle handmade items from stained glass to huckleberry jam, sweaters to silver earrings. The food booths are often a few bites beyond what you'd expect from a cart. On any given day (and especially around holidays), lively musicians, jugglers, magicians, face painters, and clowns please the crowd.

Getting there. FREE Tri-Met (231-3199) is free in the heart of downtown (fareless square). MAX light rail—also free within the fareless square—runs to the Saturday Market every 15 minutes or so. Get off at Skidmore Fountain, right in the thick of things under the Burnside Bridge. Street parking is free on Sundays.

While you're at the Market, wander through the year-round stalls in the nearby **New Market Village** and the **Skidmore Fountain** buildings (see Skidmore/Old Town below).

SKIDMORE/OLD TOWN
Skidmore/Old Town: Between Front and 4th avenues from
SW Oak to NW Glisan streets (map:H5-L5)

Once part of the city's commercial core, the restored brick buildings of **Skidmore/Old Town,** just north of the present downtown, now abound with art galleries, good restaurants, and nightclubs. Demarcated by antique street signs, Old Town runs predominantly north of W Burnside between Front and Fourth avenues. Skidmore spills over just south of Burnside. Here lawyers, architects, artists, and media folk dominate the work force. On weekends nine months a year, an open market bustles underneath the Burnside Bridge, attracting tourists and locals (see Saturday Market in this chapter).

MAJOR ATTRACTIONS

At the center of **Skidmore** is the city's most gracious fountain, **Skidmore Fountain** (where two women dispense the gift of water in drinking troughs for both man and beast), in cobblestone **Ankeny Square**. Across Ankeny Square, the **Skidmore Fountain Building** has been remodeled as a mall with a number of silly tourist-oriented shops.

KIDS FREE At the east end of the square, the **Jeff Morris Fire Museum** (55 SW Ash Street) provides what is basically a window view of vintage fire engines. Take a peek, it's free. Down the street, the **Oregon Maritime Center and Museum** (113 SW Front Avenue, 224-7724) exhibits model sailing ships, Liberty Ships, stern-wheelers, and navigational instruments. The museum is open weekends; admission is $2 for adults; children under 8 are free.

West of Ankeny Square there's a courtyard with an overflow of tables from the eateries inside the **New Market Village**, a magnificent brick and terra-cotta building dating back to 1872. A column-lined atrium with two rows of tables displays three levels of decent boutiques, jewelry shops, florists, and a number of inexpensive eateries. There are two additional wings to the south and west of what was once the New Market Theater. Public bathrooms are downstairs (they're locked, so you'll need to ask one of the merchants for a key).

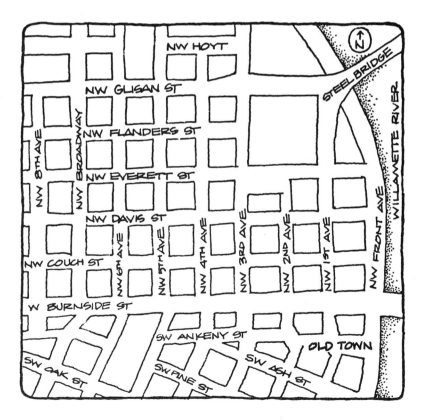

One unique street is SW Ankeny. It's only a block or so long, but for a quarter you can call upon the **World's Cheapest Psychic** and speak to the King himself at the **Church of Elvis**. Down a few mollusks at the Wachsmuth family's 75-year-old **Oregon Oyster Company** (208 SW Ash Street, 227-5906), or wish upon the hand-sewn silk shirts and boxy hats of **De La Salandra** (220 SW Ankeny Street, 226-6168). At the foot of SW Ankeny Street on Second Avenue, there's **Berbati** (19 SW Second, 226-2122), an excellent, casual Greek restaurant.

Just south along SW Second and SW First avenues is a handful of galleries. In the historic Hazeltine Building, the **Elizabeth Leach Gallery** (207 SW Pine Street, 224-0521) is a large, airy gallery well suited to large sculptures. **Gango Gallery** (50 SW Pine Street, 224-2270) has recently taken a turn toward fresh and technically accomplished Northwest contemporary artists. **Photographic Images** (208 SW First Avenue, 224-3543) exhibits excellent prints from master photographers. On the corner of SW Second Avenue and SW Ash Street, grab a cafe au lait at one of the city's finest bakeries, **Le Panier** (71 SW Second Avenue, 241-3524). France is also well represented through the large arched windows of **Crepe Faire** (133 SW Second Avenue, 227-3365). In the oldest section of town is the city's first chil-dren's bookstore, **Skidmore Village Books** (50 SW Third Avenue, 222-5076). Late in the afternoon, drop into **McCormick and Schmick's Seafood Restaurant** (235 SW First Avenue, 224-7522) for some of the best happy-hour eats in town.

Down the middle of SW First Avenue runs MAX light rail, transporting people from downtown to the east side as far as Gresham. Cross north under the Burnside Bridge to the carefully restored historic distric of **Old Town**—and the last free east-bound stop on MAX. At the corner of NW First Avenue and Burnside is a store where everything is **Made in Oregon** (10 NW First Avenue, 273-8354). The popular **Oregon Mountain Community** (60 NW Davis Street, 227-1038) stocks a good variety of outdoor sports clothing and equipment. Most of the Old Town busi-nesses center around NW Second Avenue, which begins at the offices of the city's weekly newspaper, **Willamette Week**, at the corner of W Burnside and NW Sec-ond Avenue. Across the street, the **American Advertising Museum** (9 NW Second Avenue, AAM-0000) is the country's first print-and-broadcast museum, in the 1890s former Erickson Saloon building (see American Advertising Museum in this section). At the north end of NW Second Avenue is Portland's only Native Amer-ican art gallery, **Quintana** (139 NW Second Avenue, 223-1729).

In between there's no shortage of places to eat. From the upstairs windows of **La Patisserie** (208 NW Couch Street, 248-9898), watch the activity in the streets with the octagonal One Pacific Square building in the background. Upon closer inspection, you'll find a plaque on the side that marks the high-water mark of the flood on June 7, 1894 (about 3 feet above the present sidewalk level). **Opus Too** (33 NW Second Avenue, 222-6077) dishes up excellent grilled fish. Next door, lights are low in **Jazz de Opus** (33 NW Second Avenue, 222-6077), a good choice for late-night drinks. One of the most strikingly designed Japanese restaurants in Portland is **Uogashi** (107 NW Couch Street, 242-1848). **Obi** (101 NW Second Avenue, 226-3826) creates innovative renditions of maki. Less inventive but equally satisfying is the homespun **Johnny's Greek Villa** (200 NW Third Avenue, 227-1096). There's also the staid **Couch Street Fish House** (105 NW Third Avenue, 223-6173).

▼

MAJOR ATTRACTIONS

Chinatown blends into Old Town right about at NW Third Avenue; however, the main serpent-adorned entrance to Chinatown is on Fourth Avenue. On November 21st, 1989, the area north of Burnside between NW Third and NW Sixth was designated a National Historic District, now the oldest and, technically, the largest in Oregon. However, it's still small enough that fiery red-and-yellow lampposts are needed to remind you of your whereabouts. Trucks unload bok choy at the back door of **Fong Chong** (301 NW Fourth Avenue, 220-0235), half Oriental grocery, half restaurant—Portland's finest dim sum parlor.

PITTOCK MANSION
3229 NW Pittock Dr, 248-4469 (map:FF7)

Henry Pittock had the advantage of watching over Portland from two perspectives: from behind the founder's desk at the *Daily Oregonian* and, in his later years, from his home 1,000 feet above the city. The stately **Pittock Mansion** (built by him in 1914) stands on 46 acres high above the city and stayed in the family until 1964, when the entire property was sold to the City of Portland for $225,000.

Inside, a graceful staircase sweeps from the basement to the second story (another, less conspicuous stairway leads to the servants' quarters on the top floor). The 22 rooms, furnished with antiques, include an oval parlor and a Turkish smoking room. Regular tours are conducted (1pm–5pm), and the manicured grounds around the mansion and Pittock Acres (with numerous hiking trails) are open to the public until dark. The gatehouse (once the gardener's cottage) for a time was the Gate Lodge restaurant, but it had closed at press time, and its future is uncertain.

WASHINGTON PARK
Park Place at Vista Ave, 796-5274 (map:GG7)

There are 280 parks in Portland. At 4,683 acres, Forest Park is the most sprawling and primitive, while the 24-square-inch Mill End's Park (SW Front Avenue and Taylor Street) is decidedly the city's smallest. Washington Park may well be the most civilized.

A substantial portion of the 546-acre plot, originally purchased by Portland's founders in 1871, is currently home to the well-kept trails of the **Hoyt Arboretum** (with an inspiring addition, the Vietnam Veterans' Living Memorial), as well as to the more formal **International Rose Test Garden**, the traditional **Japanese Gardens**, and the lush **Rhododendron Gardens**. In the northern end of the park, hiking trails meander through the woods. (See Gardens in the Exploring chapter.)

KIDS Also in the park is the **Washington Park Zoo** (4001 SW Canyon Road, 226-ROAR), famed for its successful breeding of Asian elephants; the informative, hands-on **Oregon Museum of Science and Industry** (4015 SW Canyon Road, 223-OMSI); and the educational **World Forestry Center** (4033 SW Canyon Road, 228-1367). (See Museums in the Arts Chapter.)

One-way roads wind through the park, and in summer a narrow-gauge train ($2

Looking for a particular place? Check the index at the back of this book for individual restaurants, nightclubs, lodgings, shops, attractions, and more.

adults, $1.50 children) runs through the zoo to the Rose Garden (limited to the zoo in the winter). Other facilities include four lit tennis courts, an outdoor amphitheater, covered picnic areas, and an archery range.

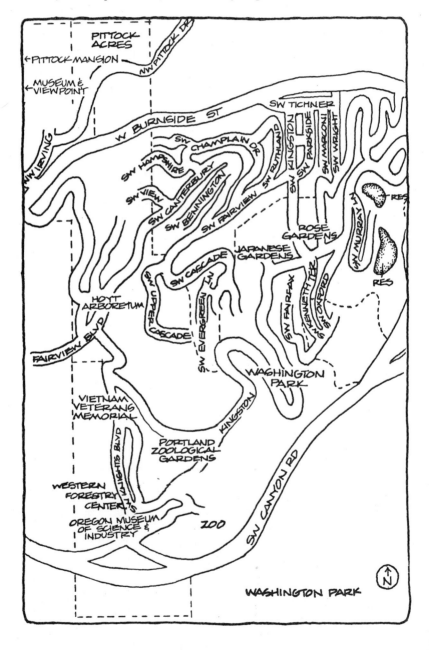

▼
MAJOR ATTRACTIONS

Hoyt Arboretum
4000 SW Fairview Blvd,
228-8732

KIDS FREE Sweeping views, miles of trails, and more than 700 species of trees and shrubs—all neatly labeled— make up Washington Park's 175-acre tree garden. It's an international collection of woody plants, including the nation's largest assortment of conifer species. Blossoms dust the Magnolia Trail in spring; a ¾-mile section of the Bristlecone Pine Trail is paved for wheelchair access. In the arboretum's southwest corner is the Vietnam Veterans' Living Memorial, an inspiring outdoor cathedral commemorating the Oregon victims of that conflict. Maps are available at the arboretum's Visitor Center (10am–4pm), and weekend guided walks (April– October) begin there.

International Rose Test Garden
400 SW Kingston Ave,
248-4302

FREE Whether for a blossom-framed snapshot of Mount Hood or to scrutinize a new hybrid, this is the obligatory first stop for any visitor to the Rose City. The garden (established 1917) is the oldest continually operating testing program in the country. Thanks to its 10,000 plants—more than 400 varieties—and a knockout setting overlooking downtown Portland, it's an unmatched display of the genus *Rosa*. The garden's 4.5 acres are a riot of blooms from June through October, from dainty half-inch-wide miniatures to great blowzy 8-inch beauties. Fragrant old-garden varieties fill the gap between the parking lot and the Washington Park tennis courts.

Japanese Garden
611 SW Kingston Ave,
223-4070

In 1988, the Japanese ambassador to the United States pronounced this the most beautiful and authentic Japanese garden, ahem, outside of Japan. In actuality, it comprises five gardens: the traditional Flat Garden, the secluded and flowing Strolling Pond Garden, the Tea Garden with a *chashitsu* (ceremonial teahouse), the stark Sand and Stone Garden, and a miniature Natural Garden. In contrast with the exuberant rose blossoms across the street, this is an oasis of lush greenery, winding paths, and tranquil ponds. Flowering cherries and azaleas accent the grounds come spring; in summer, the Japanese irises bloom. And in autumn, the laceleaf maples glow orange and red. Eaves and posts of the Japanese pavilion frame the Flat Garden to the west and Mount Hood to the east. Admission is $3.50 for adults, $2 for seniors and children over 6.

Books in the Best Places *series read as personal guidebooks, but our evaluations are based on numerous reports from local experts. Final judgements are made by the editors. Our inspectors never identify themselves (except over the phone) and never accept free meals or other favors. Be an inspector. Send us a report.*

Washington Park Zoo
4001 SW Canyon Rd,
226-1561

KIDS What began just over a century ago as a seaman-turned-veterinarian's menagerie on SW Third Avenue and Morrison Street has since grown into an outstanding 64-acre zoo in Washington Park, winning awards for exhibits such as that of the lush flora and fauna of the Cascades as well as the colony of endangered Peruvian Humboldt penguins, well protected (and thriving) here. In 1962, Packy—the first Asian elephant born in the Western Hemisphere—blazed the trail for the pachyderm breeding program. Twenty-three newborns later, the elephant grounds haven't won any prizes for looks but have received plenty of praise for functionality. The zoo's complex chimpanzee exhibit claims to be the nation's largest, with an arena architecturally designed specifically with the natural behavior of the chimps in mind. Other unique environments include the extreme climates of Alaska and the microscopic world of insects. In April 1989 the newest exhibit, African Grasslands, opened with black rhinoceros, giraffes, impalas, zebras, and birds. Plans are in the works for an African rain forest by 1991.

A small steam train chugs through the zoo year-round. In summer, jazz and blues concerts are held on Wednesdays and Thursdays respectively, at the grassy outdoor amphitheater (see Calendar chapter).

HAWTHORNE

Along Hawthorne Blvd from SE 17th Ave to SE 42nd Ave
(map:GG4-GG5)

"Loretta? Loretta, you cannot just sit here and smoke a joint. No, no. Not here in public," explained a well-dressed man to a bag lady on Hawthorne Boulevard. Fact is, you used to be able to do just about anything on Hawthorne among its disjointed architecture, fledgling businesses, and vacant buildings. Today, you can still sell off old records, clothes, or jewelry at the string of secondhand stores on Hawthorne Boulevard, from the Willamette to the foot of the country's only inner-city volcano, Mount Tabor. And in the half-dozen or so blocks between SE 32nd and SE 38th avenues you can spend late mornings reading *The New York Times* over a cup of espresso at **Cup and Saucer** (3566 SE Hawthorne Blvd, 236-6001); purchase hand-cured sausage, colorful pasta, or fine cookbooks at **Pastaworks** (3735 SW Hawthorne Blvd, 232-1010), or sniff precious fragrances from the exclusive **Perfume House** (3328 SE Hawthorne Blvd, 234-5375).

Hawthorne is also fast becoming a mecca for food critics. Until the idiosyncratic **Bread and Ink Cafe** (3610 SE Hawthorne Blvd, 239-4756) opened its neighborly doors, the dogs and burgers at **Nick's Famous Coney Island Food** (3746 SE Hawthorne Blvd, 235-4024) were Hawthorne's primary fare. Nowadays, the narrow sliver of Hawthorne Boulevard provides the diner with a good representation of international cuisines. Perhaps the most exotic is in the very simple space at **Phnom Penh Express** (4604 SE Hawthorne Blvd, 232-8608). There are also a number of Vietnamese eateries, the most popular of which is **Thanh Thao** (4005 SE Hawthorne Blvd, 238-6232). Decent Mexican fare can be had at **La Casa de Rios** (4343 SE Hawthorne Blvd, 234-2038). For breakfast, try the **Tabor Hill Cafe**'s (3766 SE Hawthorne Blvd, 230-1231) honest omelets. Veterans of the '60s hang on—and out—at the **Hawthorne Street Cafe** (3354 SE Hawthorne Blvd, 232-4982).

Even when you're not hungry, the area makes for a good snoop. Rickety steps lead into the **Knotting Chamber** (3257 SE Hawthorne Blvd, 232-1043), a two-story Victorian that beckons needlepointers and knitters; or just for thrills poke around **Murder by the Book** (3729 SE Hawthorne, 232-9995). Fanciful artwork is display in the **Graystone Gallery** (3279 Hawthorne Blvd, 238-0651), or pick up virtually anything, from costume jewelry to $450 armoires, at the **Beaver Trading Post** (3713 SE Hawthorne Blvd, 232-8482). The racks of dark retro clothing in **Grin n' Wear It** (3535 SE Hawthorne, 232-8425) are balanced with colorful cotton and rayon **El Mundo for Women** (3556 SE Hawthorne Blvd, 239-4605). But even as the boutiques and cafes spread down the street, the vestiges of Hawthorne's past life (**Beaver Book Store**, 238-1668, and **Crocodile Records**, 238-1957) assure that it will be a long while before they take over.

BRIDGES
Over the Willamette River

The bridges of Portland serve as important links between downtown commerce and the residential neighborhoods on the east side. More than simply utilitarian, however, they also help shape the city—much as the ferries distinguish Seattle or colleges define Boston. And every Portlander has a favorite span.

Many people love the **St. Johns Bridge**, a graceful suspension bridge on Highway 30 on the way to Mount St. Helens. It was constructed during the Depression and completed in 1931, the last to be built in the area for more than 25 years. Its four lanes are among the least traveled of any Portland bridge, and its location, at the base of Forest Park, is out of the way and not visible from downtown.

The downtown bridge that's cherished by pedestrians but cursed by motorists (and aesthetes) is the timeworn 1910 **Hawthorne Bridge**. Its open grating allows walkers, runners, and cyclists to view the river below, but that same grating can be as slick as ice, even on sunny days. This was the second Portland bridge to be illuminated by a citizen group called the Willamette Light Brigade, which is in the process of permanently lighting all the Portland bridges.

Just north of the Hawthorne is the **Morrison Bridge**, the first Portland-area span over the Willamette. In 1987 it became the first bridge to receive the attention of the controversial Light Brigade. Many consider the Morrison a vital route into the city. Its west end is at the foot of the hotel and shopping district, and its east end provides direct access to I-5 northbound and I-84 east (toward the airport).

Some claim the best view of Portland is from the unsightly **Marquam Bridge**, which shoulders I-5 (and 100,000 vehicles daily) across the Willamette. Unfortunately, the view can be enjoyed only at freeway speeds. A good reference for Portland bridge buffs is *The Portland Bridge Book* (Oregon Historical Society, 1989), by Sharon Wood and artist Jay Dee Alley.

THE GREAT OUTDOORS
BICYCLING

Portland's diverse topography (flat and breezy stretches on the east side, steep and breathless hills on the west) has something for every cyclist. In fact, many people bike to work, and even more—the Portland Police neighborhood patrol and the urban messengers—work on bikes.

Cyclists looking for organized 30- to 100-mile rides at a touring pace should call the **Portland Wheelmen Touring Club Hotline** (282-PWTC). Up to 120 people show up for these group rides, and you don't have to be a member to pedal along. The oldest club in town, **Rose City Wheelmen** (281-2250), has evolved into a masters' racing club primarily for ages 30 and older. RCW, known for its annual Rose Festival race at Mount Tabor and a July ride to Hood River, holds training rides every Saturday and Sunday. Serious racers opt for the **Beaverton Bicycle Club** (649-4632), which has a strong group of junior riders but no age limit. Membership in Oregon's most elite group, **Team Oregon** (620-9740), is by invitation only.

The **Oregon Cycling Association** (661-0686) holds twice-a-week events from May to mid-September: practice races are at **Portland International Raceway** on Tuesday nights, when the raceway's closed to autos, and on Thursdays across town at the **Alpenrose Velodrome** (6149 SW Shattuck Rd, 244-1133), the second-shortest track in the country (hence heroically steep), and situated next to a working dairy farm. Mountain biking, to the dismay of some hard-core environmentalists, is also beginning to make tracks through Portland parks.

The following are some of the favored bicycle routes in the area:

Columbia River Scenic Highway
NE 82nd Ave to Cascade Locks

Eighty-five miles round trip. In at least one direction you might ordinarily be cursing the famed winds of the Columbia—but most of the way you'll be loving the scenery too much to think about it. You begin at Montavilla Park (NE 82nd Avenue and NE Glisan Street), and follow Halsey to the Scenic Highway, which eventually joins I-84 at Warrendale. I-84 takes you the last few miles eastward to Cascade Locks—and here highway riding is legal. Cross the Columbia at the Bridge of the Gods; Highway 14 takes riders back on the Washington bank. Spectacular, especially amid fall foliage.

Leif Erickson Drive
NW Thurman St to

When it's light enough out to ride in the woods after work, **Portland United Mountain Pedalers** (288-9627) meet at the NW Thurman Street gate to Leif Erickson

THE GREAT OUTDOORS

Germantown Rd
(map:FF7-DD9)

Drive at 5:30pm on Wednesdays (May–September) for a fat-tire tour of Forest Park. It's rough, but possible, on touring bikes. The 11-mile gravel road (paved for only a few hundred yards) twists north along Forest Park. This is the city's only (and barely, at that) acknowledged mountain-bike area. For the first 6 miles, the road threads in and out of the gullies, offering occasional spectacular views of the river and northeast Portland. The last 5 miles are the most isolated and peaceful. Although the fragile Wildwood Trail is off limits, four new areas have been opened for mountain biking. This both extends—and shortens—the bike routes: now mountain bikers can abbreviate the trip by taking the cutoff to NW Skyline Boulevard via Fire Lane 3 (just past the 3½-mile marker), NW Saltzman Road (6 miles), Springville Road (9¼ miles), and Germantown Road (11 miles). Then loop back on busy Highway 30, or continue to the newly opened Bonneville Road and Fire Lanes 12 and 15.

Hagg Lake
7 miles southwest of Forest Grove, 359-5732

KIDS During spring and summer, cyclists swarm the well-marked bike lane around manmade Henry Hagg Lake in Scoggins Valley Park. The loop follows gentle hills and fields for 10½ miles, passing numerous picnic and swimming spots. Ambitious cyclists can start in Forest Grove and take the Old TV Highway to Scoggins Valley Road.

Marine View Drive
Kelley Point Park at the confluence of the Willamette and Columbia rivers to east end of N Marine Dr (map:AA9-BB6)

Just across the Willamette from Sauvie Island, Kelley Point Park anchors a favorite ride that follows the Columbia east along the airplane-swept flats of Marine Drive. Most just ride the river road, but you can also cross over I-205 (there's a bike lane) to Washington and back to the path alongside the roaring I-5 via Evergreen Highway and Columbia Way.

Sauvie Island
Confluence of Willamette and Columbia rivers off Hwy 30 (map:AA9)

See Daytrips in the Outings chapter.

Skyline Boulevard
Skyline Blvd between NW Cornell and Rocky Point roads (map:GG7-DD9)

Doing Skyline Boulevard as a loop requires pedaling an elevation gain of 1,400 feet, but it's truly the most scenic 17 miles around, with broad views of the Willamette Valley from this ridge-top road. Begin in Portland or in Beaverton (the climb's about the same either way).

If you've found a place around town that you think is a Best Place, send in the report form at the back of the book. If you're unhappy with one of the places, please let us know why. We depend on reader input.

BIRD WATCHING/ WILDLIFE VIEWING

Every glovebox should include a copy of the *Oregon Wildlife Viewing Guide* (Defenders of Wildlife, 333 S State Street, Suite 173, Lake Oswego, OR 97094, $5.50), published with the assistance of many of the appropriate regulatory agencies. Many of the viewing sites are also marked with state highway signs depicting binoculars. Here are a few of the more notable:

Clackamette Park
At I-205 and Hwy 99 interchange, exit 9 from I-205 (map:NN3)

A busy park for small and large boat launchings; in the spring, blue herons nest on the shores of Goat Island.

John Inskeep Environmental Learning Center
19600 S Molalla Ave (Clackamas Community College), Oregon City, 657-6958 (map:DD3)

See Gardens in this chapter.

Kelley Point Park
N Suttle Rd off west end of N Marine Dr (map:AA9-BB6)

See Parks and Waterfront in this chapter.

Oaks Bottom Wildlife Refuge
Trailheads: SE 7th Ave and Sellwood Blvd (Sellwood Park); SE Milwaukie Blvd and Mitchell St, 796-5193 (map:HH5)

These 160 acres of woods and wetlands were the first officially designated wildlife refuge in Portland. An almost 3-mile walk begins in Sellwood Park. More than 140 species of birds have been spotted here, the most popular of them being the great blue heron, which feeds on the carp in the Bottoms. Others include pileated woodpeckers and warblers (spring) and green-backed herons (spring and summer).

Portland Audubon Society Bird Sanctuary
5151 NW Cornell Rd, 292-6855 (map:FF7)

Every birder in the state ends up here eventually—in part for the winged species that flock here and in part for the excellent naturalists' bookstore. Surrounded by the vast wilderness of Forest Park and connected to the Wildwood and Macleay Park trail is a 160-acre sanctuary owned by the Audubon Society. Trails wrap around a pond and follow the creek. At the Wildlife Care Center visitors can view barn and screech owls, red-tailed hawks, and injured fowl on the mend. The society's bookstore has a viewing window overlooking feeding platforms for local songbirds.

Inspectors for the Best Places *series accept no free meals or accommodations; the book has no sponsors or advertisers.*

Powell Butte
*SE Powell Blvd and SE
58th (unmarked street)
(map:HH1)*

See Parks and Waterfront in this chapter.

Ross Island
*Willamette River, just
south of Ross Island
Bridge (map:HH5)*

Ross Island actually includes the complex of Ross, Hard-tack, East, and Toe islands. All except Toe are owned by Ross Island Sand and Gravel and are being slowly devoured by the company's backhoes. On the northwest side of privately owned Toe Island is a 50-nest great blue heron rookery in a black cottonwood grove. The rookery can be viewed only by boat or with binoculars from the mainland. Best shoreside views (try for winter, when the trees are leafless) are from the Willamette Greenway, just north of Willamette Park. Also look for belted kingfishers nesting on the island's steep banks, as well as beavers and red foxes. The nearest boat ramp is in Willamette Park, but *please* don't land on the island.

**Sauvie Island Wildlife
Management Area**
*At the confluence of the
Willamette and Columbia
rivers, north end of Sauvie
Island*

See Parks and Waterfront in this chapter.

Washington Park Zoo
*4001 SW Canyon Rd,
west of Portland on Hwy
26, 226-7627*

See Washington Park, in Major Attractions in the Exploring chapter.

CANOEING/KAYAKING

Four rivers converge on the Portland area: leisurely kayaks and canoes paddle along the shores of the Willamette and Columbia rivers watching for blue herons, which nest along the banks; whitewater kayakers surf the rapids of the Sandy and Clackamas rivers. And don't forget the 6,500 lakes and reservoirs in this state alone: pick up a copy of *Oregon's Quiet Waters: A Guide to Lakes for Canoeists and Other Paddlers* by Cheryl McLean and Clint Brown, which includes more than a dozen within two hours of Portland.

South of the city, canoe and kayak rentals are available from either of two shops on opposite sides of the Willamette. On the west side, across SW Macadam Avenue from Willamette Park, the **Ebb & Flow Kayak Center** (0604 SW Nebraska Street, 245-1756) rents canoes, sea kayaks, and all the accessories for $10–25 a day. Lessons are available. On the east side, there's the 30-year-old floating **Sportcraft Marina** (1701 Clackamette Drive, Oregon City, 656-6484). Both shops offer lessons and, in summer, are open seven days. On warm Saturdays it's best to call ahead to reserve a boat.

Whitewater enthusiasts prefer **Alder Creek Kayak Supply** (39085 Pioneer Boulevard, Sandy, 668-3121). They don't rent downriver kayaks; instead, take the $220 six-week class or sign up for $15-an-hour private lessons. In fall 1990, Alder Creek will conduct its first international trek to Rio General and Rio Paquare in Costa Rica.

CLIMBING

On July 19, 1894, aided by the complex carbohydrates of an old-fashioned bean bake, 193 persons climbed Mount Hood and initiated themselves as members of the **Mazamas** (909 NW 19th Avenue, 227-2345, map:FF6). Now 2,500 members strong, the Mazamas are Oregon's biggest climbing group and the standard local means of acquiring mountain- and rock-climbing skills. (Oddly, membership requires that you climb a glaciated peak.) This safety-conscious organization is a superb resource offering seasonal group climbs, weekly lectures (at its northwest Portland clubhouse), midweek rock climbs, day hikes, and other adventurous activities both inside and outside of the Northwest. Women who want less–structured climbing adventures and more independence can contact two organizations based in Seattle: **Women Climbers Northwest** (PO Box 20573, Seattle, WA 98102)—for social interaction, not instruction—and **Woodswomen Northwest** (1423 35th Avenue, Seattle, WA 98122, 206-325-9589) for organized trips.

Throughout the year, avid climbers hone their skills at the dynamic three-year-old **Portland Rock Gym** (2034 SE Sixth Avenue, 232-8310, map:GG5), which has finally settled into its 4,000-square-foot home with 20-foot-high indoor simulated-rock climbing walls, overhangs and all. Lessons and rental equipment are available.

The following are a few of the major climbs (alpine and rock), all within three hours of Portland:

Broughton Bluff
Lewis and Clark State
Park, above the east bank
of the Sandy River

These cliffs, 30 minutes from Portland, tend to be dirty and covered with vegetation, but the southwestern exposure protects climbers from the cold winds of the Columbia River Gorge.

Horsethief Butte
2½ miles east of The
Dalles bridge on Washing-
ton State Hwy 14

Here's a good practice spot, a basaltic rock mesa offering corridors of short climbs and top-rope challenges. Halfway back to Portland along Highway 14 is **Beacon Rock**. One of the river's prominent landmarks, this monolith provides climbers with technically difficult climbs—as well as poison oak and loose rock. Still, the climber is often safer than the many unsuspecting hikers who misnavigate the treacherous hiking trail below.

Mount Adams
95 miles northeast of Port-
land, (509) 395-2501

See Excursions in the Outings chapter.

Mount Hood
50 miles east of Portland,
666-0704

When British navigator Capt. George Vancouver first spied Mount Hood from the mouth of the Columbia River in 1792, he thought it must have been the highest mountain in the world. At just over 11,245 feet, Mount Hood is not even the highest in the Cascades, but its beautiful asymmetry and the relative ease of ascent make it one of the busiest peaks in the country. Still, due to unpredictable weather and very steep snow climbing (the last 1,500 feet), climbers should have either a skilled guide or solid mountaineering skills. **Timberline Mountain Guides** (1-548-0749) are based, in summer, at the Wy'east Day Lodge at Timberline. See also Daytrips in the Outings chapter.

Mount St. Helens
55 miles northeast of Portland, (206) 247-5473

See Excursions in the Outings chapter.

Rocky Butte Quarry
Between Rocky Butte Park and I-205 off NE 91st Ave (map:FF3)

This quarry, now abandoned, was first mined by the Works Projects Administration for the construction of the Rocky Butte fortress at the top. Its west wall is the site of the area's most popular bouldering. The cracked basalt cliffs support over 100 routes (some as high as 150 feet) and are most easily accessible by top roping. Watch out for poison oak.

Smith Rock State Park
9 miles northeast of Redmond on US 97, 3 hours southeast of Portland, 1-546-3412

Its extreme difficulty (welded tuff surfaces sometimes soft enough to tear off in your hand), its stunning scenery, and its arid climate have helped make Smith Rock a mecca for world-class climbers. The season is long (February–November), since most of the rain falls at the turn of the year. Watch climbers ascend "Monkey Face," the park's toughest climb. Bivouac camping only, no trailers, in the state park along Crooked River.

Nearby 350-foot chisel-shaped **Stein's Pillar** (east of Prineville on US 26 to the Ochoco Reservoir, follow Mill Creek Road north 7 miles) has a couple of enjoyable routes too.

FISHING

From February to June, fanatical anglers line their boats bank-to-bank across the Willamette (in formations called hoglines) and wait for the river's monsters to bite. The spring Chinook weigh 20 or 30 pounds, and otherwise responsible professionals can be found skipping work and running up huge bills at **Larry's Sports Center** (656-0321), strategically located halfway between the Willamette River hogline (at Oregon City) and the one across the Clackamas River's mouth above Willamette

Falls. There 100,000 wearying salmon wait for the muddy Willamette to clear.

The Clackamas River's year-round mix of spring Chinook salmon, summer and winter steelhead, and fall Chinook and Coho salmon lures a steady stream of fishermen to its banks and wading pools. Information and guides can be obtained from the Oregon State Marine Board, 3000 Market Street NE, Salem, OR 97310, 378-8587. Hogliners and other anglers can find **salmon and steelhead tag information** at the **Oregon Department of Fish and Wildlife** (2501 SW First Avenue, 229-5400; mailing address, PO Box 59, Portland, OR 97207). A 24-hour automated number provides answers to common questions (number not available at press time), or pick up the annual regulations at fishing goods stores or by writing the department. Following the lead of other states' fishing promotions, the state is debuting a free day of fishing on the second Saturday in June 1990, expected to become an annual event.

Two local groups have been especially active in helping to save the rivers for fishing. **Northwest Steelheaders** (PO Box 22065, Milwaukie, OR 97222, 653-4176) promotes fishery enhancement and protection programs, river access, and improved sportfishing. **Oregon Trout** (7830 SW 40th Avenue, No. 2, Portland, OR 97219, 244-2292) works through the courts and regulations processes to restore and preserve habitats.

GOLFING

Portland has more golfers than greens. In fact, a recent study by the parks and recreation department concluded that the city could easily support another 20 courses. Currently, there are at least 20 18-hole golf courses within 20 miles of the city center, though half are private. A half-dozen courses were under construction at press time, but for now the harsh reality is that every 18 holes must support an average of 3,000 golfers. And only three are considered first rate.

The most spectacular courses are private: the elite among them include the **Columbia-Edgewater Country Club** (2838 NE Marine Drive, 285-8354), **Portland Golf Club** (5900 SW Scholls Ferry Road, 292-2778), **Riverside Golf & Country Club** (8105 NE 33rd Drive, 282-7265), and **Waverly Country Club** (1100 SE Waverly Drive, Milwaukie, 654-9509).

The following are the best of the public courses:

Cedars Golf Club
15001 NE 181st St,
Brush Prairie, WA,
285-7548

Just north of Vancouver, WA the Cedars offers a long, rolling challenge with a lot of water hazards. Considered tournament quality, with nice clubhouse facilities.

Eastmoreland Golf Course and Driving Range
2425 SE Bybee Blvd,
775-2900 (map:II5)

Bordered by the Crystal Springs Rhododendron Garden and blessed with old and venerable trees and lovely landscaping, the second-oldest golf course in the state is currently undergoing cosmetic surgery by way of a new clubhouse, driving range, and some course renovation. A technically challenging and popular course.

Heron Lakes Golf Course
3500 N Victory Blvd,
289-1818 (map:CC7)

Designed by golf course architect Robert Trent Jones Jr. (even the hills are manmade), Heron Lakes is the city's only championship-quality public golf course. With 27 excellently planned holes (and only 15 minutes from downtown), it's one of the busiest in the city.

Progress Downs Golf Course
and Driving Range
8200 SW Scholls Ferry
Rd, Beaverton, 646-5166
(map:HH9)

Southwest Portland's only regulation 18-hole public golf course is especially popular on weekends. Progress Downs also has a covered, lighted driving range for night and foul-weather practice.

HIKING

It's true, the hiking in Oregon is superlative. The cascading waterfalls of the Columbia River Gorge, the alpine lakes of the Cascades, the desolate peaks of the Wallowas, majestic Mount Hood, and the rugged Oregon Coast—all (except perhaps the Wallowas) are within easy access of Portland. However, to really get away you need barely leave the city limits. In fact, a 24.6-mile hike, the Wildwood Trail, begins in northwest Portland. The Wildwood Trail (see listing) in Forest Park is part of a 140-mile hiking/biking/running loop around the city (see 40-Mile-Loop in the Daytrips section of the Excursions chapter).

One place to start, if you're unfamiliar with the region, is at **Portland Parks and Recreation** (1120 SW Fifth Avenue, Room 502, Portland, OR 97204, 796-5132) or the **Mazamas** (909 NW 19th Avenue, Portland, OR 97209, 227-2345). For a nominal fee, both schedule frequent hikes at all levels of difficulty.

For those farther afield, good maps of day- and half-day hikes in the Gorge and around Mount Hood can be found at the **US Forest Service** office (319 SW Pine Street, first floor, 326-2877). Parking lots at some trailheads are notorious for car break-ins—don't leave anything valuable behind.

The following are a few of the better close-in hikes:

Kelley Point Park
N Suttle Rd off west end of
N Marine Dr
(map:AA9-BB6)

See Parks and Waterfront in this chapter.

Lower Macleay Park
NW 29th Ave and Upshur
St (map:FF7)

Balch Creek is one of the few creeks that still flow unfettered down the otherwise developed West Hills. Lower Macleay Trail connects NW Upshur Street to Forest Park's long Wildwood Trail, but hikers can make a 2-mile loop up Balch Canyon by taking a right at the first trail intersection, then right again at the second, ending up on NW Raleigh Street. A short walk northeast to the Thurman Bridge above the park leads back down to the starting point. At the park, the creek disappears into a drain pipe.

Marquam Nature Park

Trailheads: Council Crest Park, Sam Jackson Park Rd (just west of the Carousel Restaurant); SW Terwilliger Blvd, near the OHSU School of Dentistry (map:GG7)

Just as it was becoming technologically possible to build view homes in the steep gulches of Marquam Hill, the Friends of Marquam Nature Trail were working to save this path through the forested hillside. From the parking lot off Sam Jackson Park Road (which is mostly used for overflow parking from the Oregon Health Sciences University) the trail climbs 900 feet to Council Crest. To walk to Washington Park Zoo, continue over the top to the intersection of Talbot and Patton roads. A new short downhill trail leads to a Highway 26 overpass. The trail is remarkably quiet and peaceful—even so, women should bring a friend or a large dog.

Oaks Bottom Wildlife Refuge

Trailheads: SE 7th Ave and Sellwood Blvd (Sellwood Park); SE Milwaukie Blvd and Mitchell St, 796-5193 (map:HH5)

See Bird Watching in this chapter.

Sauvie Island Wildlife Management Area

At the confluence of the Willamette and Columbia rivers, north end of Sauvie Island

See Daytrips in the Outings chapter.

Wildwood Trail (Forest Park)

Main trailheads: W Burnside gravel parking area (map:GG7), Washington Park (map:GG7), NW Cornell Rd (map:FF7), NW Thurman St (map:EE7)

One of the country's longest natural woodland trails winding through a city park, the Wildwood Trail is Portland's cherished refuge for hikers and runners. The shady trail through groves of fir and aspen officially begins at the World Forestry Center and links such attractions as the Hoyt Arboretum, Pittock Mansion, and the Portland Audubon Bird Sanctuary before it plunges into the less-trod territories of Forest Park. It ends 24½ miles later, at Germantown Road. Many spurs cross the trail, joining it to various neighborhoods and parks. The first 10 miles are well used, the last are good for solitude.

The best place to pick up the Wildwood Trail is at its origin at the World Forestry Center off Highway 26. The trail crosses W Burnside (be quick when crossing—it's the main commuter route into the city). Then follow the trail up to Pittock Mansion or farther north to NW Cornell Road. Another option is to explore the branching trails of the Hoyt Arboretum (in Washington Park). But beware, these are the most used parts of the trails, and they also are very hilly. Another trail begins across the

Highway 26 overpass (from the south end of the Wildwood Trail) and connects the Wildwood Trail to panoramic Council Crest. Not many people know about this, but it's only a mile—best when timed with sunset.

HORSEBACK RIDING

Flying M Ranch
10 miles west of Yamhill, watch for signs, 662-3222

KIDS Known for its Old West down-hominess, the Flying M is a great place to take the kids (over age 10) riding. The fee is $10 per hour, and that includes a guide. For more adventuresome travel, overnight rides up Trask Mountain are offered at $150 per person for two days and one night, including all meals, lodging, and, yes, Joe Justin's campfire songs at the mountain's top.

Lakeside Horse Rentals
162nd Ave off Foster Rd, 761-1853 (map:II1)

This stable, located near Powell Butte, has horses for every level of riding skill, and the rates are reasonable: $8 per hour. With 120 acres of trails and, on clear days, views of two volcanoes, it's a popular place. Call ahead for reservations.

ICE SKATING

Lloyd Center Ice Pavilion
2201 Lloyd Center, 282-2511 (map:FF5)

Closed at press time for the first time in 30 years, this formerly open-air skating rink will reopen in fall 1990 under a roof. The renovated facilities will include a pro skate shop. Group and private lessons available.

Valley Ice Arena
9250 SW Beaverton-Hillsdale Hwy, Beaverton, 297-2521 (map:HH9)

It's the largest around and has been a fixture of the relic Valley Plaza Shopping Center for 25 years. Lessons are available and skate rentals are free with admission. Public skating most weekday mornings, afternoons, and weekends. The Portland Winterhawks hockey team regularly scrimmages here.

RIVER RAFTING

The local rafting season generally runs from May to October. Local outfitters rent the necessary equipment to run the four closest whitewater rivers—Clackamas, Sandy, White Salmon, and Klickitat. Since river conditions can change rapidly, inexperienced rafters should stick to the guided trips. One of the most reputable rental outfitters is **River Trails Canoe and Raft Rentals** (336 E Columbia Street, Troutdale, 667-1964), through which, for $40 per raft, up to four people can float the relatively calm section of the Sandy from Oxbow Park 9 miles to Lewis and Clark Park. More confident rafters can run the longer section that starts 16 miles upriver, which is designated an Oregon Scenic Waterway and includes Class III rapids. **M'n'M Rafting** (661-RAFT) is another source for all the equipment necessary for trips.

Less than two hours from Portland, **White Water Adventure** (38 Northwestern Lake Resort, White Salmon, WA 98672, 509-493-3121) offers guided daytrips on the White Salmon and Klickitat rivers. The spring-fed White Salmon has rapids in classes II, III, and IV. From March to October, all you need to do is show up for the 2½-hour float through inspiring scenery. White Water runs three trips a day down the recently designated wild and scenic White Salmon. Snow-pack runoff keeps the season to a short three months (April–June); call for reservations. Prices for all trips start at $40 per person; group rates available.

One of the longest-running Portland-based outfitters (22 years), **Lut Jerstad Adventures** (PO Box 19537, Portland, OR 97219, 244-4364), will take groups of eight or more down Oregon's premier rafting rivers, the Rogue, Owyhee, and Deschutes. The Owyhee, in southeast Oregon, must be run in the spring—it's usually dry enough by June to roller-skate in the riverbed. Jerstad will also fill special requests to run the John Day and Grande Rhonde. Three-day trips with the works—food, guides, equipment, and four-star service—start at $325 per person.

For those on their own, a good place to start gathering equipment and information is **Andy and Bax Sporting Goods** (234-7538), Portland's premier rafting store. Or take the Mazamas' class in April (227-2345). Another way to learn the local rivers comes from **Northwest Rafters Association** (246-0386), a statewide organization of 500 self-outfitted boaters. The ecology-minded NWRA organizes river trips, holds monthly meetings on both practical and political aspects of river running, and volunteers for river cleanups.

ROLLER SKATING

Oaks Amusement Park

Foot of SE Spokane St, north of Sellwood Bridge on the east riverbank, 236-5722 (map:II5)

The Northwest's largest roller-skating rink stays open year-round (even though the park closes in winter). A live DJ rocks the rollers Friday and Saturday nights. A giant Wurlitzer pipe organ plays Tuesday–Thursday nights and Sundays. The rink's available for private parties; call ahead.

ROWING

The Willamette, smooth-flowing and right outside Portland's front door, is a prime location for many rowing clubs. The **Blue Heron Rowing Club** (0425 SW Montgomery Ave, 223-5859), located on the RiverPlace Marine Dock, is the most accessible. The Blue Heron is structured much like a health club: initiation requires $75 worth of lessons, six group or three private. Monthly rates start at $40, with sculls, sweeps, and coaching available for levels from recreational to national-champion caliber. At press time, owner/coach Tom Leonardi was considering a tourist package for rowers at nearby hotels. The **Station L Rowing Club** (1750 NW Front Ave, 222-3248) runs four- and eight-person boats April through November. The **Portland/Vancouver Rowing Association** (Route 1, Box 754, Hillsboro, OR 97124-9726, 222-3248), a consortium of local rowing clubs, holds four regattas each spring.

Portland Rowing Club (foot of SE Harney Street; mailing address: PO Box 82370, Portland, OR 97282) provides like-minded competitive company and moorage for those with their own boats.

RUNNING AND WALKING

Regardless of the weather, Portlanders like to run—a lot. And those who don't run, walk. Three distinct groups serve the various needs of the local perambulatory community (many people belong to all three): **Oregon Road Runners Club** (PO Box 549, Beaverton, OR 97075-0549, 626-2348) is in a close race for second-largest running club in the country after New York City. For $15 a year, or $20 a family, the club functions as race promoter and information network. While ORRC puts on over 25 local races—including one of the country's best 26-milers, the **Portland Marathon**, held the last Sunday of September—most of the race winners belong to **Nike-Portland Running Club** (PO Box 82694, Portland, OR 97282, 244-0225). This club meets for group training sessions and offers the services of the club coach. Membership costs $20, $25 for a family. Monthly meetings are held at 7:30pm the third Wednesday of each month at **My Father's Place** (523 SE Grand Avenue, 235-5494, map:FF5). **Cascade Rainrunners** (mailing address: Paul Vanture, 8311 SW Third Avenue, Portland, OR 97219) meets—for purely social reasons—at 7pm the second and fourth Wednesdays of each month at the **Leaky Roof Tavern** (1538 SW Jefferson St, 222-3745, map:GG6). Not coincidentally, the Leaky Roof is owned by master-class standout Mike Heffernan.

Council Crest Park
Top of Marquam Hill
(map:GG6)

Fairmount, Hewett, and Humphrey boulevards form a figure eight for one of the most popular recreation loops in the city. People walk, run, cycle, even roller-ski. The most popular portion is 3½-mile Fairmount Boulevard circling Council Crest Park, a moderately hilly course that on a clear day overlooks virtually everything from the Willamette Valley to Mount St. Helens. Take Hewett Boulevard to avoid the busier Humphrey Boulevard during rush hour—in fact a figure *nine*.

Duniway Park and
Terwilliger Blvd
North end of Terwilliger
Blvd to Barbur Blvd and
I-5 (map:GG6-II6)

Runners have worn grooves into the lanes of the Duniway Track, which now holds water like a drainage ditch. Up one terrace, however, is the quarter-mile sawdust track. The track has certain conveniences—the adjacent YMCA, an exercise and stretching area, public toilets—but parking is not one of them. At 5pm you won't find a space, legal or illegal, for your car in the tiny lot. Women should be careful, especially when venturing into the restrooms alone. The road continues all the way to Lake Oswego, although few trot that far, due to the hills and hard asphalt surface.

KIDS *means it's a good place to bring kids.*

Greenway Park
*SW Hall Blvd and Green-
way St, Beaverton
(map:HH9)*

A suburban common, Greenway is surrounded by recent commercial and residential developments. The 2½-mile trail follows Fanno Creek to SW Scholls Ferry Road, where the asphalt ribbon doubles back.

Glendoveer Golf Course
*14015 NE Glisan St,
253-7507 (map:FF1)*

The sawdust trail around the circumference measures 2 miles 95 feet, according to one coach who measured it for his team's workouts. The north and south sides border sometimes busy streets, but the east-end trail curves through a miniature wildlife refuge in woods overrun with well-fed (and fearless) rabbits.

Laurelhurst Park
*SE 39th Ave between SE
Ankeny and SE Oak
streets (map:FF4)*

Once a gully and swamp, Laurelhurst is now a lovely 25-acre parkland where paved and gravel trails crisscross the lawns under elegant shade trees and a manicured pond holds ducks. The 1 1/3-mile path rings the park, but pay attention to the kids on bikes and roller skates.

Leif Erickson Drive
*NW Thurman St to
Germantown Rd
(map:FF7-DD9)*

See Biking in this section.

Mount Tabor Park
*SE 60th Ave and Salmon
St (map:GG3)*

The only volcano within city limits in the Lower 48 has one of the better eastside views of Portland's West Hills. Tabor was named in honor of a faraway twin peak in the Biblical Palestine. Asphalt roads loop up the hill. Dirt trails stretch for 1 to 5 miles.

Powell Butte
*SE Powell Blvd and SE
58th (unmarked street)
(map:HH1)*

See Parks and Waterfront in this chapter.

Tom McCall Waterfront Park and Willamette Park
*West bank of the Wil-
lamette River, stretching
3¼ miles south from
downtown Portland
(map:K6-A6)*

Noontime runners flock to the promenade in what's considered to be the city's front yard. It only runs 1¾ miles north to the Broadway Bridge; however, south of River-Place (after a brief interruption soon to be eliminated) the path reappears along the river to Willamette Park, making a round trip of 6½ miles.

Tryon Creek State Park
*Terwilliger Blvd, 1 mile
off Hwy 43 in Lake Os-
wego, 653-3166 (map:II5-
JJ5)*

See Parks and Waterfront in this chapter.

Tualatin Hills Nature Park
SW 170th Ave, Beaverton,
645-6433

Fortunately, the Tualatin Hills Park and Recreation District has left St. Mary's Woods virtually untouched since it purchased the 180 acres from the Catholic archdiocese of Portland 10 years ago. Deer trails work their way through the woods, but the path (clearly marked) makes a 1-mile loop on the west bank of Beaverton Creek. If it's wet out, the dirt trail is likely to be quite muddy.

SAILING

Scores of speedboats chop up the water on the Willamette River, making a simple Sunday sail a fight for survival. And while sailing on the Columbia is certainly pleasant, the upstart sport of boardsailing gets more attention on that river these days (see Columbia River Gorge in the Outings chapter). Nevertheless, sailing is a business for the following organizations, who specialize in rentals and instructions:

Island Sailing Club
515 NE Tomahawk
Island Dr, 285-7765
(map:CC6)

This Columbia River club located east of Jantzen Beach offers instruction for American Sailing Association certification and rentals (20- to 25-foot crafts). Charters available; open year-round.

The Portland Sailing Center
3315 NE Marine Dr,
281-6529 (map:CC4)

Primarily a sailing school, here students practice the particulars of tacking and jibing on a range of different boats. The center also rents to certified parties and offers brokered charters far beyond the banks of the Columbia—to Baja or the San Juans, for example. The staff is terrific, but the hours are irregular (especially during the off season), so be sure to call ahead.

SKIING: CROSS-COUNTRY

The growing popularity of Nordic skiing has outpaced the availability of new snowparks and trail information. Most maps have the popular or marked trail systems on them, but the most comprehensive guide is Klindt Vielbig's *Cross-Country Ski Routes of Oregon's Cascades*. Because of the typically wet snow of Oregon, Vielbig recommends wax to smooth the pores of even waxless skis.

Mount Hood
About 60 miles east of
Portland, Zig Zag Ranger
Station, 666-0704, or
622-3191

It takes more than looking out the window to make weather condition assessments at Mount Hood. Miserable weather in Portland sometimes shrouds the excellent Nordic conditions on the mountain. Snow reports can be dialed at the four summit ski areas (the snow's rarely the same at all four): 222-2211 (Timberline), 227-SNOW (Mount Hood Meadows), 222-BOWL (SkiBowl), and 272-3351 (Summit). Road condition reports are now toll calls: 1-976-7277 in Oregon, (206) 976-ROAD in Washington. Each area on the mountain has some form of a Nordic program (see Skiing: Downhill in this section).

The Portland chapter of the **Oregon Nordic Club** (PO Box 3906, Portland, OR 97208, 220-0662) operates the popular weekend Nordic center at Teacup Lake, on the east side of Oregon 35, across from the Mount Hood Meadows parking lot. The 20 kilometers of groomed trails are open to the public for a small donation.

South of Highway 26 on US Forest Service Road 2656 just past the Timberline Lodge turnoff, the Trillium Lake Basin is especially popular. Local resident David Butt voluntarily grooms the two main areas, Trillium Lake Road and Still Creek Campground Loop, as well as six other trails. For trail information and other snowpark areas, call the Zig Zag Ranger Station.

Santiam Pass
86 miles southeast of Salem, McKenzie Ranger Station, 1-822-3381; Sisters Ranger Station, 1-549-2111

The US Forest Service trail system at Ray Benson Snopark near the Hoodoo ski area is one of the most extensive in the state with warming huts (and wood stoves) at the trailhead and beyond.

Three Sisters Wilderness
180 miles southeast of Portland, Bend Ranger Station (1-388-5664)

Fifteen miles west of Bend on the road to Mount Bachelor, the US Forest Service's Swampy Lakes trail system has warming huts and exquisitely beautiful (if hilly) terrain. Six more miles up Century Drive is the snowpark for Dutchman Flat, a trail system that connects to Swampy Lakes. Together, the systems are the best-planned web of trails in Oregon. East of Bend, overnight skiers can trek into **Paulina Lake Resort** (1-536-2240).

Southwest Washington
76 miles east of Portland, 26 miles north of Carson, WA, (509) 427-5645 (Wind River Ranger station), (206) 247-5473 (St. Helens Ranger station)

Oregon permits are valid for seven snowparks in Washington. Along the Upper Wind River the terrain is generally rolling, through heavy clearcuts and forested areas (21 miles of well-marked trails). Two areas south of Mount St. Helens are both accessible from Road 83. Recommended are the Marble Mountain–Muddy River and Ape Cave–McBride Lake–Goat Marsh areas. Unmarked roads through gentle, wide-open areas offer extensive views of the mountain itself. See also Mount St. Helens in Excursions in the Outings chapter.

Willamette Pass
69 miles east of Eugene on Oregon Hwy 58, 1-345-

The Nordic center's only three years old at this small downhill area, but there are up to 20 kilometers of groomed trails ($4). The trail goes behind the ski area, where it eventually meets superb trails in the Deschutes National Forest. Favorites include those to Gold and

7669 (ski area), 1-433-2234 (Crescent Ranger Station)

Rosary lakes (to the north) and Odell and Crescent lakes (to the south). Rentals and overnight accommodations are available at **Odell Lake Lodge** (1-433-2540).

SKIING: DOWNHILL

Cooper Spur

PO Box 977, Hood River, OR 97032, 1-352-7803
24 miles south of Hood River

One T-bar and one rope tow service the 500-foot vertical drop. Plans for a chair lift are on hold for at least another year because of nearby resident spotted owls. This is not a dramatic or particularly thrilling ski area, but it's inexpensive and has a family-style charm.

Hoodoo

Box 20, Highway 20, Sisters, OR 97759, 1-342-5540
86 miles southeast of Salem at Santiam Pass

Compared with the elaborate Mount Bachelor, Hoodoo's not too impressive. But looks can be deceiving: its three chair lifts gain 1,035 vertical feet, the top is steep enough to satisfy a mogul-crashing expert, and the bottom tapers enough to make room for a mile-long run. Seven miles of groomed cross-country trails and a full Nordic center (lessons to retail sales).

Mount Bachelor

PO Box 1031, Bend, OR 97709, 1-382-2607; 1-382-8334 in Oregon, (800) 882-2222 for reservations.
183 miles southeast of Portland (22 miles outside of Bend)

See Bend in Excursions in the Outings chapter.

Skibowl Multorpor

PO Box 280, Government Camp, OR 97028, 1-222-2695
53 miles east of Portland on US Hwy 26

Skibowl used to suffer the most during seasons with low or late snowfall, but snowmaking in the lower bowl has added consistency. A new night run in the upper bowl has helped draw skiers back to the state's lowest-elevation ski area. Lower suits beginners and intermediates, while upper is challenging enough to host ski races. Five rope tows, four double chairs. Nordic lessons on the short groomed track are available.

Summit

PO Box 385, Government Camp, OR 97028, 272-3352
54 miles east of Portland

Snow, chair lift, and rope tow aside, Summit is not really for skiing. It's for families and winter fun (inner-tubing too). With a 400-foot vertical drop and a half-mile run, it's perfect for small children and not-so-adventurous adult skiers. Lessons and rentals available (Nordic too).

Timberline
Government Camp, OR 97028
231-7979 from Portland or 1-272-3311
60 miles east of Portland, 6 miles north of Government Camp

See Mount Hood in Excursions in the Outings chapter.

Mount Hood Meadows
PO Box 470, Mount Hood, OR 97042, 246-7547 from Portland, or 1-337-2222
68 miles east of Portland

The most varied terrain of all Mount Hood ski areas (wide-open beginner slopes to steep, narrow chutes)— the longest lift lines, too. The mountain's only quad chair has sped things up a bit, and now the nine chairs can return 12,600 skiers per hour to the top. **FREE** The rope tow is free. Two day lodges, and night skiing Wednesday through Saturday. There are 10 kilometers of trails, and when they're groomed the fee is $4.

SWIMMING

Thanks to former governor Tom McCall, the Willamette River through Portland is clean enough to swim in, either from the few and rocky beaches or from a small dock just south of the Burnside Bridge. The Columbia River has two popular wading areas, Sauvie Island and Rooster Rock State Park. Blue Lake also suits swimmers (see Parks and Waterfront in this chapter).

The few indoor public pools are busy during the winter. Swimming lessons through **Portland Parks and Recreation** (796-5130) have waiting lists in the summer, although both the **Mount Hood Community College** and **Tualatin Hills** aquatic centers can handle many swimmers (see listing). The city charges $1.25 for each adult visit, unlimited four-month passes available. Most high schools have pools, but public access is usually limited to the summer months. The following is a list of the better public pools in the area:

Columbia Pool
7701 N Chautauqua Blvd, 283-6848
(map:DD7)

Portland's largest indoor pool is actually two 25-yard pools side by side. The shallow one ranges from 2 to 3 feet deep; the deep pool slopes to 8 feet.

Harman Swim Center
7300 SW Scholls Ferry Rd, Beaverton, 643-6681
(map:HH9)

No threat of hypothermia here. At 88 degrees, the water's extra 4 degrees make it noticeably warmer than the other pools in the district. Swimming instruction for all ages and therapy sessions for disabled or physically limited individuals.

Books in the Best Places *series read as personal guidebooks, but our evaluations are based on numerous reports from local experts. Final judgements are made by the editors. Our inspectors never identify themselves (except over the phone) and never accept free meals or other favors. Be an inspector. Send us a report.*

Oregon City Municipal Swimming Pool
1211 Jackson St, Oregon City, 657-8273 (map:O04)

Lap swimming, swimming lessons, and water exercise classes are all available in this 25-meter, six-lane indoor pool. Open year-round.

Mount Hood Community College (Aquatics Center)
26000 SE Stark St, Gresham, 667-7243

The Aquatics Center runs four pools: an outdoor 50-meter pool (June to early October) with morning and evening lap swims; an indoor 25-yard six-lane pool; a very warm (90–92 degrees) pool that's 4 feet deep designed specifically for the handicapped; and an oft-used hydrotherapy pool. Fee is $1.25 per visit; regulars get a discount.

Tualatin Hills Park and Recreation Swim Center
15707 SW Walker Rd, Beaverton, 645-7454

Portland's largest enclosed public swimming pool (50 meters). It's part of a large recreation complex in the Sunset Corridor whose facilities include covered tennis courts, playing fields, and a running trail. $1.25 per swim. Discounts available for district members.

Multnomah Metro YMCA
2831 SW Barbur Blvd, 294-3366 (map:A1)

If something about this place seems familiar, it's because the pool and steam room are the setting for the climax of local novelist Katherine Dunn's acclaimed *Geek Love*. Its location next to the Duniway Park track and running trail makes it very popular. Open all day for lap swimming. A $10 day pass entitles visitors to use of the entire facility. Members of other YMCAs get seven free visits; after that it's $5 a day.

YWCA Fitness and Swim Center
1111 SW 10th Ave, 223-6281 (map:G1)

A bare-bones spot, but the coed 25-yard indoor pool costs $6 for nonmembers; the price includes access to aerobics classes and the weight room.

TENNIS

Portland might be short on golf courses and indoor swimming pools, but it is well supplied with tennis courts. Portland Parks and Recreation has 177 outdoor courts at 42 sites. The favorite site in the city is **Washington Park**, which has six courts above the Rose Gardens—and a waiting line on warm weekends. **FREE** Reservations may be made May–September for individual outdoor courts at Grant, Portland Tennis Center, and Washington Park. Otherwise it's first come, first served.

In addition, the city owns two indoor tennis centers: the excellent **Portland Tennis Center** (324 NE 12th Avenue, 233-5959, 233-5950, map:GG5) was the first municipal indoor court in the Western states financed by revenue bonds. It has eight outdoor courts, four indoor ($5.75 each for singles on weekends; weekday play is cheaper). The other is **St. Johns Racquet Center** (7519 N Burlington Street, 248-4200, map:DD8), where everything's undercover—three indoor tennis courts

($5 each for singles on weekends) and Portland's only four public racquetball courts ($8.50 per court on weekends). Other area indoor courts that are open to the public, though some require a full day's advance notice, include: **Glendoveer Tennis Center** (NE 140th Avenue and NE Glisan Street, 253-7507, map:FF7); **Lake Oswego Indoor Tennis Center** (2900 SW Diane Drive, Lake Oswego, 635-5550, 636-9673 in summer, map:KK6); **Tualatin Hills Park and Recreation District Tennis Center** (15707 SW Walker Road, Beaverton, 645-7457); **Vancouver Tennis and Raquetball Center** (5300 E 18th Avenue, Vancouver, WA, 206-696-8123, map:BB5); **Western Athletic Club** (8785 SW Beaverton-Hillsdale Highway, 297-9723, map:HH8). Again, weekdays are a better deal.

Here are a few of the better courts in the area (call the Portland Parks and Recreation department, 796-5132, for others):

WEST SIDE
Gabriel Park.. SW 45 Ave and Vermont St (map:II7)
Hillside .... 653 NW Culpepper Terrace (map:FF7)

SOUTHEAST
Col. Summers.................................... SE 20 Ave and Belmont St (map:GG5)
Kenilworth.................................... SE 34th Ave and Holgate Blvd (map:HH4)

NORTHEAST
Argay .... NE 141st Ave and Failing St (map:FF1)
US Grant .... NE 33rd Ave and Thompson St (map:FF4)

WINDSURFING

See Columbia Gorge and Hood River in Daytrips in the Outings chapter.

GARDENS

Portland may or may not be, as one national magazine recently labeled it, the gardening capital of the United States, but no one would dispute the fact that it is one heck of a place to take up the trowel. The Willamette Valley's rich soil and mild climate make possible a growing season and a variety of plant life that gardeners elsewhere can only fantasize about.

Accomplished Portland gardeners are not a recent phenomenon: in 1889 the nation's first rose society was established here, soon followed by the first primrose and rhododendron societies. By the 1920s, Portland boasted more garden clubs than any other city in the nation; they now total more than 20.

FREE This predilection for plant life means that visitors will encounter gardens in unexpected places. Small bamboo, butterfly, and lily gardens, for example, are tucked between exhibits at the **Washington Park Zoo** (4001 SW Canyon Road, 226-1561, map:GG7). There's an herb garden next to the **Oregon Museum of Science and Industry** (4015 SW Canyon Road, 228-2828, map:GG7), and more than 120 named varieties of camellias on the **University of Portland** campus. A third-floor courtyard in **Good Samaritan Hospital** includes a rose garden; the **Kaiser Clinic** (in Rockwood) maintains a sinister garden of common poisonous plants, designed to alert parents to back yard dangers. The following gardens are among the city's horticultural highlights—all free and open daily, unless otherwise specified:

Berry Botanic Garden
11505 SW Summerville Ave, 636-4112 (map:JJ6)

Berry's quarter-acre rock garden is more than an extraordinary accumulation of alpine plants; it is also part of the garden's nationally recognized efforts to preserve endangered plant species. The primrose collection, for instance, is one of the world's most complete, containing several varieties that are threatened in their native habitats. Three other plant groups (lilies, rhododendrons, and Northwest natives) are featured on the 6½-acre former estate of Mrs. Rae Selling Berry. Volunteer tour guides explain the connection between the lush woodland and streamside plantings and the berry-seed bank—unique in its attempt to preserve the rare and endangered plants of an entire region. Open by appointment only, Monday through Saturday.

Crystal Springs Rhododendron Garden
SE 28th Ave at Woodstock Blvd, 796-5193 (map:II5)

Kodachrome was invented for places like this. Normally a peaceful green retreat for bird watchers and neighborhood strollers, Crystal Springs in April and May becomes an irresistible magnet for color-happy camera and video buffs. Roughly 600 varieties of rhododendrons and deciduous azaleas blaze on the 7-acre grounds. The spring-fed lake, home to a sizable colony of waterfowl, is a year-round attraction; Japanese maples, sourwood trees, and fothergillas paint fall. A small fee is charged only on Mother's Day—when Portlanders traditionally promenade through peak bloom.

Elk Rock, The Garden of the Bishop's Close
11800 SW Military Ln, 636-5613 (map:JJ6)

This 13-acre estate in the exclusive Dunthorpe neighborhood serves as the headquarters of the Episcopal Diocese of Oregon, which explains the name: "close" is an English term for an enclosed place or garden—especially one adjoining a church, where monks used to march in peace. This garden's genesis, however, dates back 75 years to the collaboration between its owner, Scottish grain merchant Peter Kerr, and New York landscape architect John Olmsted, son of Central Park designer Frederick Law Olmsted. Together the two men created an exquisite terraced garden facing Mount Hood and overlooking pristine Elk Rock in the Willamette River. Both native and rare plants are featured, including 50 varieties of magnolias (a Kerr favorite).

Other highlights are lily ponds, a natural spring channeled into a small descending trickle, a large rock garden, perennial beds, and a formal boxwood-hedged terrace. Tread respectfully.

The Grotto
NE 85th Ave and NE Sandy Blvd, 254-7371 (map:EE3)

Visitors sometimes introduce long-time Portlanders to the Grotto. Founded to honor Mary, mother of Jesus, the Grotto is a surprise to even the city's most skeptical residents—it's both a religious shrine and a lovely woodland garden. Sunday Mass (May–September) faces the Grotto of Our Sorrowful Mother, a fern-lined niche hewn from a 110-foot-tall cliff inside the Grotto—a marble replica of Michelangelo's *Pietà*; outside, cathedraling redwoods and firs frame the silence. Throughout the 58-acre grounds, rhododendrons, camellias, azaleas, and ferns shelter religious statuary, providing both the penitent and the plant lover ample material for contemplation. Upper-level gardens and a panoramic view of the Columbia River are reached via a 10-story elevator ride ($2 adults, $1 children and seniors). Noteworthy events: the 10-night Festival of Lights in December, and an outdoor ecumenical Easter sunrise service.

Hoyt Arboretum
4000 SW Fairview Blvd (Washington Park), 228-8732 (map:GG7)

See Major Attractions in this section.

Home Orchard Society Arboretum
19600 S Molalla Ave, Oregon City, 657-6958 (map:OO3)

Adjacent to the John Inskeep Environmental Learning Center (at Clackamas Community College) is a dazzling assortment of fruit-bearing plants. The Home Orchard Society cultivates dwarf fruit trees, stunted to fit the given territory. Terrific samplings of, for example, more than 10 kinds of apples and 30 pear varieties. If you've been wanting to add a blueberry bush to your yard—or a kiwi vine, persimmon, pawpaw, or plum-apricot cross—this is the place to decide on the variety. The hours are tricky: 10am–2pm on first and third Saturdays, 11am–3pm on second and fourth Sundays (March–October).

International Rose Test Garden
400 SW Kingston Blvd (Washington Park), 248-4302 (map:GG7)

See Major Attractions in this chapter.

Look for **FREE**—*it means this attraction or event is free of charge.*

Japanese Garden
611 SW Kingston Blvd
(Washington Park),
223-4070 (map:GG7)

See Major Attractions in this chapter.

John Inskeep Environmental Learning Center
19600 S Molalla Ave,
Oregon City, 657-6958
(map:003)

What once was ravaged land—the waste-water lagoons and parking lots of a berry-processing plant—is now shady paths, ponds, wildlife habitat, and alternative technologies. The learning center at Clackamas Community College demonstrates environmentally sound solutions to urban problems, incorporating recycled plastic "logs" in foot bridges and utilizing solar and compost-heated greenhouses in the nursery. A nearby recycling depot helps fund for the 8-acre center.

KIDS Kids flock to the birds of prey exhibit, and to see the muskrats and ducks in the ponds. The observatory's 24-inch telescope is open evenings on Wednesdays, Fridays, and Saturdays, weather permitting.

Leach Botanical Garden
6704 SE 122nd Ave,
761-9503 (map:HH1)

The emphasis on native Northwest plants is fitting, since one of the garden's creators discovered two genera and 11 species in Northwest wildernesses. Well-known amateur botanist Lilla Leach and her husband, John, began their 5-acre garden along Johnson Creek in the early 1930s; today it encompasses more than 8 acres and 1,500 species of winter-blooming plants, native irises, and ferns; recently, bog and rock gardens have been added. **KIDS** A rustic stone house on the grounds is used for children's nature study classes. **FREE** Free garden tours Saturdays at 10am and Wednesdays at 2pm. Closed Mondays.

PARKS AND WATERFRONT

Blue Lake
Blue Lake Rd at N
Marine Dr and NE 223rd
Ave, 248-5050, 248-5151
(map:BB8)

Although a natural wetlands area is planned, Blue Lake Park is unabashedly developed, with plenty of parking, swimming, boat rentals, volleyball courts, paved paths, play fields, and other facilities. **KIDS FREE** The Multnomah County Park Services Division holds two summer weekly entertainment series (one with blues, reggae, and Latin-jazz concerts, and another for kids with puppets, comedy, and music). Concerts are free with park admission (per-car fee). Cyclists, however, can come and go as they please.

The facts in this edition were correct at presstime, but places close, chefs depart, hours change. It's best to call ahead.

Council Crest Park

*Top of Marquam Hill, 5-
minute drive southwest of
downtown (map:GG6)*

On one of the tallest peaks in the Tualatin Mountains,
Council Crest Park is valued for its nearly panoramic
views of the Coast Range and the Cascades. Park at the
top, especially popular at sunset. The Marquam Hill
Trail crosses through the Douglas firs and maple forest
on the northwest side of the hill.

Elk Rock Island

*SE 19th Ave and Bluebird
St, Milwaukie (map:KK4)*

Each spring, high waters on the Willamette impede access to this pristine island, but at other times you can
step-stone from Milwaukie's Spring Park across the
gravel-scrubbed bedrock to the island. Heron feed in the
little bay separating the two. Migrating Canada geese
graze on the shelf of grass on the island's west side. A
sublime natural rock formation cascades out of the oak
forest on the northwest end, where the deepest waters
of the Willamette (home to many sturgeon) slice by. Un-
verified local lore attributes the name to Native Amer-
icans driving elk over the bluff and floating them to the island for processing.

Forest Park

*Boundaries: north of W
Burnside to Newberry Rd,
west of St. Helens Rd
(Hwy 30) to Skyline Rd,
248-4492 (map:FF7-
DD9)*

In 1948, after more than 40 years of citizen effort, 4,200
acres of forest land was formally designated Forest
Park. The land had survived logging, wildfire burns,
subdivision into private lots, and an aborted scenic-road
project. Now 4,800 acres of forest wilderness includes
50 miles of trails along northwest Portland's Tualatin
Mountains, all within 10 minutes (sometimes less) of
downtown. Leif Erickson Drive, a gravel road that
stretches from NW Thurman Street to Germantown
Road, is all that's left of an ambitious real estate agent's
1914 scenic drive through a planned subdivision. Now
closed to cars, the popular hiking, running, and
mountain-biking lane is paved for a short stretch near
NW Thurman Street. The rough road parallels the Wildwood Trail (see also Hiking in this chapter).

Hoyt Arboretum

*4000 SW Fairview Blvd
(Washington Park),
228-8732 (map:GG7)*

See Washington Park in Major Attractions in the Exploring chapter.

Johnson Creek Corridor

*East entrance: Tidman-
Johnson Park, 2 blocks
south of SE 37th Ave and
Crystal Springs Blvd; west*

Birding is good along Johnson Creek, and canoers and
rafters can float the creek in spring and early summer.
Two parks, Tidman-Johnson and Bundy, link the interesting creek. Though not completely developed yet (a
gravel path only extends from Tidman to SE Tacoma

Look for **FREE**—*it means this attraction or event is free of charge.*

*entrance: Bundy Park,
SE 142nd Ave and Foster
St*

Street), you can make the walk part of a loop that includes the elegant old Eastmoreland neighborhood and golf course.

Kelley Point Park
*N Suttle Rd off west end of
N Marine Dr (map:AA9-
BB6)*

An isolated park across the channel from Sauvie Island at the convergence of the Willamette and Columbia rivers. Biking, hiking, and wildlife viewing are best in the spring and fall. An easy 15-mile trail skirts the lake. In the summer, Kelley Point is inundated with picnickers and sunbathers.

Mary S. Young State Park
*Hwy 43, just south of
Marylhurst College, West
Linn (map:MM5)*

Along the Willamette River, this suburban refuge is stalwartly defending itself from surrounding development. The park has picnic spots, 2 miles of dense forest trails, and a half-mile bike path. The state maintains it in as close as possible to its original natural condition.

Oxbow Park
*8 miles east of Gresham
via SE Division St and
Oxbow Pkwy, Gresham,
663-4708*

In the oxbow bends of the Sandy River Gorge, old-growth forests and wildlife thrive. Formally the park covers 870 acres, but the ecosystem appears to extend upstream to the Sandy River Preserve (owned by the Nature Conservancy) and downstream to the YMCA camp. In late October the park hosts its annual October Salmon Festival, focusing on the spawning salmon (see Calendar). About 15 miles of hiking trails follow the river and climb the ridges, and more than half are open to horses. Call the park for information on special Sandy River fishing rules, guided raft trips, and boat rentals.

**Portland Audubon Bird
Sanctuary**
*5151 NW Cornell Rd,
292-6855 (map:FF7)*

See Bird Watching in Outdoors section of this chapter.

Powell Butte
*SE Powell Blvd and SE
58th Ave (unmarked
street) (map:HH1)*

The Portland Audubon Society's urban naturalist Michael Houck calls Powell Butte the future Forest Park of southeast Portland. From the meadows at the 630-foot summit, hikers can see north to Mount St. Helens and south to Mount Jefferson. Until the city builds and marks trails, gravel roads and rutted paths will have to do. A 2-mile loop circles the volcanic mound on the way to the top. Watch out for poison oak.

Books in the Best Places *series read as personal guidebooks, but our evaluations are based on numerous reports from local experts. Final judgements are made by the editors. Our inspectors never identify themselves (except over the phone) and never accept free meals or other favors. Be an inspector. Send us a report.*

Sauvie Island Wildlife Management Area
At the confluence of the Willamette and Columbia rivers, on the north end of Sauvie Island

In the past 20 years, both human and car traffic have tripled here. To finance toilets, parking, an interpretive center, and maintenance, the Oregon Fish and Wildlife Commission (229-5400) has initiated $2.50 daily and $10 annual car-park permits for this 12,000-acre state wildlife preserve. One of the few sandy beaches on the Columbia is Walton Beach, at the end of the paved portion of NW Reeder Road. The best picnic spot on the Columbia, however, is 3 miles away at Warrior Rock Lighthouse. See also Sauvie Island in Daytrips in the Outings chapter.

Silver Falls State Park
20024 Silver Falls Hwy SE, Sublimity Park, 1-873-8681

At least 10 waterfalls drape Silver Creek Canyon. South Falls, the most spectacular, is a short walk from the lodge and main parking area. Further up Highway 214, parking is available within a few hundred yards of Winter Falls, North Falls, and Upper North Falls. The essence of Silver Falls State Park (1½ hours southeast of Portland), however, is best taken in from the 7-mile Silver Creek Canyon Trail, constructed in the 1930s by the Civilian Conservation Corps. A conference center makes this a favorite meeting and retreat spot. Lots of other trails: 3.7 miles for bikes, 3 miles for joggers, and 12 miles for equines. Overnight facilities with electrical hookups, as well as primitive camping spots.

Smith and Bybee lakes
North Portland Peninsula between Delta and Kelley Point parks (map:CC7-CC8)

In industrial North Portland, this undesignated natural area encompassing nearly 2,000 acres of lakes and wetlands tenuously awaits its fate. At press time, an unofficial trail bordered the Columbia and Oregon sloughs and both lakes. The trails (it is hoped) will someday be incorporated into the 40-Mile-Loop. A good place to spy on wildlife, especially blue heron in the slough.

Rooster Rock State Park
Take I-84 east to exit 25, 695-2261

On a warm weekend, all 1,800 parking spaces for this mile-long sandy beach are full. The familiar Crown Point viewpoint rises on the other side of I-84. There's a logged-off swimming hole in the Columbia River, a boat launch, and docks for boats and anglers. On the far east end, a separate beach has been designated "clothing optional."

When the east wind is blowing, windsurfers crowd the beaches; call 695-2220 for wind and weather information. Park admission is $1 per car.

The facts in this edition were correct at presstime, but places close, chefs depart, hours change. It's best to call ahead.

Tom McCall Waterfront Park
Along the Willamette River from the Marquam Bridge to the Steel Bridge (map:A5-L5)

See Major Attractions in this chapter.

Tryon Creek State Park
Terwilliger Blvd, 1 mile off Hwy 43 in Lake Oswego, 653-3166 (map:II5-JJ5)

Like Forest Park, Tryon Creek Canyon was threatened with a housing project. However, the Friends of Tryon Creek State Park raised money to buy the land, and the park now consists of 640 protected acres between Lewis and Clark College and Lake Oswego, with 8 miles of intersecting trails. The paved half-mile Trillium Trail is the first handicapped-access trail in an Oregon state park. A 3-mile bike trail winds along the park's border with Terwilliger. There's also a Nature House with natural science exhibits and meeting rooms (see Essentials chapter).

ORGANIZED TOURS

BOAT TOURS

Portland Steam Navigation Company
286-7673

Rose, a 65-foot replica of the type of sternwheeler that once plied the Columbia and Willamette rivers, navigates these waters (June–September) with regularly scheduled cruises from RiverPlace Marina. Charter trips, available year-round, sometimes displace the public outings, so call for schedules and reservations. Sightseeing excursions run about $8, while the two-hour dinner cruise sets you back $30.

Rose City Riverboat Cruises
289-6665

KIDS Better known as the "Yachts-O-Fun" boat, the 49-passenger *Cruis-ader Princess* provides a good outing for all ages (the big motorboat churns up more excitement than the sternwheeler). Aim for the upriver trip (toward Oregon City), as downriver sights tend toward the industrial (April–October). Adult fares range from about $8 for the hour-long downtown moonlight cruise to $30 for the two-hour dinner trip to Lake Oswego. Open April through October (charters year-round), with annual excursions during the Christmas parade of lighted boats. Reservations recommended (required for dinner trips). Departs from RiverPlace Marina.

Looking for a particular place? Check the index at the back of this book for individual restaurants, hotels, B&Bs, shops, bars, parks, museums, galleries, neighborhoods, messenger services, nightclubs, and more.

Sternwheeler Columbia Gorge
606 NW Front Ave, #A1 (McCormick Pier), 223-3928 (map:L6)

See Daytrips in the Outings chapter.

MOTOR TOURS

Gray Line of Portland
4320 N Suttle Rd, 285-9845 (map:CC7)

This touring agency offers several choices (late April through mid-October): Mount Hood ($26), the Columbia River Gorge ($26), the northern Oregon Coast ($26), and two Portland city tours (a three-hour version for $13 and a seven-hour trip for $22). Pickup can be arranged from any major hotel (beginning at the Imperial). Reservations required.

Portland Parks and Recreation Historical Tours
796-5132

These inexpensive ($12-$21) and educational daytrips sponsored by the city parks department cover a goldmine of historic places: The Oregon Trail, Lewis and Clark's route to Astoria, the Columbia Gorge, Portland cemeteries, and even a literal gold mine—Bohemia. Portland historian and writer Dick Pintarich leads the popular van tours. Most span the entire day (8am–7pm), give or take a few good stories. April through October only. Reservations required.

WALKING TOURS

Portland Downtown Discovery Walk (recorded)

Ignore the funny looks from passers-by as you stand on a street corner and gaze–quarter–turn–gaze–quarter–turn at example after example of Portland's terra cotta. It's Architecture 101 with this 84-minute tape ($10.95), which walks you through a quick, somewhat interesting course on Portland's 145-year development. Get tape player and tape from Powell's Travel Bookstore (Pioneer Courthouse Square, 228-1108, map:H3).

Portland on Foot
235-4742

Most tour leaders merely recount Portland's history; 90-year-old veteran guide John Meynink reminisces. Meynink leads 2½-hour walking tours of Old Town or the Yamhill Historic District each Saturday (April–September). Call for schedule and gathering place. Fee is $2.50 for adults, $1 for children.

Portland Public Walking Tour
796-5111

See Art in Public Places in the Arts chapter.

If you've found a place around town that you think is a Best Place, send in the report form at the back of the book. If you're unhappy with one of the places, please let us know why. We depend on reader input.

Urban Tour Group
227-5780

KIDS FREE For 20 years, schoolchildren and adults have learned Portland history from UTG volunteers. Teachers, round up the kids—school groups are free. Video versions of the two-hour tours are available for those who live vicariously. Private tours are $3 per person ($15 minimum); reservations are a must. Most of the tours start in the South Park Blocks.

WAGON TRAIN TOURS

Wagons West Ltd
Rte 1, Box 274, Forest Grove, OR 97116,
357-5757

KIDS Only in Oregon can adventurous souls spend three days in a wagon train. Wagonmaster Lyle Spiesschaert, a former Oregon State University youth development specialist, initiated these wagon train expeditions for Japanese children and juvenile offenders. By popular demand, a select few are open to the general public. The annual Labor Day train retraces part of the original toll road connecting the Willamette Valley to the Coast. Nothing's left out: wagons, grits, campfire songs, Wild West tales—and horses, of course.

OUTINGS CONTENTS

OUTINGS

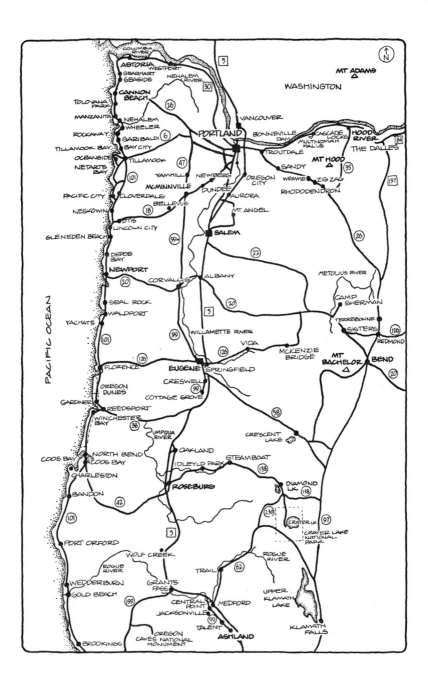

DAYTRIPS

ANTIQUING IN SELLWOOD

At the east end of the Sellwood Bridge is Portland's antique row—13 blocks of antique and collectible shops. Sellwood (essentially SE 13th Avenue from Maleden to Clatsop streets, map: II5), once a separate town on the east bank of the Willamette, was annexed to Portland in the 1890s. It is proud of its past: the community still puts out its own weekly newspaper, now in its 85th year, and shop owners have placed signs on their buildings identifying their original uses and construction dates. The better part of a day can be spent browsing. The street is a repository of American country furniture, lace, quilts, toys, hardware, china, jewelry, and trinkets.

Particularly noteworthy are the stores with specialties, such as **Nielsen Collection Antiques** (7742 SE 13th Avenue, 234-8111), where 17th- through 19th-century American and European clocks and hand tools are sold; the **1874 House** (8070 SE 13th Avenue, 233-1874), crammed with brass and copper hardware and light fixtures from old houses, and architectural fragments; and **The Roaring 20s** (8027 SE 13th Avenue, 238-1737), with restored and refinished furniture from that decade. In **Austin's Place** (8425 SE 13th Avenue, 232-4364), you might peruse the old collection of Sellwood neighborhood photographs. **The General Store** (7987 SE 13th Avenue, 233-1321) is housed in the 1905 Caldwell Grocery, whose back wall is the exterior of an old caboose from the Spokane, Portland, and Seattle Railway.

Follow SE 13th Avenue across Tacoma Street to **Old Sellwood Square** (8235 SE 13th Avenue). The **Webfoot Bookman** (239-5233) retails old books on Oregon and the West, and **Jonathan's** (233-1489) deals in estate jewelry and Victorian silver. Antique lamps and hand-sewn reproduction Victorian lampshades can be found at **Satin and Old Lace Shades** (8015 SE 13th Avenue, 234-2650)—they also do a decent job of repairing and restoring antique lamps. To restore your energy, stop in at **El Palenque** (8324 SE 17th Avenue, 231-5140), Portland's only Salvadoran cuisine.

ASTORIA

The oldest US settlement west of the Rockies, Astoria today is an unpretentious coastal town of about 10,000 people—a stop for oceangoing freighters and home port for commercial fishing boats. Fishing, canning, and logging were the mainstays of a rather unsteady local economy, which now seems to be making a recovery after several lean years.

The town is coming into its own as a tourist destination that boasts a wealth of history, Victorian architecture, and natural beauty. Many salmon- and bottom-fishing charters leave from here, the biggest of which is **Thunderbird Charters** (1-325-7990). **Sixth Street RiverPark**, with its always-open, covered observation tower, provides the best vantage point for viewing river commerce, observing bar and river pilots as they board tankers and freighters, and watching seals and sea lions as they look for a free lunch. Downtown, some new restaurants and galleries have moved in next to the fishermen's bars and the mom-and-pop cafes. Bed and breakfasts are proliferating, particularly in the lovely Victorian homes on the steep hillsides overlooking the river. Other Victorian houses are gradually undergoing restoration as well.

The history of US exploration and settlement here begins with Captain Robert Gray, who sailed up the river in 1792, naming it Columbia after his ship. (Oregon and Washington are planning a joint 200th-anniversary celebration of that journey for 1992). In 1805–1806, Lewis and Clark made their winter camp at nearby **Fort Clatsop**. Their journals tell of rain on all but 12 of the 114 days of their stay—no surprise to locals. A reconstructed eight-room fort stands at the site of their encampment at Fort Clatsop National Memorial, 6 miles southwest of town off US Highway 101. You'll see equipment used by the expedition party, and can walk the same paths they walked to the spring and the canoe landing on what is now the Lewis and Clark River.

FREE New York fur trader John Jacob Astor, at his death the wealthiest man in America, established **Fort Astoria** in 1822 for the Pacific Fur Company. The fort had all but disappeared by the mid-19th century but now has been partially reconstructed (at 15th and Exchange streets).

The first stop for most visitors is the **Astoria Column**, atop Coxcomb Hill, Astoria's highest point. Built in 1926 by the Great Northern Railway, the 123-foot-high spiraling mural was inspired by Trajan's Column in Rome. At the top of the 166 steps there's a panoramic view of the harbor, the Columbia estuary, and distant headlands of the Pacific.

The **Columbia River Maritime Museum** (on the waterfront at the foot of 17th Street, 1-325-2323) is one of the finest museums of its kind in the West. The 1951 Coast Guard lightship *Columbia* is moored outside, and inside are five historic small craft. A sixth, a replica of an early gill-netting sailboat, is now under construction. Thematic galleries depict the Northwest's maritime heritage: fishing and whaling, fur trading, navigation, and shipwrecks. Admission is $3 for adults, $1.50 for children. In the remodeled 1904 city hall building just up the hill from CRMM is another museum devoted to Astoria's history, the **Clatsop County Heritage Museum** (16th and Exchange streets, 1-325-2203). The **Flavel House** (Eighth and Duane streets, 1-325-2563), an 1883 Queen Anne mansion built by the Columbia River's first steamship pilot, Captain George Flavel, is now the home of the county historical society.

Shopping. Astoria's two downtown galleries and one bookstore are all located within a block of each other. In the **Ricciardi Gallery** (108 10th Street, 1-325-5450), you can buy an espresso up front and then browse the collection of works by regional artists. Around the corner is **Michael's Antiques and Art Gallery** (1007 Marine Drive, 1-325-2350). Look for **Parnassus Books** at 234 10th Street (1-325-1363). The **Art Center Gallery at Clatsop Community College** (1-325-0910) can be found on campus, at the top of 17th on Jerome Street. A special treat for those who love vintage clothing is **Persona Vintage Clothing** (100 10th Street, 1-325-3837), often praised for its quality goods.

Eats. Stop in at the **Columbian Cafe** (at the corner of 11th Street and Marine Drive, 1-325-2233) for gourmet pastas and omelets, luscious crepes and desserts. The next-door **Border Town Burrito Bar** is renowned for its sumptuous burritos and also serves beers and Italian sodas. The **Pacific Rim Restaurant**, next to the World War I monument (229 W Marine Drive, 1-325-4481), offers New York and Sicilian pizzas and a view of the harbor. A local favorite is the **Ship Inn** (1 Second

Street, 1-325-0033), with its seasoned fish and chips, Watney's ale, Cornish pasties, and other British fare served by expatriates Jill and Fenton Stokeld. **Josephson's Smokehouse** (106 Marine Drive, 1-325-2190) prepares alder-smoked salmon and tuna as good as any you'll find (great for a picnic on Coxcomb Hill). For a light lunch on the waterfront, try **Little Denmark** (125 Ninth Street, 1-325-2409), whose specialties are Scandinavian pastries, open-faced sandwiches on homemade bread, and imported beer.

Three blocks from downtown is the elegant **Franklin Street Station** (1140 Franklin Avenue, 1-325-4314), with five guest rooms, each with its own bath. Another good night's stay can be had at the **Franklin House** (1681 Franklin Avenue, 1-325-5044). Or try the small but tidy **Crest Motel** (5366 Leif Erickson Drive, 1-325-3141) overlooking the Columbia.

Astoria is a natural starting point for excursions to the Oregon and Washington coasts. Sweeping ocean views can be had from the **South Jetty Lookout Tower,** Oregon's northwesternmost point. The jetty marks the head of the **Oregon Coast Trail,** which extends 62 miles along the beach and over inland hills to Tillamook Bay. **Fort Stevens State Park,** 10 miles west of Astoria on US Highway 101, is a 3,500-acre park offering 605 campsites, 7 miles of bike paths, and uncrowded beaches. Walk the beach to see the rusted hulk of the British schooner *Peter Iredale,* wrecked in 1906. Fort Stevens, built at the mouth of the Columbia during the Civil War as part of Oregon's coastal defense, was fired upon in June 1942 by a Japanese submarine. It's the only military fort in the continental US to see action during the war.

BREWERIES

FREE The Northwest has become a center for craft breweries—small, independent companies that turn out special beers, generally in small batches and according to traditional methods. Aficionados argue that Northwest brews are distinctly different from even the best imports. They claim that the Western barley, Willamette and Yakima valley hops, and Cascade water give local concoctions their particular character.

The "local" brewery (actually opened by a company in Wisconsin) that enjoys big commercial status is Portland's own **Blitz-Weinhard Brewing Company** (1133 W Burnside, 222-4351, map:T1), from which you can smell steaming hops on your way to Powell's Books. Blitz tours show how their successful beers have been made for more than 100 years. Sample local favorite Henry Weinhard's Private Reserve (aka Hank's) in the Hospitality Room after the tour.

In the gleaming copper, glass, and steel pub at the **Portland Brewing Company** (1339 NW Flanders Street, 222-7150, map:L1), jazz swings on Fridays and blues on Saturdays. Sample the ever-popular Portland Ale, Timberline Ale, and Grant's Scottish Ale and Imperial Stout (they have a license to brew Grant's beer for draught sales in Oregon). The soup-and-sandwich menu features vegetarian and Italian specialties.

You can watch the **Bridgeport Brewery & Pub** (1313 NW Marshall Street, 241-7179, map:N1) at work through picture windows behind the bar. The comfortable pub with its library of periodicals and good pizza encourages lingering over beer.

B. Moloch/The Heathman Bakery and Pub (901 SW Salmon Street, 227-5700, map:G1), a bustling downtown restaurant (see Restaurants chapter), is also the home of the Widmer Brewing Company. The pub, with its floor-to-ceiling windows, is known for its Altbier, Weizenbier, and Hefeweizen brews. Seasonal beers, too.

Technically, the McMenamin joints are not breweries, they're brew pubs. The difference? A brewery is exactly what it claims to be—sometimes with a pub or tasting room attached. A brew pub is more of a novelty—a brewery that makes its beer only for a particular bar or, in the case of McMenamin's, a group of bars. Most will give tours by prior arrangement only, though there's always somewhere to get a peek at the process. Of the nearly two dozen McMenamin pubs in Portland and other Oregon cities, six have in-house breweries. In Portland try **Fulton Brew Pub** (0618 SW Nebraska Street, 246-9530, map:II6) or the original **Hillsdale Brewery and Public House** (1505 SW Sunset Boulevard, 246-3938, map:HH6). **Cornelius Roadhouse** (Sunset Highway and Cornelius Pass Road, 640-6174), in an inviting big farmhouse, is a favorite of many. Farther afield is the **Lighthouse Brew Pub** (4157 N Highway 101, Lincoln City, 1-994-7238) on the Oregon Coast, and **High Street Brewery and Cafe** (1243 High Street, Eugene, 1-345-4905), where U of O Ducks like to quaff a few. (See also Pubs and Taverns in the Nightlife chapter.)

CHAMPOEG-AURORA

The road to Champoeg (pronounced *shampooey*) off I-5 winds through amber farm fields with green patches of fir and oak, past browsing cattle and horses, and leads to some of the state's most significant historic sites. Champoeg was the home of Calapooya Indians before fur traders and settlers came in the early 1800s. In 1843, settlers here voted to form the first provisional government of the Oregon Country. **KIDS** Now a 568-acre park on the Willamette River, Champoeg on summer weekends is crowded with picnickers and kids on bikes, Frisbee throwers and volleyball players. The excellent Visitor Center (1-678-1251) tells of Champoeg's role in Oregon's history. There's an open house in a replica of a settler's cabin; tickets are $4 to $7.50.

Just west of the park entrance is the **Robert Newell House** (1-678-5537), a replica of the 1852 original, which serves as a museum of Native American and pioneer artifacts. On the grounds are the Butteville Jail (1850) and a pioneer schoolhouse. Open Wednesday through Sunday (closed December and January). Admission is $1.50 for adults, 50 cents for children.

The town of Aurora, midway between Portland and Salem on the east bank of the Willamette, is a well-preserved turn-of-the-century village that's been put on the National Register of Historic Places. Two dozen or so clapboard and Victorian houses line the highway. It's moving toward its third decade as an antique center. Fourteen shops, representing over 50 dealers, currently dot a mile-long stretch of 99E (though the population runs no higher than 530). Plans are in the works for a new antique mall, with another 30 or so shops. Most stores (and the town's only restaurant, Chez Moustache) close Mondays.

Look for **FREE**—*it means this attraction or event is free of charge.*

A Prussian immigrant, Dr. William Keil, named the town after his daughter Aurora—suggesting a new beginning for the pioneers who came here over the Oregon Trail. Property, labor, and profits were communal, and the society prospered under Keil's autocratic rule. People lived according to strict Christian principles: industry was the rule, simplicity in dress was required, and marriage with outsiders was prohibited. Farming sustained the economy, but outsiders knew the colony for the excellence of its handicrafts: furniture, clothing, tools, embroidered goods, baskets, and clarinet reeds. After a smallpox epidemic in 1862 and the coming of the railroad in 1870, the colony gradually weakened.

The **Old Aurora Colony Museum** (formerly the Ox Barn Museum) commemorates the communal society of 1857 and comprises five buildings: the ox barn, the Karus home, the Steinbach log cabin, the communal wash house, and the farm equipment shed. Open different days depending on the season; call ahead, 1-678-5754. Admission is $2.50 for adults, $1 for children. Tours are available by prior arrangement.

FORT VANCOUVER

FREE **Fort Vancouver**, first the headquarters of the Hudson's Bay Company (1825–1849) and then a US military post, has been reconstructed on the original site and is open to the public.

The grand officers' quarters along **Officers' Row** have all been restored: the George C. Marshall House, furnished in antiques, is the showpiece (the rest are townhouses and offices and a restaurant). The oldest house in the row, the **Grant House** (1101 Officers' Row, 206-696-9699, housed quartermaster Ulysses S. Grant when he was stationed here in 1852. It's now an intimate restaurant (see Restaurants chapter). The quarters of the Hudson's Bay Company's chief agent, Dr. John McLoughlin, who later founded Oregon City, are also impressive. The visitors' center (I-5 north to Vancouver, Washington, take the Mill Plain Boulevard exit) has a museum that presents a slide show of the Fort's history; (206) 696-7655.

The 1840s gardens of Fort Vancouver are being re-established and at press time were flourishing. Some consider these early gardens the seedbeds of Northwest horticulture and agriculture; this is the first known organized local planting of vegetables, herbs, and flowers in a formal plot (reflecting the garden's English origins and some exotics such as purple Peruvian potatoes and West Indian gherkins). The original master gardener was Scotsman Billy Bruce, who learned his craft from the Royal Horticultural Society on the Duke of Devonshire's estates.

FORTY-MILE LOOP TRAIL

The Forty-Mile Loop Trail is the brainchild of the Olmsted brothers, who, in 1904, at the time of the Lewis and Clark Exposition, suggested developing a park system around the city. However, it wasn't until 1980, when a private nonprofit group put together a land trust, that the idea was acted upon. The goal is to complete a hiking and biking path that will connect the parks along the Columbia, Sandy, and Willamette rivers. With help from the city and county parks systems, the Forty-Mile

Loop Land Trust (241-9105) has completed a healthy portion of what has grown to be a 140–mile loop around Greater Portland.

The main section of the **Wildwood Trail** is the longest completed segment. Combined with the 10-mile-long **Marquam Nature Park,** a continuous path snakes 33 forested miles along the west side of the Willamette. A woodsy, unpaved path leads from the Sellwood Bridge through Willamette Park, Council Crest, Washington Park, Hoyt Arboretum, Pittock Acres, and Forest Park to as far north as St. Johns Bridge. Day hikers can park either at the zoo (look for the trailhead just north of the World Forestry Center) or the Interpretive Center, on SW Sam Jackson Road just west of Duniway Park. Mountain bikers are allowed on the dirt trail but are not-so-quietly discouraged.

At the confluence of the Columbia and Willamette rivers in north Portland is **Kelley Point Park**, where deciduous forests and meadows border the Columbia Slough, an excellent vantage point for watching river steamers, tankers, and barges. Eventually there will be a connection to the **Marine Drive Trail,** a paved 12-mile segment that parallels the Columbia from I-205 through Blue Lake Park to Troutdale.

Currently, the Land Trust is working on getting access to a 12-mile stretch of railroad from Gresham to Sellwood that joins up with Powell Butte, Leach Botanical Gardens, and Tideman-Johnson (where salmon spawn in Johnson Creek) parks. Because surrounding property is private, at press time the only access to Tideman-Johnson was at the south end of SE 37th Avenue. Limited street parking.

Maps of the loop are available at REI (Jantzen Beach, 283-1300), Powell's Travel Bookstore (Pioneer Courthouse Square, 228-1108), and the Portland Parks Bureau (Portland Building, fifth floor, 796-5193).

LARCH MOUNTAIN

The best sunset-watching spot in western Oregon, excluding the summit of Mount Hood, is the top of **Larch Mountain**, about 40 miles east of Portland. Unlike the peak of Mount Hood, you can drive there.

Among the alpine firs and bear grass you'll find picnic grounds. A short trail leads to **Sherrard's Point**—the summit—a rocky promontory jutting out from the mountaintop. From here there are spectacular 360-degree views of Mount Hood, Mount Adams, Mount St. Helens, Mount Jefferson, the Columbia River Gorge, and all of Portland. (The point is fenced, but keep an eye on your kids and dogs.) If you see moving black specks in the meadows far below, they are very likely black bears that have come to feed in Larch Mountain's abundant huckleberry patches. Binoculars are a must and tend to get passed around among the strangers who meet at the top. A longer (7-mile) hiking trail leads from the mountain's top through a small patch of old-growth western hemlock and Douglas fir to Multnomah Falls in the Gorge. Closed in winter, except to those with cross-country skis.

Directions. From Crown Point on the Old Columbia River Scenic Highway, continue upriver to the Larch Mountain Road junction (also reached by turning off I-84 at Lewis and Clark State Park in Troutdale, following the Sand River past Dabney Park and the Women's Forum State Park). The road up the mountain (14.5 miles) is a pristine corridor of timber which breaks open in several places, allowing grand roadside panoramas.

LONG BEACH PENINSULA

From Astoria, journey across the Columbia on the 4-mile ($1.50 toll) **Astoria-Megler Bridge**, the longest continuous truss span in the world, to Washington. **Long Beach Peninsula**, with its 28 uninterrupted miles of beach, draws clam diggers by the hundreds. Oregonians are sometimes put off by the curious driving-on-the-beach sport that still exists here.

Ilwaco is famed among sport-fishermen for its plentiful charter fishing businesses and its treacherous sand bar. **Cape Disappointment** is the site of the **North Head Lighthouse** (1899), which stands on a headland at the river mouth. In Seaview, stop for lunch or dinner at the **Shoalwater Restaurant** in the historic Shelburne Inn (Pacific Highway 103 and N 45th, 206-642-4142). The Shoalwater's forte is fresh, skillfully prepared seafood, and the menu changes seasonally, following the local catch. Those with time to travel might want to drive the peninsula's north shore to **Oysterville**, now a National Historic District but at one time a thriving boomtown following the discovery of the rich oyster beds of Willapa Bay. Plaques mark the tidy historic homes and the restored Oysterville Church. Beyond is **Leadbetter Point Natural Area**, where the beaches, woods, and marshes draw hikers and bird watchers. **The Ark**, on the old Nahcotta Dock, serves fresh oysters and other local seafood (273 Sandridge Road, 206-665-4133). **Long Island**, a wildlife refuge in Willapa Bay, harbors one of the last old-growth cedar forests in the state. There are oysters to pick and a few superb camping sites on the island, though it can only be reached by boat. Information about the island and a boat ramp are found near the southeastern corner of the island, just off Highway 101.

MARYHILL MUSEUM

In the arid eastern reaches of the Columbia River Gorge, about 100 miles east of Portland, the **Maryhill Museum**, a massive neoclassical edifice, perches rather obtrusively upon the river's barren benchlands. Maryhill, once the palatial residence of the eccentric Sam Hill (son-in-law of railroad tycoon James J. Hill), is now a museum with a stunning collection of Rodin sculptures.

Hill bought 7,000 acres here in 1907 with the intention of founding a Quaker agricultural community. When that failed to materialize, Hill lost interest in living in the "ranch house" named after his wife and daughter. It seems that the museum came about through a little help from his friends: famed dancer Loie Fuller (also a close friend of Rodin) encouraged Hill to turn his mansion into an art museum; art collector Alma Spreckels became Maryhill's principal benefactor; and Queen Marie of Romania gave much of her royal and personal memorabilia to Hill and traveled to Maryhill for the dedication in 1926.

With one of the largest collections of Rodin works in the world (78 bronze and plaster sculptures and 28 watercolors), three floors of classic French and American paintings and glasswork, unique exhibitions such as chess sets and Romanian folk textiles, and splendid Northwest tribal art, the museum makes for quite an interesting visit. A cafe serves espresso, pastries, and sandwiches; peacocks roam the lovely landscaped grounds. Maryhill is open daily from March 15 to November 15. On Highway 14, 13 miles southwest of Goldendale, (509) 773-3733.

FREE Up the road is another of Sam Hill's bizarre creations, a not-quite-lifesize replica of **Stonehenge**, built to honor World War I veterans of Klickitat County. Unlike the original, Hill's Stonehenge (not stones but poured concrete) doesn't function as an observatory. It embodies Hill's personal vision: a pacifist, he considered his monument a statement on the human sacrifices made to the god of war.

Just 20 minutes north of Goldendale on US 97 is the **Goldendale Observatory**, a popular spot when Halley's comet dropped by. High-powered telescopes give you incredible celestial views through unpolluted skies. Open Wednesday through Sunday from April through September; call ahead the rest of the year, (509) 773-3141.

MOUNT HOOD

At 11,245 feet, Hood is not the highest in the chain of volcanoes in the Cascades, but it is one of the most developed—in part due to the easy 1½-hour trip east from Portland. According to geologists, the mountain still conceals hot magma and is anxious to spew. For now, though, all's peaceful in the towns on its flanks. On the way up, Sandy (named for the nearby river), with its white-steepled church, weekend country market, and fruit stands, makes a nice stop before heading into the mountains. Here you'll find **Oral Hull Park**, designed for the blind, with splashing water and plants to smell and feel; 1-668-6195. You'll also pass through the aptly named town of Rhododendron (rhodies bloom in July).

From Highway 26 at Government Camp, a 6-mile road twists its way to **Timberline Lodge** (elevation 6,000 feet), whose ski area provides four-season skiing and impressive frontal views of Mount Hood's glaciers. Chair lifts take skiers and photographers up over the Palmer Snowfield (technically, the glacier has stopped moving) year-round. The massive timber and stone lodge was constructed by WPA workers in the 1930s. Throughout the lodge are structural and decorative pieces made by hand from native materials: the 100-foot-high chimney and the enormous central fireplace were fashioned out of volcanic rocks from the mountain, the hand-wrought andirons from old railroad tracks, hardwood chairs and tables hand-hewn from Oregon timber. The lodge still functions as a hotel; the rooms with fireplaces get booked early. Call 231-5400 or 231-7979.

One of the best hiking trails leads 4½ miles west from Timberline Lodge to flower-studded Paradise Park. Like Rainier, this mountain is girt by a long trail (called **Timberline Trail**), a 40-mile circuit of the entire peak that traverses snowfields as well as ancient forests. The lower parts can blaze with rhododendrons (peaking in June) and wildflowers (peaking in July); all are easily reachable from trails that spread out from Timberline Lodge.

Mid-May to mid-July is the prime time for **climbing** Mount Hood, a peak that looks deceptively easy, with its last 1,500 feet involving very steep snow-climbing. **Timberline Mountain Guides** in Terrebonne (also a seasonal base camp at the Wy'east Lodge) equips and conducts climbers to the summit; 1-548-0749.

KIDS Just east of Government Camp the meadows of **Trillium Lake** beckon picnickers. On the north side of the highway is **Snow Bunny Lodge**, where you can take the kids sledding. Mount Hood's biggest ski area, **Mount Hood Meadows**, covers over 2,000 acres and with the opening of the Shooting Star chair has become one of Portland's favored areas for beginners and schussers alike. **Cooper Spur Ski Area** (on Cooper Spur Road, off Highway 35) has gentler slopes, and the year-round **Inn at Cooper Spur** (1-352-6692) has rooms, cabins with fireplaces, and a decent restaurant. Another dozen miles or so down Cooper Spur Road is the 1889 **Cloud Cap Inn**, a log landmark at the timberline on the north flank of Mount Hood. No longer a hotel, it's anchored to the mountain by cables, and the view alone is worth the detour. The lodge is also an access point for the Timberline Trail. Call the Ranger Station in Zig Zag (666-0704) or Parkdale (666-0701).

OPAL CREEK WILDERNESS

The raging old-growth controversy has probably drawn more visitors to the proposed **Opal Creek Wilderness** than to any other ancient stand. The pools of water punctuating Opal Creek are as achingly beautiful as lovers' eyes; the pine-needle-padded trail and spacious forest bring further emotional attachment. The imperial cedar grove commands the kind of hushed respect usually reserved for snow-capped peaks and lonely, windswept beaches. Two hours from Portland, Opal Creek is 36 miles east of Salem via progressively more primitive roads. A mountain bike is a great way to cover the 3 miles from the gate up to the quaint mining town of Jawbone Flat, where the trail begins (the way back is all downhill). Anyone there can point out the spot where a white water pipe marks the trailhead, across the Battle Ax Creek bridge and up a lane to the right. From there, it's about 3½ miles on an unauthorized but well-traveled trail to the cedar grove, which has trees up to 250 feet high and 1,000 years old. Here the trail fades, requiring cross-country travel on steep terrain. The hiking is predictably rigorous in spots; practically the only old growth left is in places that are difficult to log. The owners and managers of Shiny Rock Mining Company at Jawbone Flat have been working for decades to protect this gorgeous hunk of undesignated wilderness from the still-pending timber sales—thank them along your way. It's 13-plus miles for the round-trip hike; start early, bring a lunch, and dawdle in the forests. A comprehensive guide to Oregon's old-growth trees, a two-year project by the Oregon Natural Resources Council (ONRC), was just going to press as this book was. It describes a handful of places within an hour of Portland: the closest ancient forest, at Oxbow Park; examples of the Willamette Valley's unique leafy lowland forests at the **Sauvie Island Wildlife Management Area**; western hemlock and Douglas fir on the more demanding **Larch Mountain Trail** (see Larch Mountain in this chapter) behind Multnomah Falls in the Columbia Gorge. They're all worth visiting, but the stands are so small it's almost like visiting animals in the zoo. Call ONRC for the book; 223-9001.

Directions to Opal Creek: From Portland, drive south on I-5. Take the North Santiam Highway exit (Oregon Highway 22) and drive east for about 25 miles. At a flashing yellow light between the state forestry department and the Swiss Village Restaurant (look for the Elkhorn Recreation Area sign), turn left and drive 21 miles due north up the Little North Fork Santiam River. You cross the National Forest boundary, and Little North Fork Road becomes FS Road 2207. At the only major fork in the road, bear left on FS Road 2209. Watch for deer as the road surface deteriorates into rutted dirt. Park at the gate; chances are good you'll have lots of company.

OREGON CITY

Archaeologists have found evidence that the **Oregon City** area, at the confluence of the Willamette and Clackamas rivers, has been inhabited for 3,000 years. It's history that makes Oregon City. The city sits at the end of the 2,000-mile **Oregon Trail**, which brought 300,000 migrants west. The town, therefore, can lay claim to many firsts in the state's history: the first territorial capital, the first industrial use of water power, the first garden, the first Protestant church, the first Masonic lodge. Its newspaper was the first west of the Missouri. A canal and locks were built at **Willamette Falls** in 1872, which opened the area up to river traffic and thus to industrial development.

Oregon City's downtown business district begins at the east bank of the Willamette; residential neighborhoods top the bluffs above the river. Pedestrians ride the **municipal elevator** between the lower and upper sections of town. This 130-foot cylindrical structure, at Seventh Street and Railroad Avenue, zips to upper Oregon in 15 seconds. From the glass-enclosed observation deck at the top you can see the falls (actually in West Linn) and, on a clear day, Mount St. Helens.

The **Oregon Trail Interpretive Center** (657-9336), at Fifth and Washington streets, tells the stories of Oregon Trail pioneers. On the list of National Historic Sites is the **John McLoughlin House** (Seventh and Center streets, 656-5146). McLoughlin settled in Oregon City in 1829 to help protect the interests of the Hudson's Bay Company. Open Tuesday through Sunday; purchase tickets next door in the former house of Dr. Forbes Barclay, arctic explorer, physician, public official, and philanthropist.

Today the pioneers at **John Inskeep Environmental Learning Center** (19600 S Mollala Avenue, Oregon City, 657-6958) have turned what was once a parking lot for a berry-processing plant into an 80-acre environmental study area with paths, ponds, wildlife, and alternative technologies: in keeping with the center's goal of promoting recycling, 90 percent of the recently completed **observatory** was constructed from recycled materials. Adjacent to the Environmental Learning Center is the **Home Orchard Society Arboretum,** which cultivates a dazzling assortment of fruit-bearing plants.

RIVER CRUISES

KIDS Before the arrival of railroads and paved roads, people could hail a steamboat just about anywhere between Portland and Eugene, Astoria and The Dalles. Two **sternwheelers** still navigate the waters of the Columbia and Willamette rivers and offer some relief from today's highways.

From its summer base, about 45 minutes east of Portland, the Columbia Gorge sternwheeler (a triple-deck paddle-wheeler) voyages through the dramatic Columbia River Gorge. Sound a bit touristy? Portlanders confess they've taken the scenic trip several times and still love it. In late September, the 147-foot vessel returns to Portland, where it's used for wedding receptions and company outings. Holiday dinner-and-dance and occasional get-down-and-do-the-blues cruises are very popular. Fares range from $10 to $30. The monthly schedule varies, so call ahead; 223-3928.

The *Rose*, a 65-foot sternwheeler replica, sails from the RiverPlace Marina in downtown Portland. The downriver trip gets quite industrial, passing shipyards, grain terminals, seven of Portland's 12 bridges, and perhaps the world's largest drydock. The more scenic direction is upriver toward Milwaukie, passing Sellwood, Oaks Park, Johns Landing, and gracious old homes on the bluffs overlooking the Willamette. The 49-passenger vessel has a topside deck and four different tours. Call for schedule; 286-7673.

SAUVIE ISLAND

Pastoral Sauvie Island, with its farms, orchards, produce stands, waterways, and wildlife—just 20 minutes from downtown on US Highway 30 West—is a quick escape for bicyclists, bird watchers, fishermen, and boaters. Bounded on the east by the Columbia River and on the west by Multnomah Channel, Lewis and Clark named it Wappato Island after a native plant they and the local Multnomah Indians used for food. It was later renamed for a pioneer dairy farmer, Laurent Sauvie.

In summer, watch for "U-pick" signs or buy fresh produce from one of the local markets, such as the **Sauvie Island Farms Market** (621-3489) or the **Pumpkin Patch** (621-3874). If you're planning to bike, park at the east end of the bridge; you can't miss the lot. From there take the 12-mile biking loop. At the 6-mile point, if you're feeling energetic, take the 5-mile side trip down to the Columbia. There are several bird-watching turnouts along the loop. A traditional fall activity is to trek out to island farms to pick Halloween pumpkins. Be warned, though: on rainy days the broad, golden fields of the island turn into mud farms, so take your rubber boots if you're going to pick.

The northern half of the island is a **game refuge** of sorts; that is, duck hunters come in autumn (October–January), making it no place to hang around, for you or the ducks. At other times, bountiful wildlife can be seen in the marshes and open fields. Look for red foxes, black-tailed deer, great blue herons, geese, ducks, and migrating sandhill cranes. Reeder Road extends to the northern shore and to short sandy beaches that freighters and small pleasure craft pass by. The western branch of the road follows the dike of the Multnomah Channel, passing the Bybee-Howell House, humble houseboats, rickety marinas, the old site of the Hudson's Bay Company's Fort William (abandoned in 1836, nothing remains), and then eventually dead-ends.

The **Bybee-Howell House** in **Bybee-Howell Territorial Park** was built in 1858 by James F. Bybee on a donation land claim and sold to neighbor Benjamin Howell in 1860. The Classic Revival–style two-story house has nine rooms and six fireplaces. **KIDS** The hands-on **Agricultural Museum** displays agricultural equipment used in cultivating and harvesting crops, a complete harness shop, dairy equipment, and hand tools for working wood, leather, and metal. In the adjacent **Pioneer Orchard**, there are more than 115 varieties of apple trees brought here by pioneers—many of them unknown to modern-day orchardists. The house and museum are open Wednesday through Sunday, June 1 through Labor Day. Admission by donation. (Call 621-3344, open season, or 222-1741, closed season.)

Looking for a particular place? Check the index at the back of this book for individual restaurants, hotels, B&Bs, shops, bars, parks, museums, galleries, neighborhoods, messenger services, nightclubs, and more.

WINE COUNTRY

Oregon is home to over 50 bonded and licensed wine-making enterprises. While wineries are found in western Oregon as far south as Medford and Ashland, the majority are clustered west and southwest of Portland in the northern **Willamette Valley**. This quiet agricultural area is being challenged by the migration of urbanites lured by its peaceful beauty. Once best known for its filbert and prune crops, it now boasts some of the finest vineyards on the West Coast and has a growing international reputation for pinot noir. The topography is characterized by rolling hills whose verdant flanks are choice locations for vineyards due to their sunlight exposure, soil composition, and drainage. The maritime climate, with frequent gentle precipitation, cooling breezes, and long growing seasons, is suitable for wine grape varieties such as chardonnay, pinot noir, riesling, and pinot gris.

The wineries themselves are delightful to visit for those with even a passing interest in wine. Foremost among the reasons must be the settings—some of Oregon's prettiest. In all seasons, there is much to take in, from Japanese woodcut misty hills to spring buds to flaming fall colors to the harvesting of the small, intensely flavored grapes. The individual wineries range from farmhouses with adjoining production facilities to efficient modern plants. Almost all have tasting rooms staffed by either winery owners or workers with intimate knowledge of the wines and production methods. They usually welcome questions and take great pride in their products. Facility tours are often available—to be sure, you may want to call ahead. And of course there are the wines to sample, which may include vintages not available elsewhere or small lots from grapes in scarce supply. Prices are close to standard retail, though bargains are occasionally found, especially in purchases by the case.

Do take along bread, cheese, and other wine-friendly foods to enjoy, not only to enhance appreciation of the wines, but also to dampen the alcohol's effects. Many facilities have tables or grassy areas for picnicking.

To learn more about specific wineries and their specialties, get a copy of the Oregon Winegrowers' Association's booklet *Discover Oregon Wineries* (1359 W 5th Avenue, Eugene, OR 97402, 1-233-2377), available for free in most wine and food stores. Or visit a local Portland wine shop: the better ones have particularly close ties to the Oregon wine industry and can help you set an itinerary. (See Wines, Beers, and Spirits in Shopping chapter.)

Below are some recommendations for wineries to visit. These places have tasting rooms open every day (unless otherwise noted). Calling in advance is always recommended; all are closed the month of January.

WINE TOUR 1: WEST OF PORTLAND. There are several wineries due west of Portland worth visiting. Pick up a baguette and cheese and head to the Tualatin Valley. The following wineries make a good daytrip:

Ponzi Vineyards (Vandermost Road, Beaverton, 628-1227) was designed by Richard Ponzi with striking results. His bottlings (especially pinot noir, pinot gris, and dry white riesling) are first-rate. Open every day, but it's best to call ahead. **Oak Knoll Winery** (Route 6, Hillsboro, 648-8198) is one of Oregon's oldest and largest producers, famous for fruit and berry wines, plus award-winning pinot noir and riesling. Great picnic grounds. Open Wednesday through Sunday. A recent purchase of the old **Laurel Ridge Winery** (David Hill Road, Forest Grove, 1-359-5436) has resulted in a beautiful reconstruction of the facilities. Excellent sparkling wine, good sauvignon blanc, gewurztraminer, and riesling. Wonderful setting. Open Tuesday through Sunday; weekends only in winter. Bill Fuller is one of Oregon's wine producers of longest standing and a great conversationalist. His facility, **Tualatin Vineyards** (Seavey Road, Forest Grove, 1-357-5005), in lovely surroundings, was recently expanded with a new tasting room. Well known for chardonnay, gewurztraminer, pinot noir, and riesling.

WINE TOUR 2: YAMHILL COUNTY. About 45 minutes southwest of Portland is Yamhill County. There are enough producers in this area that several day-tours can be made with no repeat visits to any one winery. In fact, Oregon has designated Highway 99W the state's official wine road. Local produce stands still dot the roadside in summer, but increasingly it's the wineries, antique shops, and B&Bs that draw visitors to these lush green hills. Start by making a toll-free call to **Pinot Pete's** (Dundee, 800-422-1186), who can have a picnic packed for you to pick up en route. In Layfayette, drop into the former **Layfayette School** (1-864-2720), now a large antique mall.

Some recommended wineries along 99W include: **Rex Hill Vineyards** (30835 N Highway 99W, Newberg, 1-538-0666) which, since its opening in the early '80s, has produced a number of vineyard-designated pinot noirs that received critical attention. Its location is splendid, one of the state's best visitor facilities. The new tasting room is open every day from April through December; weekends only February through March. **Knudsen Erath** (2700 NE Knudsen Lane, Dundee, 1-538-3318) is one of the pioneer Oregon wineries, noted for wonderful pinot noirs. Dick Erath doesn't look or act anything like a stereotypical winemaker, and his successful (and good-value) wines seems to prove that that doesn't matter. A beautiful setting, just up the hill from Crabtree Park (good for picnics). One of Oregon's most commercial and successful wineries, **Sokol-Blosser** (5000 Sokol Blosser Lane, Dundee, 1-864-2282), has also been innovative at times. High on a hill overlooking Yamhill Valley, **Chateau Benoit Winery** (NE Mineral Springs Road, Carlton, 1-864-2991) is best known for its sparkling wines and sauvignon blanc.

WINE TOUR 3: SALEM AREA. Just shy of an hour south of Portland lies the state capital, Salem. North and west of Salem are several of the newest vineyards and wineries. A few are still developing their drop-in tasting trade, though here are a couple of good ones to keep in mind:

Bethel Heights Vineyards (6060 Bethel Heights Road NW, Salem, 1-581-2262) has a lovely location and a tasting room with great views. Its wines have won several awards; try the pinot noir, chenin blanc, and riesling. Closed January and February; open Tuesday through Sunday the rest of the year. **Glen Creek Winery** (6057 Orchards Heights Road NW, Salem, 1-371-9463) is a tasting stop for sauvignon blanc and chardonnay. Pretty grounds, too. A new winery (since 1987), **Schwarzenberg Vineyards** (11975 Smithfield Road, Dallas, 1-623-6420) is noted not only for its pinot noir and chardonnay but its setting near a wildlife preserve. Open Tuesday through Sunday; weekends only in winter.

EXCURSIONS

ASHLAND

The remarkable success of the **Oregon Shakespeare Festival**, now over 50 years old, transformed this sleepy town into the one with the best tourist amenities in the region. The Ashland season now draws an audience of nearly 350,000 over the eight-month season, filling theaters to an extraordinary 94 percent of capacity. Visitors pour into this town of 15,000, providing clientele for fine shops, restaurants, and bed and breakfasts. Amazingly, Ashland has not lost its soul: for the most part, it seems a happy little college town set in lovely ranch country, which just happens to house the fifth-largest theater company in the United States.

The **festival** mounts plays in three theaters. In the outdoor Elizabethan Theatre, which seats 1,200, appear the famous and authentic nighttime productions of Shakespeare (three different plays) each summer. Stretching from February to October, the season for the two indoor theaters includes comedies, contemporary works, and some experimental works; in these the large repertory company is more likely to excel, for Shakespeare outdoors takes a toll on voices and subtlety. Visit the Exhibit Center, where you can clown around in costumes from plays past. There are also lectures and concerts at noon, excellent backstage tours each morning, Renaissance music and dance nightly in the courtyard, plus all the nearby daytime attractions of the Rogue River: rafting, picnicking, and historical touring. The best way to get information and tickets is through the festival box office, 1-482-4331, or the comprehensive Southern Oregon Reservation Center, which offers ticket and accommodation packages; PO Box 477, Ashland, OR 97520; 1-488-1011, 800-533-1311 in Oregon, 800-547-8052 outside Oregon.

Last-minute tickets are rarely available, yet a persevering few can sometimes obtain them once in Ashland. Due to a number of no-shows, you're more likely to get tickets the day of the performance than the week before. Our recommendation is to get up early and wait in line for "priority tickets" at the ticket office in the courtyard of the Shakespeare complex. Persons holding high-priority numbers have a good chance of securing leftover tickets. Another method is simply to make a sign announcing you need a ticket. Many theatergoers have an extra ticket or two.

If none of these tactics works, you still won't be stuck in Ashland without a play to go to: **Actors' Theatre of Ashland**, the town's growing experimental theater program (often called **Off Shakespeare**), is worth checking into. Festival actors often join in these small productions, giving audiences a chance to see Shakespearean actors having a bit of fun and going out on a theatrical limb. A full listing is available at the Chamber of Commerce, 110 E Main Street, 1-482-3486.

Recently, a northern offshoot of the Oregon Shakespeare Festival, **Oregon Shakespeare Festival Portland**, set full-time roots in Portland's Performing Arts Center. It's not a trip to Ashland, but the theater's just as good. Call 248-6309 for information and tickets. (See also Theater in the Arts chapter.) In late October, after the curtain has dropped, locals recapture the stage with an outrageous **Halloween parade**. Participate or watch from the Mark Antony or Columbia hotels. Don't bother the Chamber of Commerce with questions—they don't like to promote such ghoulish behavior.

There is more to Ashland, however, than Shakespeare and crowds. Just beyond the city limits, the peaceful **Rogue River Recreation Area** has fine swimming for the sizzling summer days, as does the lovely valley of the Applegate River. Twenty-two scenic miles up Dead Indian Road is **Howard Prairie Lake Resort,** where you can camp, park your trailer, shower, rent a boat, and fish all day (April–October); 1-482-1979. **Mount Ashland Ski Area** (1-482-2897), 18 miles southwest of town, offers 23 runs for all classes of skiers, from Thanksgiving to April, snow willing. **Lithia Park,** designed by the creator of San Francisco's Golden Gate Park, is Ashland's central park, extending 100 acres behind the outdoor theater and providing a lovely mix of duck ponds, Japanese gardens, grassy lawns, playgrounds, groomed or dirt trails for hiking and jogging, and the pungent mineral water that gave the park its name. Great for picnicking, especially after stocking up at nearby **Greenleaf Deli** (49 N Main Street, 1-482-2808).

In town, **Manna from Heaven Bakery** is a distinguished Old World bakery famous for elaborate breads, pastries, and good coffee. Definitely worth a visit for breakfast; 358 E Main Street, 1-482-5831. **Jazmin's Bistro & Sidewalk Cafe** is the place to go dancing in town. It's a small spot, generally jam-packed on weekend nights, especially when musicians on their way to Portland or San Francisco stop in; 180 Lithia Way, 1-488-0883. The **Mark Antony Hotel,** a downtown landmark, is of some historic interest, but ownership seems to change almost yearly, with corresponding closings and reopenings; 212 E Main Street, 1-482-1721.

Weisinger Vineyard and Winery and the **Rogue Brewery & Public House** are welcome additions to the Ashland area. The winery is the perfect spot to sample Oregon products. Snuggled in a Bavarian-style building, the winery gift shop offers jams, jellies, sauces, and, of course, wines for sale (on Siskiyou Boulevard, just outside Ashland, 1-488-5989). Wash down a sandwich or a pizza with a Rogue Golden Ale at the brewery, located at 31 B Water Street, a good place to unwind after a day of theater; 1-488-5061.

Locals say the choice of best food in Ashland is a toss-up between the charming **Chateaulin** (50 E Main Street, 1-482-2264) and the **Winchester Country Inn** (35 S Second Street, 1-488-1113), the latter in a century-old Queen Anne home that looks out onto a neatly snipped garden. The jambalaya at the **Bayou Grill** (139 E Main Street, 1-488-0235) nicely extends the range of cuisine on the downtown dining strip. In summer, nothing competes with sitting outside by the creek at **Back Porch BBQ** (92½ N Main Street, 1-482-4131). Good though not entirely authentic Thai food can be had at **Thai Pepper** (84 N Main Street, 1-482-8058). Another spot, a bit quirky perhaps, is **Geppetto's** (345 E Main Street, 1-482-1138), with a conglomeration of Italian, Asian, and American dishes. Nine miles down the road is a budget Italian restaurant, once the only place to eat in the area, called **Callahan's** (7100 Old Highway 99 S, 1-482-1299). The 35-minute drive past red hills, jutting cliffs, and thick evergreens to **Green Springs Inn** (11470 Highway 66, 1-482-0614) is a guaranteed escape from Ashland's tourist crowds; this unassuming restaurant with hearty soups and pastas doubles as a neighborhood store.

Despite growing competition for accommodations, the **Chanticleer Inn** (120 Gresham Street, 1-482-1919) has maintained its position as the preferred B&B through nearly a decade of Shakespeare seasons. Also notable are the farmhouse and carriagehouse of the **Arden Forest Inn** (261 W Hersey Road, 1-488-1496). If privacy is a priority, look into the **Fox House Inn** (269 B Street, 1-488-1055) or wind your way up Mt. Ashland Road through several miles of gargantuan evergreens to the huge, custom-made, log **Mt. Ashland Inn** (550 Mt. Ashland Road, 1-482-8707). A similar sense of remoteness can be found a bit closer in at **Country Willows** (1313 Clay Street, 1-488-1590) or even on Main Street at **Morical House** (668 N Main Streeet, 1-482-2254), a remodeled 1880s farmhouse. house. The swing on the front porch identifies **Cowslip's Belle** (159 N Main Street, 1-488-2901), a charming B&B. More plush is the **Romeo Inn** (295 Idaho Street, 1-488-0884), with a baby grand piano in the library, a heated pool (summers only), and a hot tub on the large back deck.

BEND

Bend was a quiet, undiscovered high-desert paradise until a push in the 1960s to develop recreation and tourism potential tamed Bachelor Butte into an alpine playground. Then came the golf courses, the airstrip, the bike trails, the river-rafting companies, the hikers, the tennis players, the rock hounds, and the skiers. Bend's popularity and population have been on a steady increase ever since, elevating it in the last three years to serious-destination status. You may wonder what all the fuss is about as you approach the predictable main street (Third Street, here), but the town's charm, relying heavily on the blinding blue sky and sage-scented air, eventually wins over any visitor with even a moderate affection for the great outdoors. Part of the appeal is due to its proximity to the following.

Mount Bachelor Ski Area (22 miles southwest). Having recently opened four express lifts (Summit, Pine Marten, Outback Super Express Quad, and Skyliner Express), Mount Bachelor now has 11 lifts feeding skiers onto 3,100 vertical feet of dry and groomed skiing. In high winds or stormy weather the Summit Express doesn't run, but when it does it divulges spectacular views of the Three Sisters Wilderness. Even if you don't ski, we recommend you take the Express up to the new restaurant on the hill, **The Skiers' Palate** in the Pine Marten Lodge, whose ski-hill eats rank considerably above the norm. The 9,000–foot elevation at the summit makes for all-season skiing. High-season amenities include a ski school, racing, day care, rentals, an entire Nordic program with 60 kilometers of groomed trails ($8), and better-than-average ski food at six different lodges. Call 1-382-8334, 1-382-2442, or 1-382-7888 (taped ski report).

Other attractions: the **High Desert Museum**, 6 miles south of Bend on Highway 97, is a nonprofit center for natural and cultural history with live-animal presentations on birds of prey, river otters, and porcupines. Fifty acres of natural trails and outdoor exhibits offer replicas of covered wagons, a sheepherders' camp, a settlers' cabin, and an Indian wickiup. Admission is $4; call 1-382-4754. **Pilot Butte** (just east of town), a cinder cone with a road to the top, is a good first stop, offering a knockout panorama of Bend and the mountains beyond. **Lava River Cave** (12 miles south on Highway 97) is a mile-long lava tube. You'll need a warm sweater to descend into the dark and surprisingly eerie depths. **Lava Lands Visitor Center**, atop a high butte formed by a volcanic fissure, is a lookout point with accompanying geology lessons about the moonlike panorama created by central Oregon's volcanic activity; call 1-593-2421. The **Pine Mountain Observatory** (30 miles southeast of Bend on Highway 20, 1-382-8331) is the University of Oregon's astronomical research facility. One of its three telescopes is the largest in the Northwest. The

Deschutes Historical Museum (corner of NW Idaho Avenue and Wall Street) features regional history and interesting pioneer paraphernalia but keeps limited hours; 1-389-1813.

For full appreciation of the 100-mile **Cascade Lakes Highway/Century Drive** you'll need several hours and a picnic lunch. Begin in Bend along the Deschutes, using the National Forest Service's booklet "Cascade Lakes Discovery Tour"; call 1-388-5664. Twenty-two miles north of Bend in Terrebonne lies **Smith Rock State Park**. Some of the finest rock climbers in the world gather to test their skills on the red rock cliffs here. The climbers' second-favorite hangout is **La Fiesta Mexican Restaurant** (Highway 97, Terrebonne, 1-548-4848), fondly known as Rudy's.

As for eats, Bend has plenty. **Geno's Italian Specialties** (2210 E Highway 20, 1-389-3464) is the kind of place you'd want two blocks from your house (especially welcome after a solid day of skiing): reasonable prices, large servings, and outstanding food. The 54-year-old **Pine Tavern Restaurant** (967 NW Brooks Avenue, 1-382-5581) is a better choice if you're in the mood for a fancy night out. **Players Grille** (61 NW Oregon Avenue, 1-382-5859), with its neon-lit mahogany bar and the jazzy Deco intimacy of its back dining room, specializes in fresh Northwest foods. Don't be put off by the austere old church facade of **Le Bistro** (1203 NE Third Street, 1-389-7274), for the inside of Bend's finest French restaurant more resembles that of a sidewalk cafe. Also noteworthy are: the **Old Bend Blacksmith Shop and Broiler** (211 Greenwood Avenue, 1-388-1994), ranch cooking in a wonderfully frenzied atmosphere; huevos rancheros and homemade muffins at the **West Side Bakery and Cafe** (1005½ NW Galveston, 1-382-3426); Bend's first brew pub, the **Deschutes Brewery & Public House** (1044 NW Bond Street, 1-382-9242); and 6 miles north of Bend on Highway 20 W, the **Tumalo Emporium** (64619 Highway 20 W, 1-382-2202), a truly local eatery and friendly bar where dusty old cowboys are as likely to stop in as families on vacation.

Of all the places to stay, **Sunriver Lodge and Resort** (15 miles south of Bend, 800-547-3922) is the biggest and best-known. It's actually more than a resort, with everything from rooms and condos to three-bedroom houses for rent. It's an organized community with its own post office and 200 or so full-time residents. But while Sunriver may be the biggest lodgings in Bend, the **Inn at the Seventh Mountain** (18575 Century Drive, 1-382-8711, 800-452-6810 in Oregon) is the closest to Mount Bachelor, with a long roster of activities in the multi-condominium facility.

If you don't want a social chairman, can live without an adjacent dining room, and rarely need a hot-tub soak after 11pm, then the spacious rooms of **Mount Bachelor Village** (19717 Mount Bachelor Drive, 1-389-5900, 800-452-9846 in Oregon) may be your style. Less showy and more reasonably priced is **The Riverhouse** (3075 N Highway 97, 1-389-3111, 800-452-6878 in Oregon). In summer, **Rock Springs Guest Ranch** (64201 Tyler Road, 1-382-1957) is a good place for families: counselors take care of the kids in special programs all day, while adults hit the trail, laze in the pool, play tennis, or gobble down hearty meals in the ranch dining room. Try Best Western's **Entrada Lodge** (19221 Century Drive, 1-382-4080) if all you need is a sleep and, OK, maybe a soak in a hot tub. The **Lara House Bed and Breakfast** (640 NW Congress Street, 1-388-4064), once a run-down boarding house in Bend's oldest house (1910), is now a bright and homey four-bedroom inn.

Twenty-two miles northwest of Bend is **Sisters**, named after the three mountain peaks that dominate the horizon (Faith, Hope, and Charity). This little community is becoming a bit of a mecca for tired urban types looking for a taste of cowboy escapism—someplace a little less grown-up and a little more remote than Bend. On a clear day (and there are about 250 of them a year), Sisters is exquisitely beautiful and often overlooked by Bend-seekers. Surrounded by mountains, trout streams, and pine and cedar forests, this little town is beginning to capitalize on the influx of winter skiers and summer camping and fishing enthusiasts. **Santiam Pass,** wedged between two national forests, and the alpine lakes on the west side of **Three Fingered Jack** are two favorite outdoor playgrounds. Several **mountain biking trails** begin right in town and continue south into Forest Service land. Call the Sisters Ranger Station for more information; 1-549-2111.

There are mixed feelings about the pseudo-Western storefronts thematically organizing the town's commerce, but then again, Sisters does host 50,000 visitors at its **annual June rodeo.** If cowboy isn't your style, there is a very good art gallery at the corner of Elm Avenue and Main Street, a mini-mall called Barclay Square (with a nice tile boutique), and a mountain gear store with a knowledgeable staff.

While the population is about 730, more than 3,000 people receive their mail at the Sisters P.O. Many of them run boarding and ranch facilities. The most famous ranch is the **Patterson Ranch,** where Polish-Arabian horses and South American llamas are bred. Call 1-549-3831 for information.

The social centerpiece of Western-theme Sisters is **Hotel Sisters and Bronco Billy's Saloon** (corner of Fir and Cascade streets, 1-549-RIBS), dishing up Western-style ranch cooking. Pizza fiends opt for utterly fresh from-scratch pizzas at **Papandrea's** (325 E Hood Street, 1-549-6081), the original link in a growing chain. **The Gallery** (230 W Cascade Street, 1-549-2631) draws the morning crowd.

Eight miles west of Sisters, the 1,800-acre, unassumingly spectacular **Black Butte Ranch** (Highway 20, 1-595-6211, 800-452-7455) remains the jewel of Northwest resorts. Rimmed by the Three Sisters mountains, scented by a plain of ponderosa pines, the area has limitless, year-round recreation.

COLUMBIA RIVER GORGE

The Gorge once was more a terror than a scenic wonder, because of the narrow, winding highway alongside it. But now most of the traffic is out on I-84, leaving beautiful old Route 30 for the take-your-time wanderers. The scenery is partly magnificent waterfalls, partly dramatic cliffs and rock formations cut by the country's second-largest river (which, unlike the Mississippi, has a rapid downhill surge). Watch the river for colorful participants in the booming sailboard craze, for which this windy stretch of the Columbia has become world renowned.

The old **Scenic Gorge Highway** is an easy 20-mile trip from Troutdale on. But before you hit the road, stop in at **Tad's Chicken 'n' Dumplings** (a mile east of Troutdale on Highway 30, 1-666-5337), a decades-old Oregon institution popular with kids, bargain-hungry families, tourists—and chicken fanciers in general. Once on the Scenic Gorge Highway, popular viewpoints and attractions are numerous: **Crown Point,** 725 feet above the river, features an English Tudor vista house. Below, at **Rooster Rock State Park,** one of the attractions is a nude bathing beach.

Larch Mountain, 14 miles upriver from Crown Point, is even more spectacular than the more famous overlooks. **Multnomah Falls** ranks second-highest in the country at 620 feet (in two steps). The stone **Multnomah Falls Lodge,** at the foot of the falls, was designed in 1925 by Albert E. Doyle, of Benson Hotel fame, in a rustic style. Now a National Historic Landmark, the lodge houses a naturalists' and visitors' center and a large restaurant but does not have overnight facilities. Check out the Falls Room Lounge, (503) 695-2376. **Oneonta Gorge** is a narrow, dramatic cleft through which a slippery half-mile trail winds to secluded Oneonta Falls; this rugged trail, mostly through the actual stream bed, is suitable only for the adventurous.

Bonneville Dam, the first federal dam on the Columbia, offers tours of the dam itself, the fish ladders (seen through underwater viewing windows), and the locks; (503) 374-8820. You can tour the Bonneville Fish Hatchery (next to the dam) year-round, but the best time is in September and November, when the Chinook are spawning; (503) 374-8393. **Bridge of the Gods,** in the old river town of **Cascade Locks,** has a fine little museum that recounts the Indian myth about the legendary rock-arch bridge that collapsed into the Columbia River long ago. **Columbia Gorge Sternwheeler** departs three times daily in the summer from the locks, stopping at Bonneville Dam and Stevenson Landing; 1-374-8427 (see Daytrips in this chapter).

HOOD RIVER

Much of the Northwest's bounty converges in this agreeable town of 4,000. Fruit orchards are everywhere, benignly supervised by 11,245-foot Mount Hood 30 miles to the south and nourished by the Columbia River, rushing alongside the town's northern edge. From the town itself, however, the views are of Mount Adams on the Washington side, looking down upon the Columbia and its ever-present windsurfers through a fortuitous cleft in the bluff.

In summer you can't miss the "boardheads," dotting the river with their brilliant sails and lending the town a distinctly Californian quality. They've come, only in about the last half-decade, because of the roaring winds that blow opposite the current—boardsailing paradise.

While Hood River reaps all the sailboard myths, in fact the waters on the Oregon side of the Columbia are reportedly tame compared to those off the Washington banks. Boardheads claim the wind "really pulls" on the Washington side. The hottest heads circumvent rocky shores and industrial areas to surf off points like **Swell City** and **Doug's Beach.** To find them, follow the streams of vans and wagons piled high with boards and masts, or tune in to radio station KMCQ 104 for the local wind report, delivered by "Bingen" Bart live every morning (April–September).

Two fine spectator spots are located right in Hood River, the **West Jetty** and **Port Marina Park,** although sailboarders will head for any number of other roadside launching spots east, west, and north of here when changing wind conditions warrant. For lessons or for information on wind conditions, sailboard rentals, or launching spots, there is a multitude of sailboard equipment shops, including **Hood River Windsurfing** (4 Fourth Street, 1-386-5787), which has an in-house weather computer continually monitoring weather conditions along the Columbia, and **Ker-**

rits (408 Columbia Street, Suite 222, 1-386-4187), which makes Lycra outfits for fashion-conscious windseekers. In the same building, **Windwear** (504 Oak Street, 1-386-6209) features comfortable onshore clothing.

Locals will strongly attest that there was life in Hood River before the sailboarders arrived. The **Hood River County Museum** (Port Marina Park, 1-386-6772, open Wednesday–Sunday until 4pm, or when the flags are flying) exhibits, among other things, Native American artifacts of the region. It's also the town's **Chamber of Commerce** (1-386-2000). In town, you'll find **Waucoma Bookstore** (212 Oak Street, 1-386-5353) and the **Columbia Art Gallery** (207 Second Street, 1-386-4512), for contemporary local art. **Public restrooms** are located at Second and State streets in the ground floor of the city hall.

The region's main draw has always been the orchards and vineyards of the fertile valley, celebrated in a wonderful small-town **Blossom Festival** held every year in mid-April. (See Calendar chapter.) The **Mount Hood Railroad** (Hood River Depot, 1-386-3556) makes four-hour round trips from the quaint Hood River Depot into the heart of orchard country, May through October. You can buy the fruit of the orchards at **The Fruit Tree** (4140 Westcliff Drive, 1-386-6688), near the Columbia Gorge Hotel, or sip a little grape in tasting rooms at the **Three Rivers Winery** (275 Country Club Road, 1-386-5453) or **Hood River Vineyards** (4693 Westwood Drive, 1-386-3772), the latter known for its pear and raspberry dessert wines. There's even a brewery in town now, the **WhiteCap BrewPub** (506 Columbia Street, 1-386-2247), home of the hand-crafted Full Sail ales. The pub's outdoor deck (with live music on weekends) provides a fitting place for tired sailboarders to unwind while still keeping the river in their sights.

Panorama Point, a half-mile south on Highway 35, has the best view of the Hood River Valley leading to Mount Hood. Heading east out of Hood River, the **Rowena Crest Viewpoint**, just off the old Highway 30, has a grandstand vista of the rolling Columbia River.

A mile up a gravel road, **Stonehedge Inn** (3405 Cascade Drive, 1-386-3940) is a remote dining hideaway with one dressy, dark-paneled room, a homey library, a long enclosed porch with a view, an intimate bar, and superb food. A bit more casual, **Chianti's Restaurant** (509 Cascade Street, 1-386-5737) has the congeniality of a drop-in Italian eatery. **Reflections of the Past** (1302 13th Street, 1-386-2111) is an elegant, family-run place, full of honest foods such as lightly creamy broccoli soup and addicting crispy-chewy crisscross fries. Recently, locals have migrated to **The Mesquitery** (1219 12th Street, 1-386-2002) for substantial barbecue dinners. At breakfast, boardheads down carbos at **Bette's Place** (416 Oak Street, 1-386-1880).

The completed (1920) Columbia Gorge Scenic Highway was crowned by lumber baron Simon Benson's luxury hotel, the **Columbia Gorge Hotel** (4000 Westcliff Drive, 1-386-5566, 800-826-4027 in Oregon). It's been an attraction for countless tour buses and honeymooners ever since its remodel a decade or so ago. The famed (and overrated) Farmer's Breakfast ($20) is complimentary with a room. The impressive **Lakecliff Estate** (3820 Westcliff Drive, 1-386-7000) is everyone's favorite bed & breakfast, with the same stunning view of the river as at the Columbia Gorge Hotel. Another pleasure is the impeccable **State Street Inn** (1005 State Street, 1-386-1899). **Duckwall House** (811 Oak Street, 1-386-6635) is a bit more reasonably priced, though sometimes noisy from the busy street out front. An inexpensive alternative to the posh Columbia Gorge Hotel or the homey B&Bs is the modest **Vagabond Lodge** (4070 Westcliff Drive, 1-386-2992)—ask for a cliffside room.

Twenty minutes west of Hood River is **The Dalles,** *the* historical stop along this stretch. Here the Oregon Trail ended; goods from wagons were loaded onto barges for the final float to Portland. Here, until the dam submerged it, was Celillo Falls, where Indians fished for salmon. Here stood Fort Dalles, built in a peculiarly ornate style by an interesting American architect, Andrew Jackson Downing, whose 1850 surgeon's house is now a museum (15th and Garrison streets), with exceptional relics from the pioneer trails. Architecturally, the town is much more interesting than others nearby, with nicely maintained examples of Colonial, Gothic Revival, Italianate, and American Renaissance styles.

The best way to cap an afternoon of contemplating the past is to picnic at **Sorosis Park**, a large, shady park that is the highest overlook on the scenic drive through the Gorge. Or visit the **River Front Park,** adjacent to I-84, for river access and tamer sailboarding winds. A stay in the circa-1899 **Williams House Inn** (608 W Sixth Street, 1-296-2889), surrounded by a 3-acre arboretum, is a history lesson in itself. The humble-looking **Ole's Supper Club** (2620 W Second Street, 1-296-6708) in the industrial west end of The Dalles prepares an excellent slab of prime rib and has a notable wine list (the bar doubles as a wine shop).

MOUNT ADAMS

Mount Adams and the surrounding area are a natural splendor largely overlooked by visitors in favor of the mountain's "big brother" to the north, close-by Mount Hood to the east, and the show-stealing windsurfers on the Columbia to the south. Similar to Mount Rainier in terrain, but smaller (12,326 feet) and much safer, it is a good day-long (weekend, for most) climb. Besides climbing to the summit of this massive volcano, hikers and skiers can explore miles of wilderness trails in the Mount Adams Wilderness Area and the Gifford Pinchot National Forest.

Volcanic activity long ago left the area honeycombed with caves and lava tubes, including the **Ice Caves** near Trout Lake, with stalactites and stalagmites formed by dripping ice. To the southwest of Trout Lake is the **Big Lava Bed,** a 12,500-acre lava field filled with cracks, crevasses, rock piles, and unusual formations. Contact the Mount Adams Ranger Station in Trout Lake (509-395-2501) to **register for ascents** and for information on area activities. **Dog sled** excursions on the mountain are available through Wilderness Freighters Guide Service, (509) 761-7428.

In the warm months, Klickitat County is a land of abundance: morel mushrooms in the Simcoe Mountains (April–June), wildflowers in the Bird Creek Meadows (part of Track D, the only area of the Yakima Indian Reservation open to the public) in late July, and wild huckleberries—reputedly the best in the state—in and around the Indian Heaven Wilderness (mid-August to mid-September).

Most people come here to camp, but there are a couple of alternatives if you prefer a mattress to pine needles: the precious **Mio Amore Pensione** (Little Mountain Road, Trout Lake, 509-395-2264), with Mount Adams looming up over the cow pasture on the other side of Trout Lake Creek; **Flying L Ranch** (off the Glenwood-Goldendale Road on Flying L Lane, 509-364-3488), 160 acres and nothin' fancy except those huckleberry pancakes come morning (and an occasional appearance by the Philadelphia String Quartet).

Close-by options include bicycling the back roads around Glenwood, bird watching at **Conboy Lake National Wildlife Refuge**, or skiing the 3 miles of groomed trails on the ranch property. When returning, don't take the quickest route back to Portland. Instead, consider driving the spectacular loop through Goldendale.

MOUNT ST. HELENS

The temperamental **Mount St. Helens** simmers about an hour north of Portland off I-5. On a clear day it is well worth the trip to see the 8,365-foot remains, as well as the mountain's regrowth since the incredible eruption of May 18, 1980 (it's 1,300 feet shorter than before the blast). The US Forest Service's wood-and-glass visitors' center (3029 Spirit Lake Highway, Castle Rock, WA, 206-274-6644; or 206-274-4038 for weather conditions) sits in a stand of timber in the Gifford Pinchot National Forest, near Silver Lake. .
is stunning, either with the naked eye or through one of the center's telescopes. The center commemorates the blast with excellent exhibits, a walk-through volcano, hundreds of historical and modern photos, geological and anthropological surveys, and a film documenting the destruction and rebirth. A network of trails, some of which accommodate wheelchairs, are good for short, scenic strolls.

To get there, take Exit 49 from I-5 and travel 5 miles east on Highway 504. Or for the better view from the north, the side on which the blast carved out a crater 2 miles across and half a mile deep, from I-5 turn east on Route 12 into Randall, then take Route 25 to connect with 26, which will lead you to **Windy Ridge**; park at the end of the road (closed winters). Many of the trails have been created or reconstructed to allow further exploration. The big thrills are to see the volcano from the air, which can be arranged with any of the numerous charter companies in the nearby towns of Kelso and Longview, or to climb it. Most climbers take one of two trails (Butte Camp or Monitor Ridge) up the south face—more of a rugged hike than real alpine climbing, but an ice axe is still recommended. The all-day climb (8 miles round trip) is ideal for novice alpinists: the only big dangers are some loose-rock cliffs and the unstable edge around the crater. In winter you can ski down. Permits are required mid-May through October, and only 100 are given out each day (for free). *Everyone* must register with the Forest Service headquarters in Amboy; (206) 247-5473 or (206) 247-5800. A small percentage of the permits are dispensed each day at the trailhead on a first-come, first-serve basis, but don't count on it; arrive early. Fines *are* doled out—at the top.

NORTHERN OREGON COAST: SEASIDE TO NEWPORT

The Oregon Coast, notorious for its fog-gripped shoreline, is still thought of as one of the last vestiges of rugged individualism and has always been a favorite diversion for Portlanders. It used to be you could leave the city on the spur of the moment

Friday afternoon, drive to the coast, and let an oceanfront cabin for the weekend. Not so anymore. Campgrounds are often full in the summer, and many lodgings are booked weeks (sometimes months) in advance. Although much of the coastline is still untouched, in the summers many of the coastal towns are mobbed with travelers who've heard tell of the coast's wild beaches (virtually all are public), jagged promontories, and abundant marine life. But the true Northwesterner knows the beach is just as spectacular on a stormy winter day. Here's a look at the towns and attractions on the northern coast, from Gearhart south to Newport, and some suggestions of where to stay when your first choice is unavailable.

One hundred years ago, affluent Portland beachgoers rode Columbia River steamers to Astoria, then hopped a stagecoach to Seaside, the Oregon Coast's first resort town. The place seemed to become more crowded every year, so fashionable Portlanders began to put their summer cottages (some of them substantial dwellings) in **Gearhart**, which to this day is mostly residential. And the recent legal controversy over the **Pacific Way Bakery and Cafe** (601 Pacific Way, 738-0245) indicates that the townspeople want to keep it that way. The wide beach is backed by lovely **dunes**, and **razor-clam digging** is popular here—the gas stations even rent shovels. **Gearhart Golf Course**, opened in 1892, is the second-oldest course in the West—a 6,089-yard layout with sandy soil that dries quickly; open to the public, 1-738-5248.

In **Seaside**, destination resort hotels, shops, and tourist amenities of all sorts are springing up at a rapid pace. The crowds mill along Broadway, eyeing the entertainment parlors, the taffy concession, and the bumper cars, then emerge at the Prom, the 2-mile-long cement "boardwalk" that's ideal for strolling.

Surf fishing is popular here. Your best bet lies at the south end of town in the cove area (also frequented by surfers). Steelhead and salmon are taken only from the Necanicum River, which flows through town. Seaside has good **razor-clam beaches** and hiking. The trailhead for the 6-mile hike over **Tillamook Head** is at the foot of Sunset Boulevard, at the town's south end. The spectacular and rugged trail ends at Indian Beach in **Ecola State Park**, near Cannon Beach.

There's something about the beach here that gives visitors a hankering for a clam chowder or a quick seafood dinner at **Dooger's Seafood and Grill** (505 Broadway, Seaside, 1-738-3773). Another has opened up farther down the coast in Cannon Beach. The coast has been no haven for Mexican restaurants, but **Christiano's** (412 Broadway, 1-738-5058) has been getting favorable reports lately. As for a place to rest your head, here are a few of the better beach spots: **The Boarding House** (208 N Holladay Drive, Seaside, 1-738-9055), which with its fir tongue-and-groove walls and beamed ceilings retains a very beachy feel, though **Gaston's Beachside Bed & Breakfast** (corner of Avenue "I" and the Prom, Seaside, 1-738-8320) is the best deal on Seaside's Prom; **Gilbert Inn Bed & Breakfast** (341 Beach Drive, Seaside, 1-738-9770), a larger, 10-room Victorian only a block from the water; **Riverside Inn B&B** (430 S Holladay Drive, Seaside, 1-738-8254), on Seaside's main drag, a comfortable lodge with cottages to let (it's a hike to the ocean); the upbeat and stylish full-service resort **Shilo Inn** (30 N Prom, Seaside, 1-738-9571), in an excellent beachside setting.

Just north of Cannon Beach is **Oswald State Park**, with one of the finest campgrounds on any coast in the world. You walk a half-mile from the parking lot to tent sites among old-growth trees; the ocean, with a massive cove and tidepools, is a short walk further. No reservations, but the walk deters crowds who might otherwise come; call 1-238-7488 for word on availability.

Cannon Beach is the Carmel of the Northwest, an arts community with a hip ambience and strict building codes that prohibit neon and ensure that only aesthetically pleasing structures of weathered cedar and other woods are built here.

Today, the town is tourist oriented, and during the summer it explodes with visitors who come to browse through its galleries and crafts shops or rub shoulders with the coastal intelligentsia on crowded Hemlock Street. Its main draw is the spectacular beach—wide, inviting, and among the prettiest anywhere. Dominating the long, sandy stretch is **Haystack Rock**, one of the world's largest coastal monoliths. It's impressive enough just to gaze at, but check it out at low tide and observe the rich marine life in the tidal pools.

Ecola State Park (on the town's north side) has fine overlooks, picnic tables, and good hiking trails. If you hike to **Tillamook Head**, you can see the Tillamook Rock Light Station, a lighthouse built offshore under difficult conditions more than 100 years ago and abandoned in 1957. Today it is a columbarium (a facility for storing cremated remains) called "Eternity at Sea." No camping along the trail, except for summer campsites atop the Head.

Galleries abound in the Cannon Beach area, all on Hemlock Street, the main drag. Two especially good ones are the **White Bird**, which has a range of arts and crafts (1-436-2681), and the **Haystack Gallery**, which shows photography as well (1-436-2547). The **Coaster Theater** (108 N Hemlock Street, 1-436-1242) presents good summer plays, as well as local and out-of-town shows in the winter. The **Haystack Program in the Arts** (1-725-4081), offered through Portland State University, conducts arts workshops (coordinated with family vacation plans).

Other shops of interest on Hemlock Street include Once Upon a Breeze (1-436-1112), a kite store at the north end of town; Osburn's Ice Creamery & Deli (1-436-2234), with excellent picnic and take-out supplies and ice cream; Cannon Beach Baker (1-436-2592), with one of the few remaining brick oil-fired hearth ovens on the West Coast, supplying a good assortment of breads, cookies, and pastries; Cannon Beach Book Company (1-436-1301), with a surprisingly extensive selection; and El Mundo Ltd for Women (1-436-1572) and El Mundo Ltd for Men (1-436-1002), both carrying natural-fiber clothing in chic, youthful styles.

Changes in Cannon Beach over the past decade are most visible in the restaurants. The **Cafe de la Mer** (1287 S Hemlock Street, 1-436-1179), once a post-'60s coffeehouse, has been transformed into one of the beach's best eating establishments. Another chic favorite is **The Bistro** (263 N Hemlock Street, 1-436-2661). Step away from the water and into **The Brass Lantern** (1116 S Hemlock Street, 1-436-2412), where the food is exotic and the preparations daring. In the morning many locals gather at the **Lazy Susan Cafe** (126 N Hemlock Street, 1-436-2816).

There's no shortage of hotels in Cannon Beach, yet only two are recommended: the 129-room cedar-shake **Surfview Resort** (1400 S Hemlock Street, 1-436-1566), for its proximity to Haystack Rock and the expansive, sandy beach; and the two-bedroom **Tern Inn Bed and Breakfast** (3663 S Hemlock Street, 1-436-1528), which sits on a rise two blocks from the beach.

Nestled on Cannon Beach's south side, **Tolovana Park** is more kicked-back, less crowded. Leave your vehicle at the **Tolovana Park Wayside** (with parking and restrooms) and stroll an uncluttered (especially in the off season) beach. At low tide you can walk all the way to **Arch Cape**, some 5 miles south. (Be careful, the incoming tide blocks your return.) **Hane's Bakerie** (3116 S Hemlock Street, 1-436-1719) sells very good, French-inspired baked goods. The tidy and cute oceanfront **Sea Sprite Motel** (Tolovana Park, 1-436-2266) has six units.

Resting mostly on a sandy peninsula with undulating dunes covered with beach grass, shore pine, and Scotch broom, **Manzanita** is a lazy community gaining popularity as a second home for well-to-do Portlanders. The attractions are obvious: the adjacent Nehalem Bay area is fast becoming a **windsurfing mecca; Nehalem Bay State Park**, just south of town, offers hiking and bike trails as well as miles of little-used beaches; and overlooking it all is nearby **Neahkahnie Mountain**, with a steep, switchbacked trail leading to the 1,600-foot summit boasting the best viewpoints on Oregon's north coast.

A block and a half off the beach, the **Blue Sky Cafe** (154 Laneda Avenue, 1-368-5712), an unglitzy restaurant akin to a hippie cafe, offers no outward clues to its unpretentious and moderately priced culinary excitement.

The Tillamook bay front is one of the seasonal homes for the summer salmon fleet. If you don't mind wading through an RV park, greasy-spoon restaurants, and tacky surroundings, there are several establishments in **Garibaldi** that sell the area's freshest seafood, including salmon, shrimp, sole, bottom fish, and crab. **Miller Seafood** (1-322-0355), on Highway 101, is the easiest to find. Fresh salmon, lingcod, and bottom fish are featured. **Smith's Pacific Shrimp Co.** (1-322-3316) sells fine shrimp and has viewing rooms at 608 Commercial Drive. **Hayes Oysters** (1-377-2210), on Highway 101 in Bay City, is the best place to buy oysters (check whether the rare and wondrous Kumamoto oysters are available). Make a quick stop in town at **Downie's Cafe** (9230 Fifth Street, Bay City, 1-377-2220) for a rich, chunks-o'-clam chowder.

Tillamook is dairy country par excellence, a more likely spot for a convention of cows than of people. On the north end of town along US Highway 101 sits the home of Tillamook cheese, the **Tillamook County Creamery Association**. Inside the creamery (under expansion at press time), a self-guided tour offers only a glimpse of the cheese-making process, along with minuscule cheese samples, schlocky tourist trappings, overpriced Tillamook cheese, and too many tourists; 1-842-4481. Instead, go about one mile south on 101 to the **Blue Heron French Cheese Factory** (1-842-8281). Blue Heron is less kitschy and better stocked than the Tillamook Creamery and offers a variety of cheeses. The establishment also has a Knudsen Erath wine-tasting room, where visitors may sip the Oregon-made wine.

The **Pioneer Museum** (Second Street and Pacific Avenue, 1-842-4553) occupies three floors of the 1905 county courthouse. Displays re-create the pioneer past and document wildlife. West of Tillamook in Netarts Bay the **clamming** is very good.

You'll find standard but reasonably priced Cal-Mex fares at **La Casa Medello** (1160 Highway 101 N, 1-842-5768). On the outskirts of the Netarts/Oceanside area, in a little cove in one of the nation's most pristine estuaries, sits the unassuming **Whiskey Creek B&B** (7500 Whiskey Creek Road, 1-842-2408).

Eight miles west of Tillamook, **Oceanside** is part of the 22-mile **Three Capes Scenic Drive**, one of Oregon's—and perhaps the world's—most beautiful stretches of coastline. The narrow, winding road skirts Tillamook Bay, climbs over **Cape Meares,** traverses the shores of **Netarts Bay,** and runs over **Cape Lookout,** the westernmost headland on the north Oregon Coast. The trail from the parking lot at the cape's summit meanders through primeval forests of stately cedar and Sitka spruce. The lower side of the drive provides spectacular ocean vistas. Down at sea level, the desertlike dune landscape presents a stark contrast to Cape Lookout's densely forested slopes. The road to Pacific City and the route's third cape, **Cape Kiwanda,** runs through lush, green dairy country. All have excellent camping facilities.

In the evening, slip into **Roseanna's** (1490 Pacific Avenue, Oceanside, 1-842-7351) for an outstanding wedge of Toll House pie topped with Tillamook ice cream, then roll into a room at the aptly named **Three Capes Bed and Breakfast** (1685 Maxwell Mountain Road, Oceanside, 1-842-6126).

The dory fleet comes home to **Pacific City,** where salmon-fishing boats are launched from trailers in the south lee of Cape Kiwanda. This town has lately been known for another kind of fleet: hang gliders that swoop off the slopes of the cape and land on the sandy expanses below. The region's second Haystack Rock (Cannon Beach has the other) sits a half-mile offshore. Even if you've never visited before, this area may look familiar: nationally acclaimed Oregon photographer Ray Atkeson has made Cape Kiwanda the most-photographed spot on the Oregon Coast. **Robert Straub State Park,** worth visiting, sits at the south end of town and occupies most of the Nestucca Beach sand spit. The Nestucca River flows idly to the sea right outside the **Riverhouse Restaurant** (34450 Brouten Road, Pacific City, 1-965-6722), a calming, apple pie sort of place.

If you decide to forgo the Three Capes Scenic Drive, US Highway 101 will take you through Tillamook and then Nestucca dairy land, some of the most fertile in the state. Nestled in the heart of the Nestucca River Valley is **Cloverdale,** the town that became famous for a 1986–87 battle with state officials over two roadside signs (featuring Clover the Cow) that violated a state signage law. Outside Cloverdale in the middle of nowhere is the historic 1906 **Hudson House Bed & Breakfast** (37700 Highway 101 S, Cloverdale, 1-392-3533). Just south stands the attractive, substantial, cream-colored adobe hotel-condominium complex called **The Chelan** (48750 Breakers Boulevard, Neskowin, 1-392-3270).

A few miles south is the primitive **Cascade Head,** a tall promontory of rain forests, meadows, and rocky cliffs, reachable only on foot. The **Sitka Center for Art and Ecology** (1-994-5485) operates here and offers summer classes on many subjects, as well as numerous concerts, talks, and exhibits.

Otis is barely more than a junction, but the busy **Otis Cafe** (Otis Junction, 1-994-2813) and its down-home breakfasts, shakes, and homemade pies have put this tiny town on the map.

Picture the Oregon Coast without any land-use planning laws at all. It would be only slightly worse than the 10 miles of strip development collectively known as **Lincoln City.** With a few notable exceptions, Lincoln City offers little in the way of outstanding lodgings or reataurants. And if you're coming to the coast to escape the rat race, beware the congested stretch of Highway 101 between Lincoln City and Newport during the summer. The Lincoln City exceptions: **Lacey's Doll and Antique Museum** (3400 Northeast Highway 101, Lincoln City, 1-994-2392) displays more than 4,000 dolls, some of them very old, plus some antiques and curios; **Barnacle Bill's Seafood Market** (2174 Northeast Highway 101, Lincoln City, 1-994-3022) is famous for smoked fish—salmon, sturgeon, albacore, and black cod—and also sells fresh seafood; **Catch the Wind Kite Shop** (Highway 101, Lincoln City, 1-994-9500), whose owners fly some of their more spectacular designs—weather permitting—at the D River beach wayside across the highway from the shop, and at Agate Bay, north of Newport.

Time your visit to catch Siletz Bay's daily sunset light show from a table at the **Bay House** (5911 SW Highway 101, Lincoln City, 1-996-3222), a place that is, like the view, worth savoring. Locals stand in line rain or shine for half-pound burgers from **Road's End Dory Cafe** (Locan Road, one mile off US Highway 101, Lincoln City, 1-994-5180).

Flower boxes on the windows and whitewashed brick walls in a small, woodsy setting give **Gleneden's** most innovative restaurant, **Chez Jeannette** (7150 Old Highway 101, 1-764-3434), the appearance of a French country inn. The buildings at **Salishan Lodge**—perhaps the coast's best-known resort—are scattered far enough apart not to harm the delicate ecology. The beach, a half-mile away, is a splendid strand of driftwood and gulls. A standard of excellence is adhered to throughout the resort.

Once a charming coastal community, **Depoe Bay** today is only an extension of Lincoln City's strip development. Driving down Highway 101, it's hard to tell where one community ends and the other begins. Fortunately, some of the original Depoe Bay, including its tiny harbor, remains intact. During the **gray whale migratory season** (December–April), the leviathans cruise within hailing distance of the headlands. **Deep Sea Trollers** (1-765-2248) is one of several operations offering hour-long whale-watching cruises. **Depoe Bay Aquarium and Shell Shop** has a simulation of an undersea cave, plus harbor seals in a grotto.

Cape Foulweather, christened thus by famed British explorer Captain James Cook when he sailed by in 1778, is aptly named: fog often enshrouds it, even though sunny skies may appear just to the north and south. Reach the cape by the Otter Crest Loop, 2 miles south of town. It has an inspiring viewpoint for watching birds, sea lions, and surf. Adjoining it is the **Lookout Gift Shop and Observatory**, a rarity: its gifts are carefully selected items from craftspeople around the world (1-765-2270). On the Otter Crest Loop in a 100-acre parklike setting is the **Inn at Otter Crest** (1-765-2111), with exquisite landscaping but mediocre resort facilities.

One of the most popular tourist destinations on the Oregon Coast, **Newport** also demonstrates the pitfalls of development. The place has grown—in some respects not attractively. Veer off Highway 101's commercial sprawl and seek out the real Newport: the **bay front**, where fishing boats of all types—trollers, trawlers, shrimpers, and crabbers—berth year-round. Nearby, take a drive out on the **South Jetty Road** for sea-level views of harbor traffic. A walk through the congenial **Nye Beach** area offers glimpses of the old and new in Newport, a potpourri of Newport's professionals, tourists, writers, and fishermen.

Art galleries. Oceanic Arts Center, 444 SW Bay Boulevard (1-265-5963), and the Wood Gallery, 818 SW Bay Boulevard (1-265-6843), both on the bay front, each offer a fine selection—the former primarily jewelry, paintings, and sculpture, the latter functional sculpture, woodwork, pottery, and weaving.

Most **fishing charters** provide bait and tackle, clean and fillet your catch, and even smoke or can it for you. Many charter operators have initiated **whalewatching** excursions, as well as half- and full-day fishing trips. Sea Gull Charters (343 SW Bay Boulevard, 1-265-7441) and Newport Sport-fishing (1000 SE Bay Boulevard, 1-265-7558) are two popular operators. **Hatfield Marine Science Center** (Marine Science Drive, South Beach, 1-867-3011) offers displays, a replica of a tide pool, educational programs, and a full range of free nature walks, field trips, and films, especially during the summer "Seatauqua" program.

On a sunny day in town request an outdoor table overlooking the bay at the **Canyon Way Bookstore and Restaurant** (1216 SW Canyon Way, 1-265-8319). Or try a fresh jalapeno or oyster omelet at **The Whale's Tale** (452 SW Bay Boulevard, Newport, 1-265-8660).

Even though there are a number of places to stay in Newport, we wouldn't advise you to drop into town (or for that matter anywhere on the Oregon Coast these days) without a reservation. The first bed and breakfast in the County is the comfortable **Ocean House Bed & Breakfast** (4920 NW Woody Way, Newport, 1-265-6158), at Agate Beach. The **Sylvia Beach Hotel** (267 NW Cliff Street, Newport, 1-265-5428), a 77-year-old hotel, currently enjoys what must be its happiest and most imaginative incarnation, each room decorated in a different literary theme. The nautically outfitted **Oar House Bed & Breakfast** (520 SW Second Street, 1-265-9571), once a bordello, boasts a centralized location and a pleasant—if distant—view of the ocean. More predictable is **Embarcadero** (1000 SE Bay Boulevard, 1-265-8521), a huge, attractive complex situated right on the bay.

ESSENTIALS CONTENTS

ESSENTIALS

TRANSPORTATION
AIRPLANES: PORTLAND INTERNATIONAL AIRPORT (PDX)

Portland International Airport (map:DD3) is only about 20 minutes from downtown, with uncomplicated freeway access (allow extra time during rush hour). Fourteen airlines service the airport, with direct flights or easy connections to most major US cities. The airport also provides direct daily service to Seoul, Taipei, and Tokyo.

Public information centers are located on the upper and lower levels of the terminal. They are staffed from 6:30am to 11pm Sunday through Friday and 9am to 11pm Saturday. For airport information, call Port of Portland, 231-5000 ext. 411.

The **airport's paging service** (249-4747) is provided through 20 white courtesy telephones located throughout the terminal. To page from within the terminal, simply pick up a white telephone and place your request. The **Lost and Found** (249-4755) is on the lower level and is open from 7am to 9pm Monday through Friday.

Recently, the main concession area was renovated and renamed the **Oregon Market**. It's now an attractive mid-terminal mall complete with skylights. Among the shops are Powell's Books, Nike, the Real Mother Goose, Norm Thompson Outfitters, Oregon Mountain Community, Made in Oregon, and City Kids (see the Shopping chapter). Airport contracts stipulate that prices in the Oregon Market shops must match those in the stores' other Portland outlets—so shopping at PDX is actually an affordable pleasure, not just a diversion.

Off the Oregon Market, near the barbershop and the women's lounge, is a **nursery**. It has changing tables, a crib, chairs, and a private restroom, free of charge. Unfortunately, child care is not available.

The **PDX Conference Center** (249-4984), located on the mezzanine overlooking the Oregon Market, opened in February 1988 and has since become a popular stopover for business travelers. Services include a fax machine, photocopying, computer rental, typewriters, and telephones. Conference rooms are available by the hour or by the day; they start at $15 per hour or $75 per day for six people and go up to $25 per hour or $125 per day for 70 people. There's also a lounge where you can relax with a copy of *The Wall Street Journal*. Limited secretarial help is available in the business center.

Drivers have three choices for **parking** (288-7275) at PDX: short-term (in the new parking garage just off the terminal), long-term, or economy. Rates vary from 50 cents per half hour in short-term (maximum $10 per day) to $5 per day in long-term and $3 per day in economy. Free shuttle buses run between the long-term and economy lots every five minutes. All lots are open 24 hours.

Perhaps the easiest way to get from the airport to downtown Portland (and vice versa) is on the **Raz Downtowner** (246-3301). These vans depart from PDX every 20 minutes on weekdays, every 30 minutes on weekends, from 5am to midnight. One-way cost is $5. The Downtowners stop at the Greyhound station, the King's Way Inn, the Benson Hotel, the Hilton Hotel, the Heathman Hotel, the Portland Inn, and the Marriott Hotel. Allow 35 minutes for the trip.

The east side of the city is serviced by the **Eastside Airporter** (249-1837), whose vans are at the airport every hour on the hour from 5am to midnight; rates for door-to-door service in northeast Portland start at $6.50 and increase according to mileage. The Airporter vans also service Hood River/The Dalles; Vancouver and Longview, Washington; and the Troutdale and greater Gresham area; call for routes and prices.

The **Beaverton Airporter** (649-2213) leaves the airport each hour at a quarter past the hour, starting at 6:15am. Between 4:15pm and 12:15am (every day except Saturday) the vans go twice each hour, at a quarter past and a quarter till the hour. Rates are $10 one-way or $16 round trip to most major Beaverton hotels, $15 one-way or $25 round trip for door-to-door service. The Beaverton Airporters also go to Hillsboro; the fare is $18 one-way.

The most economical trip into the city is via **Tri-Met** (233-3511); one-way fare is 85 cents. Catch bus number 12 from just outside the baggage claim area; the trip to the downtown mall takes approximately 40 minutes, via Sandy Boulevard.

AIRPLANES: CHARTER

From the Portland International Airport, **Flightcraft** (281-3300) offers 24-hour service seven days a week. You can charter a plane for anywhere in the United States or Canada; call for information.

Aircraft at Your Call International (640-8294) provides charter services for passengers and freight from the Portland-Hillsboro Airport; **Aero Air** (640-3711) also charters planes here, and features a full-service maintenance center.

Aurora Aviation (222-1754), at the Aurora Airport, 20 minutes south of Portland on Interstate 5, provides charter/air taxi service. **Aero West** (661-4940) offers similar services from the Troutdale Airport, east of the city (they also conduct Mount St. Helens tours).

BUSES AND LIGHT RAIL: TRI-MET

Tri-Met (233-3511): Seventy-one bus lines and a sleek light rail called MAX make it exceptionally easy to get around the city without a car. Most buses run at 15- or 30-minute intervals throughout the week, with express service during rush hours on some routes. (There are exceptions: for instance, the bus to Tualatin goes only once every two hours. Call Tri-Met for schedules on specific routes.) Many of the buses are wheelchair accessible.

FREE Travelers in the downtown area can ride for free anywhere in the 300-block "Fareless Square." The square extends from Interstate 405 on the south and west to Hoyt Street on the north and the Willamette River on the east. Otherwise, fares are 85 cents for travel in two zones (from downtown to residential areas within the metropolitan area) and $1.15 for three zones (necessary for travel from downtown to most parts of Tigard, Beaverton, Gresham, Milwaukie, and Lake Oswego). One-month passes are available for $17 for two zones and $37 for three zones. All-day tickets are $3. Up to three children age 6 and under can ride free with a fare-paying customer. Finally, youth and Honored Citizens (those 65 and older or disabled) are eligible for discounted fares.

On its 15-mile light rail course, MAX (Metropolitan Area Express) passes through downtown and Old Town, crosses the Steel Bridge, and continues on the east side, passing the new Oregon Convention Center and the Lloyd Center before continuing on its way to Gresham. Glass-covered stations along the way maintain schedule information and ticket machines. (Fareless Square applies to MAX, too.) The comfortable trains run every 15 minutes most hours of the day. The fares are the same as those for Tri-Met buses.

You can purchase bus or MAX tickets and obtain scheduling information at Tri-Met's Customer Assistance Office in the middle of Pioneer Courthouse Square (map: H3). It's open from 9am to 5pm weekdays. You can purchase tickets onboard buses, but MAX tickets are available only from ticket machines at each stop along the line. Tri-Met runs on the honor system; that is, bus drivers only sometimes check fares from downtown and MAX drivers never check fares. However, Tri-Met inspectors randomly request proof of fare payment on buses and MAX, and passengers who haven't paid are fined or cited in district court.

Almost all of the bus lines run through the Portland Transit Mall (on SW Fifth and Sixth avenues) along Pioneer Courthouse Square.

BUSES: OUT OF TOWN AND CHARTER

Greyhound-Trailways Bus Lines (550 NW Sixth Avenue, 243-2323, map: L4) has a full schedule to and from Portland. The station, completed just a few years ago, is located about six blocks north of Burnside, within walking distance of the downtown hub. For package service, call 243-2333. You can charter a bus from **Evergreen Stage Line** (285-9845).

TRAINS

Eight blocks north of Burnside is the **Amtrak** passenger station (800 NW Sixth Avenue, 241-4290, map: M4). To reach the baggage room or package express service at Union Station, call 223-2663.

KEYS TO THE CITY
AMERICAN EXPRESS

The **American Express Travel Service** office (110 SW Sixth Avenue, 226-2961, map: F2) will cash your AmEx travelers checks. Open weekdays, 9am to 5pm.

CATERERS

Ron Paul Catering & Charcuterie (2438 NW 23rd Avenue, 223-1724, map: FF6) is one of the preeminent caterers in town, and its airy eatery in northwest Portland is the perfect place for discussing party arrangements. Also in northwest Portland is **Briggs and Crampton** (1902 NW 24th Avenue, 223-8690, map: FF6), another excellent caterer, run by Nancy Briggs and Juanita Crampton, who've been gaining a national reputation for their two-person lunch feasts. **Food in Bloom** (2701 NW Vaughn Street, 223-6819, map: FF7) in Montgomery Park is another good bet. (For other recommendations, see the Index preceding the Restaurants chapter).

CHILD CARE

The **Children's Services Division of Multnomah County** (815 NE Davis Street, 238-8300) recommends licensed day-care operators Monday through Friday 8am to 5pm. Two reputable organizations are the **Northwest Nannies Institute** (245-5288), which places course graduates for live-in or daily care throughout the metro area, and **Rent-a-Mom** (5331 SW Macadam Avenue, suite 282, 222-5779), a day-care agency in the Portland area.

CHURCHES

The **Ecumenical Ministries of Oregon** (0245 SW Bancroft Street, suite B, 221-1054, map:II6) provides counseling, education, and housing for the poor, alcohol and drug addicts, and single women and children. They also provide church referrals by denomination, predominantly for the greater Portland area but also throughout Oregon.

COMPLAINTS

To register a complaint about an abandoned automobile or a large truck parked in a residential area, call the City Neighborhood Division (796-7306). For barking dogs, call Multnomah County Animal Control (667-7387). For neglected trash pickup or accumulation of garbage in yards, call 796-7306. Anything else to gripe about? The City of Portland's general number is 226-3161; Multnomah County's general information number is 248-3511.

CONSULATES

Major consulates in the Portland area include the **French Consulate** (1849 SW 58th Avenue, 245-9311), the **British Consulate** (3515 SW Council Crest Drive, 227-5669), the **Japanese Consulate** (First Interstate Tower, 1300 SW Fifth Avenue, 221-1811), the **Swedish Consulate** (1600 SW Fourth Avenue, 224-4155), and the **Mexican Consulate** (545 NE 47th Avenue, 233-5662).

DATING SERVICE (AND ANOTHER OPTION)

For the past two years, **Great Expectations** (4247 SW Corbett Street, 226-DATE, map:HH6) has received *The Downtowner*'s readers poll award as the best dating service in Portland. It's an international franchise with approximately 1,000 members in the greater Portland area. *Willamette Week* classified ads have also worked miracles for some dissatisfied singles in Portland; call 223-1500 to place an ad.

DISCRIMINATION

The **Metropolitan Human Relations Commission** (1120 SW Fifth Avenue, 796-5136, map:G3) helps people who feel they have been discriminated against on the basis of race, gender, age, marital status, political or sexual orientation, disabilities, and so forth.

DRINKING FOUNTAINS

No one will ever go thirsty in Portland. Tapped into the city's well are a number of continuously flowing drinking fountains. The four-petaled fountains (located in many downtown public areas) were given to the city by lumberman and philanthropist Simon Benson in 1912.

DRY CLEANERS AND TAILORS

One of the most convenient dry cleaners in the downtown area is **Bee Tailors and Cleaners** (939 SW 10th Avenue, 227-1144, map: G2), which is open weekdays and Saturday mornings. Bee offers curbside service; just honk. Another good bet is **Levine's**, with several locations downtown, including one at 200 SW Broadway (222-4444), one in the PacWest Building at 1211 SW Fifth Avenue (228-6212), and the main store at 2086 W Burnside (223-7221).

FOREIGN EXCHANGE

Exchange money at any major bank or at **Tele-Trip Insurance and Foreign Currency** (281-3045), located at Portland International Airport near the TWA and United Airlines counters. Among the foreign banks in Portland are the **Bank of Tokyo Ltd** (441 SW Sixth Avenue, 222-3702, map: I3), the **Hong Kong and Shanghai Banking Corp** (300 SW Sixth Avenue, 242-1199, map: I3), and the **Mitsubishi Bank** (707 SW Washington Street, suite 1406, 242-3533, map: I3).

FOREIGN VISITORS

The **Portland School of Tutoring and Language** (1422 E Burnside, 232-7440, map: GG5) offers instruction and translation in more than 50 languages, specializing in legal, technical, and scientific translations and interpretation. They will also meet visitors at the airport and arrange for shopping expeditions and other tours. The **World Trade Center Portland/School of Languages** (121 SW Salmon Street, 464-8888, map: F5) is another excellent resource.

GROCERY DELIVERY

Strohecker's Inc (2855 SW Patton Road, 223-7391, map: GG7) offers grocery delivery service through an independent broker twice weekly, on Tuesdays and Fridays. Fees start at $5. Call Tuesday mornings and ask for Tina.

HANDICAPPED AID

SOAR (Shared Outdoor Adventure and Recreation, 324 NE 12th Avenue, 238-1613, map: FF5) offers a wide range of instruction in outdoor activities for people with disabilities. Another organization, the **Flying Outrigger Ski Club** (320 SW Stark Street, 796-5439, map: I5), offers its members ski lessons and the use of equipment at no charge. It's mainly for people with lower-body disabilities; yearly memberships cost $20. **Access Oregon** (1600 SE Belmont Street, 230-1225, map:GG5) is an excellent resource, offering a wide range of information and referrals for persons with disabilities.

LEGAL SERVICES

The **Oregon State Bar Lawyer Referral Service** (5200 SW Meadows Road, Lake Oswego, 684-3763, map:KK8) has offered referrals since 1971. Expect to pay as much as $35 for an initial office consultation. **Multnomah County Legal Aid** (310 SW Fourth Avenue, 224-4086, map:I4) offers legal services to qualified low-income citizens.

LIBRARIES

KIDS The **Multnomah County Library** has 15 branches throughout the city, with film, record, and book borrowing, plus other services. The library sponsors a variety of films, lectures, and programs for children. The **Central Library** (801 SW 10th Avenue, 223-7201, map:H1) is open seven days a week. The **Clackamas County Public Library System** has 13 branches and a Bookmobile. Call individual branches for hours and events. The **Beaverton City Library** (12500 SW Allen Boulevard, Beaverton, 644-2197, map: HH8) is available for use by citizens in Washington, Multnomah, or Clackamas counties and open seven days.

LIMOUSINE SERVICE

For the past 20 years the **Oregon Limousine Service** (809 N Portland Boulevard, 283-2275) has supplied extraordinary cars and drivers for celebs, newlyweds, execs, and others.

LOST CAR

If you suspect your car has been towed, call the **Police Bureau** at 796-3044. If there's no mention of it in their records, call 911—it's probably been stolen.

MEDICAL AND DENTAL SERVICES

Tel-Med (248-9855) maintains a tape library on topics from birth control to arthritis. Send them a stamped, self-addressed envelope, and they will mail you a list of tapes, any of which you can then request to hear over the telephone. Several hospitals provide physician referrals: **Emmanuel Hospital and Health Center** (2810 N Gattenbein Avenue, 228-5465, map:FF5); **Good Samaritan Hospital** (1015 NW 22nd Avenue, 229-7100, map:FF6); **Eastmoreland Hospital** (2900 SE Steele Street, 231-3495, map:HH4); **Woodland Park Hospital** (10300 NE Hancock Street, 238-3627, map:FF2); **Providence Medical Center** (4805 NE Glisan Street, 230-6025, map:GG4); and **St. Vincent Hospital** (9205 SW Barnes Road, 291-2188, map:GG8). The **Multnomah Dental Society** (223-4731) provides emergency and routine referral service at no charge.

NEWSPAPERS

The lone daily in Portland, *The Oregonian* (1320 SW Broadway, 221-8327, map:F2), has been published since 1850 and reigns as the king of print journalism in the city. It's joined on Wednesdays by *Willamette Week* (2 NW Second Avenue, 243-2122, map:J6), a thought-provoking, irreverent, sometimes controversial paper that covers politics, the arts, and civic matters. Both of these papers contain substantial and useful entertainment calendars. (*The Oregonian*'s is on Fridays.) *The Downtowner* and *This Week* (6960 SW Sandburg Street, Tigard, 620-4140) are sister publications that cover the downtown core and greater Portland and the Washington County suburbs, respectively. *The Business Journal* (10 NW 10th Avenue, 274-8733) and the *Daily Journal of Commerce* (2014 NW 24th Avenue, 226-1311) cover the city's business beat.

PERSONAL SHOPPER

Nordstrom (701 SW Broadway, 224-6666, ext. 1450, map:H2) provides a personal shopping service for clients. Ten people who love to shop are available to help others who are less enthusiastic about that task, for whatever reason.

PET CARE AND BOARDING

The Irwin's **Forest Glen Kennels** (Route 1, Box 442, Beaverton, 649-4962) can accommodate as many as 95 dogs and 25 cats. They've been in business for 25 years and are popular among local pet owners; call early for reservations. Karen Kovalik's **Critter Sitters** (657-1841) is an altogether different service: the Sitters come to your home and provide pet care when you're out of town. They'll also water plants and keep an eye on the place.

PIZZA DELIVERY

With some 20 stores in the Portland area, **Domino's** takes a big slice of the pizza delivery category, though **Pietro's**, with nine stores that deliver, and **Godfather's**, with seven, are also contenders. If you're in northwest Portland, let **Pizza Oasis** (2241 W Burnside, 228-5260) bring you a pie—they're a cut above the rest.

PUBLIC OFFICIALS

J.E. "Bud" Clark (1220 SW Fifth Avenue, 248-4120, map:F3) is the mayor of Portland. The city commissioners—they make up the city council—are **Earl Blumenauer** (248-5577), who heads the Department of Public Works; **Dick Bogle** (248-4682), Department of Public Safety; **Bob Koch** (248-4151), Department of Public Utilities; and **Mike Lindberg** (248-4145), Department of Public Affairs. **Barbara Clark** (248-4078) is the city auditor. The commissioners' offices and that of the city auditor are located downtown at 1220 SW Fifth Avenue (map:F3). The Multnomah County commissioners are **Gladys McCoy**, chair (248-3308); **Pauline Anderson**,

District 1 (248-5220); **Gretchen Kafoury**, District 2 (248-5219); **Rick Bauman**, District 3 (248-5217); and **Sharron Kelley**, District 4 (248-5213). Their offices are located in the Multnomah County Courthouse building at 1021 SW Fourth Avenue (map:F3).

PUBLIC RESTROOMS

The most centrally located public restrooms downtown are those in **Pioneer Courthouse Square** (map:H3), near the Tri-Met office. The lobby opens at 8:30am and closes at 5pm weekdays; it is also open during the afternoon on weekends (hours vary).

SALON CARE: HOUSE CALLS

The Bob Shop (555 SW Oak Street, 226-2886, map:I4) can often provide stylists and manicurists to come to your hotel or home; call for details. On the northeast side of town, **Salon #1** (17306 NE Halsey Street, 255-8686, map:FF1) offers similar services.

SENIOR SERVICES

In Multnomah County, the **Aging Services Divison** (426 SW Stark Street, 248-3464, map:I4) helps seniors obtain information about health services, low-income housing, recreation, transportation, legal services, volunteer programs, and other matters. The equivalent agency in Clackamas County is the **Area Agency on Aging** (821 Main Street, Oregon City, 655-8640). They also have a Washington County outpost on 150 NE Third Avenue, Hillsboro (640-3489).

SERVICE STATIONS: ALL NIGHT

Jantzen Beach Union 76 (12205 N Center Road, 285-2567, map:CC6) provides 24-hour towing and services. **Rockwood Union 76** (1545 NE 181st Avenue, 661-5608), off I-84, also provides 24-hour auto service. Closer to downtown, **Uptown Chevron** (2230 W Burnside, 224-3859, map:GG6) is open all night, and so is **Burns Brothers**, across the river (621 SE Martin Luther King Jr Way, 238-7393, map:L9).

SHOE REPAIR

Steve's Shoe Repair (1211 SW Fifth Avenue, 227-4767, map:F2), in the PacWest Building, is open from 7:30am to 5:30pm weekdays. **Dr. Sole & Mr. Heel** has won the Best Shoe Repair award in Portland in the past, but a recent split in the family-owned business resulted in two unaffiliated stores by that name: one is at 425 SW 10th Avenue (222-5456, map:I2) and the other is at 1020 SW Third Avenue (222-9647, map:F4). Call for hours.

If you've found a place around town that you think is a Best Place, send in the report form at the back of the book. If you're unhappy with one of the places, please let us know why. We depend on reader input.

TELEPHONE NUMBERS

AAA Club of Oregon 222-6734
AIDS Hotline 223-AIDS
Alcoholics Anonymous.. 223-8569
Ambulance 911
Amtrak 241-4290
Animal Control 667-7387
Auto Impound 796-3044
Battered Women's Hotline 235-5333
Better Business Bureau 226-3981
Birth and Death Records. 229-5710
Blood Bank... 223-4199
Chamber of Commerce 228-9411
Child Abuse Hotline, Children's Services Division 238-7555
CIA (in Seattle)... 206-587-5364
City Lights (outages) 238-2851
City Parks and Recreation Information.................................... 796-5193
City of Portland 226-3161
Coast Guard 240-9300
Coast Guard Search and Rescue 240-9301
Crisis Center... 223-6161
Directory Assistance (50 cents per call, in OR) 1-555-1212
Drunk Drivers Hotline 800-24DRUNK
Environmental Protection Agency... 221-3250
FBI.. 224-4181
Fire 911
Housing Authority of Portland 249-5511
Immigration and Naturalization Service 221-3006
Internal Revenue Service... 221-3960
Marriage Licenses... 248-3027
Northwest Ski Report 222-9951
Passports 294-2424
Pets (Lost).. 667-7387
Planned Parenthood 775-0861
Poison Center.. 225-8968
Post Office Information... 294-2300
Pregnancy Center (Crisis) 255-7342
Rape Hotline 235-5533
Recycling Information.. 796-7202
Red Cross.. 284-1234
Renters Hotline 299-5739
Sexual Assault Prevention—Womenstrength............................ 796-3139
Sexual Minorities Counseling Hotline 228-6785
Sports Organizations:
   Portland Meadows (horse racing) 285-9144
   Trail Blazers (basketball)... 234-9291
   Winter Hawks (hockey) 238-6366

State Patrol 238-8434
Suicide Prevention 223-6161
Time 282-2222
Tri-Met 233-3511
US Customs 221-2871
Visitors Information 222-2223
Voter Information 248-3720
Weather 236-7575
Women's Crisis Hotline 235-5333
Zip Code Information 294-2308

TELEVISION STUDIO AUDIENCES

FREE KATU (2153 NE Sandy Boulevard, 231-4222, map:GG5), Portland's ABC affiliate, is the city's only station that airs shows with studio audiences. The two programs filmed live are *AM Northwest* (321-4610), the daily interview show, and *Town Hall* (231-4620), a weekly civic affairs program. Call for reservations.

TOWING

Speed's Towing (120 SE Clay Street, 238-6211) offers 24-hour towing from any of six Portland-area locations—whether you like it or not.

UNIVERSITIES AND COLLEGES

For a city its size, Portland has many institutions of higher learning. **Portland State University** (724 SW Harrison Street, 464-3000, map:D1), the state's urban university, is located at the south end of the South Park Blocks. The **Oregon Health Sciences University** (3181 SW Sam Jackson Road, 279-8311, map:HH6), in southwest Portland, is the only academic institution in the state devoted exclusively to the study of health. In north Portland, the **University of Portland** (5000 N Willamette Boulevard, 283-7101, map:DD7) was founded early in the 20th century by the Catholic archbishop of Oregon. Another private institution, **Pacific University** (357-6151), was founded in 1842 in nearby Forest Grove. Nationally noted **Reed College** (3203 SE Woodstock Boulevard, 771-1112, map:II4) is located in southeast Portland off Bybee Boulevard. The largest privately funded college in Oregon is **Lewis and Clark College** (0615 SW Palatine Hill Road, 244-6161, map:JJ6), off Terwilliger Boulevard in southwest Portland. Its programs include the Graduate School of Professional Studies and the Law School. **Marylhurst College** (636-8141), once a women's college, became coeducational in 1976. Community colleges are also numerous in the area: **Portland Community College** (244-6111) has three campuses in the metropolitan area (705 N Killingsworth Street, map:EE5; 12000 SW 49th Avenue, map:JJ7; and 17705 NW Springville Road, map:EE9); **Mount Hood Community College** (667-6422) is located in Gresham; and **Clackamas Community College** (657-8400) is in Oregon City.

VETERINARIANS: EMERGENCY AND WEEKEND SERVICE

Dove Lewis Memorial Veterinary Clinic (two locations: 1984 NW Pettygrove Street, 228-7281, map:FF7; and 18990 SW Shaw Street, Aloha, 645-5800) is supported by the Portland Veterinary Medical Association. The northwest Portland branch is open 24 hours on holidays; call for other hours.

BUSINESS SERVICES
BUSINESS GIFTS

Sutton Place Gifts
245-4418

Several weeks before your office assistant's birthday, Beth Sutton will call to remind you of the date, then select, wrap, and deliver a nifty gift. You can also arrange business gifts for VIPs, customers, or, say, the 92 individuals who work for you. Prices start at $25 per gift, with wrapping and delivery extra. Inquire about personal gifts as well.

COMPUTER RENTALS

Bit-By-Bit
10220 SW Nimbus Ave, Ste K8, Tigard, 639-5467 (map:JJ9)

This well-established rental service will set you up with an IBM PC-compatible for a minimum of $128 per month, which includes free delivery and setup in the Portland metro area. They also lease IBMs (the real thing) and Macintoshes, as well as peripheral equipment. Ask about the rent-to-own program.

Micro-Rentals Inc
713 SW 12th Ave, 273-8787 (map:G1)

By the day or by the year, Micro-Rentals can outfit you with Hewlett-Packard, Compaq, IBM, or Apple equipment. No on-site rental; however, they guarantee immediate delivery.

CONFERENCES, MEETINGS, AND RECEPTIONS

Most hotels and restaurants have private meeting rooms for rent. The following is a list of other rental facilities appropriate for business meetings, private parties, and receptions. Private functions can also be held at the Multnomah County Library (call the branch nearest you to reserve a room), most museums, Portland State University (which has numerous halls, auditoriums, and meeting rooms), and other educational facilities.

Menucha Retreat and Conference Center
28711 E Crown Point Hwy, Corbett, 695-2243

Nonprofit religious, cultural, educational, and governmental groups are welcome at this center, perched high on a bluff overlooking the Columbia. It's part of Portland's First Presbyterian Church, and it has a kindlier, gentler atmosphere than some of the other conference locales. Trails wind through Menucha's 98 wooded acres, and a swimming pool and other diversions occupy visitors. The homestyle cooking is a draw, although no alcohol is allowed in the dining room.

Montgomery Park
2701 NW Vaughn St,
228-7275 (map:FF6)

In the last several years, Montgomery Park has become one of Portland's premier meeting places. There are numerous possibilities here: the banquet hall can accommodate as many as 350 people for a sit-down dinner, or if that's too grand, choose from four conference and meeting rooms. The (sometimes) sunny atrium is also available and can hold as many as 800 standing guests. Catering by Food in Bloom, based in the building.

Oregon Convention Center
NE Martin Luther King
Jr Wy (Union Ave) and
Holladay St, 274-6555
(map:M9)

Purposefully recognizable by its green twin towers (glowing when lit from within), this gargantuan new facility just across the river from downtown has 150,000 square feet of open exhibit space with reception, banquet, and meeting rooms which can accommodate 50 to 5,000 people in one seating. The new convention center (opening September 1990) has two separate entrances, which allows two major events to take place simultaneously (10,000 people total). Indoor parking for 900 cars (auxiliary parking at the Coliseum), wheelchair accessibility. A MAX light-rail stop at the front door makes a trip into downtown effortless.

Pittock Mansion
3229 NW Pittock Dr,
248-4470 (map:GG7)

This Portland landmark leases space during the evening for recognized organizations, commercial and nonprofit alike. The mansion, in its lofty location high above the city, can accommodate 50 for a sit-down dinner or 250 for a standing reception; you'll need to hire a caterer. It's a popular locale—reserve a year in advance for the holiday season.

Portland's White House
1914 NE 22nd Ave,
287-7131 (map:FF5)

Weddings and private parties are big events at this elegant bed and breakfast inn. The former mansion of local timber baron Robert F. Lytle, the White House has an 1,800-square-foot ballroom, with room for 100 dancers. Bring your own caterer.

Tryon Creek State Park
11321 SW Terwilliger
Blvd, 653-3166 (map:JJ6)

A meeting room in the Nature House at picturesque Tryon Creek is available, free of charge, to governmental groups. For a small charge, private environmentally oriented groups can meet as well. Other requests are reviewed on a case-by-case basis, and at press time a group of staff and friends were ironing out the ground rules for such events as weddings and receptions.

Valley Conference Center
9368 SW Beaverton-Hillsdale Hwy, Beaverton, 292-0199 (map:HH9)

Conferences are a big business here, whether the party's for five people or 500. Among the features in the nine distinct rooms are fireplaces, stage areas, service bars, and parquet dance floors. There's also a shuttle service available to local overnight accommodations.

Wapatoos Reception-Conference Hall
4144 SE 60th Ave, 775-0766 (map:HH4)

A rustic hall in the urban heartland. The Wapatoos can accommodate as many as 200 people for a fund-raising casino party, a square dance, a business meeting, or a wedding. The competent staff will give you as much—or as little—help as you need; a caterer and a disc jockey are available, or feel free to hire your own.

World Forestry Center
4033 SW Canyon Rd, 228-1367 (map:GG7)

There are two facilities available at the Forestry Center, which welcomes all kinds of parties, from class reunions to academic conferences (no proms, however). There are kitchen facilities and tables and chairs; you arrange for catering. Exceptionally nice.

World Trade Center
121 SW Salmon St, 464-8688 (map:F5)

On the mezzanine level are four rooms, the largest of which (the auditorium) seats 227 people. These rooms are available for business meetings and other events; no weddings.

COPY SERVICES

Kinko's
1525 SW Park Ave, 223-2056 (map:E1)

The service is usually helpful and friendly—even at 3am (open 24 hours)—although these shops do high-volume business, and small jobs often don't get the attention they deserve. At the new and spiffy Park Avenue location you can rent Macintosh computers by the hour. Both stores have color laser copiers and fax machines.

Clean Copy
1732 SW 6th Ave, 294-3999 (map:D1)

For high-quality business copy services, this shop comes highly recommended. It features offset printing, color laser copies, and photocopying, and has desktop publishing services. Free parking.

PrintRight
425 SW Madison St (and branches), 228-6306 (map:F3)

With some 25 locations throughout the greater Portland area (including Vancouver, WA), there's no escaping PrintRight. Expect fast service or, if you're doing the work yourself, a savings of two cents per copy over Kinko's.

MESSENGER SERVICES

Pronto Messenger Service
726 SE 20th Ave,
239-7666 (map:GG5)

It seems that when someone wants to send something by messenger in this city, they invoke the verb "Pronto," as in, "I'll Pronto it over to you." Hands down, it's the city's favorite cross-town delivery service.

TranServe Systems Inc
534 SW 2nd Ave,
241-0484 (map:I4)

By car, bicycle, plane—TranServe delivers. They offer overnight or immediate delivery whether in the city or abroad.

SECRETARIAL SERVICES

BP&K Professional Office Services Inc
317 SW Alder St (11th and 12th floors), 224-3366 (map:H4)

From personalized form letters and desktop publishing to telephone answering and conference room rental, they provide it here. BP&K also leases executive suites, short- or long-term, and offers fax and photocopying.

Executype
621 SW Morrison St (Ste 1330), 295-2260 (map:H3)

Typing is the bread and butter at Executype, which specializes in word processing, transcription, and (24-hour) dictation. They also do resumes. Laser printing available.

HQ—The Headquarters Companies
10260 SW Greenburg St, Ste 400), 293-8400 (map:JJ9)

Catering to business travelers (and particularly handy to the Washington County high-tech firms), HQ is a national company that offers word processing, phone and beeper service, mail service, binding, fax and more. Also rents office and conference space.

CALENDAR CONTENTS

CALENDAR

▼
CALENDAR

JANUARY

Annual All-Oregon Products Show
Montgomery Park, 393-4334 (map:FF6)

Everything from freeze-dried soup to hazelnuts is available at this huge sale on the third weekend in January. More than 400 manufacturers gather at the event; the public is invited to attend Friday night and all day Saturday and Sunday.

Great Northwest Chili Cookoff
Expo Center, 226-1561 (map:CC4)

For 10 years now, the chili cookoff has benefited the zoo, providing funds for expansion and for animal care. About 34 different chilis are sampled by no fewer than 3,000 visitors.

FEBRUARY

International Film Festival
Northwest Film and Video Center, 1219 SW Park Ave, 221-1156 (map:G1)

More than 40 international films are shown at the Oregon Art Institute (and select downtown theaters) during this annual film fling. For three weeks in February and March, American and foreign films, independent and otherwise, premiere in Portland. Opening and closing nights are the biggies, when major studio productions make their Portland debut. Tickets: $5 per show ($4.50 for OAI members) or $75 for festival pass.

Newport Seafood and Wine Festival
Newport, 114 miles southwest of Portland on Highways 99W and 101, (800) 262-7844

To find this three-day festival, cross the Yaquina Bay Bridge to South Beach; it all takes place in that community's exhibition hall. More than 100 exhibitors, largely seafood distributors and wineries, display their wares; of course, food and wine are plentiful. There is a gate fee: $2.50 for adults, $1 for teenagers (children free). Usually the last weekend in February.

Oregon Shakespeare Festival
Citywide, Ashland, 300 miles south of Portland, 1-482-4331

An unassuming little college town set in lovely ranch country just happens to house the fifth-largest theater company in the country. Almost 200,000 visitors a year (February-October) fill the festival's three theaters. Lectures, backstage tours, Renaissance music, and dance are other attractions theatergoers enjoy. Last-minute tickets are rare in the summer. From November to April, the Oregon Shakespeare Festival moves north to Portland (see November listing).

Books in the Best Places *series read as personal guidebooks, but our evaluations are based on numerous reports from local experts. Final judgements are made by the editors. Our inspectors never identify themselves (except over the phone) and never accept free meals or other favors. Be an inspector. Send us a report.*

**Timberline Pro-Am
Snowboard Classic**
Timberline Lodge, Government Camp, 66 miles west of Portland on Mount Hood, off Highway 26, 321-7979

Thrills abound at this professional competition, which is also open to amateurs. As many as 150 snowboarders participate.

MARCH

**Northwest Writers
LitEruption**
South Park Blocks, 222-2944 (map:F1)

Bookhounds look forward to this two-day event, which got its start in 1988. Booksellers, small presses, writers, and, most of all, readers, congregate at the Masonic Temple for readings, signings, and coffeehouse goodies from the Ann Hughes Coffee Room (of course). Admission is $1. **KIDS** Look for the film festival at the Oregon Art Institute next door, and the art show at the Heathman Hotel, held in conjunction with LitEruption.

**Oregon State Special
Olympics**
Mount Bachelor, Bend, 163 miles southeast of Portland on Highways 26 and 97, 1-382-2442

Disabled athletes compete in ice skating and downhill and cross-country skiing just prior to the big international meet (usually held a few weeks later). More than 400 Olympians participate.

Portland Saturday Market
Under the Burnside Bridge at SW 1st Ave, 222-6072 (map:J7)

KIDS FREE "Saturday Market" is a bit of a misnomer because it's open Sundays, too. Every weekend from the first of March through the Christmas season, more than 200 artists offer their handmade wares at this outdoor market in Old Town. The fast-food booths are also worth sniffing out.

Shrine Circus
Memorial Coliseum, 235-8771 (map:Q7)

KIDS Grab the kids, they'll love this. Everything you'd expect from a three-ring circus.

APRIL

Home and Garden Show
Multnomah Expo Center, 246-8291

This enormous trade show features exhibits for home decorating and remodeling, along with everything you need for the care and feeding of your lawn or garden.

Hood River Blossom Festival
Hood River, 60 miles east of Portland on I-84, 1-386-2000

The coordinators of this event assure us that any similarities between it and the one in The Dalles are purely coincidental. Tours of wineries and the blossoming fruit orchards are available; just follow the well-marked "Blossom Trail" up Highway 35.

International Children's Festival
Vancouver, WA,
(206) 695-3050
(map:AA4)

KIDS Each year the theme differs, but this week-long festival is always a sure bet for kids. In 1990 the event celebrates puppetry from around the world. There's comedy and music, hands-on activities, a toy store with international pizzazz, and a food pavilion. Open exclusively to school groups until the final weekend.

Packy's Birthday Party
Washington Park Zoo,
226-1561 (map:GG7)

KIDS Portland's famous elephant will be 28 in 1990, and all his admirers will turn out to help him celebrate. Last year everyone was invited to eat cake, play games, and sign the birthday card. Pay zoo admission and the party is free.

Trillium Festival
Tryon Creek State Park,
636-4398 (map:JJ6)

Yet another blossom festival, but this one's in the spectacular 641-acre Tryon Creek State Park. In the spring, when the trilliums bloom, the Friends of Tryon Creek host this weekend celebration featuring a native plant sale, food, music, guided walks, and other diversions.

MAY

Greyhound Racing
Fairview, 667-7700

You've seen the Kentucky Derby, right? Well, here dogs run instead of horses, the track is smaller (no more than 770 yards), and instead of a jockey urging the animals on, the greyhounds chase a little mechanical rabbit. The season runs from May to September. Admission is $1. No children under 12 are allowed during evening races.

Pole, Pedal, Paddle
Mount Bachelor, Bend,
163 miles southeast of
Portland on Highways 26
and 97, 1-388-0002

This grueling test of endurance is one of central Oregon's most popular events. In '89, 3,000 people skied, biked, canoed, and ran in teams or by themselves (brave people) past 35,000 cheering spectators. Usually the weekend after Mother's Day, the original small-town run is now a full-fledged two-day event, complete with a street fair.

Sand Castle Day
Cannon Beach, 72 miles
west of Portland on High-
ways 26 and 101,
1-436-2623

KIDS Oregon's original and most prestigious sand castle contest is more than a quarter-century old. Buckets, shovels, and squirt guns aid the 1,000-plus contestants in producing their transient creations. Upwards of 40,000 spectators show up to view the masterpieces. The event is free to spectators; participants pay an entrance fee.

KIDS *means it's a good place to bring kids.*

JUNE

Britt Festival
Jacksonville, 283 miles south of Portland on I-5, 1-773-6077

This musical extravaganza runs from mid-June through August in the hillside field where Peter Britt, a famous local photographer and horticulturist, used to have his home. A handsome shell has been constructed, and listeners sit on benches or loll on blankets under the stars. The season starts with bluegrass and ballet, then presents a full-size orchestra for three weeks, and concludes with jazz and musical theater.

Cascade Festival of Music
Drake Park, Bend, 163 miles southeast of Portland on Highways 26 and 97, 1-382-8381

This one-week festival features classical, pops, and jazz concerts in a riverside pavilion. Along with the concerts is a children's ballet performance and a picnic before Friday night's pops performance.

Chamber Music Northwest
Reed College and Catlin Gabel School campuses, 223-3202

Enjoy a pre-concert picnic before any of 25 performances during this exciting, nationally acclaimed chamber music festival, which features works from a widely ranging repertoire. Runs from mid-June through July.

Oregon Bach Festival
Eugene, 105 miles south of Portland on I-5 (take U of O exit), 1-686-5666

This celebrated festival features 30 concerts, including chamber music and recitals from baroque to jazz. You can hear music both at Beall Hall on the University of Oregon campus and downtown at the impressive Hult Center for the Performing Arts.

Portland Rose Festival
Citywide, 228-9411

KIDS FREE Now in its ninth decade, the Portland Rose Festival is a 24-day celebration that encompasses a variety of major events: three parades, a world-class rose show, an air show, an Indy cart race, a hot-air balloon race, and a ski classic at Mount Hood. It's one of the premier festivals in the nation, and an event that Portlanders are exceedingly proud of. This year, the carnival will move to the Lloyd Center's south parking lot from its usual location downtown along the Willamette; however, such attractions as the Rose Festival Amphitheater and the Oregon Pavilion will remain in McCall Waterfront Park.

Prefontaine Classic
Hayward Field, Eugene, 105 miles south of Portland on I-5 (take U of O exit), 1-683-5635

Eugene may not be the track-and-field town it was in the '70s, but it still has the Prefontaine Classic, named for the University of Oregon's 1972 Olympian, Steve Prefontaine. High-caliber athletes from around the country compete in the annual meet.

CALENDAR

Seattle to Portland Bicycle Ride
(206) 522-BIKE

Traverse the highways and byways from Seattle to Portland on a bike and have a great time doing it. The Cascade Bike Club sponsors this one- or two-day excursion (depending on individual capabilities) every June. Riders don't need to be members of the bike club, but they must register by the first of May. Last year more than 9,000 people pedaled the pavement.

Your Zoo and All That Jazz, Zoograss Family Concert Series
Washington Park Zoo, 226-1561 (map:GG7)

FREE The jazz concerts are held Wednesday evenings, bluegrass on Thursdays, for nine weeks during the summer. Bring a picnic to enjoy on the grassy slopes of the zoo amphitheater, but leave your alcoholic beverages at home; wine by the bottle is for sale on the site.

JULY

Annual Pinot Noir Celebration
Linfield College, McMinnville, 39 miles southwest of Portland (take 99W), 472-8964

Pinot noirs from around the world are showcased in this three-day event, as well as symposiums and lectures by renowned speakers. Tastings, gourmet meals, and entertainment too.

Concours d'Elegance
Pacific University, Forest Grove, 23 miles east of Portland on Highway 8, 357-6656

Those who treasure fine automobiles and love nostalgia will especially enjoy this one-day event. More than 400 classic automobiles are on display, and a barbershop quartet sets the tone.

Country Classic Horse Show
Inchinnan Farms, Wilsonville, 16 miles south of Portland on I-5, 241-1401

KIDS Horse lovers will appreciate this three-day event benefiting the Portland Opera. There are equestrian shows and activities for children (Friday is Kids' Day). Food and drink are available.

Especially for Children Program
Blue Lake Park, 224-1412

KIDS Every Wednesday afternoon for nine weeks through the summer, mimes, puppeteers, actors, musicians, and other artists entertain wee ones on the shores of Blue Lake—rain or shine. Admission is $1 per car. There are also evening concerts at the park for adults.

Fort Vancouver Fourth of July Fireworks
Vancouver, WA, (206) 693-1313 (map:BB5)

KIDS FREE The best fireworks in Oregon are across the Columbia River...in Washington. Portlanders flock to the National Historic Site of Fort Vancouver for a day of activities and stage entertainment climaxing in the largest free aerial display west of the Mississippi. The bombardment lasts a full hour.

Gorge Cities Blow Out
Columbia Gorge, east of Portland on I-84,
1-667-7778

The Blow Out, a 20-mile open-water race from Cascade Locks to Hood River, is one of the premier races of the board-sailing world. If you miss it, however, take heart: hot-dog sailors challenge the gorge en masse from the beginning of June through Labor Day, and then some.

Multnomah County Fair
Portland Expo Center,
285-7756 (map:CC4)

KIDS This is an urban county fair complete with cotton candy, prize cattle, and carnival games. The six days of festivities include big-name entertainers that have included the Dale Ridge Boys, Johnny Cash, and Lee Greenwood.

Oregon Coast Music Festival
Various coastal cities along Highway 101,
(800) 762-6278 (in Oregon)

In 1979, a musical celebration began as the Haydn Festival; four years later, it was given its current name and a broader repertoire. Today it's a two-week musical marathon: there's bluegrass and salsa, classical and jazz. Concerts are held in Bandon, Charleston, Coos Bay/North Bend, Reedsport, and Newport.

Oregon Country Fair
Veneta, 125 miles south-west of Portland (take I-5 to Eugene, then Highway 126), 1-343-4298

Entering its third decade, this festival is for many Eugeneans as much a part of summer as sunshine. Arts and crafts, educational exhibits, food, and entertainment abound at the three-day fete, which takes place in a bucolic setting a half-hour from Eugene. Traffic is also part of the party—consider riding the free bus from downtown.

Rainier Beer Columbia Gorge Pro-Am
Columbia Gorge Sailpark, Hood River, 60 miles east of Portland on I-84,
1-493-1545

Sailboarders from around the world come to participate in the week-long Pro-Am, a high-wind slalom for both amateurs and pros, usually scheduled in mid-July.

Rose City Blues Festival
McCall Waterfront Park,
282-0555 (map:H6)

FREE National blues artists (such as James Cotton) play at this three-day benefit for the Oregon Food Bank. The shows are free, although sponsors accept donations of food and money. A big event: in 1989, 30,000 fans turned out.

Street of Dreams
Portland, location varies,
684-1880

Each year more than 100,000 people flock to the Street of Dreams, a showcase of approximately a dozen new custom-built luxury homes. Street of Dreams was introduced in 1976; now there are more than a dozen of the elegant housing projects in the greater Portland area.

Look for **FREE**—*it means this attraction or event is free of charge.*

World Championship Timber Carnival
Albany, 70 miles south of Portland on I-5,
1-928-2391

What would Oregon be without its timber—the state's primary source of controversy and contention (although it's true that the tree industry ranks second in revenues to marijuana)? This colorful carnival has become a tradition, with champion loggers showcasing their talents in a variety of logging-related contests, including tree climbing, tree topping, and axe throwing. For four days, the town of Albany is in a whirl.

AUGUST

The Bite, A Taste of Portland
McCall Waterfront Park,
248-0600 (map:H6)

KIDS Eat to your heart's content and help Oregon Special Olympics at the same time. Thirty restaurants and 20 wineries offer heaps of delectables while performers at three different venues entertain you. OSO maintains souvenir and information booths; there are also hands-on activities for the kids.

Hood to Coast Relay
Timberline Lodge to
Seaside, 1-272-3707

More than 700 teams participate in this 160-mile, around-the-clock relay. Starting times are staggered; runners hit Portland continuously beginning in the evening, then on through the night and into the early morning. It's an event that's fun to watch, although veterans say it's more fun to participate—if you're up to it (teams are made up of either six or 12 people who run multiple 5-to-6-mile stretches).

Mount Hood Festival of Jazz
Mount Hood Community
College, Gresham,
666-3810

Definitely one of the premier festivals around, this weekend affair has featured in the past such greats as Lou Rawls and the Count Basie Band. About 20 bands take part each year. Sample the offerings of local restaurants in the concession area or bring a picnic lunch (no alcohol or glass containers allowed). Tickets are around $20 a day.

Oregon State Fair
Fair and Expo Center,
Salem, 51 miles south of
Portland on I-5 (take exit
258), 1-378-3247

KIDS It's everything a fair should be: food, games, rides, horse shows, and live entertainment. For 11 days, the people of Salem go hog wild. Ends on Labor Day. Admission is $5.

Scandinavian Festival
Junction City, 90 miles
south of Portland (take
I-5, Harrisburg exit),
1-998-6154

KIDS For four days, the Scandinavian population of Junction City celebrates its heritage and honors the ancestry of the area's early European settlers. Crafts, games, dancing, music, and feasting (and feasting and feasting) are the highlights.

Seaside Beach Volleyball Tournament
Seaside, 70 miles west of Portland on Highways 26 and 101, (800) 444-6740

FREE Surf, sand, and 1,500 volleyball enthusiasts combine for this competition, billed as the largest beach volleyball tournament north of California. Nonparticipants have a ball, too.

Washington County Fair
Washington County Fairgrounds, Hillsboro, 648-1416

KIDS This fair is a bit more old-fashioned than its Multnomah County counterpart. There's a rodeo, too.

SEPTEMBER

Artquake
Center for the Performing Arts and Park Blocks, 227-2787 (map:G1-E1)

FREE For three days in early September, Portlanders let loose a grand celebration of the performing and fine arts. The Center for the Performing Arts is the hub of the festival, although there are events throughout the downtown area, especially Pioneer Courthouse Square. There is no admission charge for many Artquake events; others charge a nominal entrance fee.

Cycle Oregon Bike Tour
Salem, route varies, (800) 543-8838

In 1988 the Oregon Department of Tourism introduced "Cycle Oregon" with a Willamette Valley route; in '89 it was Portland to Ashland via Bend. More than 2,000 cyclists (riders from other states as well as Oregonians) participated in the week-long tour, which organizers are planning to run each September.

Fall Kite Festival
Lincoln City, 88 miles southwest of Portland (take 99W), (800) 452-2151

FREE KIDS Lincolnites love to fly kites of all shapes and colors, and last year so did the more than 20,000 people who attended the festivities (which included a lighted show at night). Prizes are awarded for the most innovative tail and most original kite. The dates of this event change depending on the tides; call to verify.

Mount Angel Oktoberfest
Mount Angel, 26 miles south of Portland (take I-5, Woodburn exit), 1-845-9440

FREE In 1990 the Oktoberfest celebrates its 25th anniversary; maybe then it will top the 300,000-visitor mark established in '89 (although, in truth, sponsors say they can only guess at the number of attendees). It's music, art, stage shows, food booths, and, of course (with a $2 admission), a beergarden.

Pearl District Festival
Pearl District, 222-2223

For two days, artists open their lofts to the curious, galleries hold wine-tastings and sponsor bands, NW Marshall Street is closed for the social whirl around the Bridgeport Brew Pub, and sculptures decorate the district's streets.

Pendleton Round-Up
Pendleton, 210 miles east of Portland on I-84, (800) 524-2984

Yeehaw! This four-day rodeo complete with cowboys, bucking broncos, bulls, and clowns is said to be one of the biggest in the country. More than 400 contestants and 50,000 spectators make it so. Admission ranges from $6 to $12. A carnival downtown (Happy Canyon Days) keeps things hopping while the rodeo riders recover.

Wintering-In Harvest Festival
Howell Territorial Park, Sauvie Island, 222-1741 (map:AA9)

FREE The Oregon Historical Society sponsors this splendid fete on the peaceful grounds of the Bybee-Howell House, a restored pioneer homestead. Music, food, and crafts are highlights of the afternoon; there's also free apple cider.

OCTOBER

Annual Halloween Extravaganza
Northwest Film and Video Center, 1219 SW Park Ave, 221-1156 (map:G1)

Every Halloween the Film Center shows silent horror movies; last year it was *Dr. Jekyll and Mr. Hyde*. But there's a twist: real people participate in the "staging" of the films; that is, a full orchestra (conducted by Jon Newton) plays an original score. Only for those who possess a sense of Halloween adventure. Wear a costume. Admission is creeping above $10.

Eugene Celebration
Citywide, Eugene, 105 miles south of Portland on I-5, 1-687-5215

More than 150,000 people turn out for this two-week celebration of Oregon's second-largest city. There is a wide range of events, from the Mayor's Fine Art Show to the Fifth Avenue Jazz Festival to bike races. Don't miss the coronation of the Slug Queen.

Greek Festival
Holy Trinity Greek Orthodox Church, 3131 NE Glisan St, 234-0468 (map:FF4)

FREE For three days, Portland's Greek community celebrates with traditional foods, music, dancing, and various festivities. The focus is on the Greek Orthodox Church; everyone is invited.

Portland Meadows
1001 N Schmeer Rd, 285-9144 (map:BB6)

Fridays, Saturdays, and Sundays you can catch live horse racing at the Meadows, but on Tuesdays, Wednesdays, and Thursdays you have to settle for simulcasts. If you feel lucky on Monday, play the lottery instead—the Meadows is closed.

Portland Trail Blazers Basketball
Memorial Coliseum, 234-9291 (map:Q7)

The Trail Blazers are not the winningest NBA team, but Portlanders don't seem to mind. The home games are exciting (and earsplitting), and every one has sold out for the last 10 years! Tickets range from $7.50 to $29.

Portland Winterhawks Ice Hockey
Memorial Coliseum, 238-6366 (map:Q7)

See tomorrow's NHL players today in the WHL (Western Hockey League). This developmental league grooms young hockey players for the big time (34 former Winterhawks have already made it). The 72-game season runs from October through March, with prices topping out at about $9.

Salmon Festival
Oxbow Park, Gresham, 248-5050

When the salmon come home to spawn, the people of Gresham celebrate with an annual 8-kilometer run, a salmon barbecue, and arts and crafts. The name of the game here is environmental education. Salmon-viewing walks (where you can see the fish spawning in the Salmon River Gorge) and old-growth walks are conducted to teach the importance of the earth's natural resources.

NOVEMBER

Festival of the Trees
Memorial Coliseum Exhibit Hall, 235-8771 (map:FF5)

Sponsored by the Providence Medical Foundation, this event benefits needy hospital patients. Sixty 8-foot trees are thematically decorated. There are also gingerbread displays, holiday entertainment, and arts demonstrations. An auction is held on opening night; bids for trees and displays start at $500.

Oregon Shakespeare Festival Portland
Center for the Performing Arts, 248-6309 (map:G2)

In 1988, the renowned Ashland company made its first appearance in Portland. The season and the schedule differ from those in Ashland, but the same high standards apply. (See Theater in the Arts chapter.)

Pioneer Courthouse Square Holiday Happenings
Pioneer Courthouse Square, 223-1613 (map:H3)

KIDS Generally, the festivities begin the day after Thanksgiving with the lighting of the Christmas tree in the square. In 1989, a 40-by-70-foot ice-skating rink was installed for the holiday season; the rink is scheduled to open again in December 1990. Skate rental is available; admission is charged.

DECEMBER

Christmas Ships
Columbia and Willamette rivers, 223-2223

Every year, local boating enthusiasts bedeck their vessels with lights and parade the Columbia and the Willamette for several weeks in December. Call for schedule.

KIDS *means it's a good place to bring kids.*

US Bank Zoo Lights Festival
Washington Park Zoo,
226-1561 (map:GG7)

KIDS For the month of December the zoo is ablaze with lights—on buildings, trees, and animated animal sculptures. During the evenings there's live holiday music, elves bearing treats, and visits from you-know-who.

The Nutcracker
Civic Auditorium, 222
SW Clay St, 226-6867
(map:E3)

KIDS A merry production by the Oregon Ballet Theater puts even the most ferocious Scrooge into the holiday spirit. It generally runs for two weeks before Christmas.

Singing Christmas Tree
Civic Auditorium, 222
SW Clay St, 657-3096
(map:E3)

During the second weekend in December, some 130 adults from local church choirs join forces for this lavish production, which, over the last 27 years, has become a Portland holiday tradition. Artful lighting enhances the group's formation—in the shape of a Christmas tree. The six performances are usually sold out, so buy tickets early.

Timberline New Year's Eve
Timberline Lodge, Gov-
ernment Camp, 66 miles
west of Portland on Mount
Hood off Highway 26,
231-7979

All-night skiing is a long-standing New Year's tradition at Timberline. Thirty dollars buys a lift ticket valid from 9am December 31 until 9am New Year's Day; it also gets you into New Year's Eve festivities in the Wy'east Lodge, live music included. Fireworks start at midnight.

Whale Watch Week
Newport, 114 miles south-
west of Portland on High-
ways 99W and 101,
1-867-3011

During the week between Christmas and New Year's Day, volunteers from the Science Center in Newport assist visitors in sighting gray whales from various stations along the coast. The Yaquina Bay Lighthouse, Cape Perpetua, and Depoe Bay are among the best places for viewing; volunteers are available from 10am to 1pm (morning light is best).

I N D E X

INDISPENSABLE GUIDEBOOKS FOR THE PACIFIC NORTHWEST

Sasquatch guidebooks are available at bookstores and other retail outlets throughout the Pacific Northwest. To order copies by mail, complete the order form below and return it to us with your payment.

PORTLAND BEST PLACES (1st edition)
A Discriminating Guide to Portland's Restaurants, Lodgings, Shopping, Nightlife, Arts, Sights, and Outings
by Stephanie Irving. . . . . $10.95 x quantity = _____

NORTHWEST BEST PLACES 1990-1991 (8th edition)
Restaurants, Lodgings, and Touring in Oregon, Washington, and British Columbia
by David Brewster and Stephanie Irving. . . . .$15.95 x quantity = _____

SEATTLE BEST PLACES (4th edition)
Restaurants, Lodgings, Shopping, Nightlife, Arts, Sights, and Outings
by David Brewster and Kathryn Robinson . . . .$10.95 x quantity = _____

SEATTLE CHEAP EATS (3rd edition)
230 Terrific Bargain Eateries
by Kathryn Robinson. . . . .$7.95 x quantity = _____

Subtotal $ _____

WA state residents add 8.1% sales tax . . . . $ _____

Postage and handling $1.50

TOTAL ORDER = $ _____

☐ I enclose payment of $ _____(payable to Sasquatch Books).

☐ Please charge this order to my credit card:

MasterCard#_____ Exp. Date_____

VISA#_____ Exp. Date_____

Name_____ Phone_____

Address_____

City_____ State_____ Zip_____

SHIP TO:

Name_____

Address_____

_____ State_____ Zip_____

Payment must accompany order. Please allow up to four weeks for delivery. Orders shipped via UPS unless otherwise specified.

☐ Please send me a complete catalog of Sasquatch Books.

SASQUATCH BOOKS 1931 Second Avenue, Seattle, WA 98101 (206)441-5555

PORTLAND BEST PLACES REPORT FORM

Based on my personal experience, I wish to nominate/confirm/disapprove for listing the following restaurant, shop, nightspot, sight, etc.:

_____

_____

_____

_____

(Please include address and telephone number, if convenient.)

REPORT:
(Please describe food, service, style, comfort, value, etc.; include the date of visit. Continue on another piece of paper, if necessary.)

I am not concerned, directly or indirectly, with the management or ownership of this establishment.

Signed _____

Address _____

_____

Phone _____ Date _____

Send to: Stephanie Irving, editor
Portland Best Places
Sasquatch Books
1931 Second Avenue
Seattle, WA 98101

PORTLAND BEST PLACES REPORT FORM

Based on my personal experience, I wish to nominate/confirm/disapprove for listing the following restaurant, shop, nightspot, sight, etc.:

_____

_____

_____

_____

(Please include address and telephone number, if convenient.)

REPORT:
(Please describe food, service, style, comfort, value, etc.; include the date of visit. Continue on another piece of paper, if necessary.)

I am not concerned, directly or indirectly, with the management or ownership of this establishment.

Signed _____

Address _____

_____

Phone _____ Date _____

Send to: Stephanie Irving, editor
          Portland Best Places
          Sasquatch Books
          1931 Second Avenue
          Seattle, WA 98101